PASSION FOR JUSTICE

PASSION FOR JUSTICE

RETRIEVING THE LEGACIES OF
WALTER RAUSCHENBUSCH, JOHN A. RYAN, AND
REINHOLD NIEBUHR

HARLAN BECKLEY

WESTMINSTER/JOHN KNOX PRESS
LOUISVILLE, KENTUCKY

Cover photographs are credited as follows:

Walter Rauschenbusch: From *Walter Rauschenbusch: American Reformer,* by Paul M. Minus (New York: Macmillan Publishing Co., 1988). Reprinted by permission of Carl Rauschenbusch.

John A. Ryan: From *The Social Doctrine in Action,* by John A. Ryan. Copyright 1941 by Harper & Brothers. Reprinted by permission of HarperCollins Publishers.

Reinhold Niebuhr: By courtesy of Burke Library, Union Theological Seminary of the City of New York.

Book design by Christine Leonard Raquepaw

First edition

This book is printed on acid-free paper that meets the American National Standards Institute Z39.48 standard. ∞

Published by Westminster/John Knox Press
Louisville, Kentucky

PRINTED IN THE UNITED STATES OF AMERICA

9   8   7   6   5   4   3   2   1

Library of Congress Cataloging-in-Publication Data

Beckley, Harlan, 1943–
    Passion for justice : retrieving the legacies of Walter Rauschenbusch, John A. Ryan, and Reinhold Niebuhr / Harlan Beckley. — 1st ed.
        p.   cm.
    Includes bibliographical references and index.
    ISBN 0-664-21944-6 (alk. paper)

    1. Christianity and justice—History of doctrines—20th century.   2. Rauschenbusch, Walter, 1861–1918—Contributions in concept of justice.   3. Ryan, John Augustine, 1869–1945—Contributions in concept of justice.   4. Niebuhr, Reinhold, 1892–1971—Contributions in concept of justice.   I. Title.
BR115.J8B42   1992
241'.622—dc20   91-48343

To Debby,
Benjamin,
Jonathan,
and Rachel

CONTENTS

ACKNOWLEDGMENTS

Writing for publication is among the many ways we can experience how extensively the products of our work depend upon others: both institutions and persons. The following are among those to whom I am grateful.

James M. Gustafson and Charles M. Swezey provided inspiration, encouragement, and advice at many stages in the production of this volume.

Thomas L. Shaffer offered helpful comments on virtually the entire manuscript. Comments from several others have also informed the organization and content of the pages that follow. They are: William Lad Sessions, R. Neville Richardson, Mark H. Grunewald, Robin L. Lovin, John W. Elrod, Davis Perkins, Joseph L. Allen, and an anonymous referee at Westminster/John Knox Press.

I am also grateful for advice and support from James F. Childress, John P. Reeder, Jr., Lewis H. LaRue, Robert W. McArhen, Thomas W. Ogletree, and Douglas F. Ottati.

Members of my academic department at Washington and Lee have constantly expressed interest in my work and have willingly accepted duties that I could have performed rather than working on this project. I am thankful to Louis W. Hodges, Alexandra R. Brown, Richard G. Marks, and especially to Minor L. Rogers, who was department chair during the period of most intensive labor on this volume. Karen S. Lyle, secretary for the department of religion, has provided cheerful and able assistance in preparing the manuscript.

This project would not have been completed without grants and support from institutions and the persons responsible for them. I am especially appreciative to Washington and Lee University and its vice president for academic affairs, John W. Elrod. The university granted a sabbatical leave, during which I wrote the first draft of the manuscript, and subsidized additional research and publication through the John M. Glenn Grant Fund and the Philip F. Howerton Fund for Special Programs in the department of religion. The Frances Lewis Law Center at Washington and Lee furnished me with an office during my sabbatical leave. Its director, Lewis H. LaRue, and secretary, Margaret A. Williams, and the dean of the law school, Frederic L. Kirgis, Jr., were particularly gracious in accommodating an interloper in their midst.

I am also grateful to the National Endowment for the Humanities for a fellowship for college teachers that enabled me to take a full-year sabbatical leave in 1987–88.

Finally, several persons at the Colgate Rochester Divinity School/Bexley Hall/Crozier Theological Seminary and at the American Baptist Historical Society, located at the Divinity School, helped provide access to lectures and essays of Walter Rauschenbusch that are difficult to obtain.

I am most indebted to my children, to my wife, Debby, and to our parents for the sustaining care that nourishes both meaningful labor and a sense of justice.

INTRODUCTION

WHY THIS STUDY?

This is a study of the lives and thought of three persons who dedicated much of their intellectual and moral resources to justice, especially economic justice for the working class in the United States. It is not a comprehensive study of their lives or thought. It focuses on their passion for justice and their thinking about justice.

Even those who have never heard of Walter Rauschenbusch, John A. Ryan, or Reinhold Niebuhr have felt the impact of their thinking and acting for justice. Each of them changed the way in which we think about religion and its relationship to moral dimensions of the social order. Due largely to the time at which their creative work was directly influential—Rauschenbusch from 1907 until near the end of the second decade of this century and Ryan from 1906 through the thirties—Rauschenbusch's impact has been confined largely to Protestants and Ryan's to Catholics. Niebuhr's influence has been more expansive. Partly due to the time of his most influential thinking—from 1932 through the fifties—and partly due to an explicit attempt to communicate his largely Protestant insights to others, Niebuhr's writings have informed the thinking of Catholics and of non-Christians. His influence among non-Christians has been sufficiently pervasive for Morton White to refer to them as "atheists for

Niebuhr."[1] In addition to shaping our thinking about justice, within and outside the churches, each of these men advocated specific policies and attempted to bring them about through political and/or other forms of social action. Their impact has not been confined to the academy, or even to intellectuals; they had a role in the enactment of policies that they believed would effect justice for the working class. The most vivid example is Ryan's lifelong support for a minimum wage, which became law in the Fair Labor Standards Act of 1938.

This, then, is a historical study of three persons who have influenced our thinking about justice and some of the policies that shape our lives. My aim is not, however, to trace a history of ideas and social action in their cultural and social impact. This is primarily a study in theological ethics. I analyze, compare, and contrast Rauschenbusch's, Ryan's, and Niebuhr's understandings of justice with the intention of retrieving their legacies for contemporary thinking about justice. Although this book offers no full-blown constructive theory of justice, the concluding chapter sets forth a partial agenda for our thinking about justice. That agenda is derived from my assessments of the legacies these authors have bequeathed to us. This concluding agenda is not a comprehensive review of all the elements in my analysis; it emerges as much from my evaluative judgments as from our authors' legacies. For example, I find deficiencies in Niebuhr's Christian realism and affinities with Rauschenbusch's and Ryan's attempts to account for a divine ordering of human life through nature and social patterns and processes. Others may disagree with my assessments yet still discover legacies for their own thinking about justice in my analysis. In that sense, the seven chapters analyzing, comparing, and contrasting these three views of justice stand independently of the concluding chapter. This focused interpretation is intended to reveal heretofore unrecognized aspects of our authors' understanding of justice that will contribute, in its own right, to our theologically informed thinking about justice.

Few would dispute that Rauschenbusch, Ryan, and Niebuhr provide the most significant writings on justice among American theological ethicists in this century. Despite their continuing influence upon contemporary theology and ethics (Niebuhr more than Rauschenbusch or Ryan), there exist few accessible studies focusing on their understandings of justice.[2] There is, insofar as I am aware, no study that compares

---

1. Morton White, "Religion, Politics, and the Higher Learning," *Confluence* 34 (December 1954): 257. See also *Social Thought in America: The Revolt Against Formalism,* 2d ed. (Boston: Beacon Press, 1957), 404–405.

2. The most notable exception is Karen Lebacqz's treatment of Niebuhr's theory of justice in her *Six Theories of Justice* (Minneapolis: Augsburg, 1986), 83–99. In addition, Merle Longwood has written an essay in which he attempts to ferret out canons of justice

and contrasts their views on justice. I embarked on this study because I believed that a comprehensive and comparative study of their views on justice could uncover contributions, yet unrealized, that they have to make to our thinking about justice.

The idea of a comparative study first occurred to me while reading James Gustafson's brief contrast between Rauschenbusch and Ryan in *Protestant and Roman Catholic Ethics*.[3] Gustafson notes that Rauschenbusch and Ryan never responded seriously to each other's work, despite considerable overlap in their interests.[4] The same observation holds for Niebuhr's relationship to Ryan and, to a lesser extent, to Rauschenbusch as well.

These three men had much more in common than overlapping careers that influenced American social thought and public policy. All three were ordained clergymen who became seminary professors. Each of them came to think about justice in response to indignation about injustices they experienced in the capitalist economy of the United States, yet all three, sons of first generation immigrants (save Niebuhr's mother, Lydia), considered themselves patriotic Americans. Though only Ryan was educated as an ethicist, all three employed ethics, that is, reflection about moral criteria, as a crucial component of their struggle against injustice. Although none called himself a theologian, theology was a crucial component for the ethics of all three. In this sense, they were all theological ethicists. They all gained prominence through books and essays addressed to a wide audience, including laypersons in the church. None of them confined his writing and lecturing to academic peers.[5] Normally, authors with so much in common would respond to one another's work. These three did not.

Niebuhr never systematically developed. "Niebuhr and A Theory of Justice," *Dialog* 14, no. 4 (Fall 1975): 253–262. Charles Curran treats Ryan's views on justice in the context of a long chapter interpreting Ryan's social thought. *American Catholic Social Ethics: Twentieth-Century Approaches* (Notre Dame: University of Notre Dame Press, 1982), 26–91. Of interest, but less accessible, are two Ph.D. dissertations that consider justice as a part of their studies of Ryan's economic thought: *The Economic Thought of Monsignor John A. Ryan* by Patrick Gearty (Washington, D.C.: Catholic University of America Press, 1953) and "The Economic Ethics of John A. Ryan and Gustavo Gutiérrez" by David Krueger (Ph.D. diss., University of Chicago, 1988). Although there are Ph.D. dissertations that treat Rauschenbusch's concern for justice, I know of no study that attempts an analysis of his theory of justice.

3. I have subsequently come to disagree with Gustafson's interpretation of Rauschenbusch in that book. This disagreement is spelled out in the concluding chapter of this volume.

4. James M. Gustafson, *Protestant and Roman Catholic Ethics: Prospects for Rapprochement* (Chicago: University of Chicago Press, 1978), 21–26.

5. In addition to the commonalities already mentioned, both Rauschenbusch and Ryan published their major books with Macmillan, and both were influenced by an important mutual friend, the economist Richard Ely.

Rauschenbusch and Ryan make rare incidental references to each other. I am aware of only one reference Niebuhr made to Ryan. In the second volume of *The Nature and Destiny of Man,* Niebuhr criticized Ryan's "pathetic logic" regarding state tolerance of non-Catholic religion.[6] Niebuhr passed no judgment on Ryan's view of economic justice. Insofar as I know, Ryan never commented on Niebuhr's work. This scarcity of exchange between Protestants and a Catholic, given the period in which our authors wrote, is not surprising. More surprising is that Niebuhr gave very little attention to Rauschenbusch's work. Even though Niebuhr's Christian realism was, in part, a counterpoint to the social gospel, "of which Rauschenbusch was the most celebrated exponent,"[7] Niebuhr did not develop his ethics in relation to analyses of Rauschenbusch. He did, in one paragraph in a 1932 essay, contrast his realist understanding of justice with Rauschenbusch's liberal Protestantism. In that paragraph, Niebuhr wrongly asserted that Rauschenbusch ignored the class struggle and sought justice by purely educational and moral means.[8] There are other scattered references to Rauschenbusch, but Niebuhr's most extensive analysis of Rauschenbusch was in a short essay written in 1957, after Niebuhr's understanding of justice was well established.[9] This paucity of careful analysis of one another's work leaves a near vacuum the comparative analysis in this book is intended to fill.

CLUES FOR UNDERSTANDING

Before engaging my comparative analysis, readers should be alert to five features of its organization.

Theology, Ethics, and Policies

First, the analysis attends to theological, ethical, and policy components in each author's understanding of justice. I doubt that their views on justice can be understood apart from any of these dimensions of their thought. To

---

6. Reinhold Niebuhr, *The Nature and Destiny of Man,* vol. 2: *Human Destiny* (New York: Charles Scribner's Sons, 1943), 223.

7. Reinhold Niebuhr, *An Interpretation of Christian Ethics* (New York: Harper & Brothers, 1935; repr., New York: Meridian Books, 1956), 8.

8. Reinhold Niebuhr, "Is Peace or Justice the Goal?" *The World Tomorrow* 15, no. 10 (September 1932): 276; see also Ronald Stone, *Reinhold Niebuhr: Prophet to Politicians* (Lanham, Md.: University Press of America, 1981), 55–56, 249 n. 7.

9. See Reinhold Niebuhr, "Walter Rauschenbusch in Historical Perspective," in *Faith and Politics,* ed. Ronald H. Stone (New York: George Braziller, 1968), 33–45.

be sure, they articulated their views on justice without having explicitly formulated its theological basis beforehand. Ryan, as a Catholic moral theologian focusing on economic ethics, had precious little, and nothing new, to say about theology. He relied on the Thomist theology he received from his Catholic tradition. Rauschenbusch, a professor of church history, and Niebuhr, a professor of Christian ethics, did not fully develop their theologies until long after their first important books on justice. Nevertheless, the ethical justifications and criteria by which these authors made judgments about the justice of particular policies were, from the beginning of their careers, informed by their understandings, however implicit, of God and God's relations to the world. Thus, I interlace this theological dimension in their ethics with my analysis of their thinking about justice throughout the analysis in this book.

Our authors' writings on justice were not confined to theological and ethical theory. Their theologies and ethics were thought out in the context of a pressing desire to determine what policies were required to secure justice for the working class. They did not develop an academic understanding of justice and then turn to policy questions. There was constant interaction between their commitments to policies and their understandings of justice. Hence, significant portions of the analyses that follow are devoted to discussing the policies that each author believed essential to secure justice. Although I have saved the focused discussions of policies for the final section of each analysis, a strict separation between the understandings of justice and the policies required by justice is impossible. It is necessary to depict features of each understanding of justice with policy illustrations.

Finally, because economic injustice prompted each author's initial interest in academic reflection on justice, I focus on their views regarding economic justice and policies. This focus is not meant to indicate that they did not have other practical interests. Students of Niebuhr know, for example, that his interest in the justice of international relations and war and peace almost overshadowed his interest in economic issues during the forties and fifties.

Experience, Acting, and Thinking About Justice

A second prominent theme in my analysis relates our authors' understandings of justice to their broader vocations as proponents of justice. In each case, their vocations were evoked, in part, by experiences of injustice. Ryan grew up in the midst of people (Irish-American, Catholic farmers in the aftermath of the Civil War) who lived under the burdens of economic injustice. Rauschenbusch and Niebuhr did not, but they encountered injustice in their first assignments as ministers. Rausch-enbusch was repulsed by the poverty in his congregation during an eleven-year ministry in New York City. Niebuhr came to identify with the plight of American laborers through his observations of industrial relations in Detroit during his thirteen-year ministry in a middle-class congregation there. An awareness of these early experiences and the lifelong vocational interests they evoked will aid our understanding of what these authors wrote about justice. My analysis draws upon these experiences and other factors that shaped their character and their broader vocations (i.e., beyond their academic work) as advocates for justice in order to expand our understanding of our subjects' thinking about justice. This study incorporates an account of the lives of these men as it deepens a comprehension of their thought about justice.

Theories and Conceptions of Justice?

I have thus far avoided referring to our authors' "theories" or "conceptions" of justice. With the possible exception of Ryan, they did not consider themselves to be formulating theories or conceptions of justice. Only Ryan offered a systematic delineation of the criteria for justice, and this presentation was neither prominent nor developed early in Ryan's writings. It came in a brief chapter in the middle of his second major book. Our authors' "method" was to write about the theological, ethical, or policy issues raised by their concern to eliminate injustices (e.g., Ryan's dissertation, which became his first book, was an ethical and economic argument for a living wage). They did not set out to write theories of justice. Nevertheless, I believe we can, without distorting their thought, extract from their writings what John Rawls calls a "theory" and a "conception" of justice. This third feature of my analysis requires a brief preliminary explanation.

Rawls defines a "conception" of distributive justice as a "standard [or standards] whereby the distributive aspects of the basic structure of society are to be assessed."[10] Distribution concerns the benefits and burdens of social cooperation.[11] I take Rawls to mean by a "theory" of justice both a full elaboration of one's conception of justice and the various arguments adduced to justify that conception. If we can discover theories and conceptions of distributive justice in our authors' writings, we will have shown that they offer fairly comprehensive, though not systematically presented, justifications for specified criteria

---

10. John Rawls, *A Theory of Justice* (Cambridge: Harvard University Press, 1971), 9.
11. Ibid., 4.

or standards of justice. They did more than express various ruminations and assertions about justice. We can then compare their theories and conceptions of justice to one another and to contemporary theories and conceptions.

My analysis attempts to discover in the writings of Rauschenbusch, Ryan, and Niebuhr theories and conceptions of justice comparable to Rawls's theory and conception. There are, however, crucial differences from Rawls, not only in substance but in what constitutes a theory and a conception of distributive justice and their relationship. I will mention two differences in this context and a third difference below.

First, Rawls's conception of distributive justice presents only ideal principles of justice for a perfectly just society. It does not incorporate what he calls "partial compliance theory," which formulates criteria to deal with existing injustices.[12] Our authors, like Rawls, were primarily concerned with distributive justice, not with retributive or compensatory justice. But for Rauschenbusch and Niebuhr, distributive justice incorporates aspects of what Rawls calls partial compliance theory. They were concerned with distributions of power and burdensome sacrifices as a strategy for moving from injustice to greater justice. Niebuhr, indeed, rejected applicable ideal criteria for justice. Niebuhr's criteria for distributing benefits and burdens are only a strategy for approximating the ideal of justice under conditions in which attempts to apply ideal standards of justice would cause greater injustices. Consequently, my presentation of Rauschenbusch's and Niebuhr's conceptions of justice include criteria for a strategy to secure justice in situations of injustice. In the last chapter, I contrast Rauschenbusch and Niebuhr with Ryan on this point and comment on their differences.

Second, Rawls's conception of justice is concerned with the distribution of primary goods that individuals can claim for themselves in order to pursue their chosen ends in life. Rauschenbusch and Ryan construed the benefits and burdens of distributive justice more broadly. They included individuals' just claims for social institutions that, by virtue of the common values they embody, facilitate self-development. Hence, my interpretations of Rauschenbusch's and Ryan's conceptions of justice include consideration of how common goods embodied in social institutions bear on individuals' opportunities for self-development. Ryan explicitly acknowledges this broad interpretation of the scope of justice by distinguishing between distributive justice, narrowly defined, and what he calls the "distributive" aspects of social justice or the common good. This broadening of the scope of what distributive justice includes

---

12. Ibid., 8–9.

also marks a substantive difference from Rawls (and others), which I explore in the subsequent analysis and my concluding assessments.

Gustafson's Base Points

Use of James Gustafson's four base points for ethics as the organizing framework is a fourth feature of the analysis. Gustafson believes that these four base points, and an organizing principle, framework, or perspective in which they purportedly cohere, can be discerned in any comprehensive ethics.[13] My analysis of each of these theories and conceptions of justice begins with an account of what I take to be the organizing perspective. For Rauschenbusch, it was undoubtedly the kingdom of God. I believe it was human dignity for Ryan and a creative tension between the ideal of love and the actual sinful condition of humans for Niebuhr. Each analysis also includes the authors' interpretations of Gustafson's four base points: an understanding of God; an interpretation of the circumstances of nature, of history, and of the social and economic structures in which justice must be secured; an account of human nature and individual and collective agency; and the criteria by which judgments about the justice of actions and policies are made. I take our authors' interpretations of the first three base points (i.e., God, the circumstances of justice, and human nature and agency) to constitute their justifications for a conception of justice and their elaboration of criteria for making just judgments to constitute their conceptions of justice. Thus, each analysis, in treating the four base points, also presents our authors' theories and conceptions of justice.

---

13. See Gustafson, *Protestant and Roman Catholic Ethics,* 139–141; Gustafson's most recent statement of this claim appears in *Ethics from a Theocentric Perspective,* vol. 2: *Ethics and Theology* (Chicago: University of Chicago Press, 1984). He writes that any comprehensive ethics

> must be developed in relation to four distinguishable base points, or points of reference; and to be coherent there must be an organizing concept, idea, principle, analogy, metaphor, or symbol around which the base points are organized. The base points are: (a) the interpretation of God and God's relations to the world and particularly to human beings, and the interpretation of God's purposes; (b) the interpretation of the meaning or significance of human experience—of historical life and of the human community, of events and circumstances in which persons and collectivities act, and of nature and man's participation in it; (c) the interpretation of persons and collectivities as moral agents, and of their acts; and (d) the interpretation of how persons and collectivities ought to make moral choices and ought to judge their own acts, those of others, and states of affairs in the world (143).

Gustafson also holds that a nontheological ethic will substitute assumptions or beliefs about how those things ultimately and really are for beliefs about God. Thus, the four base points apply to any comprehensive understanding of ethics (143).

In this context, we can note a third crucial difference from Rawls. Rawls observes that one may agree with his conception of justice without accepting his version of contract theory that justifies it, and vice versa.[14] Presumably, one might offer alternative justifications for Rawls's conception of justice. For our ethicists, however, such a sharp separation between the justifying theory and the conception of justice is not possible. Beliefs about God, human nature and agency, and the circumstances of justice persistently enter into Rauschenbusch's, Ryan's, and Niebuhr's application of their criteria for just judgments. Their conceptions of justice do not stand independently of the theories justifying them. Thus, we will find that one who does not accept the theological and other beliefs that justify their conceptions of justice would not fully endorse their criteria for justice or their application of those criteria. My analysis will demonstrate and elaborate on this assertion. The concluding chapter will indicate its implications for our thinking about justice.

A final comment is needed regarding my use of Gustafson's base points. Gustafson observes in *Protestant and Roman Catholic Ethics* that few persons develop an ethics sufficiently comprehensive to treat each of the base points explicitly and to demonstrate their coherence.[15] This observation applies to the subjects of this study. Their ethics are not as comprehensive as Thomas Aquinas's or Karl Barth's.[16] I have tried to avoid imposing upon their ethics comprehensiveness and beliefs that cannot be inferred from their writings. A mechanical application of Gustafson's base points would distort their understandings of justice. Consequently, the analytical chapters do not devote equal space to each of the base points or show in each case how the authors explained coherence among them. Nor is the analysis of the base points symmetrically organized. I have ordered the presentation of the base points and devoted space to each in accord with each author's emphases.

An Asymmetrical Organization

This comment about organization brings us to a fifth and final observation about my analysis. Because I have tried to arrange the next seven chapters in accord with the emphases and developments in the thought

---

14. Rawls, *A Theory of Justice,* 15.
15. Gustafson, *Protestant and Roman Catholic Ethics,* 139.
16. I do maintain that each author's thinking about justice is sufficiently comprehensive to warrant analysis of all four base points in relation to an organizing perspective or theme. Gustafson has himself briefly analyzed Niebuhr's theological ethics in light of the base points. James M. Gustafson, "Theology in the Service of Ethics: An Interpretation of Reinhold Niebuhr's Theological Ethics," in *Reinhold Niebuhr and the Issues of Our Time,* ed. Richard Harries (Grand Rapids, Mich.: Eerdmans, 1986), 24–35.

of the subjects of this study, the organization is complex and may be confusing. A brief comment on the ordering and content of each of the chapters is therefore appropriate.

The first two chapters are on Rauschenbusch. The first chapter is devoted to his understanding of the kingdom of God as the organizing perspective for his theory of justice. His idea of the kingdom of God requires a lengthy analysis because his understanding of that idea and its implications for justice is quite different from what others, including Niebuhr, mean by the kingdom of God. The second chapter treats all four base points in Rauschenbusch's theory of justice and the policies he believed his conception of justice required.

The lengthy third chapter includes Ryan's entire theory of justice as well as an account of the policies he advocated in the first and second decades of this century. The concept of human dignity, which organized his thinking about justice, is dealt with rather briefly in connection with his interpretation of human nature. Due to its relative simplicity and its close connection to his interpretation of human nature, Ryan's concept of human dignity, unlike Rauschenbusch's idea of the kingdom, does not warrant a separate chapter.

The fourth chapter traces Niebuhr's formulation of Christian realism in the creative tension between the ideal and the actual. It concludes with an interpretation of the conception of justice and the policies he advocated during the thirties. This chapter omits any distinct treatment of the first three base points in Niebuhr's theory of justice during the thirties. He did not fully develop his interpretations of human nature and agency, the historical circumstances of justice, and God until after he turned more explicitly to theology in the late thirties and early forties.

The fifth chapter returns to Ryan. It explains how Ryan expanded the application of elements in his theory of justice to advocate new policies in response to the Depression, the New Deal, and developments in official Catholic teaching. It follows the first chapter on Niebuhr in order to vivify differences in Ryan's and Niebuhr's thinking about justice during the thirties.

The sixth and seventh chapters are on Niebuhr. He requires three chapters because of the breadth of his theological ethics and because he changed his mind more dramatically than Rauschenbusch and Ryan did. The sixth chapter deals with Niebuhr's attempt to provide a more extensive theological grounding for his understanding of justice. It analyzes his in-depth treatments of human nature and agency and the historical circumstances in which justice must be done. It also includes a short account of Niebuhr's understanding of God, to which he devoted less attention. Chapter 6 concludes with a revisit to his organizing idea in the context of this theological formulation of these base points. The final analytical chapter explains the modifications Niebuhr made in his conception of justice and the policies he advocated resulting from his response to new events and the deepening of his theory of justice during the forties and fifties.

DISCOVERING LEGACIES

I conclude this introduction with an observation regarding the relation between the seven chapters of analysis and the final chapter on the legacies of Rauschenbusch, Ryan, and Niebuhr. I want to emphasize that I did not undertake an analysis of justice in the thought of these three men with a concluding assessment already in mind.[17] Previous work on justice in Ryan and Niebuhr had formed a basis for analyzing their views, but I have had to refine my interpretations and assessments of them, even though there were no major surprises. My familiarity with Rauschenbusch's thought was no greater than that of any other graduate student in theological ethics who has read his major books. I was open to discoveries. My major discovery was a historical Rauschenbusch far different from the rather superficial optimist whom I thought I had read and heard about. Rauschenbusch was not, in my judgment, a liberal Protestant who thought the difficult problems of justice could be solved by applying a sentimental version of Jesus' love to social institutions in order to bring about the kingdom of God. His sociologically informed interpretation of Jesus and the kingdom of God led him to appreciate natural limits on the capacities of human agents, limits that Niebuhr's ideal of love defies. His conception of justice is inferred, in part, from a divine ordering of nature and social relations that Niebuhr's understanding of God rejects. As I began this project, I did not imagine finding similarities between Rauschenbusch's view of justice based on the kingdom of God and Ryan's understanding of justice based on Catholic natural law theory. As my analysis progressed, I found that Rauschenbusch and Ryan both emphasized that justice requires an equal opportunity for persons to develop their natural interests toward realized

---

17. Furthermore, I present the exposition, analysis, comparison, and contrast of our authors with few evaluative judgments regarding the validity of their claims. I do not bother, for example, to criticize Rauschenbusch's view that all advances in justice emerge through Christian redemption. I do attempt to point out inconsistencies or incoherences in the authors' thinking, and I sometimes qualify or try to focus obviously anticipated criticisms, for example, of Niebuhr's view that the overall problem of justice was solved by 1957. For the most part, however, I leave it for the reader to make her or his own critical judgments and wait until the last chapter to offer some of my own.

excellences of personality.[18] The analysis that follows is far more complex and multifaceted than this brief summary suggests, but as the analysis unfolds two major contentions will become obvious. First, I believe that we need to reevaluate the common interpretation of Rauschenbusch. Second, I hold that Rauschenbusch's and Ryan's notion of equal opportunity for self-development is an important legacy for our thinking about justice. It is worth retrieving.

---

18. Rauschenbusch and Ryan both used the vague and, in our context, misleading term "personality" as a normative end for self-development. What they mean by that term is not fully clear. Neither formulated a theory of virtues, character, or excellences to specify the ends of self-development. Ryan did articulate a proximate end of human nature that integrates the sense, rational, and spiritual faculties in a hierarchical ordering. Rauschenbusch, perhaps intentionally, was even less specific. What is clear from their use of the term is that they had in mind a variety of excellences, not exclusively moral, that required opportunities for persons to cultivate their natural capacities.

PASSION FOR JUSTICE

1

DISCOVERING THE CENTRALITY OF THE KINGDOM OF GOD

THE DISCOVERY

In June of 1886, Walter Rauschenbusch, age 25, arrived at his first full-fledged pastorate—the Second German Baptist Church in the Hell's Kitchen, or Clinton, section of New York City. He came from Rochester Theological Seminary with a firm conviction of the redemptive power of the "person and teachings" of Christ to regenerate individuals. In May of 1885, Rauschenbusch had written his friend, Munson Ford, from a supply pastorate in Louisville, Kentucky, that he was in the process of constructing a view of the gospel of Christ superior to the common doctrine of the imputation of righteousness through belief in the vicarious death of Christ. Rauschenbusch was convinced that the gospel must be "translated into life." He averred that as a person "begins to live a Christ-like life, . . . he will die piecemeal by self-sacrifice just as Christ did even before his crucifixion and then he is at one with Christ and placed by God into the same category."[1] In a later reflection on these seminary years, Rauschenbusch wrote that he had "felt that every Christian ought to in some way or other participate in the dying of the

---

1. Walter Rauschenbusch, a letter to Munson Ford dated May 30, 1885, in *Walter Rauschenbusch: Selected Writings*, ed. Winthrop S. Hudson (New York: Paulist Press, 1984), 55.

Lord Jesus Christ, and in that way help to redeem humanity."[2] Interpreting these remarks, Dores Sharpe, Rauschenbusch's official biographer, held that "this contact with Jesus and his decision to live Christ's way of life, had as much to do with his social enlightenment as anything else."[3] Sharpe's exaggeration is informative.

In contrast to Sharpe's view, Rauschenbusch commented in 1918 that "my idea then was to save souls. . . . I had no idea of social questions" before coming to New York.[4] In another recollection, Rauschenbusch remembered no "social note" in his earlier emphasis upon redeeming humanity through living a Christ-like life. The "social note" "did not come from the church. It came from outside. It came through personal contact with poverty."[5] Rauschenbusch's idea of redemption had indicated some independence from his conservative mentors at Rochester Theological Seminary. He was influenced in part by the liberal theologian Horace Bushnell to depart from his teacher's (Augustus Hopkins Strong) insistence on Christ's substitutionary death.[6] Yet the religion and theology Rauschenbusch received from his father August (director of the German Department at Rochester Theological Seminary) and from his education at a conservative Protestant gymnasium (secondary school) in Germany and at Rochester Seminary were insufficient for the theology and ethics Rauschenbusch would develop to address the social question. Unlike his near contemporary, John Ryan, Rauschenbusch was forced to revise his received theology in order to formulate his theory of justice.

Still, Sharpe's commentary correctly indicates that the emphasis upon redemption through the influence of Christ's person and teaching remained fundamental in Rauschenbusch's social thought. Rauschenbusch would later subsume this emphasis upon redemption under his organizing motif of the kingdom of God, but the theme of redemption would remain crucial for his theory of justice. We will see how Rauschenbusch's stress on Jesus' redemptive influence in history distinguishes his theory and conception of justice from both Ryan's and Niebuhr's.

---

2. Walter Rauschenbusch, "The Kingdom of God," in *The Social Gospel in America, 1870–1920*, ed. Robert T. Handy (New York: Oxford University Press, 1966), 265. First published in 1913.

3. Dores Robinson Sharpe, *Walter Rauschenbusch* (New York: Macmillan, 1942), 57–58.

4. Walter Rauschenbusch, "The Genesis of 'Christianity and the Social Crisis,' " *The Rochester Theological Seminary Bulletin: The Record* 69, no. 3 (November 1918): 51.

5. Rauschenbusch, "The Kingdom of God," 265.

6. Paul M. Minus, *Walter Rauschenbusch: An American Reformer* (New York: Macmillan, 1988), 42–44.

Rauschenbusch united the evangelism from his Baptist heritage with his concern for justice.

During the first few months of his pastorate, two crucial factors compelled Rauschenbusch to reconsider the religious perspective he brought to New York. First, there was the poverty. Rauschenbusch recalled:

> I saw how men toiled all their life long, hard toilsome lives, and at the end had almost nothing to show for it; how strong men begged for work and could not get it in the hard times; how little children died—oh, the children's funerals! they gripped my heart—that was one of the things I always went away thinking about—why did the children have to die? . . . [A] single little human incident of that sort is enough to set a great beacon fire burning, and to light up the whole world for you. . . . And in that way, gradually, social information and social passion came to me.

Rauschenbusch, in this context, makes a special point of the fact that this experience was not "unusual." "I had only the same kind of human information, the same human experiences you all have—or can have. . . . [I]t [the burning fire that lit up the world] did not come through the church."[7] We will find that one of the distinctive features of Rauschenbusch's thinking about justice was a remarkable intertwining of grace and nature, of gospel and social analysis.

Second, Rauschenbusch became involved—to what extent is not clear[8]—in Henry George's campaign for mayor of New York. Harrison Webster, a teacher and friend from the University of Rochester, had earlier commended George's writings to Rauschenbusch,[9] but evidently Rauschenbusch was not deeply influenced by George until 1886. In *Christianizing the Social Order,* Rauschenbusch observed, "I owe my own first awakening to the world of social problems to the agitation of Henry George in 1886, and wish here to record my lifelong debt to this single-minded apostle of a great truth."[10] Rauschenbusch would, throughout his life, remain an advocate of George's proposal for a single tax (a 100 percent tax on rent for unimproved land), though Rauschenbusch went beyond the single tax in his proposals for reforming capitalism.

---

7. Rauschenbusch, "The Kingdom of God," 265–266.
8. Minus, *Walter Rauschenbusch,* 209 n. 26.
9. Ibid., 37; Sharpe, *Walter Rauschenbusch,* 195.
10. Walter Rauschenbusch, *Christianizing the Social Order* (New York: Macmillan, 1912).

More pertinent in this context, however, is that Rauschenbusch's en-
counters with poverty and George's mayoralty campaign in 1886 changed
his reading patterns. Sharpe notes a shift in Rauschenbusch's reading from
sermons to studies of social issues.[11] Especially important among these
readings was the work of Richard Ely, the founder of the American
Economic Association, whose call to reform capitalism was informed by
biblical Christianity and the German socio-historical school of economics.[12] From reading George, Ely, and others, Rauschenbusch became
convinced that the plight of the poor was an economic problem. He gained
an interest in the social sciences that would become an important element
in his interpretation of Christianity and his theory of justice.

After 1886, Rauschenbusch had an interest in the social question
alongside his faith in redemption through a Christ-like life, but he still
had no organizing principle to unite these two seemingly disparate
aspects of life. He recalls, "I had personal religion. I now had that large
social outlook, and how was I to combine the two things? I needed a
unity of life—faith."[13] He remembered returning to scientific study of
the Bible in order to find a basis for the social gospel.[14]

The crucial ingredients for Rauschenbusch's social Christianity were
now present: a personal religious piety stressing redemption and
grounded in the scriptures' portrayal of the person and teachings of
Jesus, an interest in those social sciences that include religious and moral
concerns, and a sensitivity to the plight of the poor provoked by an
unjust economic system. Missing was an organizing principle that could
bring coherence to these disparate commitments.

The idea that would bring coherence was already present. According
to Paul Minus, Rauschenbusch's latest and best biographer, Rauschenbusch had taken courses on the kingdom of God in the Old and New
Testaments during his studies at the gymnasium in Germany[15] and
expressed a continuing interest in the idea during the early years of his
pastorate.[16] By 1889, he was connecting the kingdom of God with the

---

11. Sharpe, *Walter Rauschenbusch,* 64–65. Sharpe offers a long list of Rauschenbusch's
readings in social studies. It includes John A. Ryan. Rauschenbusch obviously would not
have read anything by Ryan prior to Ryan's first publication, *A Living Wage,* in 1906.
12. Minus, *Walter Rauschenbusch,* 63–64. See David Traynham Anderson, "Christian
Discipleship and Social Solidarity: A Study of Walter Rauschenbusch and Richard T. Ely"
(Ph. D. diss., Union Theological Seminary in Richmond, 1990) for an extensive study
comparing and contrasting the social ethics of Rauschenbusch and Ely.
13. Rauschenbusch, "The Kingdom of God," 266.
14. Rauschenbusch, "The Genesis of 'Christianity and the Social Crisis,' " 52.
15. Minus, *Walter Rauschenbusch,* 27–28.
16. Ibid., 51, 62.

social side of Christianity. Changing individual lives, he maintained, is only one half of Christianity; "the other half is to bring in the Kingdom of God."[17] The pages of *For the Right* (a monthly paper edited and published from October 1889 to March 1891 by Rauschenbusch, his friend Leighton Williams, and a few others in order to educate the working class about the social problem) reflect this same two-pronged understanding of Christianity. *For the Right* endorsed a Christian socialism that combined "personal regeneration and social reform."[18] A statement of principles of the Christian Socialist Society of New York City, which Dores Sharpe maintains was written by Rauschenbusch,[19] asserts that Jesus' "gospel of the kingdom of God" "is the good news of a Divine Order."[20] From 1889 to 1891, Rauschenbusch clearly believed Christianity involved personal regeneration and also social reform after the pattern of Jesus' understanding of the kingdom of God. Yet the idea of the kingdom was not the central organizing principle that united his thought.

In 1891, Rauschenbusch's church granted him a sabbatical for a year of study in Europe. He spent most of his sabbatical in Germany studying "the teaching of Jesus" and "sociology." "That," he allowed, "is a good combination likely to produce results." The result for Rauschenbusch was that "Christ's conception of the Kingdom of God came to me as a new revelation. Here was the idea and purpose that had dominated the mind of the Master himself. All his teachings center about it. His life was given to it." Rauschenbusch could now unite his personal piety grounded in the redemptive influence of Jesus' person and teachings with the social impulse in the kingdom of God. "When the Kingdom of God dominated our landscape," he recollected, "the perspective of life shifted into a new alignment. I felt a new security in my social impulses."[21]

This recall, reported in *Christianizing the Social Order,* of when and how the idea of the kingdom of God became the organizing principle for his theology and ethics is confirmed by Rauschenbusch's writings during the same period. Only in 1892, after his return from Europe, did Rauschenbusch promote the kingdom of God to a principle uniting both

---

17. Minus, *Walter Rauschenbusch,* 68, citing Walter Rauschenbusch, from the *Annual Report of the Baptist Congress,* 1989, 55–56.

18. Walter Rauschenbusch, "Good Men and Good Government," *For the Right* 1 (August 1890): 2; see also Winthrop S. Hudson, "Introduction" to *Walter Rauschenbusch: Selected Writings,* 19–20.

19. Sharpe, *Walter Rauschenbusch,* 91–92.

20. Editorial, "Declaration of Principles of the Christian Socialist Society of New York City," *For the Right* 1 (April 1890): 7.

21. Rauschenbusch, *Christianizing the Social Order,* 93.

the personal and social redemptive work of Christ. In "A Conquering Idea" (written in 1892), Rauschenbusch argued for a rediscovery of the centrality of the idea of the kingdom in the synoptic Jesus. He likened this recovery to Luther's rediscovery of the doctrine of justification by faith in Paul.[22] In a lecture to the Baptist Congress in May of 1892, Rauschenbusch led with the proposition that "the whole aim of Christ is embraced in the words 'the kingdom of God'; . . . and that in that ideal is embraced the sanctification of all life, the regeneration of humanity, and the reformation of all social institutions."[23] A book-length manuscript written during Rauschenbusch's sabbatical leave in Germany also reflects this important shift in his thought.[24] It was also in 1892 that Rauschenbusch, Leighton Williams, Nathaniel Schmidt, and a few other like-minded Baptists formed the Brotherhood of the Kingdom for, in Rauschenbusch's words, "the better understanding of the idea of the Kingdom of God."[25]

The revelation Rauschenbusch experienced in Europe altered his thinking in two ways. First, it unlocked a new understanding of Christ's teaching and redemptive significance. Christ was no longer a personal redeemer who was also concerned to bring in the kingdom of God in the social realm. Instead, all of his teachings "center about" the kingdom of God, an idea that "dominated" his mind. The very core of the gospel unites redemption and justice. As we will see, Rauschenbusch perceived that Jesus himself united religious redemption with keen social analysis and social reform. Second, this new understanding of Christ united Rauschenbusch's own personal piety with his concern for justice for the working class. "Here," he says in 1913, "was a religious conception that embraced it all. . . . [W]herever I touched, there was the kingdom of

---

22. Walter Rauschenbusch, "A Conquering Idea," in *Walter Rauschenbusch: Selected Writings,* 71–74. As this essay implies, Rauschenbusch thought the kingdom of God should displace the central role the Reformation gave to justification by faith. The idea of the kingdom is more inclusive. See Rauschenbusch, *Christianizing the Social Order,* 117.

23. Walter Rauschenbusch, "The Pulpit in Relation to Political and Social Reform," in *A Rauschenbusch Reader: The Kingdom of God and the Social Gospel,* comp. Benson Y. Landis (New York: Harper & Brothers, 1957), 146.

24. See Walter Rauschenbusch, *The Righteousness of the Kingdom,* ed. Max L. Stackhouse (Nashville: Abingdon Press, 1968), esp. 79. This manuscript remained unpublished until Max Stackhouse discovered and published a version of it under the title *The Righteousness of the Kingdom.* In his introduction to this volume, Stackhouse suggests that it was written during Rauschenbusch's stay in Europe (18). Paul Minus confirms this claim in *Walter Rauschenbusch,* 78–79.

25. Sharpe, *Walter Rauschenbusch,* 116, citing personal letters of Walter Rauschenbusch from 1892. Minus, in *Walter Rauschenbusch,* citing other evidence, with the exception of *The Righteousness of the Kingdom* manuscript, arrives at precisely the same conclusion that I have about when the kingdom became the organizing theme for Rauschenbusch's thought (81).

God. . . . [I]t touches everything with religion. It carries God into everything that you do, and there is nothing else that does it in the same way."[26] Now Rauschenbusch had a concept that united his emphasis upon redemption through living a Christ-like life with his passion for social justice. Evangelism includes justice, and justice requires redemption through the influence of Christ in history. To understand Rauschenbusch's conception of justice, we must begin with his convictions that the centrality of the kingdom of God in the work of Christ is a redemptive force bearing on the social order and is normative for human conduct and for social institutions.[27]

In the introduction to his first important book, *Christianity and the Social Crisis,* Rauschenbusch wrote that "the essential purpose of Christianity was [and still should be] to transform human society into the kingdom of God by regenerating all human relations."[28] That book propelled Rauschenbusch's social Christianity to national prominence in 1907, but its organizing principle had been clear to him since 1892.[29] Rauschenbusch continued to refine his thinking during the intervening fifteen years, five of those in his New York pastorate, before joining the German Department at Rochester Theological Seminary in 1897.[30] Nonetheless, after 1892 there were no breaks or major developments in Rauschenbusch's theology and ethics (as there were in Niebuhr's) or in the policies he advocated (as there were for Ryan and Niebuhr). Consequently, we can grasp Rauschenbusch's theory and conception of justice

---

26. Rauschenbusch, "The Kingdom of God," 267.

27. I am informed in this claim by an unpublished paper of Barbara Nelson Gingerich, "Rauschenbusch, Yoder, and Troeltsch's Types: Sectarianism and Social Ethics," 1981, presented for History of Christian Social Thought, a religion seminar at the University of Chicago. She argues that Rauschenbusch's ethics is similar to John Howard Yoder's in its insistence that the kingdom of God, as manifest in the life and teachings of Jesus, is directly normative for social ethics (5–9, 13–28). Although, as we will see, Rauschenbusch did not derive his principles of justice directly from Jesus, he did formulate social principles of Jesus that, when joined with his social-scientific analysis of the contemporary social order, required specific principles of justice and even specific social policies.

28. Walter Rauschenbusch, *Christianity and the Social Crisis,* ed. Robert D. Cross (New York: Harper & Row, 1964), xxiii. Originally published in 1907 (New York: Macmillan).

29. He was presumably sufficiently dissatisfied with his early attempts at a comprehensive presentation of his social Christianity that he laid aside three versions of "Revolutionary Christianity," the manuscript he started in Germany in 1891. Finally in the summers of 1905 and 1906, Rauschenbusch wrote a fourth draft, which Macmillan published as *Christianity and the Social Crisis.* See Rauschenbusch, "The Genesis of 'Christianity and the Social Crisis,' " 52; see also Minus, *Walter Rauschenbusch,* 157–158.

30. Rauschenbusch's academic talents had been noted earlier. He had twice rejected offers from Rochester and turned down a feeler to pursue graduate study and teach sociology at the University of Chicago. See Minus, *Walter Rauschenbusch,* 99. In 1902, Rauschenbusch became professor of church history in the English department at Rochester, a position he held until his death in 1918.

while treating his writings from 1892 as a whole. We will, of course, have to remain mindful of his historical context.

The remainder of this chapter delineates the major features of Rauschenbusch's concept of the kingdom of God as the organizing framework for his theology and ethics. In the second chapter we will examine Rauschenbusch's treatment of the four base points that Gustafson notes as essential elements in any comprehensive ethic. The fourth base point—how persons and collectivities ought to make moral judgments—constitutes Rauschenbusch's conception of justice. The second chapter concludes with Rauschenbusch's application of his theory and conception of justice in advocating policies for governments and churches, which he considered the most essential agents in the struggle for justice.

THE KINGDOM OF GOD
Sources

Because Rauschenbusch came to the centrality of the kingdom of God through studying both the Gospels and sociology, it is not surprising that his understanding of the kingdom reflects a confluence of these two sources.

The Person and Teachings of Jesus

Rauschenbusch believed that the Christian conception of the kingdom of God was a divine miracle initiated in its distinctive content by the personality and teachings of Jesus. It is "divine in its origin" and "miraculous all the way."[31] Although similar ideas exist before and outside the revelation of Christ, it "gets its distinctive interpretation from Christ."[32] Neither the place nor the content of justice in Rauschenbusch's thought can be understood unless we keep before us these two claims (divine initiation and distinctiveness) about this source of his social ethics.

First, advances in justice are not products of natural improvements in the moral character of humanity. They are everywhere and always products of the redemptive grace of God introduced into history through Christ. Both the love of justice and the love of humanity that propel the

---

31. Walter Rauschenbusch, *A Theology for the Social Gospel* (New York: Macmillan, 1917; repr., Nashville: Abingdon, 1990), 139.
32. Ibid., 141.

social movement come from Christ.[33] In a lecture written in 1896 for the students at Rochester Seminary, Rauschenbusch insisted that "[o]ur higher moral status is not so much due to our own ethical vigor, as to the spiritual tide that has flooded the collective life of humanity since Christ."[34] He considered it a fact that there was no social movement outside of Christianity.[35] (Christianity exists, however, in the social movement outside the church.) Jesus Christ is, then, not merely a moral example and teacher but also the miraculous source of all moral advance. Consequently, for Rauschenbusch, advances in justice are necessarily products of Christianity, that is, the spirit of Christ that is mediated through Christian institutions but not identified solely with those institutions. Justice is impossible without a "christianizing of the social order." This is why Rauschenbusch persisted in the view that justice depended on a united personal and social regeneration wrought by faith in the gospel. For him justice and evangelism could proceed only hand in hand.

Second, in addition to initiating the kingdom as a divine force in history, Jesus offered a distinctive conception of the kingdom. In each of his four major published books and in *The Righteousness of the Kingdom,* Rauschenbusch turned to Jesus' teaching on the kingdom as the primary source for social ethics. In each case, Jesus begins with the conception of the kingdom that he inherited from the prophets and modifies it to provide a distinctive ethic. Jesus advanced the approximation of the kingdom of God, Rauschenbusch claimed in *The Social Principles of Jesus,* by teaching "an advance in ethics," which is in part "a recognition of new duties and the assimilation of new and higher ethical conceptions."[36] This conception of the kingdom is the source of a higher ethic that remains in constant tension with the mores of the culture. Furthermore, there is no reason to compromise this higher ethic of Jesus. "[T]he obligation to complete what he began comes upon us with an absolute claim to obedience."[37] (In this respect, Rauschenbusch differed both from Ryan, for whom there was no distinctive ethic of Jesus, and from Niebuhr, for whom justice required a compromise of

---

33. Walter Rauschenbusch, "Christ, the Source of All Our Good," *The Treasury* 18, no. 10 (February 1901): 757.

34. Walter Rauschenbusch, "The Corporate Life of Humanity," unpublished lecture in box 17 of the Rauschenbusch Papers at the American Baptist Historical Society Archives in Rochester, New York, 1986, 22.

35. Walter Rauschenbusch, "The Ideals of the Social Reformers," *American Journal of Sociology* 2 (September 1896): 206. Also in Rauschenbusch Scrapbook I at Colgate-Rochester Divinity School Library.

36. Walter Rauschenbusch, *The Social Principles of Jesus* (New York: Association Press, 1916; repr., Darby, Pa.: Arden Library, 1985), 80.

37. Rauschenbusch, *Christianizing the Social Order,* 67.

Jesus' ethic of love.) Rauschenbusch's recurring concern was that the churches taught "the standard of respectability rather than of distinctively Christian ethics."[38] An adulteration of the ethic of the kingdom was especially likely in the churches' judgments about economic activities. The kingdom of God, Rauschenbusch thought, required a distinctively Christian and a revolutionary social ethic.

The Social Sciences

Rauschenbusch's understanding of the kingdom of God was also deeply influenced by his use of the social sciences. His use of social science influenced both his interpretation of the teachings and work of Jesus and his view of the kingdom as a redemptive force in history.

Evolutionary social science.   In order to comprehend these two points, we must see that Rauschenbusch understood social science in light of the evolutionary theories emanating from Darwin. His initial interest was sparked by Harrison Webster. Webster taught Rauschenbusch physiology at the University of Rochester in 1883, and Webster insisted that evolutionary science could be united with Christianity.[39] Dennis R. Davis, in an article challenging Richard Hofstadter's claim that the social gospel movement dissented from all Darwinian and Spencerian evolutionary theory, also notes Webster's influence upon Rauschenbusch.[40] Davis contends that aspects of Darwinian evolutionary thought "formed an essential part of [Rauschenbusch's] synthetic construct of the Kingdom of God."[41] This claim backs my analysis in the pages that follow. Rauschenbusch rejected a social Darwinist justification for the survival of the fittest in a laissez-faire economy,[42] but his view of social science was dependent upon evolutionary natural science. Two points follow.

First, although grounded in human biological nature, this science, because it was evolutionary, was fully consistent with Rauschenbusch's insistence on a historical approach to the social order and to religion. Taking biology as his model, Rauschenbusch insisted upon a historical approach to sciences dealing with human life, especially to political

---

38. Walter Rauschenbusch, "The Service of the Church to Society," *The Treasury* 17, no. 5 (September 1899): 395.

39. Minus, *Walter Rauschenbusch,* 36–38.

40. Dennis R. Davis, "The Impact of Evolutionary Thought on Walter Rauschenbusch," *Foundations* 21, no. 3 (July–September 1978): 260–261.

41. Ibid., 270.

42. Rauschenbusch, *Christianity and the Social Crisis,* 315; Davis, "The Impact of Evolutionary Thought on Walter Rauschenbusch," 265.

economy and to theology.[43] Consequently, he did not identify the kingdom of God or the social order with a static natural order. Human nature
is sufficiently malleable to change under the redemptive influence of the
kingdom, permitting compliance with higher ethical principles.

Second, because the social and natural sciences are closely linked,
Rauschenbusch's sociology was deeply grounded in nature. Thus, he did
not entertain anything like more recent theories that reality is purely a
social construction or that the kingdom of God is a radically new
creation. The kingdom of God is founded upon the given natural instincts and limitations of humans.

This second point further clarifies Rauschenbusch's relationship to the
idealism in some strands of liberalism. We have already seen how
Rauschenbusch differed from the theological liberalism of his day that
ignored the evangelical emphasis upon the redemptive work of Christ
and the distinctiveness of Jesus' ethic. Rauschenbusch also explicitly
distinguished his conception of the kingdom of God from Albrecht
Ritschl's because Ritschl was born too early to employ sociology in his
understanding of the kingdom of God.[44] Rauschenbusch's sociological
understanding of the kingdom separated him from the ethical idealism of
many liberals. Our study of the early Niebuhr will reveal an idealism that
never tempted Rauschenbusch.

Jesus' teaching.   His interpretation of Jesus' conception of the kingdom
reflects the influence of the evolutionary social science Rauschenbusch
used. He accepted a historical-critical method for interpreting scriptures, but he also specified his method in accordance with evolutionary
sociological views. Rauschenbusch insisted that every biblical book
originated from a historical environment, and only within that environment could its meaning and power be accurately understood.[45] He
criticized millenarianists for refusing to read scriptures as "portions of a
living organization of thought, belonging to one man of a certain age and
a certain nation, to be handled reverently and to be understood only in
connection with the other thoughts of that man and his time." Biblical

---

43. See Walter Rauschenbusch, "The Value and Use of History," *The Rochester
Theological Seminary Bulletin: The Record* 65, no. 3 (November 1914): 38. Also in Rausch-
enbusch Scrapbook III at Colgate-Rochester Divinity School Library. See also Walter
Rauschenbusch, "The Influence of Historical Studies on Theology," *American Journal of
Theology* 11, no. 1 (January 1907): 116–117. In both theology and political economy, German
scholarship no doubt influenced Rauschenbusch's historical method. See ibid., 126–127. In
the case of political economy, the German influence was in part mediated through the
American economist Richard Ely. See Minus, *Walter Rauschenbusch,* 62–63.

44. Rauschenbusch, *A Theology for the Social Gospel,* 139.

45. Rauschenbusch, "The Value and Use of History," 35.

prophecy, said Rauschenbusch, who favored metaphors from nature, is analogous to a caterpillar. We know it will develop, but we are incapable of forecasting how. If we try to predict the caterpillar's development, we will surely envision its future as including sixteen legs.[46] This metaphor reflects both Rauschenbusch's emphasis upon the malleability of nature and his contention that biblical interpretation, including his interpretation of the kingdom of God, must proceed within the social and natural contexts of biblical ideas.

On this approach, Rauschenbusch interpreted Jesus as accepting the idea of the kingdom of God that he inherited from the classical prophets, which was still extant in a weakened and apocalyptic form in his own day. Jesus elevated this inherited idea of the kingdom and strove to realize it in his ministry.[47] "He spoke for his own age, about concrete conditions, responding to the stirrings of the life that surged about him."[48] "Like all great minds that do not merely imagine Utopias, but actually advance humanity to a new epoch, he took the situation and material furnished to him by the past and moulded that into a fuller approximation to the divine conception within him."[49] Further, Jesus' own idea of the kingdom was constantly maturing and developing as he responded to events around him. "[H]is conception of the kingdom became vaster and truer as he worked for the kingdom."[50] Finally, Jesus' conception of the kingdom is founded on natural human desires. Jesus prepares persons for the social order of the kingdom by energizing the faculty and habits of love that are already present in the family, in friendship, and in the desire to get together.[51] His high regard for the human personality results from cultivating and elevating a humane instinct that normal persons possess.[52]

An understanding of the kingdom so closely linked to social and natural forces could not be an in-breaking of something so new that it could not even be envisioned within the current customs, laws, institutions, and conceptions of justice. "Even religion is not powerful enough to make a break in the continuity of history."[53] Though Jesus' conception of the kingdom is distinctive (even revolutionary) and commands absolute obedience, it is not such a radical alternative to the wider social

---

46. Walter Rauschenbusch, "Our Attitude Toward Millenarianism," in *Walter Rauschenbusch: Selected Writings*, 89. First published in 1896.
47. Rauschenbusch, *The Righteousness of the Kingdom*, 81.
48. Rauschenbusch, *Christianity and the Social Crisis*, 49.
49. Ibid., 54.
50. Ibid., 65.
51. Ibid., 67–68.
52. Rauschenbusch, *The Social Principles of Jesus*, 8–9.
53. Rauschenbusch, *Christianizing the Social Order*, 328.

order that the primary function of the community of faith is to witness to its distinctive ethic. In what Stackhouse calls his most revolutionary manuscript,[54] Rauschenbusch understood the early church as a base from which the "assimilating and conquering forces [of Jesus] go out to extend the territory of his dominion."[55] Under the influence of his sociological interpretation of scriptures, Rauschenbusch claimed:

> The true way of understanding [Jesus] is to watch him as he makes his way through . . . popular thought, accepting, rejecting, correcting, elevating, enlarging, and hallowing. . . . [He took] the right impulses and convictions already existing among the people and weld[ed] them into a mightier unity. . . . Jesus accepted the faith in the Kingdom of God which his prophetic forerunners held out to him from the past. . . . [H]e gave his full indorsement to the social hope which [was] an essential part of the Kingdom idea. On the other hand, he . . . refashioned it with sovereign freedom. . . . These corrections . . . embody his most distinctive contributions to the Kingdom ideal.[56]

On this method of interpretation, Jesus did not envision a kingdom created ex nihilo but a kingdom "refashioned" from the available social and natural forces. It is, pace Rauschenbusch, more like the emerging bloom of an Easter daffodil than the metamorphosis from a caterpillar to a butterfly.

The kingdom in history. The evolutionary social science Rauschenbusch employed in his interpretation of Jesus also informed his account of how the redemptive force of the kingdom actually emerged from the person of Jesus into history.

First, he insisted on understanding Christ as one who "set in motion the historical forces of redemption which are to overthrow the Kingdom of Evil."[57] This Christ could not have been one who simply taught the ideal of the kingdom. Neither could this historical force emanate from a metaphysical conjoining of divine and human natures in order to carry out ahistorical transactions between God and humanity. On Rauschenbusch's sociological interpretation, Jesus' achievement of personality (i.e., his character) influenced others, thereby initiating the kingdom as a force in history.[58] Furthermore, the influence of Jesus' personality

---

54. Max L. Stackhouse, "Editors Introduction" to *The Righteousness of the Kingdom,* 18–19.
55. Rauschenbusch, *The Righteousness of the Kingdom,* 152. In this respect, Rauschenbusch differs, at least in emphasis, from John Howard Yoder.
56. Rauschenbusch, *Christianizing the Social Order,* 56–57.
57. Rauschenbusch, *A Theology for the Social Gospel,* 147.
58. Ibid., 151.

expands through a social organization that Jesus himself put in place. In a revealing essay, "Jesus as an Organizer of Men," Rauschenbusch portrayed Jesus as one who understood "the practical workings of human life." "He knew human nature and met its needs" by organizing his disciples in a way that they could embody and transmit the ideal of the kingdom of God. Through his practical organizing skill and "by the authority of his personality he made that ideal a living energy in the midst of our sordid earthly materialism."[59]

Second, Rauschenbusch was concerned to trace the ebb and flow of the kingdom as a social force through history. Before Ernst Troeltsch's *Die Soziallehren der christlichen Kirchen und Gruppen,* though with less sociological skill and a superficial and tendentious analysis of medieval Catholicism, Rauschenbusch devoted a large portion of *Christianity and the Social Crisis* to a social and historical analysis of the transmission of the redemptive force of the kingdom through the institutions of Western civilization.

On the basis of this empirical understanding of redemption, Rauschenbusch insisted that the church is indispensable for the salvation of the social realm. In his theology for the social gospel, Rauschenbusch wrote that anyone who understands psychology and social science should

> see the possibilities of such a group [church] in arousing and guiding the unformed spiritual aspirations of the young . . . and its power of reaching by free loyalty springs of action and character lying too deep for civil law and even for education to stir. He might well imagine too how the presence of such a social group would quicken and balance the civil and political community.[60]

Rauschenbusch did claim that the kingdom of Jesus was an ideal, miraculous, and even somewhat mysterious redemptive force in history. It did not emerge and could not have emerged from natural evolution or the social sciences alone, yet he also insisted on an interpretation of the redemptive force of the kingdom that could be comprehended by the social sciences.[61] Readers of Friedrich Schleiermacher's *The Christian Faith* may be reminded of his distinction among the magical, mystical, and empirical explanations of the work of Christ. Although Rauschenbusch did not

---

59. Walter Rauschenbusch, "Jesus as an Organizer of Men," *The Biblical World* 11, no. 2 (February 1898): 102–111.

60. Rauschenbusch, *A Theology for the Social Gospel,* 120.

61. "Scientific sociology may remain academic, cold, and ineffective. We need inspiration, impulse, will power, and nothing can furnish such steady accessions of moral energy as living religion. Science and Christian faith combined are strong." Rauschenbusch, *The Social Principles of Jesus,* 195.

explicitly employ Schleiermacher's terms, he, like Schleiermacher, rejected a "magical" explanation of redemption that ignored mediation by "anything natural" and a strictly "empirical" explanation that neglected the "peculiar" and miraculous element in the redemptive activity of Christ.[62] Rauschenbusch, however, was much more interested than Schleiermacher in how redemption occurs in the social order. Rauschenbusch's view of the kingdom was grounded in the actual social and natural conditions of humanity. "The Kingdom of God is not a concept nor an ideal merely, but an historical force. It is a vital and organizing energy now at work in humanity. Its capacity to save the social order depends on its pervasive presence within the social organism."[63]

Clearly, this scientific interpretation of the kingdom calls for a conception of justice that includes an analysis of the social forces emerging within society. There can be no "ought" divorced from an analysis of what "is," or more precisely, from what is becoming. As we will see, Rauschenbusch developed his conception of justice precisely in this way in light of his analysis of the circumstances in history.

Such an approach to justice disallows deriving principles of justice directly from the teachings and person of Jesus. Nevertheless, Rauschenbusch's procedure for deriving principles of justice was fully consistent with his scientific interpretation of Jesus introducing a distinctive ethic that claims absolute obedience. Jesus' ethic is directly normative in the sense that it does not have to be compromised to accommodate an actual human nature that Jesus ignored. Jesus' ethic, however, must be specified in light of changing historical conditions. As we have seen, Jesus' distinctive interpretation of the kingdom developed throughout his ministry and was grafted onto the realities of his society so as to emerge more fully in the social forces of history. Consequently, an ethic of the kingdom for a particular period should seek to discern the distinctive elements of Jesus' kingdom as they appear in contemporary social forces. "We therefore put the problem faultily when we ask: What did Jesus think? We ought to ask: In what direction were his thoughts working? . . . If we want to be faithful to his spirit, . . . we shall not only have to trace the line along which he moved, but even prolong it beyond the point marked in his recorded teaching."[64] We should not expect Rauschenbusch to present Jesus' teachings as a fully adequate contemporary conception of justice.

---

62. Friedrich Schleiermacher, *The Christian Faith*, trans. from the second German edition, ed. H. R. Mackintosh and J. S. Stewart (Edinburgh: T. & T. Clark, 1928), 428–431.

63. Rauschenbusch, *A Theology for the Social Gospel*, 165.

64. Rauschenbusch, *Christianizing the Social Order*, 58.

In sum, Rauschenbusch drew his interpretation of the kingdom of God from his sociological interpretation of the distinctive teachings and person of Christ as a miraculous redemptive force in history. Neither social sciences alone nor Jesus, interpreted without use of the evolutionary social sciences, could issue in a similar understanding of the kingdom. Without Jesus, the miraculous and distinctive redemptive transformation of persons and social institutions would be lost. Without Rauschenbusch's sociology, the kingdom would not have been so closely connected to social and natural forces within history. Though this combination of sources may be incongruous to some, it was not to Rauschenbusch. Jesus, himself, warrants the use of social science. Rauschenbusch maintained that the "conscious evolutionary program of Jesus . . . combines religion, social science, and ethical action in a perfect synthesis."[65] "Jesus," he asserted, "thought more scientifically about moral questions than most of us."[66]

With the confluence of these two sources in mind, we are prepared to consider the salient features of Rauschenbusch's conception of the kingdom of God.

Salient Features of the Kingdom

A fully orbed presentation of Rauschenbusch's understanding of the kingdom of God would consume an entire volume. We need only consider those features that bear directly upon his conception of justice: its social dimension, its evolutionary character, and the social principles that characterized the kingdom from the time of its most complete expression in the teachings and person of Jesus.

Social Dimension

In his day, Rauschenbusch was compelled to argue long and hard against Christians who focused exclusively upon individual spiritual and moral regeneration for the sake of attaining eternal life. In two pamphlets published for the Brotherhood of the Kingdom not long after its inception in 1892, Rauschenbusch argued that the church must recover the kingdom in its full content as the organizing aim of Jesus' ministry. The loss of this focus, he believed, had led to distorting emphases upon individual salvation and future life, the individual spiritual life, and the church as coterminous with the kingdom. Millenarianists, Rauschenbusch conceded, included hope for social justice, but this hope is, he

---

65. Rauschenbusch, *The Social Principles of Jesus,* 76.
66. Rauschenbusch, *Christianizing the Social Order,* 293.

lamented, entirely future oriented. He insisted that in addition to individual salvation and hopes for justice in a distant future, the "Kingdom also means a growing perfection in the collective life of humanity, in our laws, in the customs of society, in the institutions of education, and for the administration of mercy." Yet Rauschenbusch refused to reduce the kingdom to regenerating the social order; the kingdom, he averred, is a "synthesis" combining all one-sided conceptions of it.[67]

Obviously, Rauschenbusch thought faithfulness to Christ entailed concern for a just social order, but that point alone tells us little about how the idea of the kingdom informed his conception of justice. We are primarily interested in why the kingdom requires a concern for the social realm, the nature of this social dimension, and its relation to Rauschenbusch's continued emphasis upon evangelism and personal regeneration.

The dignity of the individual, that is, the sacredness of individual life and its development unto salvation and perfection, was fundamental for Rauschenbusch. He believed Jesus offered individuals the satisfaction of all their desires and personal perfection to those who receive him.[68] Emphasis upon the dignity of the individual personality is one of the ways in which Rauschenbusch believed Jesus corrected the prophets' conception of the kingdom.[69]

Yet Rauschenbusch argued in "The Corporate Life of Humanity" that Jesus, especially in the latter days of his life, shared the prophets' view of the nation as a collective personality that acts in rough regularity across space and time.[70] The central theme of this essay was that individuals tend to act in concert with the collective personality of the nation and receive their just due when the nation suffers or flourishes. Rauschenbusch rejected what he said was his earlier view that "every man [is] a moral being, complete in himself, standing and falling on his own merits, and entitled to his just measure of happiness and unhappiness."[71] He stressed the interconnectedness of individual and collective agents.[72] "Only by this view of

---

67. Rauschenbusch, "The Brotherhood of the Kingdom" and "The Kingdom of God," in *Walter Rauschenbusch: Selected Writings,* 74–79.

68. Rauschenbusch, *The Righteousness of the Kingdom,* 97.

69. Ibid., 95–96; idem, "The Corporate Life of Humanity," 7.

70. Ibid., 7–8.

71. Ibid., 2.

72. Rauschenbusch never dealt explicitly with the obvious tension between his claims that the individual is sacred and that individuals must suffer for the sins of collective agents. Both claims recur throughout his theology and appear in his conception of justice. I suspect it never occurred to Rauschenbusch to address this apparent inconsistency because he believed that the sacredness of the individual was only a goal to be achieved in the kingdom of God. He never doubted that progress toward the kingdom required sacrifices and suffering of individuals, which no absolute assertion of the sacredness of the individual could permit.

the nation as a moral personality, which lives on and possesses moral continuity even though the citizens pass away, can the moral problems of history be solved."[73] Consequently, "if we wish merely to save souls and see the church walk in holiness of life, even if we do not feel any social enthusiasm or any longing for the Kingdom of God in its larger sense, we must seek to saturate the collective life with higher ethical convictions and purify it of temptation."[74] As he says in *The Righteousness of the Kingdom*, "the life of the individual cannot be perfected except by seeking the perfection of society."[75]

Seeking the perfection of society cannot be limited to a concern for the collective consciousness of a people. The collective personality and therefore the individual personality are rooted in the institutions of a social order.

> For a workingman salvation [development toward personal perfection] includes a happy home, clean neighbors, a steady job, eight hours a day, a boss that treats him as a man, a labor union that is well led, the sense of doing his own best work and not being used up to give others money to burn. . . . A full salvation demands a Christian social order which will serve as the spiritual environment of the individual.

It depends upon the individual living in a social organism that is ruled by justice.[76]

For Rauschenbusch, the social nature of the kingdom entails just social institutions as a necessary means for the dignity and perfection of individuals. Because the kingdom is founded upon the dignity of the individual personality, justice is not measured by maximizing the aggregate of the good of individuals nor merely by the flourishing of the collective good. Yet his fundamental concern was not with individual rights and liberties. It was with the moral and religious development of personalities. Persons are woven into the web of a collective personality and a social order. Consequently, the social nature of the kingdom requires that justice aim to form social institutions that encourage individual development. Justice is not founded upon consent among autonomous individuals.

This understanding of the social nature of the kingdom also requires a place for the church in a just social order. The interconnectedness of the collective personality of a nation and the individual agent is mediated by

---

73. Ibid., 8.
74. Ibid., 27.
75. Rauschenbusch, *The Righteousness of the Kingdom*, 115.
76. Rauschenbusch, *Christianizing the Social Order*, 116–117.

institutions such as the family and church. Like the larger collective personality of a nation, families and churches possess an identifiable character, which they transmit to individuals. Like individuals, however, families and churches are only semi-autonomous, never free from the character-shaping sanctions of the social order and the collective personality of a nation. In this network of social interdependency, the church has a capacity for grafting individual lives into the ethic of the kingdom, yet it cannot easily endure as a servant of Jesus unless the society is also christianized. On Rauschenbusch's view of the relation between the church and the social order, the proposal of Stanley Hauerwas that the church can be "faithful to the kingdom by showing the world what it means to be a community of peace" without seeking "to *make* the world the kingdom"[77] was not a viable option. For Rauschenbusch the church has only "three possibilities. It can flee out of the world [isolate itself from the influence of society]; it can become like the world; it can make the world like itself."[78] If the church, in Stanley Hauerwas's terms, rejects a "withdrawal ethic" in order to "stand within the world witnessing to the peaceable kingdom,"[79] it had better make the world like itself. Because the character of the church, like that of individuals, depends in part upon a social order for support, it cannot for long preserve values antithetical to a society in which it chooses to remain involved. Thus Rauschenbusch feared: "If society continues to disintegrate and decay, the Church will be carried down with it."[80]

In accord with this social understanding of the kingdom, Rauschenbusch gave the church a crucial role in securing justice. The church has three functions. In obedience to the redemptive influence of Christ, the church must "maintain and strengthen its own peculiar life" in order to be a source of the revolutionary power of the kingdom.[81] But because it is itself a social organism subject to "the law of social gravitation," the church must also be an effective agent in the struggle for justice. "Even religion," Rauschenbusch observes, "is not strong enough permanently to overcome profound social differences of wealth and poverty. If we want equality in the churches, we must have approximate equality in society."[82] For the church to serve the kingdom, it must work effectively for a just social order. Third, as a semi-independent agent, the church

---

77. Stanley Hauerwas, *The Peaceable Kingdom: A Primer in Christian Social Ethics* (Notre Dame: University of Notre Dame Press, 1983), 103.
78. Rauschenbusch, *The Righteousness of the Kingdom*, 160.
79. Hauerwas, *The Peaceable Kingdom*, 102.
80. Rauschenbusch, *Christianity and the Social Crisis*, 341.
81. Rauschenbusch, *The Righteousness of the Kingdom*, 152ff.
82. Rauschenbusch, "The Service of the Church to Society," 396.

can affect the collective personality through evangelism of individuals. Evangelism involves personal regeneration, not merely by conversion but through "assimilating" persons into a fellowship with its own corporate virtues of justice, generosity, and love.[83]

The social nature of the kingdom places a necessary and distinctive role upon the church in the struggle for justice. This role reflects Rauschenbusch's view that a just social order is a sine qua non for the kingdom. It also reveals his contention that the kingdom cannot be reduced to a just social order. This is so for two reasons.

First, a just social order is impossible apart from the redemptive force of Jesus' personality mediated through the evangelizing influence of the church. When Rauschenbusch claimed that the kingdom united personal religion and social reform, he did not merely mean that both were important. They are necessary for each other. He did not believe social justice could arise from education in social science and ethics alone. While the development of the person is impossible without a just social order, neither can "the perfection of human society . . . be attained without changed lives to attain it."[84]

Second, the kingdom Jesus initiated was concerned with more than the social order or morality. "Beyond the question of economic distribution lies the question of moral relations; and beyond the moral relations to men lies the question of the religious communion with the spiritual reality in which we move and have our highest being."[85] The highest goal of the kingdom is "the gladness of unhindered brotherhood and humanity" and communion with God. A just social order is the necessary "scaffolding" for obtaining this goal and must be formed to serve it, but the kingdom is more than a just social order.[86] Love is the goal of justice. Justice is necessary for love. Yet love is more than justice.

Rauschenbusch's understanding of the kingdom integrated Jesus' distinctive emphasis on the dignity of the person with a social scientific analysis of human agents and institutions. It also united the church's mission to evangelize individuals with its role as an agent for justice and connected the regeneration and salvation of individuals with reformation of the social order. These two concerns—for the individual and for the social order—are not merely two legitimate sides of Christian faithfulness; they must be united in order to comprehend either Rauschenbusch's notion of personal salvation or his conception of justice.

---

83. Rauschenbusch, "The Corporate Life of Humanity," 29.
84. Rauschenbusch, *The Righteousness of the Kingdom*, 115.
85. Rauschenbusch, *Christianity and the Social Crisis*, 48.
86. Ibid., 62–64.

Evolutionary Character

According to Rauschenbusch, the kingdom evolves through history. His argument for an evolutionary view of the kingdom was directed primarily against a conservative apocalyptic millenarianism that was, within Baptist circles, a significant obstacle to his reforming ideas. Rauschenbusch's view of the coming of the kingdom differs, however, from all forms of apocalypticism or eschatology that do not perceive history as gradually, though erratically, progressing toward perfection under the redemptive influence of Christ.

Rauschenbusch granted that this evolutionary view of the kingdom was informed by his appropriation of social science, but it was, he maintained, congruous with and informed by the thought and work of Jesus.

First, Jesus was born into a social milieu in which apocalyptic views of the kingdom were dominant, but Jesus began to purge his thinking of apocalyptic elements as his own ideas of the kingdom developed. Rauschenbusch drew attention to Jesus' organic metaphors for the kingdom (e.g., "parables of the sower, the tares, the net, the mustard-seed, and the leaven") to show that Jesus' "higher spiritual insight reverted to the earlier and nobler prophetic view that the future was to grow out of the present by divine help."[87] Rauschenbusch conceded that Jesus retained some apocalyptic elements and that apocalypticism became even more pronounced in early Christianity. Nevertheless, he insisted that when Jesus "repeatedly and emphatically explained the coming of the Kingdom in terms taken from biological growth," he was moving "in the same direction in which the modern mind has moved."[88]

Second, faith in Jesus should inform modern evolutionary thought. Jesus was more than a socialist reformer. He was "the inaugurator of a new humanity" that bore "the germs of a new social and political order." The necessity for this redemptive element in evolutionary thought was a constant in Rauschenbusch's thinking. Thus, we see that Rauschenbusch considered his evolutionary views "a combination beween [sic] the faith of Jesus in the need and possibility of the kingdom of God, and the modern comprehension of the organic development of human society."[89]

On the basis of this evolutionary conception of the kingdom, Rauschenbusch opposed the eschatological thought of his day for its pessimism,

---

87. Ibid., 59–61; see also idem, *Christianizing the Social Order,* 64–65; idem, "Our Attitude Toward Millenarianism," 89–90; and idem, *The Righteousness of the Kingdom,* 109.
88. Rauschenbusch, *The Social Principles of Jesus,* 58–59.
89. Rauschenbusch, *Christianity and the Social Crisis,* 91.

its catastrophic view of progress, and its emphasis upon consummation rather than process.

In an early article attacking millenarianism, Rauschenbusch first praised it for preserving hope for a future that is both social and connected to the attractive features of this world.[90] He then chided it for its pessimistic refusal to grant that evolutionary changes have produced "an improvement in the net quantity of God-fearing righteousness on earth." Evolution is not only change; it is moral and religious progress. "[W]e cannot cease to believe that Christianity is gaining inch by inch."[91] This optimism clearly implies that the kingdom is already partially present, a view that Rauschenbusch, in other writings, affirms and attributes to Jesus.[92] Rauschenbusch clearly possessed an ethically significant hope grounded in optimism that the kingdom was already coming; but lest we misconstrue that hope, we must interpret it in its historical context, especially his battle with millenarians.

First, Rauschenbusch opposed millenarian pessimism because it encouraged indifference toward the social order. His hope was not for a natural evolution toward societal perfection. Rauschenbusch agreed with millenarians that "the world, *minus* the redemptive forces of Christianity, sags downward instead of rising upward, that society naturally decays, that the increase in material wealth only hastens the rotting, and that the spread of intelligence but makes evil more malignant." Only when the "redemptive forces of Christ" are added do we have a basis for optimism.[93] This redemptive force of the kingdom emerges when the distinctive ethic of Jesus comes as a task as well as a gift. Jesus' ethic was not a nonassertive, disinterested love; Jesus was, though nonviolent, involved in a revolutionary and irreconcilable conflict with the powers of his age.[94] The task of advancing the kingdom "is not simply a process of social education, but a conflict with hostile forces" of evil.[95] This clash requires suffering from those who accept the task of the kingdom.[96] Rauschenbusch did not believe justice could progress through the application of social science or moral principles alone; it would require divine regeneration as well as human conflict and suffering. This said, Rauschenbusch was an optimist about progress, though not progress unto perfection.

90. Rauschenbusch, "Our Attitude Toward Millenarianism," 86–87.

91. Ibid., 90–91.

92. E.g., Rauschenbusch, *Christianizing the Social Order,* 65; idem, *A Theology for the Social Gospel,* 220.

93. Rauschenbusch, "Our Attitude Toward Millenarianism," 91.

94. Rauschenbusch, *The Righteousness of the Kingdom,* 75.

95. Rauschenbusch, *The Social Principles of Jesus,* 151.

96. Ibid., 175.

Second, Rauschenbusch's opposition to the wholly future kingdom of millenarianism was based on evolutionary thought. For him the kingdom was present in the sense that the old era was gradually passing into the new.[97] His organic idea of the presence of the kingdom left no room for notions that the kingdom was present in eschatological communities of faith or already victorious over the old era in principle by virtue of the lordship of Christ. For Rauschenbusch, the kingdom was not present unless it was penetrating the unjust social order. The kingdom was present only to the extent that it was in fact in the social order. Rauschenbusch did not intend for Christians to live "as if" the kingdom of God were already established. Rather, he intended them to discern the divine forces for justice that were actually emerging in the wider society. These redemptive forces, Rauschenbusch believed, could be nourished to move the social order toward a closer approximation of the kingdom.

Rauschenbusch also opposed millenarian apocalypticism for its belief "in salvation by catastrophe, and hence [its] lack of interest in salvation by development."[98] This theme persists throughout Rauschenbusch's writings alongside his contention that a kingdom ethic is revolutionary and conflictual.[99] These motifs, the evolutionary and the revolutionary, cohere only if we interpret Rauschenbusch as claiming that an upheaval of values and institutions is a necessary element of evolution but not the sole means of progress and never the occasion for an abrupt establishment of the kingdom.

To place hope in catastrophe is morally wrong on two counts. First, it paralyzes action until the catastrophe occurs. The millenarianists were guilty of this error.[100] Also guilty were dogmatic socialists who, awaiting the collapse of capitalism, rejected piecemeal reforms. They allowed working persons to suffer when practical ameliorative actions were possible.[101] The dogmatic socialists committed a second error in hoping that a catastrophic collapse of the social order would produce a just society. Rauschenbusch's evolutionary view offered no such hope. He argued for a steady improvement by reforms so that the people would be ready for the task of managing society when dramatic change had evolved.[102] Rauschenbusch tended to oppose violence for the same reasons. Violence, he held, is ineffective in gaining justice for the people

97. Rauschenbusch, *Christianizing the Social Order*, 65.
98. Rauschenbusch, "Our Attitude Toward Millenarianism," 93.
99. Rauschenbusch, *A Theology for the Social Gospel*, 225–226.
100. Rauschenbusch, "Our Attitude Toward Millenarianism," 94.
101. Rauschenbusch, "Dogmatic and Practical Socialism," in *The Social Gospel in America*, 318. First published in 1901.
102. Ibid., 320.

it seeks to help. Responding to the revolutionary violence advocated by some social reformers, Rauschenbusch counseled patience "not for the sake of the people who might get hurt in a scrimmage, but for the sake of the cause and its ultimate success."[103]

The expectation that the kingdom would come by evolution rather than catastrophe reveals and informs the consequentialist element in Rauschenbusch's approach to justice. Justice is not an ideal that will be established abruptly; it requires policies that will produce the best consequences for gradually approximating the kingdom.

In his later writings, Rauschenbusch also criticized eschatologies that emphasized the consummation of perfection. In his last book, Rauschenbusch states plainly: "An eschatology which is expressed in terms of historic development has no final consummation." He goes on, in a statement that sounds much like Troeltsch,[104] to declare that the astronomical clock is ticking and will ring our race to an end in due time.[105] Rauschenbusch did not infer Troeltsch's strong criticisms of anthropocentricism and Christocentrism from this fact, but his evolutionary view of the kingdom clearly did not include a hope for the final fulfillment of humanity.[106]

Rauschenbusch, unlike Niebuhr, claimed ethics should demand perfection, though this claim must be qualified in three ways. First, perfection is not expected; it is demanded only because doing so will bring a closer approximation of it.[107] (Niebuhr explicitly denied the latter assertion.) Second, perfection occurs through the "hallowing" and balancing of natural relations and desires (e.g., "natural selfishness" and the "instinct for self-preservation").[108] Human perfection is not an ideal grounded in a freedom to transcend natural desires. (Niebuhr adopted the latter view of perfection.) Third, it is not the final ideal of perfection but the process of evolving toward it that is crucial for moral reasoning.

---

103. Rauschenbusch, "A Conquering Idea," 217. Jesus supposedly resisted the temptation to violence on similar social scientific and consequentialist grounds. See Rauschenbusch, *Christianity and the Social Crisis,* 57–60; idem, *Christianizing the Social Order,* 58–59.

104. See James M. Gustafson, *Ethics from a Theocentric Perspective,* vol. 1: *Theology and Ethics* (Chicago: University of Chicago Press, 1981), 97–98.

105. Rauschenbusch, *A Theology for the Social Gospel,* 227.

106. It would be interesting to speculate how Rauschenbusch, if he had lived to develop his theology more fully, would have integrated these ideas into his theology and ethics. As it stands, he seems to reconcile this denial of eschatological consummation with his focus on God as redeemer by locating the fulfillment of redemption in ceaseless aspiring toward perfection. See ibid.

107. Rauschenbusch, *Christianizing the Social Order,* 126; idem, *Christianity and the Social Crisis,* 420–421.

108. Rauschenbusch, *Christianizing the Social Order,* 308–310.

Jesus believed in a final consummation, but the more he became involved in the power of redemptive forces to mold human life, "the more would the final act of consummation recede in importance and the present facts and processes grow more concrete and important to his mind."[109] "[W]hat is the use of a perfect ideal which never happens? . . . The life of the race is in its growth."[110]

Rauschenbusch was more concerned with the ethical significance of redemption as progress, improvement, or growth than he was with an idea of final perfection. Nearly all of his numerous references to utopian thought were critical of its idealism.[111] For Rauschenbusch, justice was not a perfect ideal by which to judge individuals and institutions. He formulated and applied his conception of justice by discerning how various sectors of the social order were evolving toward the values of the kingdom embodied in the nonutopian teachings and work of Jesus.

In sum, Rauschenbusch's evolutionary conception of the kingdom is optimistic about religious and moral progress, rejects the notion that progress will come through catastrophe, and is inspired by hope in progress toward perfection while eschewing hope in a final eschatological perfection.

Social Principles

For Rauschenbusch, the kingdom was more than a social and evolutionary perspective or a few ideal values. An understanding of the kingdom must provide moral direction to be effective in penetrating the social order. Rauschenbusch's did. In *Christianizing the Social Order,* Rauschenbusch went so far as to call demands to democratize industry, eliminate monopolies, and so forth, "laws of the Kingdom of God on earth."[112] But these "laws" (they were more like guidelines) get ahead of our story, depending as they do on Rauschenbusch's analysis of the contemporary social order as well as on Jesus' distinctive ethic of the kingdom. Even prior to this analysis, Rauschenbusch believed Jesus' ethic of the kingdom could be specified in general social principles. These principles appear throughout Rauschenbusch's writings, but he summarized them in *The Social Principles of Jesus,* a simply written monograph he intended as a study guide for college

---

109. Rauschenbusch, *Christianity and the Social Crisis,* 63.
110. Rauschenbusch, *A Theology for the Social Gospel,* 227.
111. E.g., Rauschenbusch, *Christianity and the Social Crisis,* 33–34, 54, 108–112, 420; idem, *Christianizing the Social Order,* 64–65, 329; idem, *The Social Principles of Jesus,* 58, 191.
112. Rauschenbusch, *Christianizing the Social Order,* 372–373.

seniors. There are three key principles and several supplemental principles that indicate how the key principles can be realized. Two preliminary observations provide necessary context for understanding these principles.

First and most crucial, these general principles (as well as the principles of justice and all other moral duties) are rooted in love as a natural instinct that unifies humanity. This natural instinct is raised to its highest level by Jesus' teachings and personality.

> Love is the force that draws man and man together, the great social instinct of the race. It runs through all our relations and is the foundation of all our institutions. . . . The social mission of Christianity is to make this natural instinct strong, durable, pure, holy, and victorious over all selfish and hateful passions. The spirit of Christ allies itself with all other social forces that make for love.[113]

Love is not a transcendental ideal that Christ introduces into history or a norm counter to all natural desires and interests. Rauschenbusch's most succinct definition of love appears in *Dare We Be Christians?*, a short monograph reflecting upon 1 Corinthians 13. This love has its beginnings in sexual love and sexual love's most powerful forms in familial affections, which are then expanded to include larger associations, the nation, and finally all of humankind.

> In all [these] forms love creates an enjoyment of contact and a desire for more of it, a sense of the worth and human beauty of those we love, pride in their advancement, joy in their happiness, pain in their suffering, a consciousness of unity, an identity of interests, an instinctive realization of solidarity.[114]

This understanding of love differs emphatically from Niebuhr's view of love as agapeic, nonassertive self-sacrifice detached from its consequences for finite interests and mutuality.[115] Rauschenbusch retained a significant place for sacrifice insofar as it is effective in producing greater solidarity, but it is not a universal norm. Sacrificial love that leaves no room for "selfish interests" is a "contrivance" that is "too good to be good for anything." Properly understood, love is a natural human

---

113. Ibid., 262.
114. Walter Rauschenbusch, *Dare We Be Christians?* (Boston: Pilgrim Press, 1914), 22–35.
115. Niebuhr correctly observed that Rauschenbusch would have been "outraged" by Andres Nygren's interpretation of agape. See Niebuhr, "Walter Rauschenbusch in Historical Perspective," 39.

capacity for devotion to the common good that can be tapped by a christianized social order.[116]

This understanding of love as a kingdom-building force is obviously informed by Rauschenbusch's social scientific interpretation of Jesus. This love undergirds all of his social principles, including his principles of justice, and it is the root of his differences from Niebuhr.

The second observation concerns the imprecise expression of these general principles. This imprecision reflects the audience to which *The Social Principles of Jesus* was addressed as well as Rauschenbusch's characteristic lack of interest in a refined clarity of principles philosophers often demand. It also reflects the functions he intended these principles to perform. They are not direct action-guides but guides for asking questions that illumine the course to action.

In light of these observations, the key social principles of Jesus are "simple human principles which are common and instinctive with all real men." Jesus expands, clarifies, and lifts them to the high level of religious principles.[117] They are: "the sacredness of life and personality, the solidarity of the human family, and the obligation of the strong to stand up for all those whose life is impaired or whose place within humanity is denied."[118] Each of these principles requires a brief description to determine the kind of questions they raised for Rauschenbusch.

The sacredness of life and personality does not indicate, as might be implied, any inviolate individual rights to life, liberty, property, and so forth (recall his reasons for opposing violence). It is more a teleological than a deontological principle. On the basis of Jesus' respect for the divine worth of each individual, Rauschenbusch considered the goals of a "human environment in which the life of man could unfold in freedom and strength" and of industry organized to give all "the maximum opportunity of a strong normal life."[119] Individual sacrifices have been made and should continue to be made to bring about this social order in which each person has an opportunity to develop. Thus, this principle does not entail rights that protect individuals from restrictions imposed by society for the sake of the common good. It directs Rauschenbusch's

---

116. Rauschenbusch, *Christianizing the Social Order,* 330. This appreciation for the natural basis of love appears to be one area in which Rauschenbusch's thought changed. In *The Righteousness of God,* he wrote of the baser animal desires being broken by the revolutionary power of the Spirit of God. Even here the old desires are not annihilated but given a new center of gravity (134–135). Nevertheless, the tone is quite different from later passages in which the spirit of Christ is understood to hallow and to train natural relations and instincts. E.g., Rauschenbusch, *Christianity and the Social Crisis,* 308–310.

117. Rauschenbusch, *The Social Principles of Jesus,* 49.

118. Ibid., 190; see also 43.

119. Rauschenbusch, *Christianizing the Social Order,* 327–328.

attention to eradicating conditions in the present social order that are obstacles to the self-expression of individual personalities, especially obstacles for the working class.[120]

The principle of solidarity simply extends to all humans this care for the development of each individual personality. The principle does not aim initially at instilling in individuals a sense of solidarity with all other individuals nor at achieving the flourishing of the "collective personality." It is concerned with the common life for the sake of encouraging mutual affection among individuals. It aims to extend the natural care for each member, characteristic of familial solidarity, to a similar societal-wide fellowship.[121] It asks whether the social order contributes to or frustrates this solidarity. This focus leads Rauschenbusch to inquire if competition, the law of the market, and the wage system break down solidarity among groups in the industrial economy.[122]

The third principle follows from the first two. Jesus' concern for the poor followed from his feelings for the sacredness of life and for the familial unity of all humans. This principle demands not merely care for the poor but partiality for "those who live by productive labor" over "those who live on the productive labor of others whom they control." Jesus' feeling for the poor was not merely compassion; it was based on an evaluation of their "sound nature" and their "lovable and hopeful" qualities as distinguished from the "disquieting and dangerous" qualities of the rich.[123] The poor deserve preferential treatment on two grounds. Their personalities evince actual and potential worth, and inequalities in the social order impede their development. This partiality is not arbitrary; its justice follows from the first and second social principles. On this basis, Rauschenbusch asked his college-educated readers whether they feel social unity with the working class and whether they propose to use their privileges and capacities for the social redemption of this class.[124]

To these three key principles, which elevate universal human instincts, Rauschenbusch added supplemental principles for progressing toward the kingdom. These principles are based upon the redemptive process Jesus introduced into history. They are intended to be consonant with the universal human instincts, yet they are distinctively Christian. They grow out of the inevitable conflict of the redemptive force of the kingdom with "recalcitrant social forces" and with "evil." Though based

---

120. Ibid., 12.
121. Rauschenbusch, *The Social Principles of Jesus*, 24.
122. Ibid., 25–26.
123. Ibid., 39–40.
124. Ibid., 44. See idem, *Christianity and the Social Crisis*, 82–85, for another elaboration of Jesus' partiality toward the poor.

upon Jesus' particular initiative in history, these principles are not merely demands upon Christians surpassing what justice requires of all persons. They are pertinent to the determination of just policies because justice is not possible apart from the redemption (which for Rauschenbusch meant christianizing) of the social order.

These principles of strategy for realizing the kingdom are suggested in various places throughout later portions of *The Social Principles of Jesus*. They can be summarized as a single principle: Loyalty to the redemptive work of Christ requires "heroic service" (sacrifice symbolized by the "cross") for the "collective ideal" of the kingdom in the struggle against "evil in individuals and society."[125] The social ideal that Jesus initiated "began with repentance, faith, and self-sacrificing action, and it will always have to advance by the same means."[126] Here Rauschenbusch locates the necessity of sacrifice in Jesus' ethic of love, but sacrifice is "arbitrary and mechanical" apart from its positive consequences for mutuality in the social order.[127]

In contrast to Niebuhr, Rauschenbusch believed Jesus offered a realist ethic in juxtaposition to the idealists of his day. "He was trying to bring their feet to the ground, turn their mind to realities, and make their religion socially efficient."[128] Loyalty to Jesus' redemptive work requires finding efficient ways to create the social virtues each generation needs.[129] In order to meet this "social test," Jesus' ethic allows and even demands a fitting response to the complex needs of modern industrialism.[130] The cross is a social principle because it "is a law of social progress."[131]

Unlike the first three principles, which must become universal in the kingdom of God, Rauschenbusch did not believe the kingdom can or should rely upon universal acceptance of this principle of heroic self-sacrifice. It does, however, pertain to justice. It reinforces his view that solidarity with the poor, on which justice depends, includes a costly and effective opposition to the class that uses the powers of government, the courts, and the instruments for forming public opinion in order to protect its unearned incomes and wealth.[132] For Rauschenbusch, the determination of what is just must begin with a recognition of unjust privileges, which can only be eradicated by costly and effective actions.

---

125. Rauschenbusch, *The Social Principles of Jesus*, 75, 125, 158, 175.
126. Ibid., 190.
127. Rauschenbusch, *Christianizing the Social Order*, 340.
128. Rauschenbusch, *The Social Principles of Jesus*, 137.
129. Ibid., 139.
130. Ibid., 144.
131. Ibid., 193.
132. Ibid., 161–162.

Rauschenbusch did not believe he could derive a full conception of justice from Jesus' teachings and work. He did believe that Jesus' ethic of the kingdom entailed these general social principles that establish clear parameters within which more specific principles should be located. Jesus' understanding of the kingdom includes ethical content that bears directly on practical moral reasoning.

CONCLUDING IMPLICATIONS FOR JUSTICE

This understanding of the kingdom of God was the organizing framework for Rauschenbusch's social ethics. Its determinative role for his interpretation of history, his view of moral agency, his criteria for moral judgments, and even his understanding of God is well-established. There is nothing new in my claim that the kingdom was the organizing principle for all of Rauschenbusch's thought.

Perhaps, however, there is something new and controversial in my interpretation of Rauschenbusch's discovery and understanding of the kingdom. I claim that Rauschenbusch's understanding of the kingdom of God combined an evangelical social ethic, based upon the teachings and redemptive work of Jesus, with an evolutionary view of nature and history that is nonapocalyptic and, in the strictest sense, noneschatological. We cannot, I contend, understand Rauschenbusch's conception of justice unless we keep two things before us. First, justice requires a collective conversion and an assimilation of the social order into the ethical content and redemptive force of the kingdom Jesus initiated. The kingdom will not come through educational, moral, or natural evolutionary influences alone. It depends upon an evangelical regeneration. Second, a social scientific interpretation of Jesus' teachings and person indicates that his understanding of the kingdom was moving away from the emphases of his day on an apocalypse and on a final consummation of the kingdom. Jesus was growing in the direction of an evolutionary view of the kingdom that mobilizes the available natural and social resources toward a social order of love and equality. Hence, Rauschenbusch understood the kingdom as building upon natural human instincts, especially the desire for fellowship, and upon existing social forces. A kingdom this close to natural and social forces must also embody principles that illumine the realities of the social order.

This view of the kingdom will guide our analysis of the four base points in Rauschenbusch's theory of justice.

2

JUSTICE AS THE FOUNDATION FOR THE KINGDOM OF GOD

For one who believes that the Christian life centers in serving the redemptive force of the kingdom Jesus initiated, social ethics begins with discerning which movements in a historical period are advancing the kingdom and what obstacles impede this progress. When the advance of the kingdom depends on the collective personality of a nation and its social order, this task of discernment involves a theologically informed sociological analysis of the ever-changing institutions in society. Rauschenbusch's two books that dealt most comprehensively with social ethics begin with such an analysis of the socio-historical circumstances in which justice must advance, a prodigious task indeed.

It is not surprising, then, that Rauschenbusch was unable, under the demands of his pastorate, to write a draft of his manuscript on social Christianity that met his own standards. After coming to the German Department at Rochester Seminary in 1897, Rauschenbusch was burdened with an enormous teaching load, fifteen hours of class each week in preparatory courses (e.g., literature, physics, political economy, etc.) as well as in theology (viz., New Testament).[1] When he was appointed to teach church history in the English Department in 1902, prospects for completing this manuscript improved considerably. His teaching load

---

1. Minus, *Walter Rauschenbusch*, 110.

was lightened, and Augustus Strong, the conservative president of the seminary, assured Rauschenbusch that church history included "the history of the Kingdom of God on earth" as well as the "doings of an organization."[2] This teaching assignment fit well with Rauschenbusch's view that social ethics should be grounded in a scientific analysis of the advance of the kingdom Jesus had initiated in history. Rauschenbusch's 1905 lecture notes began with the claim that Christian history traces how the "new type of life and new creative force [that] have entered humanity" in Jesus Christ have fared in "regenerat[ing] all human relations and transform[ing] natural humanity into Christian humanity."[3]

Another factor delaying satisfactory completion of the manuscript may have been Rauschenbusch's doubts about how his argument for social reform would be received. In 1918 he described *Christianity and the Social Crisis* as a "dangerous book," which "I wrote with a lot of fear and trembling. I expected that there would be a good deal of anger and resentment."[4] He apparently thought the book might jeopardize his job.[5] Rauschenbusch was not cowardly, but he was cautious and prudential in a way that cohered with his understanding of the kingdom of God. His social Christianity was based on encouraging the advancement of the kingdom in history rather than on prophetic pronouncements of how Jesus would condemn the present social order. Subsequent to the publication of *Christianity and the Social Crisis* but before the generally positive response to it, Rauschenbusch was invited to lecture in Boston. Worried about his position with the conservative constituency of his seminary, Rauschenbusch wrote the inviter: "I do not propose to suppress God's message in me, but neither do I want to forfeit the position which enables me to pass it on most effectively."[6] He clearly tried to calculate when the time was propitious for his message to have a maximum positive effect.

---

2. Ibid., 117; Sharpe, *Walter Rauschenbusch,* 156.

3. Minus, *Walter Rauschenbusch,* 148, citing Walter Rauschenbusch from lecture notes, "Introduction to the Study of Church History," 1905, 1–4.

4. Rauschenbusch, "The Genesis of 'Christianity and the Social Crisis,' " 52.

5. Minus, *Walter Rauschenbusch,* 158; Sharpe, *Walter Rauschenbusch,* 233 n. 2.

6. Minus, *Walter Rauschenbusch,* 173. He later accepted the invitation. He was right to accept it on his own criterion, for when Rauschenbusch returned to Rochester in 1908, after a year-long sabbatical leave in Germany, his life was irreversibly changed by constant invitations for popular and scholarly lectures. Lectures he gave at Pacific Theological Seminary and at Ohio Wesleyan University led to the publication of *Christianizing the Social Order* in 1912. In that same year, Rauschenbusch was compelled to contract with a speakers' bureau to handle his speaking engagements. See Minus, *Walter Rauschenbusch,* 174–175. He had become something of a national celebrity and an agent for the causes he associated with the kingdom of God. The timing of Rauschenbusch's books on social Christianity—the first fifteen years after he had settled on the centrality of the kingdom of God—must have seemed to him to fit his analysis in both books that history had reached the point at which a social mission to advance the kingdom was possible. See Rauschenbusch, *Christianity and the Social*

By 1905,[7] he was intellectually and morally prepared to articulate his theological and sociological analysis of the historical circumstances he considered an important basis for a conception of justice.

THE HISTORICAL CIRCUMSTANCES OF JUSTICE

To this task Rauschenbusch devoted major portions of *Christianity and the Social Crisis* and *Christianizing the Social Order*. For Rauschenbusch, formulating principles of justice began with this analysis of the kingdom of God in history. "[T]o trace the moral evolution of those institutions which have to some degree been christianized," Rauschenbusch asserted, is a more fruitful way to proceed than testing the existing social order by Christian principles.[8] The social principles Rauschenbusch identified with Jesus did, however, inform his highly evaluative description of evolving social institutions. "Christianizing the social order means bringing it into harmony with the ethical convictions which we identify with Christ."[9] Such a value-laden description naturally melds into the criteria for moral reasoning that constitute his conception of justice.

In both books, Rauschenbusch assessed the contemporary situation as a continuation of the story of the kingdom throughout the history of Christendom. This procedure fit with his view that present movements toward the kingdom were products of God working in history through the redemptive influence of Christ. He understood the present situation as an evolutionary product of natural, social, moral, and divine phenomena in history. As we noted above (see note 6), Rauschenbusch thought this situation held significant opportunities for advancing the kingdom, but it also held possibilities for the "decay and extinction of Western

---

Crisis, 209–210; idem, *Christianizing the Social Order,* 29, 40. In retrospect, Rauschenbusch observed that *Christianity and the Social Crisis* "came out at a psychological moment, and was taken as an expression of what thousands were feeling." See Rauschenbusch, "The Genesis of 'Christianity and the Social Crisis,' " 53. This observation is, of course, compatible with an interpretation that attributes the success of Rauschenbusch's books with the rise of progressivism that had nothing to do with the kingdom of God. Rauschenbusch, however, insisted that the progressive trends of his day were part of the historical circumstances to be interpreted in light of the advancing kingdom of God.

7. *Christianity and the Social Crisis* was written during the summers of 1905 and 1906.

8. Rauschenbusch, *Christianizing the Social Order,* 127.

9. Ibid., 125. Notice how this procedure follows from Rauschenbusch's understanding of the kingdom. The general social principles of Jesus indicate the direction in which the kingdom is emerging, but the kingdom evolves in relation to changing social and natural forces in history. Thus, the specific criteria of moral reasoning for a particular period must incorporate a descriptive analysis of the social order.

civilization" from which "God will have to try once more." It was, then, a pivotal period at which there would be a "parting of the ways."[10] Rauschenbusch attributed this confluence of forces partially to intellectual influences in the culture (e.g., Reformation theology, eighteenth-century philosophy and science, modern evolutionary ideas, biblical sciences).[11] Nonetheless, the focus, for this man who saw God's redemptive work so closely connected to the social order, was on social institutions in five areas: family, church, education, politics, and economics.

Description of the Social Order

Rauschenbusch's most extensive and best-organized treatment of these social institutions is in *Christianizing the Social Order,* a book motivated by practical questions evoked by the success of *Christianity and the Social Crisis.*[12] His thesis was that the family, church, education, and politics were sufficiently redeemed to offer a realistic opportunity to establish justice in the economic realm. On the other hand, economic institutions were generally unregenerate and threatened to corrupt the regenerate institutions unless the nation seized this temporary opportunity to correct economic injustices. Why did Rauschenbusch judge these five institutions to be more or less Christian? And how did this description inform his conception of justice?

Family

The family was the most Christian of all institutions.[13] It had not always been so; it had evolved through the redemptive influence of Christianity working alongside "wholesome tendencies in the common life of men."[14] It had become Christian to the extent that it had abandoned patriarchal autocracy and was characterized by love as mutual helpfulness, by democratic equality, by economic cooperation, and by fathers making reasonable sacrifices for their children.[15] This christianized fam-

10. Ibid., 40; idem, *Christianity and the Social Crisis,* 209–210.
11. Rauschenbusch, *Christianizing the Social Order,* 86–89; idem, *Christianity and the Social Crisis,* 208–209.
12. Minus, *Walter Rauschenbusch,* 168; Rauschenbusch, *Christianizing the Social Order,* vii.
13. Rauschenbusch, *Christianizing the Social Order,* 128.
14. Ibid., 134–136.
15. Ibid., 128–133 passim. Rauschenbusch's views on women (as on other matters in his evaluative description of social institutions) were in part products of his time and place. He, for example, thought women's suffrage would be one of the final steps in the ascent of women. See ibid., 131. His contention that thought and action are colored by the social order acknowledges an inevitability to such limits on one's moral vision. It is important that

ily had not been primarily the product of moral achievement by its individual members; he emphasized the family as an institution. That institution had become "an ennobling and restraining force in the life of all."[16] The institution nourishes proper development of personalities.

The institution of the family relates to justice in two ways. First, it "furnishes the natural habitation for a Christian life and fellowship."[17] It nourishes the kind of character that challenges the absence of fellowship or solidarity in the economic realm. Second, the family is under attack from "disintegrating forces" in the social order, namely, economic injustices. If these forces are not christianized, the "christianized family cannot survive."[18] The preservation of the regenerate family requires justice. Thus, one purpose of justice is to support the christianized family.

Church

Rauschenbusch thought the church had also gradually come under the redemptive influence of the kingdom. For a variety of reasons, including but not limited to the influences of Constantine and Augustine,[19] the early church gradually abandoned the centrality of the kingdom, and its institutional character became monarchical, hierarchical, tyrannical, and self-aggrandizing. As with the family, the regeneration of the church was measured more by its institutional character than by the attitudes of individual members. It had surrendered its wealth and power and had become a democratic and cooperative organization, resting on equality and liberty and held together by good will. It had come under a law of

---

we assess Rauschenbusch's method of proceeding to justice through a description of the socio-historical situation without challenging, at least initially, particular aspects of evaluative analysis of social institutions.

I will add, however, that his judgments about justice for women may deserve a historical study of their own. He acknowledged, for example, that the church had often taken "reactionary positions" regarding the emancipation of women. (See ibid., 135). In *The Righteousness of the Kingdom,* he argued that Jesus' teaching restricting divorce was intended to protect women from exploitation and that one of the ways to decrease divorce is for "girls" to have an "education and independent position" so that they will be equal partners in marriage and not suppliants waiting for somebody to support them. See Rauschenbusch, *The Righteousness of the Kingdom,* 241–242. In *Christianizing the Social Order,* Rauschenbusch observed that women were not free to develop a fully "christianized personality" as long as "[m]en kept them ignorant and oppressed." See Rauschenbusch, *Christianizing the Social Order,* 353.

16. Ibid., 134.
17. Ibid., 133.
18. Ibid., 136.
19. See Rauschenbusch, *Christianity and the Social Crisis,* 143–200; idem, *Christianizing the Social Order,* 69–82.

love and service, marked by social enthusiasm and increasing solidarity with the labor movement.[20] These changes were wrought by social forces that stripped it of unearned wealth and privilege as well as by preaching the purified gospel.[21] Here again, Rauschenbusch's analysis was illumined by the social principles of Jesus, especially solidarity and identification with the defenseless, and by a sociological interpretation of the redemptive work of Jesus.

This regenerate church, like the family, is "a powerful member in the alliance of forces that are redeeming the social order."[22] Also like the family, its existence is endangered by injustices in the economic order.[23] Consequently, the church has a huge stake in the social movement for justice.[24] For Rauschenbusch, the regenerate church is both an essential agent for justice and a beneficiary of advances in economic justice.

Education

In *Christianizing the Social Order,* Rauschenbusch included education among those institutions that have "passed through a regenerating process . . . from tyranny to freedom, from aristocratic privilege to democracy of opportunity, from self-seeking to the enthusiasm of service."[25] Unfortunately, his evidence for this regeneration was largely limited to the public financing of universal education. He said little here, or in his other major writings, about the characteristics of regenerate education and nothing about how education instills virtues that make it a force for redeeming the social order. His comments regarding the threat economic injustice posed to education were limited. In one paragraph, Rauschenbusch observed that business encouraged education for immediate and material results at the cost of learning for its own sake.[26] Still, we can say that Rauschenbusch considered education among those key regenerate institutions that influenced and were influenced by the unregenerate economic system.

---

20. Ibid., 139–142 passim and 12, 91.

21. Ibid., 140–142. This passage diminishes the direct influence of Christ more than Rauschenbusch's other writings. Paul Minus cites Rauschenbusch as saying in lectures written in 1907 that "every reformatory movement has thrust the New Testament in the face of a degenerate Church." See Minus, *Walter Rauschenbusch,* 149, citing Walter Rauschenbusch from a lecture, "The Development of the Catholic Church," February 1907.

22. Ibid., 141.

23. Ibid., 142.

24. See Rauschenbusch, *Christianity and the Social Crisis,* 287–342.

25. Rauschenbusch, *Christianizing the Social Order,* 145.

26. Ibid., 316–317.

Politics

The political arena was the latest and most unstable of the regenerated areas of life. It was regenerate to the extent that it had become democratic. Rauschenbusch attributed the development of the democratic state to forces within and outside the church (especially the French Revolution), but he interpreted all of these influences as part of the redemptive influence of Christ. Even infidels, such as Voltaire, voice the spirit of Christianity. The better we understand the history of the last cight centuries, "the more influence will we attribute to Christianity in the rise of modern democracy." Rauschenbusch came close to identifying Christian redemption with democracy: "Democracy is not equivalent to Christianity, but in politics democracy is the expression and method of the Christian spirit."[27]

We will misunderstand this close connection Rauschenbusch asserted between Christian redemption and his conception of justice unless we comprehend his description of democracy. Two distinct points are in order.

First, not every form of government that is called democratic is regenerate. Rauschenbusch argued that political democracy in the United States, including its legislatures and courts, was often used by economic oppressors to defeat the just demands of the people.[28] Like Niebuhr following him, Rauschenbusch had no illusions that American democracy was automatically a force for political and economic justice, yet for Rauschenbusch this problem was attributable to business interests subverting the move to purer democracy. Pure democracy, applied to institutions in all five areas of the social order, was a solution to the social problem. Moves toward direct primaries, direct election of senators, direct legislation, recall of public officials (including judges), and control of election financing were moves toward redemption.[29] The solution to the faults of democracy is more democracy: "The people always seek to remedy the faults of democracy by still more democracy."[30]

Second, it simply did not occur to Rauschenbusch that pure democracy could be an occasion for the majority to oppress a minority or for encouraging the pursuit of individual interests at the expense of human solidarity and common care for the defenseless. When Rauschenbusch used the term "democracy," he meant more than democratic proce-

---

27. Ibid., 147–154 passim.
28. Ibid., 2–3.
29. Ibid., 281–282, 2, 151.
30. Ibid., 354–355.

dures; he was also referring to equality and solidarity with the poor. Hence, Rauschenbusch referred to the prophets' special concern for the poor and equal distribution as "primitive democracy."[31] Jesus, he claimed, democratized the kingdom of God because he emphasized service rather than being served and because he raised the value of the human personality.[32] Jesus could be readily united with democratic movements because he was on the side of the common people, that is, the poor.[33] When Rauschenbusch described the increasing democratization of politics as redemptive, he was describing the application of the cooperative idea to politics, the guarantee of freedom and protection for the helpless, and an organization for the common good.[34] Moreover, the freedom associated with democracy is to character ("a christianized personality") what fresh air is to blood.[35]

Rauschenbusch identified democracy with Christian redemption because he considered democracy a positive influence for developing each individual personality in solidarity with equal others and in care for the poor and defenseless. We distort his strong normative claim for democracy and freedom as essential to justice insofar as we associate it with contemporary descriptions of democracy as individual freedom to pursue arbitrary preferences or as indifference to developing a virtuous character.[36]

This description of democratic politics as an element in Christian redemption was the basis for Rauschenbusch's quite positive assessment of the democratic state as an instrument of justice. Thorough democratization of politics was assumed to entail government action on behalf of the people to promote equality and solidarity throughout the social order. "[T]he more democracy makes the State and the People to be identical in extent and interest, the less reason is there to fear state activity. Under true democracy state action comes to mean action of the People for their own common good."[37] In an earlier essay, "State-Help Versus Self-Help, or Paternalism in Government," Rauschenbusch also dismissed the claim that state activity in the economic order must be paternalistic interference on behalf of single classes. His argument was

---

31. Rauschenbusch, *Christianity and the Social Crisis*, 13–16.
32. Rauschenbusch, *Christianizing the Social Order*, 60–61.
33. Rauschenbusch, *The Social Principles of Jesus*, 43.
34. Rauschenbusch, *Christianizing the Social Order*, 152–153.
35. Ibid., 353.
36. To the extent that Rauschenbusch's description of democracy is inaccurate, his conception of justice is, of course, also morally inadequate. It is important, however, that we locate this inadequacy in his description of the circumstances of justice so that we do not misconstrue his normative intentions.
37. Rauschenbusch, *Christianizing the Social Order*, 430.

that actions by a truly democratic state, including "common ownership" of property, are "cooperative self-help on a large scale" because such a state is an instrument of the people.[38] Consequently, the advance of the democratic state is the primary reason for hope that the regenerate sectors of the social order can save the economic order from injustice. "[D]emocracy has put the levers where the people can reach them whenever they need them badly." It is a "point of vantage" for the next move, christianizing the economy.[39] Yet democratic politics is not enough. Political institutions are, of all the regenerate institutions, the most unstable and most vulnerable to corruption from the influence of economic institutions. Thus, politics is the primary battleground between the "Christian principle of liberty and equality lodged in our democracy, and of the mammonistic principle lodged in our business life."[40]

Economy

These four regenerate sections of the social order were, according to Rauschenbusch's analysis, pitted against the economic order and business life, "the unregenerate section of our social order."[41] The test for economic institutions, like the others, is not solely one of distributive justice. The first test is whether the economic order "creates sound and noble manhood," makes it easy or hard to do the right, rewards or penalizes "fraternal action."[42] In short, does it encourage habits of character that embody the social principles of the kingdom? Rauschenbusch answered emphatically: "No!"

According to Rauschenbusch, the capitalist economy was dominated by owners who were themselves ruled by the law of profit.[43] Profit includes interest on capital, reward for managerial performance, and insurance against risks. These returns are earned. But Rauschenbusch believed there was also an "unearned profit" gained by the power of owners to extract a tribute from the productive contributions of laborers and from the resources of the community.[44] Rauschenbusch offered no moral or economic calculus to determine the amount of this "unearned profit." Unlike Ryan, he did not isolate the contributions of each of the

---

38. Walter Rauschenbusch, "State-Help Versus Self-Help, or Paternalism in Government," in *The Social Gospel in America, 1870–1920*, 290–292. First published in 1898.

39. Rauschenbusch, *Christianizing the Social Order*, 411.

40. Ibid., 152.

41. Ibid., 156.

42. Ibid., 158.

43. Ibid., 222.

44. Ibid., 223–330 passim.

factors of economic production, that is, labor, capital, land, and entrepreneurship. Rauschenbusch took a broader sociological approach in determining the occurrence and sources of unearned gain. In an unpublished and untitled lecture on justice delivered in 1916, Rauschenbusch argued that unearned gain can be presumed wherever a laboring poor class exists alongside a class of leisure and plenty.[45] Because he rejected the notion of a class of idle poor, Rauschenbusch believed in practice that wherever gross inequalities exist they result from privileges that enable the wealthy to extract unearned gain from the productive process. He identified these privileges through a socio-historical examination of the institutions that created the background conditions for economic production. These privileges, sustained by many aspects of private productive property and unrestrained in free markets, created the occasion for "unearned profit" in the economic order.[46] For Rauschenbusch, pursuit of this "unearned profit" was the primary source of corruption in the economic order.

First, profits compete with the value and development of individual personalities. The inevitable conflict between maximizing profits and the comfort and safety of workers and consumers places an undue strain on the natural capacity of managers for human kindness. In addition to competing with the physical well-being of the working classes, unearned profits rob the masses of leisure and resources that would help raise them "to real culture, to artistic taste, and to refinement of manners."[47] The grievance of the working class is not only with the unjust distribution of benefits. "They also feel that they are not being treated as free men and of equal worth with the other class." They want justice because they want a "fuller and freer manhood."[48]

Perhaps these sacrifices of the masses could be justified if the beneficiaries of the unequal distribution of wealth were developing a higher humanity with which they could reorganize society and save the rest. But unearned wealth also undermines the moral character of those who possess it. It separates the nexus between income and work. The wealthy

---

45. Walter Rauschenbusch, [Untitled lecture on justice], in Box 20 of the Rauschenbusch Papers at the American Baptist Historical Society Archives, Rochester, New York, 1916, 3.

46. These contrasting approaches to the determination of unearned gain are a crucial difference, perhaps the crucial difference in Rauschenbusch's and Ryan's remarkably similar views on economic justice. Ryan's narrower economic approach was probably due to his extensive use of British economic theory. Rauschenbusch was more heavily influenced by the socio-historical economics of Germany and no doubt by the social and evolutionary emphases of the kingdom of God, a concept that Ryan believed was irrelevant to justice.

47. Rauschenbusch, *Christianizing the Social Order*, 242–251.

48. Ibid., 194.

are free to be idle. When they do work, it is for the senseless accumulation of wealth and power totally unrelated to enhancing their capacity to serve the community. This power and wealth robs its possessors of a proper sense of dependence that encourages persons to find their "true life only as serviceable members of the social organism." Rauschenbusch professed high regard for the natural moral instincts of persons in business, but he concluded that they also "are the [tragic] victims of our social system."[49]

Second, the rule of profits enabled by privilege also undermines human solidarity and care for the defenseless. It "trampled down the humane considerations of mercy and fraternity which had to some extent prevailed."[50] It discourages cooperation that calls out instincts of good will and solidarity and encourages unrestrained competition that represses good will and calls out selfishness and jealousy.[51] It nourishes an overgrowth of private interests that oppose a proper concern for the common good.[52] It generates hatred between the classes.[53] Christian love, including care for the weak, is not possible in the midst of inequality among classes.[54] In sum, the economic order was unregenerate because "[a] Christian social order must . . . develop and educate mutual interest and good will, and equip workmates with the sense of comradeship and solidarity to which they are entitled."[55] An economy under the law of unearned profits is alien to the kingdom; it is unredeemed and unredeemable. It must be terminated for redemption to advance.

Whatever moral goodness remains in the business life of the economic system comes from the fundamental soundness of human nature[56] and from the regenerate institutions in other areas of the social order, which send wholesome impulses into economic relations.[57] But the low value business life places upon the individual personality and upon solidarity also penetrates these other institutions.[58] Low wages and the unavailability of land make it difficult to maintain homes, which are crucial for the flourishing of familial love,[59] and marriage and family are undermined in a variety of other ways. The inequalities produced by this

---

49. Ibid., 291–310.
50. Ibid., 167.
51. Ibid., 172.
52. Ibid., 290.
53. Rauschenbusch, *Christianity and the Social Crisis*, 238–239.
54. Ibid., 247–248.
55. Rauschenbusch, *Christianizing the Social Order*, 179.
56. Ibid., 213–214.
57. Ibid., 238–239.
58. Ibid., 239–240.
59. Ibid., 262–265.

economic system create class conflict, which is especially detrimental to the church's mission to build love and unity.[60] Inequalities of economic power coupled with inflated self-interest also "threaten the very stability of the State as the organ of the common welfare."[61] Finally, in addition to corrupting regenerate institutions, an economic order that allows permanent inequalities corrupts moral reasoning. It generates theories justifying inequality.[62] One reason public opinion does not despise unearned incomes, Rauschenbusch asserted, in his unpublished lecture on justice, is that moral standards are established by the beneficiaries of injustice.[63]

Despite the unredeemable character of a purely capitalist economic order, there were, Rauschenbusch claimed, signs of regeneration in the economic realm. The interests of the laboring class and the socialist movement were both redemptive forces. Rauschenbusch did not praise the laboring class for its loyalty to the ideals of the kingdom, but its self-interest in "bread and butter" coincided with the ideal of "organized fraternity."[64] He considered the possibility that self-interests of the working class could threaten justice,[65] but Rauschenbusch also believed idealism unsupported by class interests could never produce great social change.[66] He concluded, "[I]f the banner of the Kingdom of God is to enter through the gates of the future, it will have to be carried by the trampling hosts of labor."[67] Socialism, which he viewed as closely allied with the labor movement, Rauschenbusch called "the most powerful force for justice, democracy, and organized fraternity in the modern world."[68] Socialism included elements repellent to Christianity, but Rauschenbusch thought it was more closely linked to the redemptive influence of Christ than either most socialists or most Christians realized. Its fundamental aims were part of the mission of Christianity. God raised it up because the church was too slow to realize God's ends.[69] We

---

60. Rauschenbusch, *Christianity and the Social Crisis*, 291–331 passim; see also idem, "The Stake of the Church in the Social Movement," *The American Journal of Sociology* 3 (July 1897): 21–24. Also in Rauschenbusch Scrapbook I at Colgate-Rochester Divinity School Library.

61. Rauschenbusch, *Christianizing the Social Order*, 273–274.

62. Rauschenbusch, *Christianity and the Social Crisis*, 253.

63. Rauschenbusch, [Untitled lecture on justice], 4; idem, *Christianizing the Social Order*, 166. Rauschenbusch anticipated Niebuhr's realism in both the claim that economic power can control democratic government and the claim that economic interests can subvert moral reasoning.

64. Rauschenbusch, *Christianity and the Social Crisis*, 403.

65. Rauschenbusch, *Christianizing the Social Order*, 454–455.

66. Rauschenbusch, *Christianity and the Social Crisis*, 400–401.

67. Rauschenbusch, *Christianizing the Social Order*, 449.

68. Ibid., 397.

69. Ibid., 405.

have here perhaps the best illustration of the practical implications of Rauschenbusch's belief that the history of Christian redemption is larger than church history.[70]

Implications for Justice

This evaluative description of the social order informed Rauschenbusch's conception of justice in several ways.

Justice Has Descriptive Justifications

First, Rauschenbusch's principles of justice depended heavily upon his description of the contemporary social order. He did not propose ahistorical universal principles of justice. Rauschenbusch's emphasis on the importance of justice, his assertion that the time was opportune to advance justice, and the content of his conception of justice were all grounded in this analysis of socio-historical circumstances.

Rauschenbusch concluded his analysis of the social order in *Christianity and the Social Crisis* with the claim that nations die by injustice.[71] Distributive justice is important not merely for its own sake; it is the key for the future flourishing of civilization. This is so because the principal obstacles to progress are unearned profits and concomitant undemocratic inequalities of power in the economic order. Without the remedies of justice, the materialist spirit of capitalism will penetrate the character of all institutions and persons. Repentance and the way to regeneration will be blocked.[72]

Rauschenbusch was, however, optimistic because the regenerate institutions in society provided a historical moment for advancing justice. Neither commitment to the ideals of justice nor even commitment to the social principles of Jesus is alone sufficient to secure justice. The opportunity for justice had arrived due to the historical situation.[73] "If rightly directed, a little effort in this time of malleable heat will shape humanity for good more than huge labor when the iron is cold."[74] If there is to be progress, it will occur because Christians and others align themselves with the remarkable confluence of redemptive forces in the present social situation. This opportunity will be short-lived. "Historical oppor-

---

70. See Minus, *Walter Rauschenbusch,* 148; *infra,* 71.
71. Rauschenbusch, *Christianity and the Social Crisis,* 284ff.
72. Rauschenbusch, *Christianizing the Social Order,* 319.
73. Rauschenbusch, *Christianity and the Social Crisis,* 332.
74. Ibid., 336.

tunities rarely last long."[75] Progress is not inevitable. "History laughs at the optimistic illusion that 'nothing can stand in the way of human progress.' "[76] If Rauschenbusch was naively optimistic, it was due to a misreading of the social forces of his time and place, not to an overestimation of the power of ideals to effect justice.

The substance of Rauschenbusch's principles of justice also depended upon his description of the social order. His principles of justice were, in part, a response to his description of the economic order as a system of privileges that permitted unearned profits, sustained autocratic power, and encouraged class conflict and selfishness. This description was, of course, informed by the values Rauschenbusch identified with the kingdom of God. It was not value-free, but neither were his principles of justice deduced from a priori reason or from the ethics of Jesus apart from his description of the evolving social order. These principles were developed in the context of his description of injustice.

The Kingdom in History Bears on Justice

Rauschenbusch's description of the social order made no pretense of neutrality. He was explicitly describing the advance of the kingdom of God in history. This perspective informed his descriptive analysis in several ways, thereby shaping his conception of justice.

First, his description of social institutions was guided by the character traits they sanctioned. Do these institutions produce the sort of persons who will advance the social principles of Jesus? Thus, the economic order was failing because unearned profits and inequalities of power hindered the development of personalities, undercut human solidarity, and encouraged neglect of the poor. Further, the economic order sanctioned habits that undermined these values in the other crucial social institutions. Distributive justice is important because it is required as a foundation for institutions which sustain virtues that characterize the kingdom. The principles of justice must, therefore, serve the good of the kingdom. Just institutions should make good persons, that is, persons disposed to serve the common good and care for the defenseless. The economic order should also support the kind of family, church, educational system, and political institutions that nourish these dispositions. Justice is more than fairness; it must advance God's kingdom.

Second, Rauschenbusch described the social order as a struggle be-

75. Minus, *Walter Rauschenbusch,* 177, citing Rauschenbusch, Address to Religious Citizenship League, January 30, 1914, manuscript.
76. Rauschenbusch, *Christianity and the Social Crisis,* 279.

tween redemptive forces initiated by Jesus and unregenerate forces of evil. The economic order is not a concatenation of social facts to be molded according to principles of justice. It is more akin to an agent than a passive object. "It is alive, vibrant, strong, assertive. . . . It will maul, ride down, and trample any force that interferes with its profits." The struggle for justice is a "conflict with principalities and powers." Big business, necessarily pursuing profit in an unrestrained capitalist economy, was a "personal power of malicious evil" ("the Devil").[77] These metaphorical descriptions of the economic order indicate the evangelical basis for achieving justice. For Rauschenbusch, justice cannot be envisioned, let alone achieved, apart from Christian regeneration, not just of persons but of the collective personality of business.

A third respect in which the centrality of the kingdom bore on Rauschenbusch's description of the social order specified his understanding of this redemptive process. The social nature of the kingdom allowed Rauschenbusch to discern the redemptive work of Christ in social institutions outside the church. As we have seen in his descriptive analysis, the kingdom Jesus initiated "overlaps and interpenetrates all existing organizations, raising them to a higher level . . . [or] resisting them."[78] He was convinced "that there is a great untapped reservoir of religion in the interests which lie outside the Church but inside the Kingdom."[79] Jesus' redemptive work was present even in movements (the democratic movement, the class interests of labor, and socialism) that do not acknowledge faithfulness to him. These are christianizing forces.[80] The task of regeneration includes bringing these movements to a consciousness of their alliance with the Christian mission and criticizing aspects of them that are antithetical to the cause of Christ. But the regenerative task also requires aligning explicitly Christian institutions with these redemptive forces in history. The pursuit of justice requires distributing power to these regenerative movements. The evangelical mission of Christianity, the social forces in history, and justice were inextricably commingled in Rauschenbusch's thought.

Finally, because of the evolutionary character of the kingdom, an adequate description of the social order must be historical. Synchronic

---

77. Rauschenbusch, *Christianizing the Social Order,* 240–241.

78. Rauschenbusch, *The Social Principles of Jesus,* 196–197.

79. Rauschenbusch, *Christianizing the Social Order,* 95.

80. This claim may seem inconsistent with Rauschenbusch's contention that there is no real good in civilization that does not emanate from the redemptive work of Christ. He apparently believed that the regenerative aspects of these movements could be empirically traced to the influence of Christ's personality. If he did hold this belief, he never provided evidence for it. Rauschenbusch was unable to complete a book on "social redemption" that in 1914 he agreed to submit to Macmillan. See Minus, *Walter Rauschenbusch,* 185.

descriptions of the social order or descriptions of the permanent laws of human nature ignore the dynamic redemptive force of the kingdom. This diachronic description of the social order is not, however, a story of the construction and reconstruction of a social artifact. As we have seen, Rauschenbusch describes how social institutions channel and balance ineradicable human instincts for pursuing self-interest and solidarity with others. He was describing a symbiotic growth of interdependent institutions rather than a construction of the social order. Mending the social order, Rauschenbusch observed, is like restoring diseased tissues, not like mending a clock.[81] On this description, the principles of justice are neither permanent natural laws nor divine or human impositions on a totally plastic nature. They should change in response to the redemptive forces in history, but they should also account for natural human instincts. This point can be further developed in light of Rauschenbusch's interpretation of human agency.

INDIVIDUAL AND COLLECTIVE AGENCY

Rauschenbusch devoted considerable effort to his evaluative description of the social order. He gave less attention to an interpretation of moral agency, but what he said about moral agency coheres with his description of the historical circumstances of justice. We will examine three aspects of this interpretation: the goodness and ineradicability of natural human interests, the relation between persons and collective agents, and the nature of sin and redemption.

Natural Interests

Humans are not entirely free from their common natural interests. First, as we have noted, love is not a free and disinterested giving of oneself to meet the needs of the other. It arises from a natural interest; it is a desire for solidarity issuing from the cultivation of natural affections for others (including sexual and familial attractions).[82] Second, it is neither possible nor desirable to eliminate all interest in ourselves. "The self-interest of the individual is a necessary part of human nature and may be a beneficent force in human society. It would be a calamity to rob this instinct of its incentives. . . . We want free, strong, self-reliant men."[83] Among these

---

81. Rauschenbusch, *Christianizing the Social Order,* 465.
82. *Supra,* chapter one, 52–53.
83. Rauschenbusch, *Christianizing the Social Order,* 290.

self-interests is a natural "acquisitive instinct." This interest deserves moral respect when wealth is saved to raise and educate children or to achieve some social good. The problem occurs when it is ravenous, untempered by social feeling, and centered on the self.[84] There is also an "instinct of self-preservation," which Rauschenbusch describes as a "natural selfishness of human nature." This "selfishness" is not a "hostile force" but an attribute necessary for survival.[85]

These two forms of interest, the interest in fellowship and the interest in one's own well-being, are both natural necessities. Both are also good. Thus, unlike Niebuhr, self-sacrificial love that rises above all interests is neither possible nor the mark of moral perfection. This acknowledgment that love for others and care for oneself depend on natural interests does not mean that human behavior is wholly determined. Humans are agents capable of disposing their interests. The task of moral agents, however, is not to free themselves from interests but to order, balance, and integrate their natural interests into habits of character that serve the common good.[86]

> Selfishness [presumably he means interests in one's well-being] and the social spirit both belong to the make-up of human nature. Egoism is the original warp, and self-sacrificing devotion for others is the woof that is woven in if character develops well. Both are necessary and useful. . . . [I]f the two come into conflict, the common good suffers. . . . The ideal situation is when self-interest and the common good run in the same direction, and selfishness of its own will bends its stout shoulders to the yoke of public service.[87]

There is here no ideal of love that transcends all natural interests. Acts of sacrificial love are sometimes morally required, but total self-sacrifice is neither sustainable nor desirable as a common practice. Rauschenbusch endorses Edmund Burke's view that a " 'human system which is founded on the heroic virtues is doomed to failure and even corruption.' "[88]

For Rauschenbusch, unlike Niebuhr, this combining of love and interests does not compromise Jesus' ethic. Jesus did not teach disinterested love but "encouraged" the "natural instinct of social attraction."[89] Thus,

---

84. Rauschenbusch, *The Social Principles of Jesus,* 118, 124.
85. Rauschenbusch, *Christianity and the Social Crisis,* 309–310.
86. Rauschenbusch's view of the relation between moral agency and natural human interests is remarkably similar to the understanding of human agency James M. Gustafson states in *Ethics from a Theocentric Perspective,* vol. 1, 286–287, 291.
87. Rauschenbusch, *Christianizing the Social Order,* 272.
88. Ibid., 330.
89. Rauschenbusch, *The Social Principles of Jesus,* 23.

the ethic of Jesus begins with natural human interests. This point is vividly illustrated in Rauschenbusch's idiosyncratic gloss on Jesus' command not to be anxious about one's future material well-being (Matt. 6:25–34). "It is comparatively easy," Rauschenbusch observed, "to venture on a life of obedience to this command if one is sure of an opportunity to earn a living through every coming year." On the other hand, we should expect workers whose employment is uncertain to "scrape together treasure while there is anything to scrape." The workers' anxiety is unfortunate, but their inability to satisfy Jesus' ethic lies in the economic system and not in their reasonable anxiety about material security for themselves and their families.[90] A healthy anxiety about one's future security is a natural interest that spurs labor class solidarity and promotes social salvation.[91]

On this view of agency, justice is not inferior to love when justice discriminates among interests, affirming some interests as deserving and opposing other interests. Love does not completely transcend human interests either. Like justice, it is rooted in and affirms natural human interests. Love as solidarity affirms and cultivates others' interests in self-preservation and in caring for their own and their family's reasonable needs. These interests serve the common good of the social order. Under just conditions, humans are enabled to weave these "selfish" interests together with their natural desire for solidarity into a fully virtuous moral character. Love and justice are both enabled and limited by natural human interests.

Persons in Relation to Collective Agents

There are also social limitations on individual freedom for which justice must account. Individual agents are limited by the collective personalities in which they participate. Statistics about morality demonstrate that "apparently free and unrelated acts of individuals are also the acts of the social group."[92] In his earlier lecture on "The Corporate Life of Humanity," Rauschenbusch argued that statistical variations show that individual freedom of choice is also operative. The personal life of the

---

90. Rauschenbusch, "The Stake of the Church in the Social Movement," 28.

91. See, e.g., Rauschenbusch, *Christianity and the Social Crisis*, 404–405. For Niebuhr, this command calls for a "perfect trust in God's providence" and a "perfect unconcern for the physical life," creating "a state of serenity in which one life would not seek to take advantage of another life." Anxiety inevitably results in "undue self-assertion." See Reinhold Niebuhr, "Why the Christian Church Is Not Pacifist," in *The Essential Reinhold Niebuhr: Selected Essays and Addresses,* ed. Robert McAfee Brown (New Haven: Yale University Press, 1986), 108. First published in 1940.

92. Rauschenbusch, *A Theology for the Social Gospel*, 81.

individual and the larger collective life interact to produce regularity of behavior with some individual variations.[93] This assertion that collective entities and individuals interact was a constant element in Rauschenbusch's theory of justice.

On the one hand, individuals are insufficiently independent to order their natural desires into an integral moral character. Neither virtues nor vices are primarily products of individual agents. "Religious faith in the individual would be weak and intermittent unless it could lean on permanent social authorities. Sin in the individual is shame-faced and cowardly except where society backs and protects it."[94]

As we have seen, these social authorities are themselves collective personalities possessing virtues and vices. A nation, for example, may have a Christian character.[95] This assertion of a collective character is crucial for Rauschenbusch's understanding of the social conditions for personal agency. We are not dealing merely with social factors that influence individual behavior nor with stories and moral heroes in the culture that shape individual character. We are dealing with collective entities that possess a character semi-independent from each other and from the individuals who participate in them. Neither, as in Niebuhr's thought, are groups viewed negatively as an occasion for individuals to express sublimated self-interests in a collective egoism. The groups' character may be more or less virtuous than the individuals in them. This character is constituted by social structures, by cultural values like the story of Jesus, as well as by the influence of individuals who sustain it and dissent from it. It is not, however, reducible to any one of these factors or to a calculable combination of them. It has a life of its own.

We also know from Rauschenbusch's descriptive analysis in *Christianizing the Social Order* that a national character is made up of various collective personalities, which are themselves only semi-independent. They are similar to individual agents in this respect. Only the character of a nation is relatively independent of external influences. The character of a society's institutions and orders—family, church, education, politics, and economics—are mutually interdependent and also interdependent with the character of the national social order. No one of these subnational orders possesses its own character independently of national character.

Individuals participating in the character of these collective personalities are necessarily shaped for better or worse. The collective personality

93. Rauschenbusch, "The Corporate Life of Humanity," 17.
94. Rauschenbusch, *A Theology for the Social Gospel,* 62.
95. Walter Rauschenbusch, "What Is a Christian Nation?" *The Standard* 54, no. 26 (February 23, 1907): 757.

"educates them upward, if its standard is high, and debases them, if it is low."[96] There is no radical independence from this influence. The collective personalities, in which individuals participate, either cultivate a proper balance among their natural desires[97] or stimulate and sanction their self-interest to the point that their natural capacity for love and justice is vitiated. Corrupt collective personalities even give them "an outfit of moral and political principles which will justify their anti-social activities."[98] Hence, we cannot expect to derive the criteria for justice from consent among autonomous individuals. Autonomous individuals do not exist, and the principles of justice, for which individuals offer "justifications," are subject to the goodness or corruption of the collective agents of which they are a part.

Rauschenbusch rejected the view that individual character is totally determined by these collective personalities. This view, of course, would be incoherent for one who is conscious of the influence of the collective character. In affirming collective influence on individuals, Rauschenbusch described an unchristian social order as making good persons do bad things.[99] If these persons are better than what they do under the influence of the collective agents, there exists some individual character independent of the social order. This character is due partially to the ineradicable social impulses of humans and partly to qualities instilled by the more virtuous institutions in the social order.[100] But in one lecture, Rauschenbusch also indicated a modest capacity to "train ourselves and our children" to such a standard that we may be material sound and fair

---

96. Rauschenbusch, *A Theology for the Social Gospel*, 71.

97. Consistent with his view that a sound moral character balances and harmonizes natural desires for one's own welfare and for fraternity, Rauschenbusch thought collective entities could blunt a proper interest in self-preservation as well as stimulate self-interest to corruptive proportions. In *Christianizing the Social Order,* Rauschenbusch, citing Graham R. Taylor, offered examples of how individuals' dependency on private business interests inhibited their "instinct for self-preservation" and their capacity to express "resentment" against injustices done to them (287–288).

98. Rauschenbusch, *A Theology for the Social Gospel,* 71, 73. This view of the relationship between collective and individual agency allowed Rauschenbusch to write a book condemning the immorality of business life without attacking individuals in business (see Rauschenbusch, *Christianizing the Social Order,* 313) and to note the virtues of the labor movement without claiming that individual laborers were any better than persons from other classes (see ibid., 457).

This attitude may be what enabled Walter and Pauline Rauschenbusch to establish an enduring and fascinating relationship to John D. and Laura Rockefeller. The Rauschenbusches corresponded frequently with the Rockefellers. They sent them inscribed copies of Walter's books. There was no substantive response to Walter's books, but the Rauschenbusches received approximately $8,000 in personal gifts from the Rockefellers between 1900–1918. See Minus, *Walter Rauschenbusch,* 133–134.

99. Rauschenbusch, *Christianizing the Social Order,* 127.

100. Ibid., 312–314.

enough to be built into a better humanity.[101] It seems that natural instincts, integrating influences from diverse collective personalities, and an ability to train our character combine to give humans a limited capacity for individual moral agency. All three elements necessarily contribute, in ways that can be either positive or negative, to developing individual moral character.

Rauschenbusch never systematically explicated these sources of the capacity for personal agency, but he clearly believed that individuals are, to some extent, morally accountable. They are sufficiently independent to dissent from unjust social orders, and they may be morally delinquent in a just social order.[102] His claims for individual responsibility for justice did not always cohere easily with his views on individual and collective agency. At one point he asserted that the "doctrine of moral freedom and personal accountability" places the responsibility for social reform on the business persons, who alone have the power to effect change.[103] At another point, however, he claimed more modestly that some individuals in business can respond to the call for redemption and justice. This limited capacity for individual responsibility is necessary for an advance in the emancipation of the poor.[104]

Rauschenbusch certainly could have said more, more consistently, about collective and individual agency. Still, we can easily discern the impact of what he said on the place and role of justice in his ethics. Discrimination among conflicting human interests plays a necessary and significant role in the development of collective and individual character. As long as the economic order sanctions unearned profits, the human capacity for the virtue of Christian love is constricted. In a capitalist economy, the collective character, upon which individual character depends, sanctions acquisitive interests and discourages the natural human instinct for solidarity. It fosters covetousness.[105] Moreover, the regenerate character of the family and church depends upon the character of the economy and of the nation.[106] In the absence of justice, fraternity between the classes depends upon heroic love,[107] a virtue that

101. Walter Rauschenbusch, "How Can the Aims of the Social Movement Be Realized?" Fragments of an unpublished lecture in Box 19 of the Rauschenbusch Papers at the American Baptist Historical Society Archives, Rochester, New York, no date, 26.

102. Rauschenbusch, *Christianizing the Social Order,* 466–470.

103. Ibid., 200–201.

104. Ibid., 467–468.

105. Rauschenbusch, *Christianity and the Social Crisis,* 265.

106. Rauschenbusch understood the church as a community of character formed in part by its memory of Christ's life (see Rauschenbusch, *A Theology for the Social Gospel,* 125), but he did not believe that the character of the church could be sustained by this memory alone. It also depends upon the sanctions of the social order.

107. Rauschenbusch, *Christianizing the Social Order,* 332.

is sometimes called for but is neither sustainable nor desirable as a common practice. More preferable is a just social order that taps and cultivates the natural human capacity for devotion to the common good.[108]

In light of this understanding of the natural and social limits upon individual freedom, justice is fully compatible with love. Moreover, just social conditions are indispensable for enabling individual agents to train their natural desires for the virtue of love. Again, his conception of justice is formulated in accord with this goal of developing individual character.

Sin and Redemption

Justice is a necessary means for personal regeneration, yet it cannot be achieved through the existing moral capacities of individual and collective agents. In *A Theology for the Social Gospel,* Rauschenbusch set forth a version of the doctrine of original sin. He understood original sin as the transmission of selfishness through biological propagation and through social assimilation.[109] This affirmation of a biological transmission of sin corroborates his reliance upon evolutionary science and his view that ethical theory must be based upon natural human instincts. Both orthodox theology and evolutionary science, he maintained, point out that "faulty equipment has come down to us through the reproductive life of the race." He evidently believed that moral traits such as "weakness of inhibition, perverse desires, stubbornness and anti-social desires" were, in part, genetically based. This biological basis for human moral capacities is not static, however. The "social, altruistic, and spiritual impulses are of recent development."[110] Furthermore, an overemphasis upon the biological transmission of sin and evil has neglected recognition of the transmission through social tradition.[111] Together, these two forces of evil constitute obstacles to justice and to an advance of the kingdom that natural human capacities are unable to overcome. Yet his emphasis upon the social transmission of sin gave Rauschenbusch reason to hope that sin could be partially overcome through religious forces.[112]

Unfortunately, Rauschenbusch never worked out the apparent contradictions in his conjoining of the biological and social determinants of

---

108. Ibid., 330.
109. Rauschenbusch, *A Theology for the Social Gospel,* 61.
110. Ibid., 58–59.
111. Ibid., 59–60.
112. Ibid., 67–68.

sin. It begs many questions. How can biologically determined characteristics be considered sinful or evil? How can persons who are morally and intellectually unequal due to biological causes be considered equally sacred personalities? In one passage, Rauschenbusch even asserts that raising the moral stature of humanity depends upon propagation of the fittest.[113] How can biologically determined traits be redeemed through the influence of Christ's personality? Dennis Davis suggests that Rauschenbusch may have accepted a Lamarckian view that socially acquired characteristics can be genetically inherited.[114] Perhaps Rauschenbusch could have answered these questions on the basis of a socially determined biological evolution. Without speculating on how he might have dealt more coherently with these issues, we can note two elements of his understanding of sin that were crucial to his theory of justice.

First, sin is selfishness resulting from the failure to discipline and balance natural impulses; it is not rebellion or pride issuing from an individual free before God.[115] Like love, sin has roots in natural desires rather than in transcendental freedom. These natural desires are channeled in part by social institutions. Consequently, in contrast to Niebuhr, who, in the forties, claimed that pride inevitably corrupted all institutions, Rauschenbusch understood individual selfishness as largely dependent upon the character of collective personalities. Under the rule of profit, the natural instinct for acquisition and power can expand almost without natural limit, as if the digestive organs (note the natural metaphor) expanded to the size of a Zeppelin.[116] Like Niebuhr, Rauschenbusch did not place narrow limits on the desire for wealth and power. These sinful desires are not easily satiated. Unlike Niebuhr, he did think sin was subject to correction and control through social institutions.[117] Sin and evil, which Rauschenbusch did not clearly distinguish, are variable factors. They are not unvarying endowments.[118]

Second, Rauschenbusch believed that the social gospel had retrieved an early Christian belief in a Satanic kingdom designating the social and political realities with which Christians contended.[119] The collective personalities, which have the potential to reduce our individual selfishness, have themselves become a "Kingdom of Evil." They are possessed by "the supernatural power of evil."[120] Modern sociology, reducing the

---

113. Rauschenbusch, *Christianity and the Social Crisis,* 254–275.
114. Davis, "The Impact of Evolutionary Thought on Walter Rauschenbusch," 265.
115. Rauschenbusch, *A Theology for the Social Gospel,* 47–50.
116. Ibid., 66–67.
117. Ibid., 60, 68.
118. Ibid., 43.
119. Ibid., 87.
120. Ibid., 90.

mystery of this power of evil, enables a hope for success in contending with it. Yet sociological analysis, informed by the kingdom of God, points to superpersonal forces sufficiently formidable to be called a reign of evil. This view of collective agents guards against a superficial understanding of redemption.[121] These collective agents cannot be made just by political dickering or even by moral suasion. Reform depends upon the miraculous redemptive work of Christ.

On this view of sin and evil, evangelism is both a necessary and a potent force for justice. It is necessary because justice depends upon the salvation (regeneration) of both persons and superpersonal agents. It is powerful because the redemptive force of the kingdom Jesus initiated in history is sufficient to transform the variable selfishness of universal human sinfulness.

Because these agents are in need of redemption, the church has an indispensable role in the struggle for justice. Insofar as it performs its mission to embody the gospel of the kingdom Christ introduced into history, the church becomes "the social factor" that rises above the common morality and carries the distinctive ethic of Jesus into human thought and affairs.[122] The evangelical mission of the church is to regenerate individuals and institutions, enabling them to become agents of justice.

Grace and redemption are not confined to the church. Historical forces such as socialism and the labor movement are also vehicles of Christian grace. Where "composite personalities" are compelled to operate democratically and by the rule of reward for service, they are saved from the evils of autocracy and unearned gain. Thereby they are assimilated to the law of Christ in the kingdom of God.[123] Justice itself can be a means of grace. Rauschenbusch calls the rights to property and to a job a "means of grace" for laborers.[124] How can social movements and just social institutions be means of redemption when justice is dependent on the redemptive influence of Christ? The answer lies in Rauschenbusch's understanding of the advance of the kingdom in history. The redemptive influence of Christ's personality penetrates history beyond the church. It is present in these reforming movements and in social institutions, enabling them to redeem other institutions and persons from the common morality.

Rauschenbusch's view of the kingdom as a miraculous redemptive force informs his interpretation of individual and collective agents as enmeshed in sin, from which they cannot free themselves without Christ.

---

121. Ibid.
122. Ibid., 119–120.
123. Ibid., 114, 117.
124. Rauschenbusch, *Christianizing the Social Order,* 341–351.

His belief that the kingdom is a social and evolutionary force subject to sociological analysis convinced him that grace is transmitted through a variety of ostensibly non-Christian movements. Thus, justice is both dependent upon Christian redemption and a mediator of it.

GOD

Rauschenbusch believed that a people's conception of justice coheres with their understanding of God. In a chapter on his conception of God in *A Theology for the Social Gospel,* he asserted a close connection between "a distinctively Christian experience of God" and "the struggle of humanity with autocratic economic and political conditions."[125]

This chapter was, however, Rauschenbusch's only sustained statement about God, and it does not offer a fully developed conception of God. Its stated purpose is to indicate how the social gospel's doctrines of sin and salvation "re-act" on the doctrine of God.[126] What we get, therefore, is a declaration of those aspects of the traditional understanding of God that require revision in light of the rediscovery of the centrality of the kingdom in Jesus' mission. Nevertheless, the chapter's emphasis upon God as redeemer accurately reflects Rauschenbusch's understanding of God. The little he has to say elsewhere about God as creator, orderer, and judge is secondary to God's redemptive purposes.

Redeemer

Rauschenbusch's understanding of God begins with the personality of Jesus. God is present in the personality of Jesus. Jesus' personality is "the full and complete expression of the character of God."[127] Because the purpose of all that Jesus said and did was the "social redemption of the entire life of the human race on earth," redemption is God's chief purpose.[128] In his chapter on God, Rauschenbusch revised what he calls the traditional conception of God in three ways. Each revision reflects his belief that God is present in the redemptive work of Christ's personality.

First, the old conception of a God who transcends humanity must be replaced. God is immanent as one "who strives within our striving" as our "chief fellow worker."[129] God present in the personality of Jesus is a

---

125. Rauschenbusch, *A Theology for the Social Gospel,* 187, 174.
126. Ibid., 167.
127. Ibid., 264, 273.
128. Rauschenbusch, *Christianizing the Social Order,* 67.
129. Rauschenbusch, *A Theology for the Social Gospel,* 178–179.

God whose purposes for history we can know with confidence. In Christ "we see God; in him we possess God; in him God possesses us."[130] "[R]eligion is the life of God in the soul of man."[131] Furthermore, because the redemptive force of Christ's personality can be identified in movements that are advancing the kingdom, God is immanent in specific groups in history. God takes sides. "God must join the social movement. . . . The failure of the social movement would impugn his existence."[132]

Second, the old autocratic conception of God must be democratized. One of the highest redemptive services of Jesus occurred when he took God by the hand and called him "our father," thereby democratizing the understanding of God.[133] Jesus' teaching did not immediately establish a democratic conception of God because all views of God are partially products of social conditions.[134] During most of the history of Christendom, social conditions favored an autocratic image of God. Only as the redemptive influence of Christ's personality has advanced the kingdom in modern democratic movements have we been enabled to retrieve Jesus' democratic conception of God. The redemptive force of Christ's personality, and thus of God, is immanent in democratic movements. This distinction between God as democratic and as despotic is the decisive distinction in theology.[135] It is decisive because a democratic conception of God "teaches us to prize liberty and love love," whereas a despotic conception makes "autocratic conditions look tolerable, necessary, desirable."[136] God in solidarity with the people, which is Rauschenbusch's understanding of democracy, is God redeeming humanity for the kingdom.

Third, theologies that attempt to account for the isolated sufferings of individuals or groups as part of God's justice and benevolence must be abandoned. What happens, for example, when individual suffering is facilely explained as divine justice chastening and sanctifying the individual? It silences the warning that suffering ought to convey to society. Society accepts suffering caused by social injustice as a part of God's justice for individuals.[137] Attempts to account for God's justice in relation to individuals impede the advance of social justice. Rauschenbusch asserted that an individual's sin and suffering should be understood as

---

130. Walter Rauschenbusch, "Revelation: An Exposition," in *Walter Rauschenbusch: Selected Writings*, 122. First published in 1897.
131. Rauschenbusch, *Christianizing the Social Order*, 105.
132. Rauschenbusch, *A Theology for the Social Gospel*, 178.
133. Ibid., 174–175.
134. Ibid., 167.
135. Ibid., 175.
136. Ibid., 177.
137. Ibid., 183.

sins and sufferings of the whole society. On that view, social suffering is a disease in the society, which all feel. Thus, all are moved to heal the society with social justice. God is just because God allows the suffering of the innocent to become an occasion for redeeming society from its injustices.[138] This understanding of God's justice is consistent with Rauschenbusch's notion of individual participation in collective personalities, and it allows divine justice to permit the sacrifice of individuals for the good of the whole. The suffering of these individuals has meaning because it "helps to redeem the rest from a social evil."[139]

These comments are so fragmentary and unqualified that it is impossible to determine if they could be made to cohere with a fuller conception of God that would back the remainder of Rauschenbusch's theology and his ethics. They, nevertheless, bear on his conception of justice.

If social redemption, through the personality of Jesus in history, is God's primary mode of relating to humanity, God's will for justice is fully known only in particular historical events: in the teachings and personality of Jesus of Nazareth and in those historical movements in which we discern the redemptive force of Jesus' person. There is no basis here, for example, for universal principles of justice derived from the eternal law of God implanted in the natural order. The principles of justice are distinctively Christian. They become universal only as the kingdom advances, that is, as the world is christianized.

If God is immanent in these particular events, Christians can have confidence that a conception of justice that advances the kingdom can be known and that God is on the side of social movements that promote justice. If, for example, God is immanent in democratic movements, democracy (as Rauschenbusch understood it) becomes a principle of justice that ought to be imposed on all social institutions, including economic institutions, through collective action. Epistemological uncertainty is not a reason for tolerating pluralism, in this case "undemocratic" conduct.

Finally, if God is just in relation to societies rather than in relation to individuals, justice may permit or even require individual sacrifices for the good of advancing the kingdom. Ideally, individuals should not be sacrificed for the sake of the good of society. The development of each individual personality is sacred in the kingdom of God. "When it [the kingdom] is fully come, the cross will disappear."[140] Nevertheless, permitting individual and group suffering that serves to advance society

---

138. Ibid., 183–184.
139. Rauschenbusch, *The Social Principles of Jesus*, 179–180.
140. Ibid., 180.

toward just conditions in which each personality can develop is itself just.

Creator and Orderer

This centrality of God as redeemer is fully consistent with Rauschenbusch's conception of the kingdom and his description of its advance in history, yet Christ redeems by elevating, balancing, and integrating natural human instincts. We should expect Rauschenbusch to have held a belief about God as creating and ordering human existence through nature. No such belief appears in his statements about God in *A Theology for the Social Gospel*. However, Rauschenbusch developed the basis for this belief in two early essays.

An 1897 article on revelation avowed a "general revelation of God in the structure and order of the material universe and in the moral processes of history." There are "immutable laws of nature," which are "solemn preachers of his justice."[141] Despite this general revelation, we remain in darkness until God reveals himself in "a special historic process aiming toward the establishment of the Kingdom of God on earth."[142] Presumably, the "immutable laws of nature" must be revised in light of the redemptive force of the kingdom.

A lecture written in 1900 follows a similar pattern. It, however, clearly demonstrates that the phrase "immutable laws of nature" did not cohere with Rauschenbusch's understandings of God or of nature. This later essay expanded Rauschenbusch's treatment of general revelation by entertaining the possibility of a teleological argument for God's existence. Rauschenbusch observed that the old argument from design cannot be sustained in the face of evolutionary science. There is no immutably ordered existence that points to a designer. Under the light of evolutionary science, the question has become whether a designing or ordering mind is behind the evolutionary changes in nature. Rauschenbusch answered that the element of design is not missing in an evolutionary view of the world; it "has only receded and is waiting for us at the beginning of all things. . . . The world is not a shifting mass of phenomena." There is a "Cause" in which there is "direction, purpose, and immeasurable intelligence."[143]

These statements are remarkably similar to Roman Catholic arguments for God that back natural law. There are two differences. First,

---

141. Rauschenbusch, "Revelation," 113.

142. Ibid., 114.

143. Walter Rauschenbusch, "Religion: The Life of God in the Soul of Man," in *Walter Rauschenbusch: Selected Writings,* 128–129. First published in 1900.

Rauschenbusch's notion of purposive evolution backs constantly changing natural laws. Moral laws, including principles of justice, must therefore be based, in part, upon a description of developments in history. Second, this essay, like his earlier one, insists that full knowledge of the character of God occurs only in Jesus Christ. Knowledge of God based on the ordering in the universe is inadequate even for that part of morality that pertains to justice. According to Rauschenbusch, evolutionary science assures us only that God is ordering the world in a way that calls upon us to develop our moral instincts so that humanity will be fit for survival. This view of God reduces morality to its utility for the race. "[I]n the face of Nature as we know her, it is a tremendous affirmation to assert that God is not only just, but that he is love. For myself I need all the assurance contained in the self-consciousness of Christ to brace my faith." The ensuing sentences indicate that Rauschenbusch thought others also need this assurance.[144] Unless our natural moral instincts are elevated by the person of Christ, we will not know God's character nor the justice that promotes God's kingdom.

Though these articles lack a systematic statement relating God as creator and orderer to God as redeemer, what they say about God as creator and orderer coheres with Rauschenbusch's understanding of redemption. Humans are not, by God's redeeming love in Christ, freed from the natural ordering of life. This ordering includes human desires that are given by nature. A Christian conception of justice must be grounded in these desires. Yet there are no natural laws of justice. The natural ordering of God is, first, ever changing and, second, an insufficient basis from which to derive moral principles. Inferences from the natural order that do not account for Christ's redemptive influence can and will be used to sustain conceptions of morality and justice that are less than Christian, for example, utilitarian conceptions. Adequate knowledge of God's will for justice depends upon our natural moral instincts being elevated by the redemptive influence of Christ. Yet God's redemptive love is fully congruent with principles of justice that discriminate among natural interests, sanctioning our interests in solidarity and reducing our distended self-interests.

Judge

Rauschenbusch's emphases on sin and the need for repentance entail an understanding of God as judge, but he apparently never explicated this belief. His statements about God as judge occur incidentally in the

---

144. Ibid., 130–131.

context of other topics. Two aspects of these allusions bear on his conception of justice.

First, humans discern God's judgment in suffering caused by the social order and interpreted as a disease of the whole society. Sin has natural consequences. It causes individuals to suffer, some more than others. Yet as we have seen, this suffering is not a judgment upon particular individuals but upon the sins of the whole society. In short, God's judgment does not fall upon isolated individuals. Nor is it experienced primarily by measuring ourselves and our deeds against a divine ideal. It falls principally upon collective agents, and it is experienced in the natural consequences of failures to comply with God's ordering of life. In his treatment of the atonement, Rauschenbusch wrote: "Suffering is Nature's publicity method to secure attention to something that is wrong."[145]

This natural suffering, however, does not effectively arouse humans' awareness of the sin that is destroying them. Arousal of our consciousness of God's collective judgment comes in the cross of Christ. Only the cross effectively publicizes collective injustice against the innocent who suffer. Thus, an accurate perception of God's judgment is enabled by the redemptive work of Christ, a work that simultaneously displays God's redemptive love as the basis for a new social order.[146]

Had Rauschenbusch developed this notion of God as judge, he could have related it to both divine ordering and redemption. God's judgment, manifest in the suffering that is a consequence of violations of the divine ordering, is fully comprehended only when that suffering is seen as analogous to the innocent suffering of Christ. We see, then, that God's judgment is upon the collective injustices of society. We also see the redemptive purpose of divine judgment. "The death of the innocent, through oppression, child labor, dirt diseases, or airless tenements, ought to arrest the attention of the community. . . . In that case they have died a vicarious death which helps to redeem the rest from social evil."[147] Correctly discerning God's judgment in contemporary events is the first step in the redemptive process.[148] It is occasion neither for despair nor merely for trusting in divine forgiveness and justification. It is the starting point for a future realization of justice and solidarity.

The second pertinent aspect of divine judgment is its immanence. It is present in specific movements in history and against specified social institutions. In an 1896 essay on the social movement, Rauschenbusch

145. Rauschenbusch, *A Theology for the Social Gospel*, 269.
146. Ibid., 269–274.
147. Rauschenbusch, *The Social Principles of Jesus*, 180.
148. Rauschenbusch, *A Theology for the Social Gospel*, 270.

asserted: "[I]t is a river flowing from the throne of God, sent by the Ruler of history for the purification of the nations. We see God's hand in it; we see Christ's blood in it."[149] God is not a transcendent judge condemning all schemes of justice. Though all humans sin insofar as they participate in unjust collective personalities, God's judgment is discriminate. God is on the side of the social movement, judging the business life of capitalist economies.

This understanding of God's judgment contrasts sharply with the transcendent judge in Niebuhr's theology. Niebuhr's understanding of God's judgment backs an attitude of contrition in applying any standards of justice. By contrast, the immanence of divine judgment backs Rauschenbusch's confidence in specifications of justice that condemn the privileges of the wealthy and enforce opportunities for the poor. Instead of working standards of justice that stand under God's judgment because they inevitably assert the sinful interests of some group, we get specifications of justice that reflect God's judgment against sin. Justice is not a compromise with the realities of sin but an immanent divine judgment against sin and an application of redemptive love.

In sum, Rauschenbusch's understanding of God backs a conception of justice that is enabled by the redemptive force of Christ's personality present in events and movements of history. Justice in turn supports the advance of the kingdom by condemning exaggerated self-interests and enhancing natural interests in human solidarity.

"CHANNEL BUOYS" FOR JUSTICE

Rauschenbusch's description of the struggle between the kingdom of God and the forces of evil in the early twentieth-century social order fixed attention on economic justice as the crucial moral issue. First, Rauschenbusch believed the time was right. Regeneration of the family, church, education, and especially politics had created an opportunity for advancing justice in the economic order. The pace of changing social conditions made it urgent to seize this opportunity. The insidious influence of the economic system as a collective agent threatened to undermine the character of individuals and of the regenerate collective personalities. Second, economic justice was the appropriate moral force to advance Rauschenbusch's understanding of the kingdom. By affirming justified self-interests and restraining selfishness, justice could foster the development of individual character. By sanctioning support for the defenseless, it

---

149. Rauschenbusch, "The Ideals of the Social Reformers," 202.

could nourish the natural human interest in solidarity. Economic justice could not assure love and fraternity, but it could provide necessary enabling conditions.

One who comes to the importance of justice in this way does not formulate principles of justice that stand independently of the descriptive analysis that justifies them. For Rauschenbusch, practical reasoning about justice was not simply a matter of applying principles in order to determine just distributive policies. Rauschenbusch did not even formulate distinguishable principles of justice until 1912, in the fifth part of *Christianizing the Social Order*. In that section, "The Direction of Progress," he referred to his guidelines for justice as "channel buoys" anchored in a divine instinct in humans and in historical experience and informed by Christ.[150] These guidelines provide focus and direction rather than stipulating just policies. Even this part of *Christianizing the Social Order* is not primarily a formulation of principles of justice. It and the sixth part are actually exercises in practical reasoning in which descriptive analysis and views on moral agency are combined with prescriptive principles to argue for specific economic and political policies. These other base points of his ethic, which constitute his theory justifying the principles of justice, enter into his moral reasoning about distributive policies.

Moreover, the principles that emerge are developed in response to his description of injustice. Consequently, his principles of justice include prescriptions for distributing resources, namely, power, intended to advance the kingdom against injustice, as well as principles for an ideal distribution. They incorporate what John Rawls calls a partial compliance theory of justice, that is, "principles that govern how we are to deal with injustice."[151]

Though he did not explicate principles of justice independently of his theory and application of justice, Rauschenbusch was not adverse to the language of principles. We can extract principles without distorting his thought as long as we keep in mind that his practical moral reasoning was also informed by the base points that justify his principles, that is, his interpretations of history, moral agency, and God in Christ. This relatively independent delineation of his principles will demonstrate that his social thought was more than a "prophetic" cry for love and justice. His legacy includes a normative conception of justice, namely, criteria for discriminating among conflicting interests in distributing benefits and burdens. These criteria can be divided into two parts. First, he articu-

---

150. Rauschenbusch, *Christianizing the Social Order*, 326–327.
151. Rawls, *A Theory of Justice*, 8.

lated principles that constitute a vision of an ideal, yet possible, distribution. Second, he added guidance regarding the redistribution of benefits and burdens required to redeem society from injustice.

The Ideal That Is Now Possible: Opportunity for Individual Development

The time was propitious, Rauschenbusch thought, for a social order incorporating Jesus' principle asserting the sacred worth of each individual's opportunity to develop. This opportunity is more than a fair chance to go as far up the ladder of success as one is willing and able. The economic order will be Christian, said Rauschenbusch,

> when all industry is consciously organized to give to all the maximum opportunity of a strong and normal life. . . . It will be Christian when it is organized to furnish the material foundation for love and solidarity by knitting men together through common aims and united work, . . . and by making the material welfare of each dependent on the efficiency, moral vigor, and good will of all.[152]

The content of opportunity is determined by its role in fostering the development of human character. Justice is oriented to a goal rather than to protecting individual rights. Opportunity is concerned with how the organization of the economy benefits or burdens moral development, as well as with the distribution of goods (e.g., income, wealth, and liberties) individuals can possess and use for their own ends.

Opportunity is diminished where privilege denies equality, autocracy destroys freedom, or competition stifles fraternity. Rauschenbusch revised the motto of the French Revolution[153] to specify his general principle of opportunity in more exacting requirements. Although Rauschenbusch's use of the term "justice" refers only to equality, all three requirements—equality, liberty, fraternity—pertain to how society's major institutions distribute benefits enhancing opportunity and burdens that obstruct it.

Equality as Earned Income and Wealth

Equality requires "a just return for the labor and service [persons] contribute to the life of society."[154] In itself, this principle was not a basis

---

152. Rauschenbusch, *Christianizing the Social Order,* 328.
153. Ibid., 366, 150, 327.
154. Ibid., 337.

for Rauschenbusch's radical criticism of the economic order. The principle demands neither absolute equality nor distribution according to need. Persons should be paid only on the basis of the quantity and quality of their work.[155] However, when this principle was informed by Rauschenbusch's evaluative description of the industrial economic order, it became the basis for his attack on economic inequalities. As we have seen, he believed that unequal classes signify legalized privileges, which permit the capitalist class to receive unearned income and wealth. "Easy money" or massive wealth warrants an investigation of claims to have received rewards for service rendered.[156] Rauschenbusch's investigation uncovered privileges in private control of land, private control of the means of traffic and intercourse, patent rights, and the power of large corporations to fix prices and wages.[157]

The privilege to receive rent and capital gains from land, a principal concern of Rauschenbusch since his association with Henry George, illustrates his interpretation of this principle. Rauschenbusch did not deny that land contributed to the economy or that strategically located land contributed more than other land. But, unlike Ryan, his determination of productive contributions did not focus on the immediate factors of production. His sociological approach to economics broadened his view of the variables in the process of production to include the environment for production. The right to receive income from rent on land and from increases in land value is an unjust privilege because the value of the land is created by the community. Where land is not improved by the owners, they do not contribute to its value. The value of the land is determined by external factors in the surrounding community and by pressures of demand. "Thus the community . . . creates an increasing value for city land. But our laws give this social product away to individuals." The result is "unearned gain" allowed by the legal privilege to reap return without contributing to the product.[158]

From this sociological perspective, the principle that income and wealth should be earned directs us to discover unjust privilege wherever massive individual income and wealth depend on the community. In a highly interdependent industrial economy, this situation exists in all cases of significant inequalities. Thus, this principle of justice is crucial and largely negative. "The fundamental step toward christianizing the social order, therefore, is . . . abolition of unjust privilege."[159]

---

155. Rauschenbusch, "Dogmatic and Practical Socialism," 310.
156. Rauschenbusch, *Christianizing the Social Order*, 336.
157. Ibid., 337–338.
158. Rauschenbusch, *Christianity and the Social Crisis*, 226–227.
159. Rauschenbusch, *Christianizing the Social Order*, 337.

Rauschenbusch believed this step toward justice would be redemptive because unjust privilege obstructs the opportunity to develop character. Not surprisingly, he employed a biological metaphor, "parasite," to describe those who profit from unjust privilege. Plant and animal parasites "are always defective in the essentials of life." On the obverse side, the hosts (i.e., "the people of the exploited class") "are deprived of an equal opportunity to develop their gifts."[160] The problem of injustice is not merely unfairness. The character of a social order marked by unjust privilege makes solidarity between the classes impossible.[161] It also debilitates the capacities of both classes to contribute to society. It undermines natural human instincts for self-improvement and for love and fraternity.

Freedom Through Economic Democracy

The opportunity to develop character is also enhanced by freedom. Here again Rauschenbusch developed what he meant by freedom as the converse of his description of capitalist autocracy. Only in this context is the content of his principle of freedom and its challenge to the economic order obvious. Autocracy reigns in capitalism because management has unequal power. In reality there are not, in capitalism, free competition, free contracts for labor, or free markets. Even the benevolent employer is paternalistic, "leaving the working class in a dependent attitude and fail[ing] to call out qualities of independence and initiative."[162] Freedom exists only where equals participate together in pursuit of individual and collective aspirations. To Rauschenbusch, this meant industrial democracy. He cites John Stuart Mill's call for an "association of the laborers themselves on terms of equality, collectively owning the capital . . . and working under managers elected and removable by themselves."[163] In the absence of the freedom secured by economic democracy, workers would continue to have a grievance against the capitalist class, even if they received a just share in the proceeds of their joint labor.[164]

For Rauschenbusch, freedom is neither the absence of state participation in the economic system nor the liberty of individuals to pursue their own ends. The state is intended to facilitate economic democracy,[165] and individuals are restrained by common ends of democratic cooperation.

---

160. Ibid., 334.
161. Ibid., 333.
162. Ibid., 356.
163. Ibid., 357.
164. Ibid., 193–198.
165. Ibid., 360.

Freedom is a necessary means for "creating strong and saved characters, and [for] establishing a redeemed and fraternal social life."[166] In short, freedom is justified as an opportunity for individual and collective personality development.

Moreover, this opportunity, embodied in democratic institutions, undergirds an integrated balance between self-interest and the instinct for solidarity. Freedom promotes a sense of equal worth that makes fraternal relations possible and eliminates the servility that robs a class of its virility.[167] Economic democracy cultivates healthy interests in economic advancement and work that contribute to economic efficiency and the good of the society.[168] This is not anarchy in which individuals are unrestrained by their own interests and freely love others in a utopian harmony. Freedom gives sufficient room in the social order for individual self-initiative and self-improvement that serve the common good. It conflicts with hierarchy and autocracy but not with democratic restraints on individual liberties.

Fraternity Through Socialist Cooperation

Equality and freedom are necessary but insufficient for love and fraternity. It is possible to imagine the achievement of liberty and equality without an economic basis for fraternity.[169] Fraternity cannot be sustained unless an economy based on competition is replaced by "a great cooperative system of production" with only scattered sections of private and competitive effort.[170] "Mere democracy" must be complemented by socialism.[171] As Rauschenbusch used this term, socialism did not refer, in the first place, to public ownership of public property but to making property serve the public good so that it is available to the service of all.[172] It included public ownership of much of productive property but only as a means to its aim: "harmonious cooperation of all individuals for common social ends."[173] Thus, socialism is not primarily an economic program but a moral principle justifying a variety of policies.

As a principle of justice, socialism directs institutions to create opportunities for persons to develop their fraternal instincts. Rauschenbusch did not believe such opportunities were available. Competition had been

---

166. Ibid., 352–353.
167. Ibid., 353.
168. Ibid., 195–196.
169. Ibid., 366.
170. Ibid., 365.
171. Ibid., 367.
172. Ibid., 420.
173. Ibid., 366.

forced on persons by the economic order. Individuals cannot decide whether they will enter into cooperative or competitive arrangements of organized life. The competitive organization of economic life "has overdeveloped the selfish instincts in us all and left the capacity of devotion to larger ends shrunken and atrophied."[174] When formed under the influence of a competitive economic order, individuals are not free to choose cooperation and fraternity. Yet economic life organized for cooperation could change individual character. It would free persons for fraternity.[175] This opportunity for cooperation would benefit individual development, but it was denied individuals under the burdens of competitive economic institutions. Justice requires a socialist organization of economic life, an economic order in which there are opportunities for cooperation.

Rauschenbusch's views on moral agency, especially sin and redemption, informed this principle of socialism. Individuals are not totally free to choose between selfishness and public spiritedness. Collective agencies channel natural desires. Evil collective personalities embolden the human tendency to selfishness and sin. Yet human selfishness is variable. Just collective personalities can redeem us from sin. Because the democratic and social movements were evolutionary forces enabled by the advancing kingdom Jesus initiated, Rauschenbusch could describe the opportunities wrought by these increasingly just collective agents as the redemptive work of God. He commingled the gospel and justice in a sociological analysis justifying socialism: as socialism provides opportunities for solidarity, it regenerates individual character.

In sum, the "channel buoys," or principles, that focused Rauschenbusch's moral reasoning about distributive policies were economic reward according to contributions, democratic organization of all sectors of the social order, and socializing property. Each principle specifies opportunities required for individuals to develop their personalities in solidarity. Together, these principles focus the general social principles of Jesus in relation to the contemporary social order.

"The great aim underlying the whole social movement is the creation of a free, just, and brotherly social order. . . . Its accomplishment is the manifest will of God for this generation." Yet despite this evangelical dimension of justice, Rauschenbusch did not identify justice with the kingdom Jesus sought.

> In the best social order that is conceivable men will still smolder with lust and ambition, and be lashed by hate and jealousy. . . . [A fully just social

---

174. Ibid., 369.
175. Ibid., 370.

order cannot] satisfy the restless soul in us and give us peace with ourselves. All who have made the test of it agree that [personal] religion alone
holds the key to the ultimate meaning of life, and each of us must find his
way into the inner mysteries alone.[176]

Justice is the necessary scaffolding for the kingdom, but it is also enabled
and completed by personal regeneration. Justice never displaced
Rauschenbusch's early commitment to evangelizing individuals.

The Strategy Required: Individual Sacrifice and Redistribution of Power

Neither did Rauschenbusch believe that the combination of personal
regeneration and ideal principles of justice could, of themselves, advance the social order toward the kingdom. The economic order, he
thought, remained an unregenerate evil personality possessing power to
resist moral and religious suasion. A capitalist class capable of deceiving
itself and others with "a protective integument of glossy idealization"
defending the "justice" of the present order[177] will not succumb to
religious and moral argument. A capitalist class tempted to tyranny by
the subtle intoxicant of unequal power[178] will attempt to subvert the
democratic political institutions that are instruments for justice.[179] Although democratic government figures as the crucial positive instrument
of justice, the struggle for justice is a class conflict within the arena of
democratic politics.

Rauschenbusch described that struggle as

> a war of conflicting interests which is not likely to be fought out in love and
> tenderness. The possessing class will make concessions not in brotherly
> love but in fear, because it has to. The working class will force its demands,
> not merely because they are just, but . . . because it is strong enough to
> coerce.[180]

As Donald Meyer observed, in *The Protestant Search for Political Realism,*
Niebuhr obfuscated this aspect of Rauschenbusch's thought. Niebuhr
incorrectly criticized Rauschenbusch for ignoring the realities of the class
struggle on the basis of a naive hope that justice could be achieved by
purely educational and moral means. Rauschenbusch's analysis of the class
struggle as a necessary means for justice, according to Meyer, spoke a

---

176. Ibid., 104.
177. Rauschenbusch, *Christianity and the Social Crisis,* 350–351.
178. Rauschenbusch, *Christianizing the Social Order,* 181.
179. Ibid., 281.
180. Rauschenbusch, *Christianity and the Social Crisis,* 411.

language similar to Niebuhr's attacks upon moralism.[181] There is, however, a difference. Rauschenbusch believed his time was ripe for a realistic strategy that would not compromise Jesus' ethic of solidarity. Niebuhr favored the proletarian movement as part of a balance of power strategy that he believed was tragically inconsistent with Jesus' ethic of love. This disagreement is sufficiently complex that we must await an analysis of Niebuhr to comprehend it fully, but it is located in large measure in contrasting interpretations of the ethic of Jesus.

Recall that Rauschenbusch understood Jesus' conflict with the forces of evil to require self-sacrifice, not as a universal principle, but selectively as part of an effective strategy for achieving mutuality in the social order.[182] Rauschenbusch held no illusions that fraternal love and the sacredness of individual personalities were adequate guides to the struggle for justice. The ideal of fraternal organization, he noted, cannot be realized by idealists only.[183] He believed, however, that Jesus' redemptive work as a force in history provided a basis for an effective strategy for justice consonant with the goals of the ideal principles of justice. This strategy was three-pronged.

Personal Regeneration and Voluntary Self-Sacrifice

First, Rauschenbusch concluded both his books on the social order with a claim that personal regeneration and voluntary self-sacrifice are necessary. They are among the "practical means" for christianizing the social order.[184] We must, he asserted, begin at both ends. We need a new economic system to preserve our conscience and religious faith, but we also must renew religion in order to change our economic system.[185] Religious renewal produces loyalty to Jesus' ethic of the cross, a necessary means for social progress. The cross calls persons to accept suffering in stands against the injustice of the social order. Rauschenbusch suggested that championing social justice was almost the only remaining avenue to Christian martyrdom.[186] Indeed, these sentences must have

---

181. Donald B. Meyer, *The Protestant Search for Political Realism, 1919–1941* (Berkeley: University of California Press, 1961), 259–260, 88–89. Meyer goes too far when he says that the issue between Niebuhr and Rauschenbusch was not in politics as such but in religion. See ibid., 260. Unlike Niebuhr in the thirties, Rauschenbusch never wavered in his commitment to democratic government, nor did he believe selective violence would be a useful instrument for approximating justice.

182. *Supra,* chapter one, 55.

183. Rauschenbusch, *Christianity and the Social Crisis,* 414.

184. Rauschenbusch, *Christianizing the Social Order,* 465.

185. Ibid., 459–460.

186. Rauschenbusch, *Christianity and the Social Crisis,* 417–418.

reflected his fear that *Christianity and the Social Crisis* would jeopardize his credibility or even his job. In the preface, he wrote, "Let us do our thinking on these great questions, not with our eyes fixed on our bank account, but with a wise outlook on the fields of the future." He understood the book itself as an obligation of justice. He wrote it to "discharge a debt" to his former parishioners in Hell's Kitchen. His hope for the book was that it "in some far-off way helps to ease the pressure that bears them down and increases the forces that bear them up."[187] Rauschenbusch undoubtedly perceived this book as a part of his strategy, a strategy that could exact personal sacrifice, for advancing justice. It was not only sacrifices by committed reformers that were needed. Rauschenbusch also believed a successful emancipation of the poor depended upon personal regeneration and sacrifices by individuals in the capitalist class.[188]

Rauschenbusch never thought that personal regeneration and voluntary self-sacrifice could stand alone as an effective means for obtaining justice. Nor did Jesus' ethic require it alone. Heroic sacrifice is only an essential part of a strategy for justice. The strategy also requires use of the redemptive possibilities in suffering inflicted upon innocents and in the force available through the interests and powers of the working class.

Justly Inflicted Individual Sacrifice

A second element in Rauschenbusch's strategy was the necessity for and the justice of involuntary suffering by individuals. He did not believe socialism could be achieved without inflicting some individual suffering. The suffering inflicted by the reorganization of property has to be weighed against the vaster suffering that is and will be inflicted by the capitalist system of private property.[189] This consequentialist calculation is consistent with Rauschenbusch's view that God judges justly when the suffering of the innocent has redemptive meaning for the whole. "[H]umanity is so closely bound together that the innocent must weep and die for the sins the dead have done."[190] Rauschenbusch was not as reluctant as Ryan was to violate previous "contracts" between individuals and society for the sake of moving toward a more just economic system. Rauschenbusch did not allow the sacredness of the individual personality, which he incorporated into his ideal principles of justice, to place absolute constraints upon his strategy for attaining the goal of justice.

---

187. Ibid., xxv.
188. Rauschenbusch, *Christianizing the Social Order,* 467–476, esp. 468.
189. Ibid., 429.
190. Ibid.

Redistribution of Power

Finally, a realistic strategy for justice must redistribute power to the labor movement. This strategy includes expressions of partiality and support for the self-interests of this relatively defenseless and impoverished group. Jesus' ethic of self-sacrifice does not require the laboring class to sacrifice its interests in the conflict with capitalism. The progress of the laboring class "can come only through class struggle."[191] Labor solidarity in the pursuit of class interests is an effective virtue for redeeming the present economic order.[192] Consequently, Christian idealists should not "hold the working class down to use of moral suasion only, or be repelled when they hear the brute note of selfishness and anger."[193] "Christianity should enter a working alliance with this rising class, and by its mediations secure the victory of these principles [i.e., solidarity and cooperation] by a gradual equalization of social opportunity and power."[194] Rauschenbusch did not think the interests of labor could or should be advanced by "outsiders." Labor must win its own prizes by its own efforts. But to do so labor needs laws that will "facilitate," not merely tolerate, the "organization of industrial workers" and their demand for collective bargaining. It also needs increased power for its cause that can come through more democratic economic and political institutions.[195]

Rauschenbusch, unlike Niebuhr, considered a Christian alliance with labor interests fully consistent with Jesus' ethic and an effective means to achieve cooperation and fraternity. The tensions are patent. First, how can fraternity arise out of the class conflict required to achieve justice for the laboring class? Rauschenbusch lamented that class violence and strikes generate hatred. He, nevertheless, thought that strikes, especially "sympathetic strikes," manifest the virtues of altruism and solidarity within the laboring class and that the disruptive activities of strikers were more righteous than the protests against them.[196] Yet insofar as I know, Rauschenbusch never fully endorsed labor strikes. Did fear of the hostility that strikes induce cause Rauschenbusch to waffle in supporting use of an instrument labor needed to carry out his strategy for justice? Was his goal of fraternity in irreconcilable tension with his strategy to attain justice through working class interests? A second tension is this: if

---

191. Ibid., 453.
192. Ibid., 388–389.
193. Rauschenbusch, *Christianity and the Social Crisis,* 410.
194. Ibid., 414.
195. Rauschenbusch, *Christianizing the Social Order,* 453–454, 359–362.
196. Rauschenbusch, *Christianity and the Social Crisis,* 238–239, 324–325; idem, *Christianizing the Social Order,* 389–390.

labor's interests and power are encouraged, will labor secure privileges for itself at the expense of others and of the common good? Rauschenbusch saw this possibility as remote, a risk worth taking. After all, God is immanent in the social movement. Democracy and training in the virtue of solidarity would restrain the overgrowth of labor's self-interests.[197] Niebuhr would come to view both these tensions as inevitable and irreconcilable.

In sum, Rauschenbusch supplemented his ideal principles of justice with a strategy for doing battle with the evil forces of injustice. His strategy combined, once again, the distinctive ethic of Jesus with his description of the redemptive and evil forces in the social order. It requires selective voluntary and inflicted individual sacrifices and a redistribution of power from the capitalist to the labor class. Despite their tensions with the sacredness of the individual personality and the goal of fraternity, these guides to strategy, Rauschenbusch believed, provided necessary and sufficient means for progress toward justice and the kingdom of God.

POLICIES OF GOVERNMENT AND CHURCH

The interpenetration of theory, principles, and practical moral reasoning about justice in Rauschenbusch's thought has required discussion of the policies he advocated in order to clarify the principles in his conception of justice. Yet the task remains to examine the coherence of those policies. The principal agents he called upon to change their policies were governments and the churches. In addition, the effectiveness of Rauschenbusch's policies depended upon his assessment of the interests of the working class.

Government

Rauschenbusch never lost faith in the capacity of democratic government to bring about a just economic order. He thought the democratic state had already supplied "Christian virtues" to business by putting limits on the immoralities of capitalism,[198] and he expected more from democratic politics. To be sure, he did not think these changes would come until organized labor wrested control of the democratic process from the capitalist class, but his hope in gradualism and distrust of

---

197. Ibid., 360, 388–389, 454–455.
198. Ibid., 239.

catastrophic change succored his belief that justice could and should come through the constituted government. Thus, government was the principal agent to which Rauschenbusch appealed for administering just policies.

Despite his appreciation for the socialist movement, Rauschenbusch never joined the Socialist Party.[199] His principal reason appears to have been the dogmatic socialists' insistence that change can occur only through catastrophe.[200] For Rauschenbusch, piecemeal changes were possible and were also a necessary preparation for a virtuous socialist economy. He dismissed Marx's claim that the transition to communism would come through a dictatorship of the proletariat. Rauschenbusch charged that a dictatorship of the proletariat, in the absence of an established organization of the people, would mean rule by "club orators" (socialist intellectuals). "Lord have mercy upon us!" Rauschenbusch retorted.[201] We, therefore, find Rauschenbusch advocating that the present government enact a series of practical measures en route to democratic socialism.

The centerpiece of those piecemeal reforms was Henry George's single-tax proposal. Rauschenbusch's enthusiasm for the single tax never flagged, even after the political movement for it waned. In addition to taxing nearly all rent on land, Rauschenbusch favored taxing increases in land value. He conceded that this policy would inflict sacrifices upon present landholders, but selectively inflicted sacrifices were a part of Rauschenbusch's strategy for securing justice. He believed that the suffering of landholders could be minimized by a gradual phasing in of the tax.[202] As previously noted, Rauschenbusch also justified this proposal on the principle of earned income. In addition, he held that the single tax would partially fulfill the principle of socializing property. Taxing land instead of improvements on the land (an empty lot would be taxed as much as a lot with improvements) would encourage develop-

---

199. Rauschenbusch, in an unpublished manuscript, said he would regard political control by the Socialist Party, "in its present untrained personal equipment," a public calamity. He simultaneously declared his distance from the "old parties," which, he judged, needed to be purified by the election of socialist minorities. See Walter Rauschenbusch, "The Contributions of Socialism to the New Social Feeling," manuscript in Box 22 of Rauschenbusch Papers at the American Baptist Historical Society Archives, Rochester, New York, no date, 11. Rauschenbusch, unlike Ryan and Niebuhr, never became involved in party politics. This reticence about involvement in politics may have been partially due to his deafness after 1886. It must have also been based upon Rauschenbusch's judgment that the church could perform its function better by remaining outside electoral and legislative politics.

200. Rauschenbusch, "Dogmatic and Practical Socialism," 310.

201. Ibid., 320.

202. Rauschenbusch, *Christianizing the Social Order,* 423.

ments on the land. These developments on idle land held for speculation would "turn to the public uses a value created by the public" and also increase revenues for public use.[203]

Rauschenbusch did not believe that land taxes alone could satisfy his principle of socialism. Taxes merely socialize unearned land values, leaving the title with individuals.[204] Henry George, Rauschenbusch asserted, was a new-school individualist and an advocate of the highest form of laissez-faire economics.[205] The single tax was the last opportunity to give competition a protracted lease on life.[206] Rauschenbusch viewed the single tax as only an important step on the way to a fully socialized and cooperative economic system.

Rauschenbusch also advocated other steps in the interim before socialism. First, he favored what he called "paternalistic" labor legislation to replace the fiction of the "freedom of contract" between business and workers (Rauschenbusch's quotation marks). This legislation should include limitations on hiring children, pregnant women, and mothers; maximum hours and a living wage sufficient to support families for all workers; safety regulations; compensation for disabled workers; and assistance for workers beyond their prime or handicapped. He considered these policies a minimum basis for developing the personality.[207]

Second, Rauschenbusch argued that the principle of earned wealth (in addition to eliminating the privileges previously noted) required the laborer's right to share in property through increases in public property and services, through compulsory insurance against sickness and old age, and through labor sharing in the profits and ownership of industry. The most important form of this right to property should be a job, guaranteed by law, for anyone who does "honest and efficient work."[208]

Third, where monopoly power has created privileges, which government must revoke to comply with the principle of earned income, Rauschenbusch favored public ownership rather than regulation or antitrust action. He believed that the increasing size of corporations was a natural evolution toward greater mastery of nature and efficiency. Fur-

---

203. Walter Rauschenbusch, "The Practical Cures for Social Wrongs Under Individualism," *The Treasury* 17, no. 2 (April 1900): 931; idem, *Christianizing the Social Order,* 393, 420, 423.

204. Rauschenbusch, *Christianizing the Social Order,* 423.

205. Rauschenbusch, "Dogmatic and Practical Socialism," 309; idem, "On Monopolies," in *A Rauschenbusch Reader: The Kingdom of God and the Social Gospel,* 142. First published in 1889.

206. Rauschenbusch, "How Can the Aims of the Social Movement Be Realized?" 9.

207. Rauschenbusch, *Christianizing the Social Order,* 412–417; idem, "The Practical Cures for Social Wrongs," 931–932.

208. Rauschenbusch, *Christianizing the Social Order,* 343–350.

ther, a return to competition, though it would protect persons against monopolistic power, "is a denial of fraternity." Thus, "enforcing the Sherman Antitrust Law [works] against manifest destiny and the law of evolution."[209] For Rauschenbusch, public ownership was not a human contrivance to restrain the excesses of humans' competitive nature; it was the end toward which "free play" of economic forces was moving. "*Laissez faire* to-day means public ownership."[210] Moreover, he considered regulation a "halfway house" inviting private interests to corrupt the process.[211]

He conceded that there would be difficulties in public management, but overcoming them was possible through more democratic control of the civil service. Also, democratic public management would summon qualities of public-spirited service.[212] Socialized institutions would displace the competitive character with a disposition to serve the public good. On these grounds, Rauschenbusch argued that "railways, surface lines, elevated roads, subways, water ways, telegraph and telephone systems, gas and electric light and power systems . . . are the irreducible minimum which must come under public ownership."[213] He also included mines, oil and gas wells, and the distribution of sensitive products—ice, coal, milk, drugs, and burial services—as candidates for public ownership.[214] These were still immediate and piecemeal steps; like other practical measures he proposed, Rauschenbusch viewed public ownership of monopolies as a necessary preparation for the ultimate goal of socialist cooperation.

Fourth, Rauschenbusch argued for a progressive inheritance tax and direct taxation (e.g., as contrasted with tariffs) of corporations and individuals as the best means to socialize income and wealth. These taxes are justified in part by the principle of earned income, but great fortunes, even if accumulated justly, are threats to the public good.[215] The principle of socializing property for the sake of the health of the society

209. Ibid., 163, 178.

210. Ibid., 433–434. Rauschenbusch had clearly altered his understanding of laissez-faire economics since 1889 when he called Henry George's thought the highest form of laissez-faire economics. This revision, probably unconscious, coheres with his developing views on the limits of individual freedom and on the increasing interdependence of economic institutions and economic life. The interdependence of persons and institutions had developed naturally in the modern industrial economy. Returning to competition among small enterprises was anachronistic and artificial in the context of these natural developments.

211. Rauschenbusch, *Christianizing the Social Order*, 436–437.

212. Ibid., 438–440.

213. Ibid., 435.

214. Ibid., 424, 442–445.

215. Ibid., 426–429.

and of all persons in solidarity prohibits private control of massive wealth. In one of his homier similes, Rauschenbusch compared wealth to manure. When it is spread widely, the whole flourishes. When it is left in heaps, nothing can grow under it and everything else is left impoverished.[216]

These piecemeal policies (save effective management of publicly owned industry) could be enacted by government with only political support from laborers. Complete satisfaction of the principle of industrial democracy and of Rauschenbusch's ultimate hope for economic cooperation depended upon the organized power and initiative of workers. He supported economic cooperatives because their democratic organization "combine[s] a wholesomely selfish desire to get ahead with genuine fraternal sympathy and solidarity." He did not, however, expect that the cooperative movement alone would displace capitalism.[217] Complete industrial democracy will come only when labor unions, fully enfranchised by law, press for property rights in the instruments of production, a voice in management of the workplace, and jurisdiction over output. Workers may even dispense with the employer.[218] Here the role of government is to empower unions. The unions must, then, take initiative to end the autocracy of corporate management.

Industrial democracy following from a redistribution of economic power to labor was still an intermediate step toward the ultimate goal of the principle of socialism, that is, a cooperative economy founded upon the public management of a largely publicly owned economy. Industrial democracy was, however, a necessary step. Placing power in the hands of labor was not merely a strategy to achieve justice through the class struggle; it was also intended "to create a social organization of people, on which the social management of industry can devolve when it becomes necessary."[219] Rauschenbusch's understandings of economic democracy and of the gradual training of character through institutional influences persuaded him that socialism would have to come through labor initiative. It would have to come slowly, only as laborers, through industrial democracy, gained the moral and economic skills to participate in public management. Thus, socialism could not and should not come primarily through the efforts of socialist intellectuals or abruptly through political action.

Nevertheless, Rauschenbusch envisioned a future "communistic organization" of the economic order. This "communism" would "afford a

---

216. Rauschenbusch, *Christianity and the Social Crisis,* 281.
217. Rauschenbusch, *Christianizing the Social Order,* 385–388.
218. Ibid., 198, 359–360.
219. Rauschenbusch, "Dogmatic and Practical Socialism," 321.

far nobler social basis for the spiritual temple of Christianity," that is, "a society organized on the basis of solidarity and cooperation."[220] He refused to stipulate how far this "communistic ownership" should go. Neither personal property—a person's "toothbrush" and "love-letters"—nor productive property would come entirely under public ownership.[221] Rauschenbusch expected, at the least, the continuation of family farms and businesses and small democratically organized private enterprises. Nor did he expect elimination of self-interest within a communistic organization. He rather envisioned an economic organization in which persons' "natural ambition to make themselves felt, to exert power and get honor, runs in the same direction with public needs."[222]

Despite criticisms of dogmatic socialist tactics, Rauschenbusch went further than Ryan and as far as the early Niebuhr in advocating socialist economic policies for a distant future. Still, he remained tentative about how far public ownership and public management should go. In an 1896 article, Rauschenbusch expressed (in a passage befitting Niebuhr after 1944) the fear that state management of all productive property could be "a real menace to individual liberty."[223] That theme disappears in his later writings, but Rauschenbusch never identified his principle of "socializing" all property with complete public ownership of public property. Furthermore, he did not expect socialism to usher in altruistic cooperation. Rauschenbusch's hope was that "socializing" property would encourage a balance and coordination between the natural human desires for self-welfare and for solidarity. His understanding of the kingdom of God neither envisioned nor demanded total altruism.

Rauschenbusch's hope for justice depended on democratic government empowering unions, which, he presumed, would bargain for industrial democracy and use their political influence to work for more public ownership. Given the descriptive grounds of his conception of justice, he would have had to revise it in the thirties when unions, before and after the Wagner Act, pursued narrower economic goals than Rauschenbusch envisioned for the working class. (The narrow economic aims of unions persuaded Niebuhr to de-emphasize them in favor of a more radical proletarian movement.) Speculation about how Rauschenbusch would have revised his policies and conception of justice is further complicated by the failure of the church to pursue the policies he advocated for it.

---

220. Rauschenbusch, *Christianity and the Social Crisis*, 397–398.
221. Ibid., 396.
222. Ibid., 399.
223. Rauschenbusch, "The Ideals of the Social Reformers," 211–212.

Church

Rauschenbusch had no expectation that the state and the labor movement would approximate justice apart from a concomitant advance in the redemptive force of Jesus' personality.

He saw no hope for the government policies he advocated without changes in the religious ethos. "The real advance . . . will have to come through those social forces which create and train the sense of right. The religious and educational forces in their totality are the real power that runs the cart uphill; the State can merely push a billet of wood under the wheels to keep it from rolling down again."[224] "The State," he observed, "can protect the existing morality and promote the coming morality, but the vital creative force of morality lies deeper." Religion "creates" it.[225] Although Jesus' redemptive influence exists outside the church—God being immanent in the social movement—the self-consciously Christian redemptive mission of the church makes it the crucial agent for establishing the religious basis for justice. In his writings prior to *Christianizing the Social Order,* Rauschenbusch devoted more attention to the church's evangelical role in redeeming the social order than he did to advocating government policies.

He also thought the churches would play a large role in determining the direction of the labor movement. An emancipation of the working classes was inevitably coming. Whether it would come gradually by peaceful evolution or by a catastrophe analogous to the "Civil War" depended largely upon support from the churches.[226] His point was not that the churches should preach sacrifice and nonviolence to the working class. He considered that strategy both morally wrong and ineffective. His point was that the churches' role in regenerating the capitalist ethos was likely to determine whether inevitable changes in the economic order would move toward greater justice and fraternity.

The role Rauschenbusch advocated for the church is more evangelical and ethical than political. He had no interest in Christian political parties, and he saw little reason for ministers to align themselves with the extant political parties in the United States.[227] The church has a right to lobby in the political arena, but an emphasis on direct political influence exaggerates the importance of law and blinds the church to its more important task.[228] Without repentance and faith in the gospel, political action or even ethics would be ineffective.

---

224. Rauschenbusch, *Christianity and the Social Crisis,* 377.
225. Ibid., 374.
226. Rauschenbusch, *Christianizing the Social Order,* 36–37.
227. Rauschenbusch, *Christianity and the Social Crisis,* 362–363.
228. Ibid., 372–373.

The connection Rauschenbusch made between evangelism and justice was based upon his distinctively sociological understanding of the evangelical process. According to Rauschenbusch, the church had never merely taught the gospel and moral ideas. The church is a social organization that shapes character as it enforces its prevailing sentiments by putting offenders under the ban of its disapproval. Absent this enforcement, moral ideas are strangely powerless.[229] The question was not whether the evangelical mission of the church needed to be supplemented by a social ethic. The church inevitably shapes moral values. The question was what the church would assimilate persons into: the distinctive ethic of the gospel or an ethic that supported the present injustices? Does the substance of the evangelical message incorporate the distinctive ethic of the kingdom, and do the social sanctions of the church back the ethic it preaches? Rauschenbusch repeatedly chided the church for excluding drunkards without expressing disapproval of covetous businessmen.[230] The church may take the side of the poor in theory, but it rarely sanctions its teachings by actually taking the side of the labor movement.[231]

Rauschenbusch challenged the church to accept a "new evangelism" that combined the two sources of his understanding of the kingdom of God: the distinctive ethic of Jesus and an application of that ethic in light of a disciplined social analysis of the age.[232] The first task of the church is to free itself from the ethic of respectability, which has put it under the dominion of the capitalist class.[233] The church should proclaim the distinctive ethic of Jesus that is "so high above [the] actual lives [of the capitalist class] that it will smite them with conviction of sin." Condemning capitalist sins is not sufficient, however. The church's ethic should not be "remote" from all human interests. The second task of the church is to "appeal to the motives which powerfully seize men."[234] For Rauschenbusch, this meant to identify with the needs and cause of the working class. This class is developing a powerful ethic of solidarity, an ethic more Christian than the covetousness and selfishness that undergird commerce.[235]

Rauschenbusch's evangelism did not detach the gospel from the interests of persons and groups. Applied to the modern social order, the

---

229. Rauschenbusch, "The Service of the Church to Society," 394.
230. E.g., ibid., 395; idem, *Christianizing the Social Order*, 456.
231. Rauschenbusch, "The Service of the Church to Society," 395–396.
232. Walter Rauschenbusch, "The New Evangelism," in *Walter Rauschenbusch: Selected Writings*, 136–144. First published in 1904.
233. Ibid., 142–143.
234. Ibid., 139.
235. Ibid., 142.

gospel is on the side of the working class. The church ought not remain neutral in the class struggle. The church's mission is evangelical, but evangelism sanctions moral and political interests without being directly political. This evangelical mission of the church was an essential part of Rauschenbusch's strategy to redistribute power to the working class and to convert some individuals to sacrifice their interests for the cause of justice. Through this evangelism, the church was to provide the indispensable redemptive force enabling governments to adopt just policies. Without this ingredient, progress toward justice would be seriously hindered.

The church, so conceived, is not primarily a community for moral discourse if that means a collective effort to discern what is morally right in the context of shared loyalty to the cause of God in Christ. Ethics and the gospel are closely enough connected that the evangelical mission of the church incorporates the standards of justice. The principal need is not for moral discourse to discern what is just but for new disciples of Jesus' ethic of the kingdom. The church's primary mission is to establish the religious foundation that will advance economic justice.

Neither should the church seek to embody the sociopolitical ethic of the kingdom of God merely as a witness to an alternative to the ethic of the nation. Rauschenbusch called the church to a distinctive evangelical ethic for the purpose of raising the ethical standards of society. He believed Protestant Christianity had "gained amazingly in its spiritual effectiveness on society." Moreover, churches are "no longer the sole sphere of action for the religious spirit." Churches should align themselves with nonecclesial social institutions that embody the redemptive force of Jesus. The churches "exist to create the force which builds the kingdom of God on earth. . . . By becoming less churchly Christianity has, in fact, become fitter to regenerate the common life."[236] Consequently, Rauschenbusch thought the new evangelism to which he called the church was fully consonant with his reliance upon government to enact just policies. Although the church and the state have distinct functions, their respective tasks "must mingle . . . to make social life increasingly wholesome and normal. . . . Their common aim is to transform humanity into the kingdom of God."[237]

As we now know, Rauschenbusch wrote these words in *Christianity and the Social Crisis* in some trepidation that the book would provoke resentment that might make him a martyr for the kingdom he proclaimed. The favorable reception the book actually evoked, including by

---

236. Rauschenbusch, *Christianity and the Social Crisis,* 207.
237. Ibid., 380.

many churches, no doubt contributed to what interpreters agree is the more optimistic tone of *Christianizing the Social Order*.[238] The latter volume begins by describing the social awakening of the nation and the churches, including a much more hopeful assessment of what the Catholic Church might contribute.[239] Although this hopefulness about the church does not mark a shift in Rauschenbusch's theory or conception of justice, it helps to explain why *Christianizing the Social Order* devotes more attention to advocating government policies than to changes in the church's evangelical mission. By 1912, Rauschenbusch was gaining confidence that the redemptive forces in society were providing a foundation for policies that would advance justice.

The advent of war, accompanied by severe criticism of Rauschenbusch's pacifist and perceived pro-German stand, and criticism by theological conservatives later chastened Rauschenbusch's optimism.[240] He died in 1918. We can only wonder how he might have responded to postwar realities that shaped Niebuhr's thought. He certainly would have responded. A theory of justice sensitive to changing realities in the social order invites continuing revision. Rauschenbusch no doubt would have had to reassess aspects of his theory and conception of justice in light of his overestimation of how far the churches would move toward his new evangelism. Would he have placed more emphasis upon redemptive influences outside the church? The labor and socialist movements also took directions different from those Rauschenbusch anticipated. Could he have continued to hope for christianizing society? We need not speculate on these and other questions in order to note and assess his enduring legacy, or to conclude that his is not the legacy that has been transmitted through the filter of Christian realist interpretations.

SOME CONCLUSIONS

Rauschenbusch's theory and conception of justice was deeply influenced by his belief that history can and should progress toward the kingdom of God. His ethic of the kingdom was not, however, an attempt to apply an idealist conception of love to the realities of the social order. Nor did he envision a radically new order to which an idealist conception of love

---

238. E.g., Robert D. Cross, "Introduction to the Torchbook Edition" to *Christianity and Crisis* (New York: Harper & Row, 1964), xix; Minus, *Walter Rauschenbusch*, 169–170.

239. Rauschenbusch notes John Ryan's "far-reaching program of reform" as part of the evidence for his assessment of the Catholic Church. See Rauschenbusch, *Christianizing the Social Order*, 27.

240. Minus, *Walter Rauschenbusch*, 177–184, 189–190.

could be applied. To be sure, the centrality of the kingdom in Rausch-enbusch's thought backed an application of the distinctive ethic of Jesus to the social order. But Rauschenbusch's understanding of the kingdom also backed a sociological interpretation of Jesus and of Jesus' redemptive influence in history. This sociological interpretation led Rauschenbusch to understand the distinctiveness of Christian love as an elevation of natural human interests. For Rauschenbusch, redemption from the overgrowth of selfish interests inculcated by competitive capitalism was necessary for justice, and this redemption could be hoped for. He did not believe, however, that persons could be raised above their natural human interests or their universal proclivity for sin. Rausch-enbusch's Christian ethics was never detached from his description of social and natural realities.

Thus, Rauschenbusch affirmed that justice is fully consistent with the distinctive ethic of the kingdom, even though justice discriminates among conflicting interests and requires coercion. Perfect justice demands equality, but equality according to what is due persons for their contributions in a highly interdependent economy. It requires democratic liberties, but only those liberties that provide opportunities for individuals to develop personalities in relation to the common good. It aims for cooperation and fraternity, but not for a harmony that eliminates all pursuit of self-interests. Unlike Niebuhr, Rauschenbusch never entertained the possibility of a transcendent kingdom of God in which absolutely equal and free individuals would be joined in a community of uncoerced harmony. Nor did he share Ryan's view that God has ordered the world so that justice could be achieved without violating the dignity of individuals. The goal of justice was, for Rauschenbusch, a social order in which individual dignity is sacred, but a just strategy for moving toward that goal requires that individuals will, at times, have to suffer for the good of the whole.

Rauschenbusch's theory of justice is subject to criticism for excessive optimism about redeeming human nature and history. Nevertheless, it does not display the naive liberal optimism about human evolution toward utopia that was the foil for Niebuhr's Christian realism. There are good reasons for calling Rauschenbusch's ethic and conception of justice evangelical, but it is not the gospel ethic that Niebuhr asserted was inapplicable to issues of justice. Indeed, we will discover remarkable similarities between Rauschenbusch's conception of justice and the conception of justice Ryan developed on the basis of Catholic natural law theory. They both founded economic justice and policies on notions of how society's major institutions should provide opportunities for individuals to develop their natural capacities toward the highest moral character. In grounding justice in opportunities for individuals to de-velop their personalities in the context of social interdependence, Rauschenbusch and Ryan mounted a more severe challenge to liberal rights-based theories of justice than did Niebuhr. We now turn to Ryan's version of a character-based theory of justice.

3

JUSTICE BASED ON HUMAN DIGNITY

THE INHERITANCE

John A. Ryan shared Rauschenbusch's passion for economic justice as a necessary means to provide opportunities for developing the personality. He also shared Rauschenbusch's and Niebuhr's special concern for the working class. Yet Ryan came to focus his career on economic justice via a route different from that of Rauschenbusch before him and Niebuhr following him. Rauschenbusch, who grew up in a rather aristocratic and academic Baptist household in Rochester, was "converted" to an interest in justice through experiencing economic deprivation strike at family life and destroy the lives of children in his parish in Hell's Kitchen. Niebuhr, growing up in a middle-class German Evangelical parsonage in Lincoln, Illinois, was not "converted" to his earliest radical approach to economic justice until he confronted labor issues through a middle-class pastorate in Detroit. Ryan needed no special parish experience to become concerned for economic justice.[1] He was born into it. He grew up in the home of Irish-Catholic farmers in an Irish com-

---

1. Although both Rauschenbusch and Niebuhr looked back on their parish experiences as transforming their thinking, Ryan's parish experience was brief and uneventful. Ryan devoted a paragraph of his autobiography to his three months of parish work. He reported that they were among the "happiest weeks" he had ever known, but immediately allowed that "I did not request, or even desire the opportunity to continue in parish work." Ryan's

munity in Minnesota. This background shaped Ryan's concern for and approach to economic justice in two ways: one by virtue of his ethnic heritage and his location and one through his appropriation of Catholic moral theology.

One could not grow up in a community of Irish immigrant farmers in the Midwest after the Civil War without having his or her attention turned toward economic reform. First, Irish immigrants carried with them memories of the economic deprivation and injustice from which they had fled.[2] On the first page of his autobiography, Ryan recalled stories from his parents about economic injustices visited upon his grandparents in Ireland.[3] He also remembered having read the *Irish World and American Industrial Liberator*,[4] a monthly publication that supported reform movements such as the Knights of Labor.[5] Second, economic practices following the Civil War that produced deflation, declining farm prices, high railroad rates, and high interest rates—Ryan reported that his father paid 12 percent on a twenty-year mortgage[6]—fueled Populist sentiments among many farmers.[7] Patrick Gearty observes that Ryan's first interest in economic issues came from listening to the complaints of farmers in his community, as well as from reading the *Irish World*.[8] Ryan reported that he was later influenced by the Populist politics of Ignatius Donnelly, a supporter of the National Farmers' Alliance who was from a community near the Ryan family farm.[9]

Ryan's early support for the politics of radical economic policies—he voted for the Populist candidate for president in 1892[10]—emerged naturally from his Irish, farm background. He would later align with the more comprehensive and more mainline Progressive movement. The point remains that Ryan's reforming inclinations did not require a "conver-

---

interests coincided with his archbishop's intention to send him to graduate school in preparation for teaching at St. Paul Seminary. See John A. Ryan, *Social Doctrine in Action: A Personal History* (New York: Harper & Brothers, 1941), 60–61. The development in Ryan's thought was more rational and academic and less volatile than that of either Rauschenbusch or Niebuhr. As we will see, that fact befits Ryan's theory of justice, especially his understanding of moral agents.

2. Gearty, *The Economic Thought of Monsignor Ryan*, 1–2.
3. Ryan, *Social Doctrine in Action*, 1.
4. Ibid., 8.
5. Gearty, *The Economic Thought of Monsignor Ryan*, 2.
6. Ryan, *Social Doctrine in Action*, 6.
7. Gearty, *The Economic Thought of Monsignor Ryan*, 8–9; Francis L. Broderick, *Right Reverend New Dealer: John A. Ryan* (New York: Macmillan, 1963), 8–9.
8. Gearty, *The Economic Thought of Monsignor Ryan*, 6.
9. Ryan, *Social Doctrine in Action*, 12–18.
10. Ibid., 18.

sion," nor even the authority of Catholic moral teachings on economics.[11] He grew up with them.

In addition, these ethnic and farm influences stimulated an interest in economic thought that Ryan never relinquished. Ryan recounted that in 1882 or 1883, at the age of 13 or 14, he borrowed a copy of Henry George's *Progress and Poverty* from a neighboring Catholic farmer. He recalled having read only part of the book, but he comments that it strengthened his interest in social questions and his sympathy for the weaker economic classes.[12] The remarkable fact is that the Minnesota farm boy, Ryan, nearly eight years younger than Rauschenbusch, read George in the same year that Rauschenbusch, the son of a New York academic, was introduced to George by his teacher, Harrison Webster.[13] Unlike Rauschenbusch, Ryan would later reject George's economics, but he retained a much deeper interest in economic thought than did Rauschenbusch. While in seminary at St. Paul in the 1890s, Ryan studied economics, including Richard T. Ely, even though these materials were not part of the seminary's course offerings.[14] While at Catholic University from 1898–1902, Ryan wanted to take economics as his second major along with moral theology. Degree requirements did not permit it. He, nonetheless, took courses in economics and studied economics, including John Hobson—advocate of a then heterodox theory of underconsumption—in preparation for his dissertation, published as *A Living Wage* in 1906.[15] Back at St. Paul Seminary teaching from 1902–1915, Ryan argued that priests must know the industrial world. He devoted one fourth of his course in moral theology to economic history and political economy[16] in addition to teaching a course in economics.[17] When he returned to Catholic University as a member of the faculty in 1915, Ryan continued to teach economics as well as moral theology.[18] One year later, Ryan published his most important book, *Distributive Justice,* which used economic theory and analysis much more extensively than any of Rauschenbusch's or Niebuhr's writings.

In sum, Ryan inherited, from his ethnic and farm background, an

---

11. Joseph M. McShane, S.J., *"Sufficiently Radical": Catholicism, Progressivism, and the Bishops' Program of 1919* (Washington, D.C.: Catholic University of America Press, 1986), 32–33.

12. Ryan, *Social Doctrine in Action,* 9.

13. Minus, *Walter Rauschenbusch,* 37.

14. Gearty, *The Economic Thought of Monsignor Ryan,* 21–22; Broderick, *Right Reverend New Dealer,* 21.

15. Ryan, *Social Doctrine in Action,* 62–69.

16. Broderick, *Right Reverend New Dealer,* 52.

17. Gearty, *The Economic Thought of Monsignor Ryan,* 31.

18. Broderick, *Right Reverend New Dealer,* 94.

interest in reading economics with an eye for its significance for reform movements. He later formally combined his moral concerns with economic analysis in a canon of human welfare that accounts for economic "expediency."[19] This attention to analysis of the economic circumstances of justice developed quite naturally out of Ryan's adolescent inclinations.

Ryan brought these reforming tendencies and interests in economics with him to St. Thomas Seminary (later St. Paul) in 1892, but he did not have a moral theory to give them coherence. This moral theory came via the academic appropriation of his Catholic tradition. In 1894, Ryan read Pope Leo XIII's encyclical, *Rerum Novarum*. Forty-five years later, Ryan remembered that reading of *Rerum Novarum* as a Catholic affirmation of the ideas of state regulation that he had received from the Populists and the Farmers' Alliance.[20] Ryan emphasized the pope's support for state intervention in the economy, but he got more than that from the encyclical. It opened up for him a way to apply traditional Catholic moral theology (more specifically, Pope Leo's revitalization of Thomism) to modern industrial problems.[21]

Here again, Ryan needed no "conversion," and there was no need for him, as there was for both Rauschenbusch and Niebuhr, to revise the theology and ethics he received. Ryan's writings on theology consist of only passing references to God who created and ordered nature so that there is a telos for individual humans. He contributed little that was new to Catholic moral theology. His genius was in uniting Catholic natural law with similar ideas in American progressivism[22] and in applying natural law to economic conditions in the United States.

I am not implying that Ryan's intellectual task was merely technical, nor that his career path was not fraught with obstacles from fellow Catholics that called forth his courage. We must not assume that *Rerum Novarum* was widely promoted among Catholic clerics or that it was commonly used to support economic reforms. *Rerum Novarum* first came to Ryan's attention when it was assigned in a postgraduate English class at St. Thomas three years after its publication. Ryan lamented that this lack of interest in the encyclical was typical of Catholics in the United States. Furthermore, Ryan's immediate perception that *Rerum Novarum* backed his reforming ideas was not so obvious to others. Many

---

19. See John A. Ryan and Morris Hillquit, *Socialism: Promise or Menace?* (New York: Macmillan, 1914), 58; Gearty, *The Economic Thought of Monsignor Ryan,* 247–249; Curran, *American Catholic Social Ethics,* 38–41.
20. Ryan, *Social Doctrine in Action,* 44.
21. McShane, *"Sufficiently Radical,"* 31–32.
22. Ibid., 7–56, esp. 49.

American Catholics were stressing the encyclical's antisocialist elements rather than its potential as a basis for a new social program. Joseph McShane comments that Ryan's position in the church was a rather lonely one to take in the 1890s.[23]

Later, Ryan garnered considerable Catholic support for his proposals for economic justice, but even then he encountered opposition from high places. For example, when in 1924 he helped formulate and publicly supported an amendment to the Constitution limiting child labor, Ryan became embroiled in a row with Cardinal O'Connell of Boston. In the course of the dispute, O'Connell wrote to Ryan's archbishop about this "soviet legislation" and suggested that Ryan and others "either cease their crooked and false activities or leave the University and the offices of the N.C.W.C. [National Catholic Welfare Conference]." Ryan did not back off.[24] Never contumacious with respect to Catholic authority, neither was he obsequious. Ryan exhibited courage and independence of mind in his application of Catholic moral theology to industrial problems.

Ryan's creative contribution to Catholic ethics was in his application of resurgent Thomist moral theology to the issues of economic justice in his day. McShane observes that Ryan's "Leonine Thomism" was a version of neo-Thomism freed from a wooden application of Thomistic natural law. This idea of natural law was grounded in the norm of a reasonable human life that allows "a certain latitude of judgment within the natural law framework and demand[s] ingenuity and adaptability on the part of the ethician."[25] We will see how teleological elements in Ryan's theory of rights and justice enabled him to consider the consequences of economic policies and institutions. The scope that Ryan gave to prudence, or what he called "expediency," in his practical judgments about economic justice distinguished him from some of the Catholic moral theologians of his day. It led him, for example, to criticize Catholic just-price or just-wage theories that focused almost exclusively upon facts intrinsic to a contract. He also rejected justifications of private property as an intrinsic and absolute right that were characteristic of some Catholic moral theology, probably including *Rerum Novarum*.[26]

The point remains that Ryan did not push at the frontiers of Catholic moral theology.[27] Rather, he selected from among and integrated op-

---

23. Ibid., 33–34.

24. Broderick, *Right Reverend New Dealer*, 156–159.

25. McShane, *"Sufficiently Radical,"* 34–39.

26. See Curran, *American Catholic Social Ethics*, 46.

27. In a recent article, Richard Gaillardetz challenges this widely held view that Ryan contributed little to fundamental moral theology. Gaillardetz proposes that Ryan's work anticipated the modern revisionists' inductive approach to natural law. See Richard R.

tions available in his received tradition. Ryan's emphasis upon the pertinence of economic study came, in part, from Joseph Bouquillon, his professor of moral theology at Catholic University. Bouquillon confirmed the importance of Ryan's already developed interest in economic analysis by emphasizing its neglected relevance for moral theology.[28] Even more significantly, Ryan inherited the starting point for his ethics—the equal dignity of persons founded on a proper understanding of human nature—from his academic appropriation of Catholic moral theology. Jean-Yves Calvez and Jacques Perrin, in their prominent study of the social teaching of the popes, observe that the dignity of the human person was the starting point of the social doctrine of the church.[29] Further, we will see that Ryan's interpretation of this crucial concept was fully in harmony with Catholic teaching. Thus, although Ryan combined social ethics and his study of economics in a way that was distinctive among American Catholics, the major elements of his theory of justice were retrieved from his Catholic tradition.

Francis Broderick writes that when Ryan read *Rerum Novarum* in 1894, "his career stretched out before him." "Always at the core of his social philosophy was the natural law as expounded by Leo XIII."[30] The contrast with Rauschenbusch and Niebuhr is apparent and significant for Ryan's approach to securing economic justice. Rauschenbusch discovered the centrality of the kingdom of God only after an emotionally wrenching experience in his pastorate and a trip to Germany to study sociology and the New Testament from a new perspective. His discovery forced him to rethink his own theology and much in his Baptist tradition. Niebuhr developed his Christian realism, based on a creative tension between the ideal and the actual, through a long and grueling reflection on economic and political realities in the twenties and early thirties. His Christian realism compelled him to react against the theological and

---

Gaillardetz, "John A. Ryan: An Early Revisionist?" *The Journal of Religious Ethics* 18, no. 2 (Fall 1990): 107–122. The issue here is not whether Ryan's use of economic studies constituted a distinctive contribution to American-Catholic thinking about economic justice. On that point I agree with Gaillardetz. My interpretation emphasizes Ryan's contribution in introducing economic considerations into his precise determination of what rights require, his canons of justice, and his application of them to policy judgments. The issue is at what point inductive reasoning entered into Ryan's ethics. I believe that Ryan deduced a conception of rights from the essential features of the constitution and telos of rational human nature independently of his use of empirical studies. Thus there is no reason to challenge the view that Ryan merely adopted his received tradition in moral theology, though, as McShane observes, Ryan adopted a neo-Thomism that allowed for latitude of judgment within the natural law framework.

28. Ryan, *Social Doctrine in Action*, 63; Broderick, *Right Reverend New Dealer*, 32–33.
29. Jean-Yves Calvez, S.J., and Jacques Perrin, S.J., *The Church and Social Justice* (Chicago: Henry Regnery, 1961), 103–104.
30. Broderick, *Right Reverend New Dealer*, 19, 21.

secular liberalism he had accepted from his formal education. Ryan's theory of justice emerged rather spontaneously from his Irish-American, farm upbringing and from his academic preparation to be a Catholic priest and professor.

Ryan's struggle with American Catholics was based on an academic claim that Catholics had not taken seriously prominent elements in their recent moral and theological tradition. For him, justice depended little on redemption of individual and collective agents (Rauschenbusch) or on political confrontation to secure a balance of power (Niebuhr). It depended on rational moral argument and political action within established democratic institutions. We will have occasion to observe how Ryan placed his hope for advancing justice in direct moral appeals to political leaders, especially the New Deal. There is some irony in the fact that Ryan, the Catholic, was much more involved in the mainstream of American politics than either of these Protestants.

By the time his academic formation had taken shape, the two fundamental and relatively independent elements of Ryan's theory of justice were in place: the concept of human dignity understood in light of a Catholic view of human nature (that informed his understanding of human nature and agency) and the emphasis upon economic study (that established his analysis of the circumstances of justice). This fact shapes the way I organize the ensuing discussion of Ryan's theory and conception of justice.

First, because there were only subtle changes in Ryan's moral theory from 1906, when he published *A Living Wage,* until 1944, when he published *The Theory of Morality,* I will draw freely upon his later writings to explicate his concept of human dignity and his theory of rights.[31] Second, in contrast to Rauschenbusch and Niebuhr, for whom the kingdom of God and Christian realism respectively pervaded the treatment of all the base points of their theories of justice, Ryan established relative independence between his ethics, based on human dignity, and his analysis of the circumstances of justice, namely, his economics.[32] Consequently, we will consider the organizing concept of Ryan's theory of justice, that is, human dignity, in the context of treating his understanding of human nature and agency. We will then examine his economic analysis. Despite the relative independence of economics from moral theory, Ryan believed

---

31. Broderick observes that after the publication of *Distributive Justice* in 1916, Ryan "left scholarship behind." His career after that was as an "active apostolate for social justice." Ibid., 92. Broderick's claim may be stronger than the evidence warrants, but it serves to demonstrate that Ryan's intellectual development was complete once he had written his comprehensive conception of justice.

32. See Gearty, *The Economic Thought of Monsignor Ryan,* 98.

that his determination of what is expedient for the economy ultimately should and does support the dignity of every individual. It remains proper, therefore, to designate human dignity the organizing concept of his whole theory of justice. Third, although an understanding of God and God's relations to the world was crucial for Ryan's emphasis upon and conception of human dignity, he did not attend explicitly to this base point in his theory of justice. He simply assumed it from his neo-Thomist heritage. Consequently, our treatment of Ryan's understanding of God will be brief and will follow more extensive examinations of his views on human nature and agency, and on economics.

Although Ryan did not revise significantly his early formulation of a theory and conception of justice, there was development in the policies he advocated. In response to the Depression, Pope Pius XI's encyclical *Quadragesimo Anno,* and the New Deal, Ryan, in the thirties, began to emphasize the problem of unemployment and his programs for economic democracy and the occupational group system. Prior to the thirties, Ryan gave these matters less or even marginal attention. We will reserve treatment of these policies to a later chapter following an initial analysis of Niebuhr's Christian realism, thereby vivifying the contrast with Niebuhr during this period. Even here, however, we will find these policies congruous with the policies Ryan advocated earlier and backed by greater stress on elements already present in his moral theology and economic analysis.

HUMAN NATURE AND AGENCY
The Dignity of Human Nature

The immediate basis for Ryan's theory of justice is a theory of rights, which I will delineate below. His theory of rights is, however, based upon an even more fundamental concept, the dignity of human rational nature. "Man possesses rights because of his dignity as a person." Moreover, this dignity, at least at its most abstract level, is equal for all persons.[33] Consequently, in order to understand Ryan's conception of

---

33. John A. Ryan, *The Norm of Morality: Defined and Applied to Particular Actions* (Washington, D.C.: National Catholic Welfare Conference, 1944), 15, 44. I will cite *The Norm of Morality* throughout this section. It is peculiar to cite a monograph written near the end of Ryan's life to explicate the organizing concept for a theory of justice he developed thirty to forty years earlier. This procedure is justified because *The Norm of Morality,* although fully consistent with the chapter on rights that Ryan wrote for *A Living Wage,* published in 1906, is a more comprehensive statement of his moral theology. Thus, the latter essay tells us more about the concept of dignity, which Ryan said, in *A Living Wage,* is entailed by his theory of rights. See John A. Ryan, *A Living Wage: Its Ethical and*

rights, we must first know what he meant by the equal dignity of all persons.

Dignity in Relation to a "Teleology of the Human Person"

The emphasis, in the Catholic tradition, on the fundamental importance of individual dignity can be confusing. David Hollenbach, in an interpretive essay on the most recent American Catholic bishops' statement on economic justice, observes that the letter's insistence upon the dignity of all persons reflects elements of the liberal tradition in moral theory emanating from Immanuel Kant and others. He cites the bishops' affirmation of individual dignity as backing the Kantian claim that individuals are ends in themselves with rights and not means for achieving the goals of others. This commonality with Kant has, Hollenbach observes, led some interpreters to view the letter as a Catholic capitulation to liberalism. Hollenbach contends, however, that the letter unites an emphasis upon individual dignity with a communitarian stress on the common good that mitigates the priority of individual moral rights to the good that characterizes liberal moral theory.[34]

There are similarities between Ryan's use of the concept of dignity and this more recent use of it by the bishops. Ryan's emphasis upon dignity certainly shares Kant's affirmation that individuals are ends, not mere means. When Ryan asserted the dignity of persons, he intended to claim that they have intrinsic and sacred worth.[35] Kant also believed that the dignity of persons constitutes an intrinsic worth that requires us morally to treat them as ends in themselves.[36] Thus, we find recurrent in Ryan's writings the Kantian claim that "[e]very person is an end in himself; none is a mere instrument to the convenience or welfare of any other human

---

Economic Aspects (New York: Macmillan, 1906), 53. The consistency in Ryan's moral theology over these years is evidenced not only by a summary of his understanding of rights in *The Norm of Morality* but also by a virtually word-for-word reprinting of the chapter on rights from *A Living Wage* in the second chapter of *The Catholic Principles of Politics*, published in 1940. There can be little doubt that Ryan's later, more expansive writings on the concept of dignity underlay his earlier theory of rights.

34. David Hollenbach, S.J., "Liberalism, Communitarianism, and the Bishops' Pastoral Letter on the Economy," in *The Annual of the Society of Christian Ethics*, ed. Diane M. Yeager (Washington, D.C.: Georgetown University Press, 1987), 19–40, esp. 25–26.

35. Ryan, *A Living Wage*, 53; idem, *Distributive Justice: The Right and Wrong of Our Present Distribution of Wealth* (New York: Macmillan, 1916), 358–359. Because this chapter focuses on Ryan's understanding and application of justice prior to the thirties, most of the citations to *Distributive Justice* are to the first edition. See also Ryan, *The Norm of Morality*, 50, 55.

36. Immanuel Kant, *Grounding for the Metaphysics of Morals,* in *Immanuel Kant Ethical Philosophy,* trans. James W. Ellington (Indianapolis: Hackett Publishing Co., 1983), 40.

being."[37] Further, both Kant and Ryan associated dignity with a rational nature that is different in kind from human animal nature.[38] In this respect, Ryan differs from Rauschenbusch, for whom love (from which our sense of the worth of others emerges) and justice are rooted in our animal as well as our rational desires.

Here the similarity between Ryan and Kant ends. The Catholic emphasis upon dignity, which Ryan adopted, associates human dignity with an ideal of the perfection of human nature that places external limits on the moral freedom of the will. Kant associates human dignity with freedom from all determinants of the will except for pure practical reason, which is not bound by an ideal of perfection given from outside the will.[39]

For Kant, a person is "free as regards all laws of nature, and he obeys only those laws which he gives to himself. . . . Hence autonomy is the ground of the dignity of human nature."[40] When Kant referred to our dignity as rational beings, he meant that we are able to regard ourselves "with reference to all laws to which [we] may be subject as being at the same time the legislator of universal law."[41] The inviolability of persons' dignity requires that they remain free to choose their aims in life, except for the aim of moral excellence attained by obedience to the moral law self-legislated through pure practical reason. Hence, for Kant the universal principle of justice requires "that the freedom of the will of each can coexist together with the freedom of everyone in accordance with a universal law."[42] "[T]he concept of justice does not take into consideration . . . the end that a person intends to accomplish by means of the object that he wills."[43]

For Ryan, the dignity of the individual is based, not on the autonomy of the human rational will, but on the constitution and end of rational human nature, which are knowable by reason and intuition.[44] What we

---

37. Ryan, *Distributive Justice*, 358; idem, *A Living Wage*, 46; idem, *The Norm of Morality*, 14; and John A. Ryan and Francis J. Boland, S.J., *Catholic Principles of Politics* (New York: Macmillan, 1940), 15.

38. Ryan, *The Norm of Morality*, 10; Kant, *Grounding for the Metaphysics of Morals*, 40–41. On the basis of humans' difference in kind from animals, Ryan denied, as did Kant, that we have duties "to" animals. Both refer to duties "concerning" animals based on a person's duties to human nature. Ryan was even bolder than Kant in claiming that animals are instrumental to human ends. See Immanuel Kant, *Metaphysical Principles of Virtue*, in *Immanuel Kant Ethical Philosophy*, 105–106; Ryan, *The Norm of Morality*, 48–49.

39. Kant, *Grounding for the Metaphysics of Morals*, 47–48.

40. Ibid., 41.

41. Ibid., 43.

42. Immanuel Kant, *The Metaphysical Elements of Justice*, trans. John Ladd (Indianapolis: Bobbs-Merrill, 1965), 35.

43. Ibid., 34.

44. See Ryan, *The Norm of Morality*, 7–28, esp. 16, 23; idem, *A Living Wage*, 62. Ryan's moral theology could be interpreted using "rational human nature" as the organiz-

can and should know about the constitution and end of our rational nature provides knowledge about the good for individuals upon which rights and justice are based. I will focus on what Ryan called rational nature "described in terms of teleology."[45] This teleological dimension of Ryan's moral theory is crucial for his theory of rights. It also demonstrates how Ryan's conception of dignity differs from Kant's and is similar to Rauschenbusch's principle of the sacredness of the personality.

We can better understand this teleological dimension of Ryan's thought by employing a distinction Frederick Carney makes between a "teleology of the human person" and a "teleology of obligation." According to Carney, a "teleology of the human person" "addresses the problem of moral action by first asking what the proper purpose (telos) or function of a human person is, that is, what constitutes the characteristic excellence (arete) or well-functioning of a fully-developed person." A "teleology of moral obligation" "asserts that the moral rightness of an act . . . depends upon its being the most effective act (or rule) available within the designated circumstances for serving good ends or bringing about good (or less evil) consequences." A "teleology of human persons" can be combined with either a "deontological theory of obligation" or a "teleology of obligation."[46] Ryan's moral theory is, in contrast to Kant's, based on a "teleology of the human person." He then combined this teleology with a "deontological theory of obligation" for determining the moral rightness of some actions and with a "teleology of obligation" for determining the right regarding other actions and institutions.

Ryan's "teleology of the human person" is apparent from his claim that morally good acts may be defined by the "proximate end" toward which human rational nature tends, that is, "the development and

---

ing concept. He did argue that human rational nature is the norm of morality. Nevertheless, because his conception of human dignity contains the same content, I use it. It conveys more directly the intrinsic and sacred worth of individuals upon which justice is based, and it is most easily compared and contrasted with Kant's and Rauschenbusch's use of the same term. I am not alone in making human dignity fundamental for Ryan's moral theory. Patrick Gearty observes that the principle that pervades all of Ryan's social writings is "the intrinsic worth and dignity of the human person." See Gearty, *The Economic Thought of Monsignor Ryan,* 129, see also 155, 255, 300. David Krueger, in a recent dissertation on Ryan's economic ethics, writes that "human dignity and welfare functions as *the* critical theological assumption which guides Ryan's entire economic ethic." See Krueger, "The Economic Ethics of John A. Ryan and Gustavo Gutierrez," 19. Richard Gaillardetz states that the "affirmation of human dignity was in fact the linchpin of Ryan's social ethics." See Gaillardetz, "John A. Ryan," 112.

45. Ryan, *The Norm of Morality,* 16.
46. Frederick Carney, "On McCormick and Teleological Morality," *The Journal of Religious Ethics* 6 (Spring 1978): 81–86.

perfection of personality."[47] Human dignity is, thus, based on all humans' potential for excellence,[48] where excellence is defined in terms of an ideal of individual perfection and not as the autonomy of the rational will. This ideal for perfection is known when we understand human nature as a set of distinct and hierarchically ordered capacities or faculties. The lower physical or "sense" faculties ought to be subordinate and instrumental to the higher "rational" faculties. Both the "sense" and "rational" faculties are further subordinated to the development of the whole person, which includes physical and mental health as well as the "spiritual soul."[49] From knowledge of this ordering of the faculties and of their proper ends, Ryan believed he could deduce natural laws imposed by God as the Author of nature.[50]

In sharp contrast to Kant, the dignity of human rational nature, as Ryan conceived it, imposes natural laws and ends to which the will is morally obligated apart from its self-legislation of moral maxims. For Ryan, adequate education of the will demands habitual actions according to natural laws required by the "constitution [and ends] of rational nature and the dignity of personality."[51] From the perspective of Kant's conception of dignity based on autonomy, in which the principles or morality "are not to be sought at all in the knowledge of human nature,"[52] Ryan's moral theory is heteronomous. The conception of dignity upon which Ryan's theory of justice is based entails moral content that goes far beyond the right to individual autonomy. Respect for the sacred dignity and intrinsic worth of individuals requires that justice provide each person with the opportunity to develop his or her personality in accord with this ideal of moral excellence.

On Ryan's conception of dignity, respect for individuals' autonomy is neither sufficient nor always necessary to respect their dignity. It is insufficient because freedom of the will is not the only means required for perfecting the personality. Respect for dignity demands that we provide other goods (e.g., a decent livelihood) and institutions (e.g., labor sharing in management) that are necessary means for developing the higher faculties. Respect for autonomy is not always necessary, because dignity demands respect for the freedom of others only when freedom is a means to the end of human rational nature. Individuals have

---

47. Ryan, *The Norm of Morality*, 16; Ryan and Boland, *Catholic Principles*, 10–11.
48. John A. Ryan, "The Dignity of the Personality," in *Democracy: Should It Survive?* issued by the William J. Kerby Foundation (Milwaukee: Bruce Publishing Co., 1943), 15.
49. Ryan, *The Norm of Morality*, 9–14, esp. 13.
50. Ibid., 27; see also Ryan and Boland, *Catholic Principles*, 9–10.
51. Ryan, *The Norm of Morality*, 29–44 passim, esp. 34.
52. Kant, *Grounding for the Metaphysics of Morals*, 21–22.

no right to liberties or to choose their own ends when these liberties or ends are unnecessary or detrimental to the end of their rational nature.[53]

For Ryan, the dignity of an individual requires, not respect for his or her autonomy, but provision for "the opportunity of pursuing self perfection through the harmonious development of all of his faculties. . . . [M]an shall have the opportunity of becoming not only physically stronger, but intellectually wiser, morally better, and spiritually nearer to God."[54] Accordingly, Ryan asserted that the true formula of justice, which he explicitly contrasted with Kant's principle quoted above, is "that the individual has a right to all things that are essential to the reasonable development of his personality."[55]

We see then that Ryan, like the recent Catholic bishops' letter on economic justice (as interpreted by Hollenbach), affirms the sacred dignity of each individual while rejecting that moral rightness can be determined independently of a theory of the good, at least the good for individuals. This linking of dignity with an ideal of personal perfection requires that justice provide what individuals need to develop their personalities.[56] This focus on needs essential for developing the personality, rather than on maximizing equal liberty, had enormous implications for Ryan's conception of justice and the policies he advocated.

Dignity in Relation to a "Teleology of Obligation"

In addition to distinguishing his moral theory from Kant's, the conception of dignity Ryan inherited from Catholicism also opposes various uses of what Carney calls a "teleology of obligation." We will consider two kinds of criticisms Ryan proffered against a "teleology of obligation."

The first of these criticisms, in addition to distinguishing Ryan's moral theory from consequentialist ethics, actually widens the gulf between Ryan's conception of dignity and dignity based on individual autonomy. In 1907, Ryan published an essay objecting to an excessive use of the teleological method in Catholic ethics. He argued that the moral goodness of acts should be determined by their conformity with the norm of human rational nature and not by their usefulness for obtaining humans' ultimate end in God or the proximate end of their nature. He criticized Aristotle, and Thomas by implication, for emphasizing "man's ultimate

---

53. Ryan and Boland, *Catholic Principles*, 114–115.
54. Ryan, *Distributive Justice*, 361–362.
55. Ryan, *A Living Wage*, 64–65; see also idem, *Social Doctrine in Action*, 58; idem, *The Supreme Court and the Minimum Wage* (New York: Paulist Press, 1923), 42; Ryan and Boland, *Catholic Principles*, 110, 116–117.
56. Ryan, *Distributive Justice*, 244.

end"—especially when it is presented as happiness—in determining the goodness of moral acts. Ryan asserted that this emphasis upon the ultimate end was to some degree responsible for "too much teleology of proximate ends or consequences" in Catholic moral theology.[57] Ryan's concern was that an emphasis upon teleology could undermine the view that some acts—he names "self-pollution," "fornication," and "lying"—are intrinsically wrong. Acts of unchastity are wrong, regardless of their consequences, because they subordinate the higher rational faculties to the lower sense faculties and thus fail to conform to human rational nature.[58]

Ryan's argument in this essay would have benefited from Carney's distinction between a "teleology of the human person" and a "teleology of obligation." When he argued that conformity to human rational nature determines some acts as intrinsically wrong, he was claiming that these acts are wrong regardless of circumstances and consequences because they violate what Carney calls "the proper purpose (telos) or function of a human person." Charles Plater made this point in commenting on Ryan's essay in a subsequent issue of the same journal. Plater reminds Ryan that a moral norm based on conformity to human rational nature is "very good teleology," consistent with the spirit of Aristotle, even though the application of this norm is "fatal to Utilitarianism."[59] Whether or not he read and agreed with Plater, in *The Norm of Morality* Ryan accepted the teleology of rational nature as a starting point for ethics while continuing to maintain that some acts (e.g., blasphemy, murder, theft, fornication, and contraception) are always and intrinsically morally wrong.[60]

The crucial point is that despite apparent protestations to the contrary in his 1907 essay on the teleological method in ethics, all of Ryan's moral judgments were rooted in an understanding of the telos toward which human rational nature tends. It was on the basis of his "teleology of the human person" that Ryan formulated the right to a living wage prior to 1907. The dignity of persons, upon which the right to a living wage was based, was associated with an ideal of perfection.[61] The rights that secure individual dignity are means to the end appointed to persons by nature.[62] Human dignity provides no basis for an individual's right to choose his or

57. John A. Ryan, "The Method of Teleology in Ethics," *The New York Review* 2, no. 4 (January–February 1907): 418–419.

58. Ibid., 423.

59. Charles Plater, S.J., "A Starting Point in Ethics," *The New York Review* 3, no. 2 (September–October 1907): 160.

60. Ryan, *The Norm of Morality*, 26, 38–39.

61. Ryan, *A Living Wage*, 50–51.

62. Ibid., 44.

her own ends. Rights do not exist except as a means to the good for individuals. The fact that Ryan's "teleology of the human person" determines some actions to be intrinsically wrong, no matter what the consequences or circumstances, only broadens the restrictions he was willing to place on the right to liberty. When liberty is directed to purposes "inconsistent with the true welfare of its possessor, it is a bad thing for him." In such cases, curtailment of liberty is a positive good.[63] For examples: The state can, at least theoretically, restrict religious worship when it includes "practices contrary to good morals, or forms unauthorized by God" and restrict speech in order to "prevent the diffusion of false or immoral notions and doctrines."[64]

Ryan did not eschew a "teleology of obligation" in all aspects of ethics. Even in his essay criticizing teleology in ethics, Ryan allows that the determination of the morality of actions by their consequences is legitimate in its proper sphere.[65] There are primary principles of natural law, which are obligatory in all conditions, and there are secondary principles of natural law, which are not absolutely entailed by conformity to human rational nature but depend to some extent on circumstances and consequences.[66]

In matters of justice, all actions and institutions, save the direct killing of innocents, are governed by secondary principles of natural law. Thus, for the issues that concern us most in this treatment of Ryan, he was both a teleologist of human persons and a *kind of* teleologist of obligation. The justice of institutions and policies is determined by their consequences in providing the essential means for persons to perfect their character. This openness to consequences explains why Ryan emphasized economic analysis and his principle of economic expediency in affirming the justice of a living wage, private productive property, rent- and interest-taking, high profits, as so forth. For Ryan, prudence was an essential virtue for determining what is just.

It is important, however, to understand what *kind of* consequentialist Ryan was. This understanding exposes a second criticism Ryan made of some "teleologies of obligation." Even for those moral judgments in which he used a "teleology of obligation," Ryan was concerned to specify which consequences count in determining the rightness of moral actions. He considered only those consequences that affect the capacity of individuals to perfect their personalities. He opposed the determination of rights and policies solely on the basis of whether these rights and

---

63. Ryan and Boland, *Catholic Principles*, 114.
64. Ryan, *The Norm of Morality*, 61, 62.
65. Ryan, "The Method of Teleology," 426–427.
66. Ryan, *The Norm of Morality*, 25–26; Ryan and Boland, *Catholic Principles*, 4–5.

policies produce consequences that redound to the benefit of the "social welfare." By "social welfare" Ryan meant any conception for the good of the whole of society conceived independently of the intrinsic dignity of individuals. Ryan argued that theories of rights that measure what individuals are due according to consequences for some notion of social welfare reject "the essential and absolute dignity of every human being." On the basis of his conception of dignity, Ryan opposed "social utilitarians" and "Hegelians" because their singular emphasis upon social welfare does not account for individuals as ends in themselves.[67]

Ryan incorporated his "teleology of obligation" into what he called the principle or canon of "human welfare." When he introduced his notion of economic expediency in a published debate with the socialist Morris Hillquit, he claimed in the same paragraph that human welfare is the ultimate test of any social system.[68] He further insisted on a distinction between human welfare and social welfare in order to clarify that his concern was for the well-being, not only of a social group, but also of individuals. Human welfare requires that the vital needs of the individual be safeguarded.[69] Ryan's canon of human welfare requires that the economic consequences of policies be taken into account, but the consequences that count are those that, at least in the long run, protect each individual's opportunity to perfect his or her personality.

In the long run is an important qualification. Ryan did not confine his analysis of economic consequences to their immediate implications for the well-being of individuals. The health of a society or economy should be considered independently of benefits to individuals as long as this health can be foreseen to accrue to the eventual benefit of individuals. In the context of his criticism of "social utilitarianism" in *A Living Wage,* Ryan conceded that society is something more than the sum of its component individuals and that it has rights that are distinct from the individuals composing it. Society's rights are, however, "ultimately for the sake of individuals."[70] In a later discussion of a legal minimum wage, Ryan contended that

> the welfare of society can and ought to be considered, in itself, as something immediately and formally different from the welfare of its members. . . . In the long run, however, social and individual welfare are interdependent. . . .

---

67. Ryan, *A Living Wage,* 53–62.
68. Ryan and Hillquit, *Socialism,* 58.
69. Ryan, *Distributive Justice,* 252, 109; see also idem, *Distributive Justice: The Right and Wrong of Our Present Distribution of Wealth,* 3d ed. (New York: Macmillan, 1942), 30 n. 19.
70. Ryan, *A Living Wage,* 56–57.

[While society's] immediate and formal end is the common good, its ultimate and concrete object is the good of all its component individuals.[71]

Ryan's practical judgments reflect and illustrate this theoretical distinction between immediate benefits to individuals and long-run benefits that accrue to individuals only by attending first to social welfare. On some matters, such as in his argument for a legal minimum wage,[72] immediate benefits to individuals are also judged to benefit the social weal. On the other hand, Ryan justified the state's authorization of interest because prohibiting interest could result in a decline in savings and capital that would worsen the condition of every class. Human welfare justifies permitting interest even though the immediate benefits of suppressing "workless" incomes and equalizing incomes would be desirable.[73]

Ryan's theoretical specification of what consequences count was neither completely consistent nor always precise. Although he was adamant about the distinction between rights based on individual dignity and rights based on social welfare, in other contexts, such as the passage above on a legal minimum wage, he virtually identifies social and individual welfare. They are so interdependent that they are "fostered by the same means and hindered by the same obstacles."[74] Furthermore, it is not always clear whether his requirement that consideration for the welfare of society ultimately benefit its component individuals means the dignity of every individual or of individuals collectively. Are there occasions when some individuals' rights have to be sacrificed to secure similar rights for others?

Nevertheless, as we interpret these passages in the context of his whole thought, we will find a coherent and fairly precise "teleology of obligation." The justice of economic policies should be determined by their consequences for safeguarding the dignity of every individual, that is, her or his opportunity to develop toward the end of her or his rational nature. Safeguarding individual dignity requires that we consider the well-being of society, but the social welfare should never be advanced at the expense of an individual's opportunity to pursue the ideal of self-perfection. In the final analysis, Ryan, unlike Rauschenbusch, left little room for individual sacrifice for common good.[75]

---

71. John A. Ryan, *The Church and Socialism and Other Essays* (Washington, D.C.: The University Press, 1919), 78.
72. See ibid., 76–99.
73. Ryan, *Distributive Justice*, 199. See also Ryan's justification for permitting unlimited profits under competitive conditions, ibid., 255–258.
74. Ryan, *The Church and Socialism*, 78.
75. Ryan, *A Living Wage*, 58.

In sum, Ryan's conception of the sacred dignity and intrinsic worth of every individual entails an ideal of individual perfection that determines some actions as intrinsically wrong regardless of their consequences. In most matters of justice, however, this "teleology of the human person" requires a principle of human welfare that considers the consequences of policies for safeguarding each individual's intrinsic dignity. Concern for the consequences that policies have for the well-being of the relevant whole, whether society or the economy, should never override an individual's dignity. Yet consideration for the social welfare is always relevant and sometimes crucial, in the long run, for protecting every individual's dignity. Consequently, the principles of justice should never allow individual rights inessential for self-perfection (e.g., some liberties, and we will subsequently include equalities) to interfere with obligations to the common good. Preserving the common good is necessary to provide all individuals with the opportunity to develop toward the end determined by their rational nature. Ryan understood this Catholic conception of dignity to put his theory of justice at odds with elements both of Kantian liberalism and of utilitarian and communitarian theories of justice.

Dignity: A Comparison with Rauschenbusch

The similarities with Rauschenbusch's principle of the sacredness of the personality are apparent. Both Ryan and Rauschenbusch affirmed the intrinsic worth and dignity of individuals. Both cited Kant's imperative to treat persons as ends in themselves. Yet both shared a teleological view of individual dignity based (only in part for Rauschenbusch) on God's natural ordering of human life. Justice is, thus, associated with an ideal for developing the personality rather than with a conception of autonomy in which the right is conceived independently of a prior conception of the good for individuals. Neither Ryan nor Rauschenbusch believed justice requires individual liberty to pursue one's chosen ends in life. Consequently, we should not be surprised that opportunity for their respective conceptions of self-development was a central theme in both Ryan's and Rauschenbusch's conceptions of justice, or that the policies they advocated were similar.

There are also differences. Most fundamentally, Rauschenbusch affirmed the sacredness of the personality in the context of his conception of the kingdom of God. Accordingly, for Rauschenbusch the affirmation and realization of individual dignity arises through the redemptive influence of Jesus. This redemption raises humans' natural instinct for love to a higher level, putting it in balance with the natural inclinations toward self-interest. Ryan, perhaps with Rauschenbusch in mind, explicitly rejects the idea of the kingdom of God on earth. It is strictly a heavenly reality.[76] Ryan's association of dignity with human rational nature led him to construe both love and justice and their interrelations somewhat differently from Rauschenbusch. First, for Ryan both love and justice arise from rational faculties more than from the regeneration of natural desires.[77] Second, because the dignity, which justice safeguards, is understood in terms of the constitution and end of individuals, Ryan can say that justice "considers human persons as mutually independent and as possessing individual rights." Justice, thus conceived, can be formulated (though not fully motivated) without love, which arises from the bonds that unite humans.[78] These differences have implications for their respective conceptions of justice.

First, for Ryan, individuals can develop their personalities through their rational capacities if society provides them with the means they need. Individuals depend upon the common good to fill those needs, but because dignity is not fundamentally dependent upon solidarity, justice focuses first on individual needs rather than on equality in solidarity. We have seen how his conception of the kingdom compelled Rauschenbusch to view equality as fundamental because self-development occurs, from the beginning, in the context of interdependence. For Rauschenbusch, rent on land is an unjust privilege because rent pays individuals for the value land derives from contributions by the community. Inequalities arising from such privileges make love and solidarity difficult. This contrast with Rauschenbusch's emphases on equality and solidarity was reduced in the last fifteen years of Ryan's life as he began to accent the importance of the common good in providing the means for securing human dignity.

Second, due to his emphasis upon the rational basis of self-development, love, and justice, Ryan saw less need for and placed less hope in evangelism and the redemptive influences of institutions as means for securing justice and for shaping character. Ryan did suggest that great advances in justice were contingent upon more effective love and saner conceptions of welfare. He thought such changes in values were dependent, in part, upon a religious reformation of human hearts and minds. Nevertheless, the place for evangelism is muted by reasoned appeals for love and a less materialistic conception of welfare. Ryan made these rational appeals independently of his hope for religious regeneration.[79]

---

76. Ryan, *The Church and Socialism*, 153.
77. See Gearty, *The Economic Thought of Monsignor Ryan*, 300.
78. Ryan, *The Norm of Morality*, 52–53.
79. E.g., Ryan, *Distributive Justice*, 316–318, 424–425.

Moreover, Ryan, unlike Rauschenbusch, never integrated religious regeneration into his conception of justice. Nor did Ryan believe changes in institutions could significantly alter character. One of his arguments against socialism was that its success depends upon an increase in altruism, which new institutions could not generate.[80] He was not always consistent on this point. He did suggest that economic cooperatives, which he favored, could provide "the atmosphere for a greater development of the altruistic spirit."[81] Generally, however, Ryan argued for structures of economic cooperation because they could provide the means for self-development rather than because they transform character. The state, for example, can only provide the opportunities for self-development; the individual must take advantage of them.[82]

Ryan's conception of dignity in terms of individual rational nature led him to believe justice could and should be achieved on the basis of individuals' existing moral capacities. From that perspective, Rauschenbusch's strategy for justice through evangelism and transforming individual character by altering the institutions seems unnecessary and unduly evolutionary. Human nature is not that changeable.[83] Consequently, Ryan's hope for advances in justice was more dependent upon rational appeals to individuals than upon a grand strategy of transforming character through church evangelism, the labor and social movements, and changing economic structures. Ryan did call upon the church to use "moral suasion" and upon labor unions to use their power,[84] but he gave neither the church nor the labor movement the crucial roles they had in Rauschenbusch's strategy for justice.[85]

Third, Ryan's starting point with persons as "mutually independent and as possessing individual rights" in a rather static natural order reinforced his claim that individuals are ends in themselves. Individual dignity should not be sacrificed for some greater good, not even for a future state of affairs in which each individual's development might be more fully realized. Whereas Rauschenbusch's perspective of human life in evolutionary solidarity envisioned individual dignity, in part, as a goal to be realized by a strategy permitting the sacrifice of some legitimate individual interests, Ryan regarded such sacrifices as unnecessary and

---

80. Ibid., 165–167.
81. Ibid., 229.
82. John A. Ryan and Moorhouse F. X. Millar, S.J., *The State and the Church* (New York: Macmillan, 1922), 205.
83. Ryan, *The Church and Socialism*, 150.
84. Ryan, *A Living Wage*, 329–331.
85. See Curran, *American Catholic Social Ethics*, 66–67; Ryan, *Distributive Justice*, 417–420.

morally impermissible. Ryan, for example, although holding that a large tax on capital gains from the sale of land was just, also insisted that an implicit promise from the state that its policies would not lower land values gave landholders a right to compensation. This right required the state to reimburse capital losses occurring as a result of this capital gains tax.[86] Whereas Rauschenbusch had no theory of rights, Ryan's conception of dignity provides the basis for a theory of inviolable individual rights, which just persons and institutions are obligated to protect. We are now prepared to examine that theory of rights.

These differences between Ryan and Rauschenbusch should not be allowed to obfuscate their more significant agreements. In contrast with many other theories of justice, including Niebuhr's, they agree that the purpose of justice is to provide opportunities for natural self-development. And in contrast to what we will find in Niebuhr, they were prepared to develop principles of justice that discriminate between legitimate natural interests and interests that violate the natural order (Ryan) or ordering (Rauschenbusch) of human relations.

Rights Based on Human Dignity

A set of natural, absolute, equal, and specific rights links Ryan's conception of human dignity with his conception of justice. Justice determines what is due persons, which is "neither more nor less than that action or that good which belongs to them, as a matter of right."[87] Proceeding on the basis of Ryan's account of human dignity, we can see in what sense these rights are natural, absolute, and equal claims of independent individuals (rather than dependent upon a prior conception of the common welfare). We can also see the sense in which they are specific means to an ideal of self-perfection (rather than claims upon resources for pursuing whatever ends a person chooses).

Of the three justifications that Ryan offered for natural rights in his first book—reprinted in a 1940 essay—he found the first two, based upon an ideal of self-perfection, most compelling.[88] According to the first justification, every person has a right to the essential means for self-perfection because human dignity imposes a duty for self-perfection that cannot be adequately fulfilled without natural rights.[89] The second justification, which Ryan noted is "logically sufficient," bases rights on every person's "moral privilege" to pursue self-perfection. Thus, indi-

---

86. Ibid., 111–113; cf. Rauschenbusch, *Christianizing the Social Order*, 429.
87. Ryan, *The Norm of Morality*, 53.
88. Ryan, *A Living Wage*, 50–53; Ryan and Boland, *Catholic Principles*, 17–19.
89. Ryan, *A Living Wage*, 50.

viduals do not forfeit their rights by failing to fulfill their duties. The right to a living wage sufficient to support a family does not, for example, depend upon an individual fulfilling his (Ryan considered this the duty of the husband and father) duty to his family.[90] Three points follow from this justification for rights.

First, consistent with his view that rights are justified by the moral privilege to pursue self-perfection, Ryan generally limited the scope of justice to providing the means for self-perfection. He did not include positive or negative sanctions for the duty of self-perfection within the scope of justice. In this respect he differed from Rauschenbusch, whose understanding of individual agents as dependent upon collective agents did not allow for a distinction between means and sanctions for self-development. For Rauschenbusch, institutions necessarily do more than provide the means for self-development. They either encourage or discourage good character. Rauschenbusch's argument for limiting profits included the claim that excessive wealth encumbers character development and hinders the prospects for solidarity between the classes, as well as the claim that most profits are unearned.[91] Ryan, on the other hand, countenanced the justice of unlimited profits, fairly earned. Unlimited profits can be just even though charity (but not justice) obligates persons to give from their superfluous wealth and a sane conception of individual welfare limits the amount a family can spend to between five and ten thousand dollars per year.[92]

Second, rights are instrumental, not intrinsic. Individuals, due to their dignity, have intrinsic worth, but because dignity is constituted by the potential for self-perfection, the rights that secure this dignity are but means to Ryan's "teleology of the human person." Although Ryan claimed that the right to life is intrinsic, this seems to be so only because there are no circumstances in which it is not directly necessary for self-development.[93] Elsewhere Ryan stated, "All rights are means, moral means, whereby the possessor of them is enabled to reach some end. [They are] means or opportunities by which the individual attains the end appointed to him by nature."[94] Thus, Ryan's conception of justice is not constrained by individuals' rights to pursue whatever ends they choose. The purpose of justice is to secure the goods, which can be specified in kind and amount, that are essential for self-perfection. It is

---

90. Ibid., 50–51.
91. See Rauschenbusch's chapter "The Tragedy of Dives," in *Christianizing the Social Order*, 291–310.
92. Ryan, *Distributive Justice*, 255, 303–318.
93. Ibid., 57.
94. Ibid., 44.

not a denial of a person's dignity and rights to deprive one of goods inessential to one's self-development.[95]

Third, rights are "fixed by and based upon the intrinsic worth of the human person and the individual's distinction from and independence of all other individuals."[96] Thus, rights are natural, not only in the sense that they arise from a natural order of human life, but also in the sense that they are derived from the nature of an individual and exist for his or her welfare.[97] Ryan rejected "civil" or "positivist" views of rights, by which he meant not only rights posited by civil authority, but rights conferred on individuals for the benefit of social welfare.[98] When Ryan said rights are natural, he meant that they exist for an individual exclusive of his or her relation to society. Consequently, though rights are instrumental to an ideal of individual perfection, they are not instrumental to social welfare. These rights are absolute in the sense that each individual has an inviolable claim upon the means for self-development. They are also equal to the extent that the dignity of each individual—one's capacity for self-perfection—is equal.

Understanding the implications of these last two points for Ryan's conception of justice requires that we elaborate on his claims that rights are absolute and equal and on the significance of his specification of the kinds and amount of goods to which persons have rights.

Absolute

Individual rights are absolute because they are necessary for respecting the intrinsic worth of persons. Neither the claims of social welfare nor the will of others can override their moral inviolability. Ryan, however, qualified the absoluteness of rights in two ways, one on the basis of his "teleology of the human person" and a second as a result of his "teleology of obligation." Rights, Ryan wrote, "are absolute in existence but not in extent."[99] His illustrations of this distinction appear to indicate two "reasonable limits" on the inviolability of rights.

First, Ryan noted that the reasonable limits upon the absoluteness of

---

95. William Galston, a contemporary theorist who understands himself to be drawing on an ethical naturalism and an Aristotelian tradition at odds with Anglo-American liberalism and utilitarianism, argues for a similar view of rights as instrumental to a conception of the good. Galston criticizes recent rights-based theories of justice (as distinguished from goal- or good-based). See William A. Galston, *Justice and the Human Good* (Chicago: University of Chicago Press, 1980), ix–xi, 127–142.
96. Ryan, *The Norm of Morality*, 53.
97. Ryan, *Distributive Justice*, 56.
98. Ibid.; Ryan, *A Living Wage*, 55.
99. Ibid., 45.

the rights to liberty and property are "always determined by the essential needs of personal development."[100] His point was that these rights always "exist," but their "extent," that is, the amount and kind of liberties and of private control of property, is limited by the extent to which they are essential for an individual's proper development. Thus, rights are absolute insofar as they are necessary to assure the privilege for self-perfection. They are not qualified by their consequences for the social welfare. Yet they are not intrinsic. They are absolute only as they are necessary means to the telos of human rational nature.

Ryan also illustrated his distinction between "existence" and "extent" with the right to life. The point of this illustration is more ambiguous. As we have seen, Ryan considered the right to life intrinsic in the sense that it is always essential to self-development. Yet following Catholic tradition, Ryan allowed exceptions to the absoluteness of this right when persons forfeit their right to life by murdering or attempting to murder others, when the state places its citizens at risk in time of war, or when noncombatants are killed incidentally in a just military action.[101] I am uncertain what Ryan intended by these qualifications on the absoluteness to the right to life. His claim that self-defense and executions for murders are permitted do not easily jibe with his view that rights are not forfeited by one's failure to do his or her duty.[102] The justifications for the state to place its citizens at risk or to kill noncombatants incidentally appear to be based more upon consequences for the social welfare that, in the long run, bear on the individual welfare of others. Perhaps Ryan intended, in part, a consequentialist qualification on the "extent" to the right to life. If so, his distinction between "existence" and "extent" can be applied to other rights where he clearly places consequentialist limits on the absoluteness of rights.

Ryan believed, at least theoretically, that the right to a decent livelihood, which is just as absolutely demanded by the intrinsic dignity of humans as the rights to subsistence and life, is "limited by the actual

---

100. Ibid., 46, see also 71–72.

101. Ibid., 45–46.

102. One of my referees rightly observes that Ryan, had he been a consistent Thomist, would have justified self-defense through the principle of double effect rather than on the grounds that the person attempting murder forfeits his rights. Ryan, however, explicitly states that a person attempting murder forfeits his rights. He even emphasizes this point by contrasting his justification for self-defense with situations in which it is just for innocent persons to be "indirectly" and "incidentally" but "unavoidably" killed for the sake of a "lawful end." See ibid., 45–46; and Ryan, *The Norm of Morality*, 56–57. Odd as it is, Ryan consciously omitted application of the principle of double effect to cases of self-defense, even though it would have been more consistent with his own justification for rights and with his Thomistic moral theology to have applied it.

conditions of production and distribution."[103] The right to a decent livelihood is clearly a necessary means to self-development. It is limited to the extent that attempting to satisfy it is economically infeasible or would have adverse consequences for other equally inviolable rights. Thus Ryan, after asserting that a living wage is the only way the right to a decent livelihood can be secured in a modern industrial economy, devoted an entire section of *A Living Wage* to the economic feasibility of paying a living wage to all, and most of another chapter to the practicality of state enforcement of a legal minimum living wage.[104]

The point of this example is that Ryan thought that absolute rights were, in theory at least, contingent upon circumstances. This contingency does not impugn Ryan's assertion that these rights are absolute in "existence." Individuals would continue to hold claims that others would be obligated to satisfy in other circumstances, and these claims would not be subordinated to some notion of social welfare. Nevertheless, the "extent" to which rights are absolute was for Ryan contingent upon his "teleology of obligation," that is, the economic and social expediency of satisfying them in a way that is consistent with long-run human welfare.

In actual practice, I know of no case, except the indirect killing of innocents, in which Ryan conceded that rights crucial for perfecting the personality had to be totally surrendered due to practical considerations. Ryan's general answer to his own query about the practicality of satisfying the right to a decent livelihood reflects his perspective: "[T]he concrete existence of the right in all supposes that the total amount of goods to be distributed is sufficiently large to afford a decent livelihood for all."[105] Ryan concluded from his exhaustive investigation of the consequences of a living wage that its universal application would "cause an immense improvement in our industrial and social conditions."[106] Despite the fact that Ryan's economic analysis was relatively independent of his moral theory, he asserted in the Hillquit debate that "moral values and economic expediency are in the long run identical."[107] This statement was not, as Hillquit suggested,[108] a subordination of moral values to economic expediency[109] but a profession of Ryan's optimism. Ryan was confident that the world is ordered so that the essential means

---

103. Ryan, *A Living Wage,* 74, 79.
104. Ibid., 100–101, 151–233, 302–318.
105. Ibid., 79.
106. Ibid., 328.
107. Ryan and Hillquit, *Socialism,* 58.
108. Ibid., 184–185.
109. Ibid., 260.

to self-development can be provided to every person. We will see later how this remarkable correlation between individual rights and economic expediency coheres with Ryan's understanding of God.

Ryan's confidence in the harmony of the natural order no doubt provided a perspective that influenced his economic analysis of the circumstances of justice. One notable example is his shifting views on the efficiency of labor sharing in management. In his debate with Hillquit, Ryan opposed labor sharing in management on the grounds that the laborers' productivity depends upon competition and incentives that laborers would not impose upon themselves.[110] Later, when he decided that labor sharing in management was a means for laborers to develop creative and directive faculties essential for self-perfection, Ryan praised it for the economic benefits cooperation would produce.[111]

Ryan's optimism about satisfying all rights essential for individual dignity does not mean that he did not take consequences seriously at the level of practical judgments or that he never allowed them to qualify rights. In his debate with Hillquit, Ryan, after defending the right to private property against socialist claims that property can be justly confiscated, conceded that in a supreme emergency the state may confiscate property without compensation.[112] Although "theoretical justice" gives wage earners a right to a living wage that takes precedence over a landholder's right to rent and a lender's right to interest, Ryan rejected, as impractical, a laborer's right to have that living wage paid out of funds owed employers for rent or interest.[113] Furthermore, Ryan's justifications for rent, interest, and profits were largely based on their positive consequences for long-run human welfare rather than on their direct contributions to self-development. In all of these examples, Ryan's "teleology of obligation" concerns rights that are less than absolute, that is, only indirectly or remotely related to opportunities for self-development.

In sum, Ryan held that individual rights essential for self-perfection are absolute. These absolute rights are, however, limited. First, these rights apply only to the amount and specific kind of a good, for example, liberty or private property, that is essential for Ryan's ideal of individual perfection. Second, even the right to these essential goods is qualified to the extent that the consequences of providing for them immediately endangers provision for them, or other essential rights, in the long term. As a practical matter, Ryan never or only rarely found that rights

---

110. Ibid., 59–66.
111. Ryan, *Distributive Justice*, 3d ed., 334–336.
112. Ryan and Hillquit, *Socialism*, 52–55.
113. Ryan, *A Living Wage*, 263–264.

essential for self-perfection had to be qualified due to economic and social circumstances and consequences. His economic analysis did, however, place practical limits upon some less than absolute rights and justified other "presumptive" rights for the sake of their long-run consequences in respecting individual dignity.

Equal

Ryan also maintained that persons are equal in their claims to the means for self-perfection. Their claim on rights is equal because all persons possess the faculties of will and reason that enable them to master all their faculties and direct their actions toward the end of rational nature. Consequently, persons "have equal natural rights to the means without which these ends cannot be achieved."[114] Because persons are equal in their capacity for attaining a basic level of perfection, they are equal in their claims on the goods, for example, a decent livelihood, essential for that perfection.

Ryan immediately qualified this assertion that rights are equal. Persons, he said, are equal in the abstract but not in the concrete. Persons are equal in the *"number"* of rights they hold but not in the *"extension,* or content" of each member of that set of rights.[115] Persons are, for example, equal in their right to a decent livelihood, but the quantity of income required for a decent livelihood varies.[116] Every individual has a right to a certain minimum of goods, which is "determined by the reasonable needs of personality." Once that minimum is satisfied for all, the rights of persons vary according to "a variety of circumstances, individual and social."[117] These unequal or proportional rights are attributable to three distinguishable factors.

First, some persons have special needs associated with normal self-development. Ryan, for example, opposed a proposed amendment to the Constitution requiring that "men and women shall have equal rights." He held that women are equal in their claim on rights for reasonable living, but he also insisted that women stand "in peculiar need of . . . legal protection." Ryan favored discriminatory protective labor legislation for women and children on the grounds that justice should be proportional to unequal needs.[118]

---

114. Ibid., 46–47; idem, *The Norm of Morality,* 50.
115. Ryan, *A Living Wage,* 47–48.
116. Ibid., 75.
117. Ibid., 47.
118. See John A. Ryan, *Declining Liberty and Other Papers* (New York: Macmillan, 1927), 101–114.

The second variable factor is that some individuals have a capacity for higher levels of perfection. "Although men are equal in personal dignity [i.e., a capacity for a basic level of self-perfection] they are unequal in their individual powers and needs." Those who have greater capacities and greater needs possess rights to more income for a decent livelihood and more opportunities for education.[119] Ryan's persistent association of greater needs with greater capacities suggests that his allowance for unequal rights in proportion to needs usually referred to this variation in capacities for self-development. This justification for unequal rights was based on differences in individuals' potential for achievement, not on actual achievements.

"Another objection to . . . absolute equality in distribution arises out of the principle of productivity."[120] Ryan did not give claims based on productivity equal status to claims based on needs, but once the rights to basic needs have been met, less pressing needs ought "as a matter of *social welfare* and of concrete justice to be satisfied unequally" in accord with various considerations that contribute to economic well-being. Some of these considerations, for example, the title to productive property, are based on individuals' circumstances unrelated to their active contributions to the social weal. Other considerations, for example, efforts and sacrifices that contribute to social utility, are related to meritorious actions by the individuals rewarded.[121] This justification for unequal rights is largely dependent upon the positive economic consequences gained from permitting inequalities that are only indirectly related to moral excellence.

In sum, Ryan deemed rights equal insofar as they are essential means to the basic level of self-perfection of which all humans are capable. Yet these basic needs vary among different classes of persons (e.g., women, children, and adult males), and rights vary accordingly in order to assure the equal right to the means for self-perfection. These means for the self-perfection of all should be provided before unequal capacities are considered.[122] Once these universal basic needs are satisfied, however, rights and justice are proportional. They are proportional to greater capacities and needs of those with potential for higher levels of self-development and/or to the actions or the fortunate circumstances of individuals that contribute to economic well-being.

---

119. Ryan, *A Living Wage*, 75, 47.
120. Ibid., 75.
121. Ibid., 76–78.
122. Ryan, *Distributive Justice*, 32.

Specifiable

Ryan's justification for rights as means to his ideal of personal perfection led him to assert an array of specific rights. To the extent that the means essential for self-perfection are definable, Ryan specified rights in number, content, and quantity. In *A Living Wage* he named life, liberty, property, a livelihood, marriage, religious worship, intellectual and moral education.[123] In *The Norm of Morality* he asserted rights to life, reputation, liberty, property, a livelihood, marriage, religious worship, education, association, and freedom of speech and of publication.[124] In the twenties and thirties, opportunities to develop the creative and directive faculties in economic production became a right for Ryan, even though they did not make his later list.

These rights provide individuals with absolute, at least in practice, and equal claims against society. They are not amendable on the basis of their consequences for the social welfare. In this way, Ryan's rights protect individuals from policies that aim merely to promote the public good. These rights are not based on maximizing the aggregate good. The high level of specification of these rights also distinguishes them from the abstract rights justified by rights-based theories of justice, that is, theories in which an overall right is a fundamental and intrinsic value independent of any particular conception of the good.[125] For Ryan, individuals are not protected from actions of the state or of others that deprive them of goods other than those specific ones essential for self-perfection. To illustrate the significance of Ryan's specification of rights, let us briefly compare his theory with rights-based theories that make liberty or equality the basis for justice. These are the two abstract rights Ronald Dworkin claims are candidates for rights-based theories of justice.[126]

A libertarian, such as Robert Nozick, claims that individuals' right to liberty places "moral side constraints" on policies designed to achieve goals, for example, to assure all persons the means to self-perfection.[127] Although Nozick's just society would protect some of the specific means to self-perfection that Ryan lists, it would not include the rights to a decent livelihood or opportunities to develop one's creative and directive faculties in the productive process. By contrast, Ryan's specification

---

123. Ryan, *A Living Wage*, 47.

124. Ryan, *The Norm of Morality*, 56–62.

125. See Ronald Dworkin, *Taking Rights Seriously* (Cambridge: Harvard University Press, 1978), 168–183, esp. 178.

126. Ibid., 178–179.

127. See Robert Nozick, *Anarchy, State and Utopia* (New York: Basic Books, 1974), 26–35.

of liberty in terms of the means to self-perfection limits the extent of this right to "merely a means to right and reasonable self-development." Liberty is "baneful and false" when it "does not tend toward this good."[128] Thus, Ryan contrasts the Catholic view of rights with what he calls the revolutionary philosophers of eighteenth-century France and England who exaggerate the rights of the individual so as to allow the strong to oppress the weak. The right to the liberties that are specific means for reasonable development does not extend so far that it prevents the state from safeguarding the welfare of all its citizens.[129] The state is, for example, obligated to restrict liberties in order to provide a living wage. We have also seen that Ryan was willing to limit the rights to religious worship and free speech when they are detrimental to self-perfection.

John Rawls, as Dworkin points out, makes equality rather than liberty the abstract right upon which a conception of justice is based.[130] Starting from this right, Rawls, unlike Nozick, develops a conception of justice sufficiently egalitarian to provide each person with income adequate to constitute Ryan's right to a decent livelihood. Rawls does not, however, limit persons' rights to income and liberty to amounts that are essential means to a conception of the good for individuals. For Rawls, income and liberty are called primary goods because persons can use more of them, whatever their ends in life.[131] Within practical limits, persons have a moral right to equal access to liberty, income, and other primary goods even if these goods are not necessary for a life plan of which we approve. The right to equality is independent of any goal or good for individuals. Not for Ryan! "After all," Ryan wrote, in a review of *The American Philosophy of Equality* by T. V. Smith, "equality and natural rights . . . are not ends in themselves. They are means to human welfare."[132] Thus, Ryan specified the equal right to a decent livelihood as an amount of income essential for self-perfection. After that equal right is satisfied, income and wealth are to be distributed on the basis of rights proportional to capacities for self-development and to contributions to economic well-being. Ryan's specification of rights restricts individuals' right to equality of goods more than Rawls's more general right to equality permits.

---

128. Ryan, *The Church and Socialism*, 145.
129. Ryan, *A Living Wage*, 62–64; see also idem, *The Supreme Court and the Minimum Wage*, 29–43.
130. Dworkin, *Taking Rights Seriously*, 179ff.
131. Rawls, *A Theory of Justice*, 62, 92.
132. John A. Ryan, *Questions of the Day* (Freeport, N.Y.: Books for Libraries Press, 1931), 305.

By specifying rights as the means to self-perfection, Ryan severely qualified the role of both liberty and equality in his conception of justice. We will see that neither liberty nor equality (of goods) is among Ryan's principles of justice. In this sense, Ryan's conception of justice differs not only from rights-based theories but also from Niebuhr's use of liberty and equality as ideals to be approximated in the midst of the realities of politics and economics.

This view of rights, as absolute, equal, and specific claims that individuals hold against society for the means to their basic level of perfection, constitutes the foundation for Ryan's conception of justice. As we have noted, this theory also allows for presumptive rights to unequal shares of income and wealth. It was his view of rights as claims to the means for self-perfection, however, that provided the moral integument for human dignity that Ryan sought to preserve against economic injustices.

Before turning to his analysis of the economic circumstances in which these rights had to be satisfied, we will briefly examine how assumptions about moral agents' capacity for justice influenced Ryan's strategy for overcoming injustice.

Rational Moral Agents

How can the agents responsible for justice be moved to support policies that will approximate it? Rauschenbusch devoted much of his creative thought to this question. It was the question that led Niebuhr to adopt his distinctively realist conception of justice. It did not frustrate Ryan's hope for justice nor detain him long from attending to more crucial questions.[133]

After all, human nature is constituted so that the rational faculties master the whole person and direct his or her actions.[134] The will is a distinct faculty, but it can be trained to comply with what one knows is right.[135] The influence of institutions on individual character is marginal; Ryan never introduced the concept of collective agency so important to Rauschenbusch or the notion of collective egoism that concerned Niebuhr so much. "Every man is independent in the sense that he is morally complete in himself."[136] Humans are not free to transcend the natural

---

133. Ryan and Niebuhr were almost opposites in this regard. Niebuhr never doubted that absolute freedom and absolute equality in collective harmony constituted the ideal of justice. He did not tarry over the question of what is ideally just but puzzled over how sinful agents could approximate this ideal. Ryan devoted most of his early scholarly efforts to justifying a conception of justice, which he merely assumed agents were sufficiently free and rational to act upon.

134. Ryan, *A Living Wage,* 46.

135. Ryan, *The Norm of Morality,* 34.

136. Ryan, *A Living Wage,* 46.

order, which determines their proper moral interests and the proximate end for their rational faculties. They are, however, free to alter the "laws" of a particular economic system because economic conditions "are in large measure under the control of men."[137] Individual rational agents are free to know and bring about what justice requires.

The theological doctrines of sin, redemption, and grace, which were so crucial to Rauschenbusch's and Niebuhr's understandings of agency and theories of justice, were for Ryan largely irrelevant to justice. As we have noted, Ryan's hope for justice did not presuppose the redemption of individual and collective agents that was fundamental to Rausch-enbusch's strategy for obtaining justice. Neither did the realities of individual and collective sin, which compelled Niebuhr to adjust his conception of justice, cause Ryan to compromise the rights essential for human dignity. To be sure, the impossibility of altruism—both because it is not possible for the human race[138] and because ordinary humans fall short of what they are capable[139]—figured in Ryan's practical judg-ments. Natural limitations and foibles (sins?) have to be considered. Socialism is, for example, a threat to liberty because it lodges so much power in one agency.[140] Yet Ryan never developed a doctrine of sin or considered that justice would have to incorporate a balance of power that compromised individual rights.

In short, independent rational agents are capable of acting in unison to obtain justice. Injustice exists because some persons are puzzled about what is just. Others allow selfish interests to enervate their commitment to what they know is just. These are obstacles to justice that can be overcome through appeals to right reason and by actions within the mainstream of politics.

Ryan's own participation in the struggle against injustice reflects his view of human agency and his differences from Rauschenbusch and Niebuhr in this regard. His method was to employ reasonable arguments to influence his Catholic constituency and policymakers in government. No issue was dearer to Ryan than state enforcement of a universal living wage. His first book was an ethical argument for the justice and practi-cality of this policy. *A Living Wage* and *Distributive Justice* are not books about how human agents have to be transformed in order for the kingdom of God to progress or about how moral reasoning is so debili-tated by sin that it must be compromised with political realism in order to approximate justice. These books propose to convince readers (agents

---

137. Ibid., 7–9.
138. Ryan, *Distributive Justice*, 36.
139. Ibid., 165.
140. Ibid., 169.

for justice) that a living wage and other natural rights are rationally justified and practical in the present social and economic conditions.

Ryan used the reputation he had established from *A Living Wage* to join the political crusade for minimum wage laws. He did not focus his campaign on building a constituency of politically marginal movements, but directly upon the state legislatures. Broderick observes that no name was more common than Ryan's in the fight to persuade state legislatures to pass minimum wage laws for women.[141] (Men and families would have to wait until a stronger moral and political base was established.)

During the war and after, as political support for progressive reforms dissipated, Ryan continued the political struggle from positions he sought on the faculty at Catholic University and, beginning in 1919, as head of the new Social Action Department of the National Catholic Welfare Council. Ryan had located himself so as to carry his arguments for a living wage both to his Catholic constituency and to the federal government, but the twenties was a decade of defeat for Ryan's view of justice. It was a time when Ryan's assumption that moral agents are capable of rational action for justice could easily have been shaken. Perhaps the most momentous defeat for Ryan's conception of justice occurred in 1923. The United States Supreme Court declared, in *Adkins v. Children's Hospital,* that a Washington, D.C., minimum wage statute was unconstitutional. The Court held that the statute denied employers' liberties (viz., freedom of contract) without due process. This ruling outlawed most legislation restricting labor contracts until it was reversed in 1937 by *West Coast v. Parrish.*[142]

Ryan's response to the Court's decision in *Adkins v. Children's Hospital* illustrates the differences between his understanding of moral agency and that held by either Rauschenbusch or Niebuhr. He wrote a 56-page pamphlet entitled "The Supreme Court and the Minimum Wage." Ryan's essay did not suggest that the majority's legal and moral reasoning was unregenerate, that is, distorted by economic and class interests. He did not focus beyond the judicial process on a class struggle to change, or even circumvent, constitutional law through sheer political power. Rather, Ryan presented legal and moral arguments to counter the "faulty" reasoning of the Court. Legally, the Court's interpretation of the Constitution on the basis of its social philosophy wrongly usurped legislatures' prerogative to act when their statutes do not explicitly contradict the Constitution. (The Fifth Amendment does not specify freedom of contract. In today's parlance, Ryan could have accused the

141. Broderick, *Right Reverend New Dealer*, 81–86.
142. See Ryan, *Social Doctrine in Action*, 218–222.

conservative Court of "judicial activism.") Morally, the social philosophy the Court employed was wrong because it was based upon the
eighteenth-century individualistic rights theory that Ryan had disputed
in *A Living Wage*.[143]

During this darkest period in his struggle for the centerpiece of his
view of economic justice, Ryan responded to defeat with a reasoned
appeal to moral agents and not with an analysis of movements for justice adapted to the corruption of human agents. The contrast with
Rauschenbusch is apparent, and we will see that the difference from
Niebuhr is even sharper. Ryan did not believe moral suasion could
totally replace political power. He later observed that Roosevelt's
Court-packing attempt was justified because despite its ostensible failure, it successfully pressured two justices to change their interpretations
of the Constitution.[144] Yet Ryan never considered the mainline politics
in which he was involved to be far removed from moral argument. He
viewed the participants in politics as rational agents who could be moved
to just political action by right reason.

It was no accident that Ryan's friends in seminary nicknamed him
"Senator"[145] or that Father Charles Coughlin spoke of him as the "Right
Reverend spokesman for the New Deal," taunting Ryan for his close
association with Roosevelt.[146] When Brodcrick selected Coughlin's sar-
castic appellation as the title for his biography of Ryan, it aptly distinguished Ryan from Rauschenbusch, whom Dores Sharpe readily called a
prophet,[147] and from Niebuhr, whom Ronald Stone has characterized as
a "prophet to politicians."[148] Ryan was too interested in arguments for
justice to have actually become a politician, but he thought political
agents would listen to his rational moral arguments for justice. Thus, he
did not seek the detachment from politics that a prophet requires but
located himself in a position to be an "ethicist to politicians."

This understanding of moral agency, about which Ryan wrote little but
which was reflected so vividly in his life's work for the cause of justice,
explains why his conception of justice, unlike Rauschenbusch's and
Niebuhr's, does not incorporate a strategy for achieving justice. Ryan's
strategy was contained in his argument for the principles of distribution.
Rational agents can act on rationally justified principles without a

143. Ryan, *The Supreme Court and the Minimum Wage*, 1–43.
144. Ryan, *Social Doctrine in Action*, 250–257.
145. Broderick, *The Right Reverend New Dealer*, 12; Ryan, *Social Doctrine in Action*, 12.
146. Broderick, *Right Reverend New Dealer*, 227.
147. Sharpe, *Walter Rauschenbusch*, 231, 402.
148. Stone, *Reinhold Niebuhr*, title page.

redistribution of power to the social, labor, or proletarian movements or a regeneration of moral character through evangelical efforts by the church. Moreover, this understanding of agency coheres with Ryan's analysis of the circumstances of justice. Instead of Rauschenbusch's sweeping socio-historical analysis of the redemptive transformation of collective and individual agents, Ryan focused upon whether narrower economic realities are subject to the control of rational agents seeking to secure the individual rights justice demands.

THE ECONOMIC CIRCUMSTANCES OF JUSTICE

Ryan's analysis of the circumstances of justice relied upon economics as a relatively autonomous discipline. Relative to Rauschenbusch and Niebuhr, he viewed economics as autonomous in two senses. First, economics is relatively independent of other "descriptive" disciplines, namely, sociology and history. Second, economics is a descriptive science with its own integrity independent of the normative science of ethics. Together, these two aspects of the autonomy of economic studies narrowed the scope of circumstances Ryan considered relevant to justice.

In this section, I will first explicate more fully Ryan's understanding of the relative autonomy of economic studies. Although Ryan's economic analyses were narrower and less interwoven with evaluative judgments than Rauschenbusch's (or Niebuhr's), they were broader and more closely related to moral theory than most of the economists and many of the moral theologians with whom Ryan was in conversation. Having examined the nuances of Ryan's understanding of the relation of economics to other "descriptive" and "normative" disciplines, we will consider the implications of Ryan's economic analysis of the circumstances for his conception of justice. I will first note how his extensive, though not exclusive, use of neoclassical economic theory differed from Rauschenbusch's use of the German, socio-historical approach to economic institutions.[149] Second, I will show how the relatively broad scope of justice, issuing from Ryan's notion of human dignity, induced him to go beyond the neoclassical focus on the individual firm to consider institutions (e.g., private property and corporate structures) and macroeconomic theories that focus on the economy as a whole (viz., John Hobson's theory of underconsumption). In the thirties, when Ryan gave

---

149. See Gearty, *The Economic Thought of Monsignor Ryan*, 64–68, 78–79, 93–99, for brief descriptions of differences between the neoclassical and the German historical schools of economics and of how Ryan drew upon both schools.

more emphasis to institutional and macroeconomic issues, the economic policies he advocated became closer to Rauschenbusch's.

The Relative Autonomy of Economics

As we have seen, Ryan's keen interest in economics began early in his life and in connection with his concern for justice. Joseph Bouquillon, who taught moral theology at Catholic University, impressed upon Ryan the importance of this connection. Bouquillon insisted that moral theology had underestimated the importance of the social sciences.[150] Ryan's interest in economics was never separate from his primary commitment to justice based on human dignity. Thus, whatever importance and autonomy Ryan granted to economics were meant to be consistent with his understanding of individual dignity. And so it was.

Ryan's assertion of the intrinsic dignity of individuals is established by understanding the constitution and end of the rational nature of individuals independently of empirical findings from the social sciences. Dignity establishes the most basic rights of individuals, for example, to life and to a decent livelihood, without inferences from the social sciences. We have seen that basic individual rights are established independently of any analysis of the circumstances. The circumstances of justice became important for Ryan in determining how these means for individual perfection can be secured in social relations. For the right to a decent livelihood, which was central in Ryan's early writings, the question of circumstances is, Can and how can economic institutions provide a decent livelihood for every individual? Furthermore, rational agents are capable of knowing what these individual rights require apart from an understanding of how economic relations influence their character. These agents need technical knowledge about how it is possible for an economic system to deliver the goods to which individuals have a moral right, not an understanding of how economic institutions shape character.

This understanding of how individual dignity is safeguarded in the economic life of a society backs the relative autonomy Ryan granted to economics.

From Other Social Sciences

When the question about circumstances is the rather narrow one of how individual rights, such as a decent livelihood, can be delivered to indi-

---

150. Broderick, *Right Reverend New Dealer*, 32; Ryan, *Social Doctrine in Action*, 63; Gearty, *The Economic Thought of Monsignor Ryan*, 23.

viduals, the answer hinges on an analysis of whether and how the existing market forces can be adjusted to secure this right for everyone. Ryan's framing of the question allowed him to draw heavily upon neoclassical economics, emanating from Alfred Marshall, which viewed economics as an autonomous discipline studying market forces independently of sociological and historical factors. As Gearty notes, *A Living Wage* and *Distributive Justice* deal extensively with how the market forces of supply and demand determine the distributive shares (rent, interest, profits, and wages) of the four factors (land, capital, management, and labor) that contribute to the product of a firm.[151] The problem of distributive justice is organized on the basis of these four factors of production.[152]

By contrast, Rauschenbusch, beginning from the perspective of the kingdom of God, analyzed economic activities and institutions with the broad socio-historical approach of the German school. He was concerned with the role of economic institutions in shaping individual and collective character and in establishing human solidarity. Rauschenbusch attended extensively to how economic interests impinge on the character of democratic politics. When, in his debate with Ryan, Hillquit argued that capitalist economic interests were gaining control of the culture and politics, Ryan retorted that the Wilson administration had the will to dissolve powerful corporate trusts. Ryan focused instead on the need for "specific reforms" of "economic defects of the existing system."[153] Such narrow studies of how economic forces distribute the products of industry could not have provided adequate answers for the broader questions Rauschenbusch was posing.

Ryan was not bound by neoclassical economics. Its perspective was too narrow to account for his ethical concerns. His arguments for the economic feasibility of a decent livelihood through a minimum wage and for the other means to self-perfection pushed him beyond analysis of the market forces bearing on individual firms. Even in his early books, Ryan considered the stability of the whole economy, that is, macroeconomic issues, and how economic institutions—private property and the structure of economic enterprises—affect the means to self-perfection. Nevertheless, the credence he gave to economic analysis of productivity within the competitive market impinged on Ryan's conception of justice.

---

151. Ibid., 172ff.
152. Ryan, *Distributive Justice*, xiii–xvii.
153. Ryan and Hillquit, *Socialism*, 27–42, esp. 28, 39.

From Ethics

In addition to focusing his analysis more narrowly on economics, Ryan's understanding of individual dignity accounts for the relative independence he gave descriptive economic analysis from normative moral theory. A theory of rights essential for self-perfection can be formulated independently of economic analysis, but it cannot explain how rights are fulfilled. Economics determines whether and how a good can be distributed. Economics, for example, plays no role in determining that a decent livelihood is a necessary means for self-development, but it determines that in the modern market economy this need must and can be adequately met by a living family wage. Thus, in contrast to Rauschenbusch, whose principles of justice were derived from an evaluative description of evolving social (including economic) institutions, Ryan viewed the analysis of the circumstances as a separate and largely descriptive task for economics. The question of expediency, that is, whether and how a right can be satisfied, is relatively independent of determining what those rights are. Thus, Ryan advised Catholic economists that "our *first* task [is] a full description of economic phenomena, pointing out the laws or uniformities involved. . . . [E]conomics should be treated as a positive science."[154]

Insofar as Ryan considered economics a positive science, he was again in league with the neoclassical school, which tended to separate moral values from economic laws and values that are determined by market competition.[155] Ryan, however, refused to accept economic laws as intractable. Citing Marshall himself in support, Ryan observed that "a particular economic law merely declares that, given certain external conditions, men may be expected to perform such and such economic actions."[156] As we have seen, human agents are free to alter those conditions and thus to alter, to some extent, economic laws and values, making them more consistent with moral laws and values. In arguing for a minimum wage, for example, Ryan pointed out that laws of supply and demand in free competition can be altered by monopolies, labor unions, and legal regulation.[157] He did not consider all these ways of altering present economic laws as equally expedient. An economic law such as the law measuring a laborer's productivity should not be ignored, but it is imprecise, manipulable, and indeterminative for economic policy, even

---

154. John A. Ryan, "Two Objectives for Catholic Economists," *Review of Economy* 1, no. 1 (December 1942): 2–3.
155. Gearty, *The Economic Thought of Monsignor Ryan*, 64.
156. Ryan, *A Living Wage*, 7.
157. Ryan, *The Supreme Court and the Minimum Wage*, 37; see also idem, *A Living Wage*, 8–9; idem, *Social Doctrine in Action*, 75.

if it holds as an economic law.[158] The passages cited above from Ryan's essay on the vocation of Catholic economists were qualified immediately by the following claims. To the descriptive task, "[w]e should add a moral evaluation of the economic practices and suggest remedies for bad practices." Economics "is in large part also a normative science."[159]

The interconnectedness of economics and ethics also runs in the other direction: the description of economic realities informed Ryan's conception of justice. What individuals need for self-perfection is established by moral theory alone. This need is paramount for distributive justice. Nevertheless, long-run human welfare requires that laws of economic expediency, namely, productivity and scarcity, should be secondary canons for the distribution of goods. In presenting his canons of distributive justice, Ryan explicitly stated that the canons of productivity and scarcity "measure economic value rather than ethical worth."[160] They are based on economic efficiency rather than moral desert. Here Ryan was opposing a strict moral absolutism that ignores the economic consequences of policies of distribution. These considerations of economic productivity and efficiency do not modify absolute rights to the needs for self-perfection. They do require, however, inequalities of distribution that promote human welfare, that is, a society's long-run provision for the means essential for individuals' self-development.

Conclusions

Gearty accurately characterizes Ryan's approach to practical judgments about economic policy as comprising "two relatively autonomous sciences or disciplines, namely, economic analysis, as such, and ethics, as such."[161] He also observes that Ryan combined the "orthodox" economics of the neoclassical school with "heterodox" approaches to economics that go beyond the neoclassical focus on the firm in a competitive market. From the broader scope of "heterodox" economics, Ryan gained tools to consider the stability of the whole economy and to consider social institutions beyond market forces.[162] We will examine first the influence of the more narrowly focused "orthodox" economics of Ryan's day. To the extent that Ryan accepted analyses of economic productivity in terms of market forces of supply and demand, he was inclined to an inegalitarian conception of distributive justice.

---

158. Ryan, *A Living Wage,* 243–249.
159. Ryan, "Two Objectives for Catholic Economists," 4–5.
160. Ryan, *Distributive Justice,* 247.
161. Gearty, *The Economic Thought of Monsignor Ryan,* 98.
162. Ibid., 93, 68.

Autonomous Economics Bears on Justice

Ryan's view that the equal dignity of persons requires equal rights only to the extent that specific goods are essential to a basic level of self-perfection left room for an unequal distribution of goods on the basis of economic expediency. His judgment that expediency is determined to a large extent by a comparatively narrow economic analysis of productivity led him to affirm a conception of justice less egalitarian than Rauschenbusch's. Rauschenbusch understood contributions to economic value in terms of communal influences far removed from immediate market forces. Ryan focused more on how market forces distribute the products of industry to land, capital, management, and labor as the four factors of production.

Ryan most definitely did not claim that the distributions of competitive markets were rewards for productive contributions, let alone just rewards. Rent and interest are most especially not based solely on the economic contributions of the landholder and capitalist. Both rent and interest are "workless income."[163] Neither is justified solely on the grounds of the productivity of land or capital.[164] Yet Ryan rejected the arguments of Henry George, so influential upon Rauschenbusch, that looked beyond the market to the community for the "real" contributors to economic value. Ryan admitted that the community indirectly, as a by-product of activities with other specific purposes, creates an increase in land values, but "its productive action is indirect and extrinsic, instead of direct and intrinsic." Consequently, "social production does not constitute a right to land values nor to rent."[165] "Direct and intrinsic" here means productive acts within a specific economic operation, such as clearing the land for building, that create land value. In another context, Ryan asserted that "social production of increases in the value of land involves no special expenditure of labour or money."[166] Productivity measures only direct and intrinsic contributions to economic welfare. Ryan clearly took a narrow view of what constitutes productive contributions deserving of what Rauschenbusch called "earned income." Thus, the community's indirect and extrinsic contributions to land values give neither it nor the government a right to income from the land.[167]

This argument against the community's right to collect a 100 percent tax on rent was purely negative. Ryan did not intend it as an argument

---

163. Ryan, *Distributive Justice*, 67–68.

164. Ibid., 180. The passage cited refers to interest, but Ryan believed the arguments for the right to receive rent parallel the arguments for the right to receive interest, ibid., 68.

165. Ibid., 39–47.

166. Ibid., 108.

167. Ibid.

for the landholder's right to receive rent. As we noted, he did not believe this right could be justified solely on the basis of the landholder's direct and intrinsic productive activities. Nevertheless, insofar as Ryan counted productivity as a principle of distributive justice, he understood it largely in terms of the activities of specific economic operations conditioned by immediate market forces. He was less willing than Rauschenbusch to count forces extrinsic to the market in calculating what is due persons for their contributions to economic value. Ryan's narrow notion of productivity did, however, back his justification for the right to receive rent. In his parallel discussion of interest, Ryan asserted that the productivity of capital constitutes a possible though doubtful title to interest. It helps to justify a presumptive right to receive interest.[168]

This narrow notion of productivity influenced even more directly Ryan's justification for "business men" to "all the profits they can get" (after they have paid a living wage) under conditions of competition.[169] Where Rauschenbusch thought all large profits were due to privileges extrinsic to "real" economic value of a product, Ryan associated profits, at least in part, with entrepreneurial productivity. He wrote:

> This is particularly true of those exceptionally large profits which can be traced specifically to that unusual ability which is exemplified in the invention and adoption of new methods and processes in progressive industries. The receivers of large rewards have produced them in competition with less efficient business men.

He went on to say that though the title of productivity is not entirely satisfying, it is stronger morally than other considerations that can be invoked.[170] Economic productivity is more compelling in considering the distribution of profits, because the manager, like the laborer and unlike the landholder and capitalist, is actively involved in the productive process.[171] As this distinction implies, Ryan also considered productivity

---

168. Ibid., 204–209, see also 345.
169. Ibid., 255.
170. Ibid., 255–256.
171. Ibid., 178. This tendency to associate productivity with active contributions to an economic enterprise convinced Ryan to change his views on dividends. In the first edition of *Distributive Justice,* he argued that superior efficiency should be "credited" to the stockholders, giving them title to a share of profits, ibid., 257–258. In the third edition, Ryan claimed that profits should be shared among the managers and workers, excluding stockholders, because rewards should be related to "efforts and productivity, not to mere proprietorship." See idem, *Distributive Justice,* 3d ed., 192–193; see also idem, *The Christian Doctrine of Property* (New York: Paulist Press, 1923), 18–30; and idem, *Seven Troubled Years, 1930–1936: A Collection of Papers on the Depression and on the*

important for justifying the distribution of wages above the minimum living wage.[172]

To the extent that Ryan's analysis of the circumstances of justice relied upon the autonomous discipline of neoclassical economics, it contributed to a conception of justice less egalitarian than Rauschenbusch's. We must not, however, overestimate the impact of this narrow economic analysis on Ryan's interpretation of the circumstances. As is apparent, even from this account indicating that his interpretations of rents, interest, and profits were influenced by neoclassical economics, Ryan neither accepted a narrow economic definition of productivity as scientifically precise nor considered it an unalterable law governing economic distributions. In a discussion of John Bates Clark's theory of productivity, Ryan first challenged its descriptive accuracy. He then claimed that even if it were accurate, it would not justify the market's distribution of income.[173] One reason for the second criticism of Clark's productivity theory was that markets can and should be adjusted to provide needs essential for self-development. Ryan did not allow the narrow perspective of "orthodox" economics to control his interpretation of the circumstances of justice.

The primacy of needs for individual self-development directed Ryan's attention to the relevance of economic productivity, but it also expanded the scope of justice in ways that induced him to look beyond the economics of the firm in a competitive market. We will now examine how Ryan considered the effects of general economic stability and of institutions on opportunities for self-development. Not all of these broader considerations challenged the existing economy or supported a more equal distribution of income and wealth, but they tended in that direction.

Expanding the Relevant Circumstances to Account for the Purpose of Justice

The purpose of justice, as Ryan conceived it, is to safeguard the right of every individual to the means for self-perfection. An economic distribution that sustains productivity is relevant to this purpose, but it is not the only relevant consideration. The full scope of circumstances and consequences of which Ryan took account can best be understood in the context of his distinction between three species of justice. These species

---

Problems of Recovery and Reform (Ann Arbor, Mich.: Edwards Brothers, 1937), 230. Here again, we see that Ryan was never fully satisfied with productivity as measured by existing competitive markets.

172. Ryan, *Distributive Justice*, 385.

173. Ibid., 347–351.

of justice, which he inherited from his Catholic tradition, are commutative justice, distributive justice, and social justice.

Three Species of Justice

Commutative justice, according to Ryan, governs the relations between persons, between persons and associations (e.g., a corporation and its stockholders), or between associations.[174] It "requires equality in values, . . . between what is given and what is received in exchange."[175] From the perspective of commutative justice, only factors relating to exchange equivalence between individual entities are relevant for justice. We will see that Ryan's teleological conception of rights required a broader view of the circumstances of justice.

Distributive justice differs from commutative justice in that it considers what the whole (for which the state is the primary agent) owes the parts. Distributive justice is governed by the principle of proportionality according to needs and capacities.[176] It looks beyond the contracting parties to consider how the whole can meet the needs due each individual, but it fails to consider how distribution has consequences for the well-being of the whole.

Social justice extends beyond distributive justice in that it considers the common good, yet it is not concerned with the common good as such but "the common good as comprising the welfare of all society's members." Ryan described this dual aspect of social justice by saying that it combined legal justice (a fourth species of justice), which considers what individual entities owe to the common welfare, and distributive justice, which is concerned with what is due to individuals from the whole.[177] Social justice is concerned with the "collective good," not for its own sake, "but for the sake of each of the members of society."[178] From the perspective of social justice, Ryan was concerned with the consequences policies have for the common good so that individual rights could be secured in the long run. Although Ryan did not use "social justice" as a technical term until after the publication of *Quadragesimo Anno* in 1931, he thought it expressed the same content, albeit "better and more accurately," as the term "human welfare," which was prevalent in his earlier writings.[179] Inasmuch as the notion of human welfare, as we have

174. Ryan, *The Norm of Morality*, 53.
175. Ryan and Boland, *Catholic Principles*, 140.
176. Ryan, *The Norm of Morality*, 53.
177. Ryan, *Seven Troubled Years*, 174.
178. Ryan and Boland, *Catholic Principles*, 144.
179. See Gearty, *The Economic Thought of Monsignor Ryan*, 116; Ryan, *Distributive Justice*, 3d ed., 188.

noted above,[180] linked Ryan's theory of individual rights to a concern for the common good, it, like social justice, expanded the circumstances and consequences he deemed relevant to justice.

Ryan sometimes wrote as if social justice were fully congruous with distributive and commutative justice, merely incorporating what these narrower views of justice require.[181] A reasonably close interpretation of Ryan's application of these concepts to specific issues shows, however, that each step up in the scope of justice supplemented and qualified the narrower conceptions. As we have noted, Ryan's understanding of human dignity committed him to secure for each individual the means for self-perfection. Safeguarding human dignity in the context of an industrial economy required Ryan to expand the scope of justice to account for circumstances that commutative and even distributive justice (by his restrictive definition) ignore. This broadening of the relevant circumstances can best be seen in three illustrative issues: a living wage, rents and interest, and private property.

A Living Wage

In the course of justifying the right to a living wage, Ryan criticized all theories that attempt to establish a just wage solely on the basis of equality of things exchanged between contracting parties. Not surprisingly, he objected to the determination of wages by a "free" contract or the market rate. Contracts, he argued, are not free when the employer possesses the economic force to compel low wages, and contracts and markets ignore the material requirements for a reasonable life.[182] More interesting, Ryan also considered Catholic attempts to establish just wages on the basis of medieval just-price theory erroneous. Some applications of just-price theory were adequate in practice. These adequate applications actually put aside the ideal of equivalence between the laborer's work and the wage, and based justice on the cost of a decent livelihood. But when just-price theorists attempt to establish justice on the basis of the strict definition of commutative justice, that is, equality of things exchanged, they fail to take account of human dignity, namely, the right to a decent livelihood. In *A Living Wage*, Ryan concluded that the Schoolmen never made practical use of a theory of equal gains. He expressed his wish that modern Catholics should discard this theory entirely.[183] Finally, Ryan also rejected theories

---

180. *Supra*, 125–127.
181. E.g., Ryan, *Seven Troubled Years*, 175.
182. Ryan, *Distributive Justice*, 328–332.
183. See Ryan, *A Living Wage*, 86–99, esp. 97; idem, *Distributive Justice*, 332–340; idem, "The Economic Philosophy of St. Thomas," in *Essays in Thomism*, ed. Robert E.

of economic productivity as a basis for wage justice. As we have seen from his criticism of Clark's theory, productivity is inadequate as an objective measure of economic value and, like just-price theory, fails to account for the dignity of the laborer.[184]

These methods for determining a just wage are inadequate because they attempt to establish just wages on the basis of factors intrinsic to the contract, namely, the comparative value of labor and compensation in wages. In 1933, Ryan wrote that these attempts to establish the "moral equivalence" between labor and wages are tantamount to comparing light and water.[185] Justice cannot be satisfied by measuring the value of things exchanged in a wage contract (commutative justice). Wage justice, Ryan maintained, should consider the "extrinsic principle" of personal dignity. Justice requires that wage compensation be equivalent to a living wage. Thus, the determination of a just wage requires the perspective of distributive justice, which considers how society will carry out its obligation to provide for the needs of individuals. Ryan wrote: "[T]he habit of looking at the wage contract as a matter of commutative justice . . . is radically defective. . . . The employer has obligations of justice, not merely as the receiver of a valuable thing through an onerous contract, but as the *distributor* of the common heritage of nature."[186] He expanded the relevant circumstances of justice beyond laborers' productive contributions to a firm. The circumstances include the laborers' needs and the best means an economy has available for satisfying those needs. Under the conditions of modern industrial organization, the best means is by wages.[187]

The perspective of distributive justice is not sufficient either. Ryan claimed that the employer's function is social as well as distributive,[188] and in the third edition of *Distributive Justice,* he referred to this social function as including social justice.[189] Although he did not develop how social justice is pertinent to wages in these passages, Ryan did, as we have observed in discussing his "teleology of obligation," consider the consequences of a living wage for the common good. It was in this

---

Brennan, O.P. (New York: Sheed & Ward, 1942), 249–252. Although Ryan argued, in an essay on Thomas's economic philosophy, that determination of a just wage by the cost of a decent livelihood is consistent with commutative justice (see Ryan, "The Economic Philosophy of St. Thomas," 251), it clearly violates his own definition of commutative justice as equality of things exchanged.

184. Ryan, *Distributive Justice,* 347–355.
185. Ryan, *Seven Troubled Years,* 112.
186. Ryan, *Distributive Justice,* 370–371.
187. Ryan, *A Living Wage,* 100–101.
188. Ryan, *Distributive Justice,* 371.
189. Ryan, *Distributive Justice,* 3d ed., 280–281.

context, in which human welfare (social justice) requires an assessment of the consequences of a living wage for economic welfare, that the laborer's productive contribution to an economic enterprise became a relevant issue for Ryan. It was relevant because the capacity of an economy to provide for individual needs depends upon the relation between the cost of production (including wages) and productivity (including labor). Ryan, of course, believed a living wage would increase the efficiency of labor, thereby benefiting the common good.[190]

This consideration of the consequences of wage policy for the common good also impelled Ryan to draw on John Hobson's "heterodox" theory of underconsumption and oversaving.[191] Hobson claimed that the stability of the economy depended upon increasing demand for consumer goods. Thus, this theory about the economy as a whole supported Ryan's argument for a living wage. A living wage would increase consumer demand and decrease unemployment by bringing unutilized industrial capacity into the productive process.[192] Ryan did not, until the thirties, fully develop the implications of Hobson's theory. His limited use of it in his early writings, nonetheless, demonstrates how the perspective of human welfare (social justice) induced him to broaden the scope of his economic analysis. The theory of underconsumption was more concerned with the economy as a whole than with the economics of the firm. We will see in Chapter 5 how Ryan's more extensive use of this larger perspective after the Depression led him to advocate policies to reduce unemployment through a more equal distribution of income.[193]

Rents and Interest

Ryan's justifications for rent and interest were even more dependent upon the broad perspective of human welfare. He began his treatment of interest by asking whether interest, if it is justified, is justified by intrinsic relations existing between the owner and the user of capital or by its effects in social welfare.[194] (He surely meant human welfare.)[195] Ryan concluded that the intrinsic justifications for interest (including productivity) are either doubtful or partial. Therefore, "its justification

190. Ryan, *A Living Wage*, 182–184; idem, *The Church and Socialism*, 88–91.

191. Ryan, *A Living Wage*, 168–175.

192. Ryan, *The Church and Socialism*, 93; idem, *A Living Wage*, 186–187.

193. See Gearty, *The Economic Thought of Monsignor Ryan*, 183–195.

194. Ryan, *Distributive Justice*, 171.

195. Because interest is generally paid to the wealthy and others who could receive a decent living by other means, Ryan did not consider justifying interest from the perspective of distributive justice.

must be sought in extrinsic and social considerations."[196] These social considerations, primarily the uncertainty that a sufficient supply of capital could be maintained without interest, convinced Ryan that the state was most likely justified in permitting interest.[197] It was, then, from the perspective of human welfare, which included the consequences of interest for the stability of the economic system, that Ryan decided interest is just.

His justification for rent was based on a similarly broad interpretation of the relevant consequences. The issue, said Ryan, in arguing against the single tax, is whether Henry George's proposal to confiscate rent meets the test of human welfare. It does not because its consequences for economic and political stability would be more injurious to social welfare, and ultimately to individual welfare, than the present policy of permitting rent.[198]

Ryan's justification for interest and rent on the basis of social justice appears to be as conservative and inegalitarian as if his judgments had been based solely upon the capitalist's and landholder's rights to income for their productive contributions to a single economic enterprise. Two factors mitigate this conclusion.

First, having justified interest and rent on the basis of their consequences for human welfare, he also limited the right to interest and rent on that basis. In the thirties, Ryan utilized John Hobson's theory of underconsumption more extensively because it helped to explain the Depression. Interest payments, Ryan maintained, are made to wealthy persons inclined to save rather than to consume. He argued, therefore, that the government should restrict the market rate of interest to 2 percent in order to bolster consumer demand.[199] In *Distributive Justice*, Ryan argued for taxes on capital gains from land sales, a transfer of taxes from buildings and personal property to land, and a supertax on large landholdings, because these taxes would promote the common good.[200]

---

196. Ibid., 177–186, esp. 186.
197. Ibid., 188–201.
198. Ibid., 37–39, 53–55.
199. Ryan, *Seven Troubled Years*, 252–253; idem, *Social Doctrine in Action*, 239–241.
200. Ryan, *Distributive Justice*, 100–133. Two qualifications on these proposals for land taxes accentuate Ryan's differences from Rauschenbusch. First, Ryan was concerned that these taxes, especially taxes on capital gains from land sales, would lower land values sufficiently to cause the present owners a positive loss. He proposed that the state compensate owners for any such loss. This compensation was to fulfill an "implicit promise," made at the time of the purchase, that the state would not interfere with the normal course of land values, ibid., 112–113. Ryan was less willing than Rauschenbusch to allow consequences for the common good to override contractual justice, even implicit contracts. Second, Ryan never thought these qualifications on the rights of landowners were crucial for justice, and he de-emphasized the importance of these reforms in later years because the sharp increases

These arguments were made from the perspective of social justice. Had Ryan justified interest and rent primarily on the basis of productivity or some other circumstance intrinsic to relations among the parties directly involved in economic transactions, these limitations upon returns due to landholders and capitalists would not have been warranted.

Second, because human welfare concerned how the common good affects individuals, it directed Ryan's attention not only to how the stability of the whole economy affects opportunities for self-development, but also to how the character of economic institutions affects such opportunities. In the chapter immediately following his justification for interest, Ryan advocated expansion of various kinds of consumer and productive cooperatives. These cooperatives, he maintained, would transfer the distribution of interest, profits, and power to the working class and would foster qualities (e.g., initiative, self-confidence, and cooperation) that are essential for self-development.[201] Ryan thought economic cooperatives would mitigate the disadvantages of ownership of capital by only a few without precipitating the adverse economic and social consequences of capitalism without interest or, worse yet, of socialism. He conceded that the applicability of cooperative enterprise to a complex industrial economy is somewhat limited.[202] Nevertheless, this early interest in the cooperative movement presages his later proposals for reorganizing capitalist enterprises into industrial democracies and competitive industries into occupational groups.

---

in land values that threatened economic stability had diminished. (See Ryan, *Social Doctrine in Action*, 110.) Ryan's concern for economic consequences was not directed to securing equality but to providing each individual with the needs for independent self-development. When increases in land values no longer threatened economic stability, these rights of landownership no longer conflicted with human welfare.

201. Ryan, *Distributive Justice*, 210–234, esp. 228–230. This view that institutions "foster" qualities of character approaches Rauschenbusch's understanding of institutions as collective agents that shape individual character. Ryan made a similar claim for cooperatives in an earlier essay. That essay referred to the "educational value" of cooperatives in developing the laborers' business capacities, initiative, sense of self-reliance, and so forth, in ways that would make them better citizens and Christians. See John A. Ryan, *Social Reform Along Catholic Lines* (New York: Columbus Press, 1913), 9. Still, in the same essay he maintained that individuals are free agents capable of modifying their environment, ibid., 4. Ryan never shared Rauschenbusch's sense of urgency that a missed opportunity for reforming institutions could weaken individual character and lead society to greater injustice. Nor did he share Rauschenbusch's hope that changes in the character of institutions could shape or mold individual character for the better. When Ryan spoke of institutions fostering qualities of character, he was thinking more in terms of providing opportunities or means for self-development. than in terms of how collective agents shape character.

202. Ryan, *Distributive Justice*, 232.

Private Property

The basis for these later proposals, which we will examine in Chapter 5, can best be seen in Ryan's defense of the natural right to private productive property. Here Ryan's expansion of the relevant economic circumstances to include the consequences of economic institutions is most apparent. He did not consider private property an intrinsic natural right or a contracted right. Nor did he justify it simply on the basis of its productive efficiency. He rather defended, and limited, the right to private property on the basis of its consequences as a social institution.

According to Ryan, the right to own and control productive property is neither intrinsic, like the right to life, nor directly necessary for every individual's development, like the rights to own consumption goods or to freedom. The right to own productive property belongs to a third class of natural right. It is not directly necessary for the development of any particular individual; that is, no individual needs to own productive property for one's self-development. It cannot be justified by any account of the relations between an individual and property, for example, occupancy of land or mixing one's labor with material goods. It can be justified only as a "social institution" that has positive consequences for "individual and social welfare," that is, human welfare. Thus, Ryan claimed private property as a natural right because it is "*indirectly* necessary . . . as a *social institution* . . . capable of promoting the welfare of the average person, of the majority of persons."[203]

From this perspective, the existence and extent of the right to private property is established by asking what and how the institution of private property contributes to the common good insofar as the common good bears on individual self-development. Ryan offered the following kinds of arguments in defense of private property: it is a "stimulus to the energy and ambition of all persons";[204] it provides a sense of "independence, manliness, self-reliance, self-respect, and economic power," which includes the "psychic goods which are an integral element of normal life"; it also protects individual liberty and provides the "indispensable incentive" for economic efficiency;[205] it makes possible "personal development, personal security, and adequate provision for family life."[206] Despite their differences, all of these arguments blend Ryan's

---

203. Ryan, *Distributive Justice,* 57–62, 29, 35–36. Once private productive property is justified as a social institution, the right for individuals to possess it is based on titles established by commutative justice (e.g., first occupancy of land, purchase, inheritance) or distributive justice (i.e., according to needs and capacities).

204. Ibid., 60.

205. Ryan, *The Church and Socialism,* 4, 6.

206. Ryan, *The Christian Doctrine of Property,* 12.

economic analysis and his theory of rights in examining the consequences of the social institution of private property for economic welfare
and/or self-development.

Having granted the moral relevancy of the social effects of the institution of private property, Ryan also limited the rights of private property
on this basis. He was bound neither by arguments based on the productivity of land or capital nor by arguments that private property is an a
priori moral right. If private property cannot be shown to be necessary
for human welfare, the justification for the institution disappears.[207] In
his argument that the right to own land does not include the right to
capital gains from the sale of land, Ryan contended:

> No principle, title, or practice of ownership . . . has intrinsic or metaphysi-
> cal value. All are to be evaluated with reference to human welfare. Since
> the right of property is not an end in itself, but only a means of human
> welfare, its just prerogatives and limitations are determined by their
> conduciveness to the welfare of human beings.[208]

This expansion of economic analysis to include an examination of the
social consequences of the institution of private property informed
Ryan's judgments about the justice of private property. It helped Ryan
to limit the rights of land and capital owners to returns on their property.
It led Ryan to argue that economic cooperatives are, in many cases,
more just institutions than either enterprises owned by single persons or
joint stock corporations. This focus on institutions goes beyond the
distribution of goods individuals can possess. It broadens the scope of
analysis to include how the common good provides individuals with
opportunities for self-development. This perspective on the relevant
circumstances for justice allowed Ryan to develop his later claims that
social justice requires a reorganization of the corporation and of competitive industry. We will see in Chapter 5 that Ryan's proposals for
industrial democracy and for the occupational group system were similar
to Rauschenbusch's proposals for economic democracy and for socializing business. Both were concerned with how the organization of economic institutions bears on the development of moral character.

Some Comparisons and Conclusions

These accounts of how Ryan argued for the justice of rents, interest,
profits, a living wage, and private property display his understanding of

---

207. Ryan, *Distributive Justice*, 61.
208. Ibid., 109.

the relevant circumstances of justice. He organized his treatment of distributive justice around an analysis of the four factors of production in each economic enterprise. Ryan was not bound, however, by a narrow economic description of productivity. In addition, his concern for distribution based on need and for human welfare (social justice) expanded the scope of relevant circumstances to include the stability of the economy as a whole and the social effects of economic institutions. These broader considerations brought him closer to Rauschenbusch, in both method and content. Yet Ryan never went as far as Rauschenbusch in considering the historical evolution of economic institutions in their relations to other social institutions, most especially democratic government. He was also, more than Rauschenbusch, concerned with descriptive accounts of the efficiency or expediency of economic institutions independent of an ideal of distributive justice. Even in his examination of private property, which went far beyond a narrow economic analysis of its efficiency, Ryan accounted for stimulating incentives and ambition for economic gain. Thus, Ryan admitted that private ownership can never bring about ideal justice in distribution.[209] Economic analysis had, for Ryan, a relative autonomy that Rauschenbusch never conceded to it.

Despite this relative independence of economic descriptions from moral values, Ryan did not think an individual's right to the means for self-perfection would have to be sacrificed due to economic realities. Whatever adjustments he had to make in distributive justice to account for economic practicalities, Ryan believed the world is constituted so that in the long run economic expediency and moral values are identical. This ultimate unity between Ryan's conceptions of human dignity and rights and his description of the circumstances of justice was presupposed by his understanding of God.

GOD'S NATURAL ORDER

Unlike Rauschenbusch, who offered only brief sustained statements about his understanding of God, Ryan offered none. This absence was not due to a belief that knowledge of God does not inform justice. In the foreword to *The Norm of Morality*, Ryan wrote that his moral theory should appeal "to all persons who believe in God as Creator and Ruler of the Universe." Although some of the reasoning might be accepted by "believers in an 'independent morality,' " those who deny a spiritual soul and view man merely as a highly organized animal would, Ryan

---

209. Ibid., 32.

believed, reject his central thesis.[210] In the closing pages of *Social Doctrine in Action*, Ryan noted that it is the worth of humans in relation to God that justifies social reforms intended to provide persons with the goods that are necessary for them to "develop personality and pursue perfection."[211] To be sure, Ryan based his theory of justice on natural law theory, but he recognized that Catholic natural law depended upon theism.[212] Indeed, it depended upon a particular kind of theism in which God is the telos of the created order. It was crucial to Ryan's conception of human dignity and of justice that God had ordered the world so that each individual could have the means to seek his or her ultimate end in God by perfecting his or her rational nature. We can, however, have knowledge of the moral requirements of this natural order through our natural capacities (unaided by revelation, grace, or redemption) for reason and intuition.

Ryan did not need to write about this understanding of God. It was presupposed in his Catholic tradition. David Krueger observes that Ryan used a Thomistic theology in which God is divine reason that directs and orders the world toward divine purposes that humans, created in the image of God, can know by reason.[213] Ryan had no need to revise this conception of God that he inherited. If we assume Ryan's theory of justice presupposed this divine teleological framework in which a knowable natural order directs humans toward their ultimate end in God, we can utilize his incidental references to God to see why he was confident that (1) rights based on human dignity can be united with economic analysis to construct a conception of justice that assures all persons the means for self-perfection and (2) the requirements of justice can be known independently of revelation, grace, or redemption.

God's Order and the Means to Natural Self-perfection

Ryan affirmed Thomas's view that God is eternal law directing all creatures to their final end in God.[214] For humans, this ultimate end is complete happiness and all conceivable goodness and perfection in union with God.[215] The human personality is created by God with rights and duties through which it is destined for this eternal end.[216] An infinitely

---

210. Ryan, *The Norm of Morality*, v.
211. Ryan, *Social Doctrine in Action*, 288.
212. Ryan, *The Norm of Morality*, 56.
213. Krueger, "The Economic Ethics of John A. Ryan and Gustavo Gutierrez," 17.
214. Ryan and Boland, *Catholic Principles*, 2, 4.
215. Ryan, *The Norm of Morality*, 7–8.
216. Ryan and Boland, *Catholic Principles*, 1.

wise, good, and truthful God has created the universe so that this end is somewhere attainable.[217]

Humans cannot attain their ultimate end in this life; nor does this ultimate end serve as an adequate criterion for morality.[218] But God, through the eternal law, has also appointed an end and law of human nature.[219] This natural and proximate end of humans does provide an adequate basis for moral judgments. Further, humans can attain or nearly attain the perfection of their natural proximate end, which, given the wisdom of God's ordering, is "obviously in harmony with and conducive to the *ultimate* end."[220] In some passages, Ryan goes beyond this claim that natural self-development is merely conducive to the ultimate end. Although he explicitly avoids asserting that natural self-perfection is necessary for eternal union with God, the connection between the natural order and eternal law is such that "man's final condition of existence is dependent on his earthly conduct."[221] Moreover, rights are, as we have seen, essential means to this self-perfection. If a person is deprived of these rights, "he cannot realise the potentialities of his nature nor attain the divinely appointed end of his nature."[222]

Thus, we see that God has ordered the universe so that eternal bliss is possible for every person, and individual rights, such as a decent livelihood, are essential means for natural self-perfection that is conducive to, and to some extent crucial for, attaining this eternal bliss. It is important for Ryan that the eternal end is not entirely contingent upon the natural end. This two-tiered ordering leaves room for eternal happiness and goodness beyond what can be conceived of in humans' natural end. In addition, the break between the eternal and natural allows those who have failed to attain their natural end to continue to aspire to a "blessed existence in their everlasting home."[223] In other words, there is a place for God's grace, a notion Ryan never developed, in this divine ordering.

---

217. Ryan, *The Norm of Morality*, 7.
218. Ibid., 7–8.
219. Ryan and Boland, *Catholic Principles*, 2, citing Thomas.
220. Ryan, *The Norm of Morality*, 16–17.
221. Ryan, "The Method of Teleology," 411.
222. Ryan, *Distributive Justice*, 362. This connection between the divine natural and supernatural ends of the human person is, for Ryan, the basis for the church's interest in social reform. The church's principal concern is to save individual souls for eternal union with God, but this responsibility requires that the church teach charity and justice for the economic order because they are means for attaining eternal union with God. See Ryan, *The Church and Socialism*, 152–155; idem, *The Christian Doctrine of Property*, 31–33. In addition, "[i]t is good, noble, and Christlike to battle for social conditions which will permit an ever-increasing host of persons to live in a manner worthy of adopted children of God." See Ryan, *Social Doctrine in Action*, 289.
223. Ibid., 289.

The point remains, however, that God has ordered the universe so that natural rights are conditional for an individual's normal development toward his or her appointed eternal end.

In accord with this connection between the eternal and natural end of humans, God, who governs for the good of God's subjects, rules by an eternal law that comprises the laws of physical nature no less than the moral laws.[224] All the universe, including human economic life, is divinely ordered so that the natural perfection of each individual is possible. Although Ryan never said so explicitly, his understanding of God's order appears to include a belief that the satisfaction of all individual rights is a practical possibility. He approached this affirmation, when, in one of his arguments for the right to a decent livelihood, Ryan wrote: "Since God has imposed upon [humans] the obligation of attaining [their] eternal end, . . . God wishes [them] to have the means [i.e., rights] which are adequate for that purpose."[225] I suspect Ryan would have accepted "God orders reality so that they can have" as a substitute for "God wishes [them] to have." If so, this belief would explain his enigmatic statements that the right to a decent livelihood supposes that there are sufficient goods to provide for it[226] and that moral values and economic expediency are identical in the long run.[227] This belief that God has ordered nature for humans' natural and eternal end ultimately unites Ryan's economic analysis and his theory of rights.

We should note that Ryan did not view this divine order to be constituted by rigid natural laws that govern the details of economic life. The harmony between nature and individual self-development is achieved only by flexible application of natural laws on the basis of analyses of economic consequences. In his 1907 article against overemphasis upon teleology in ethics, Ryan wrote that the natural law is expressed by "conforming" to human rational nature.[228] By 1940, Ryan was saying that conformity to the natural law is adequately expressed in acts that are "conducive" to the end of human rational nature.[229] In his judgments about such economic matters as a living wage and private property, Ryan was clearly guided by what actions and policies are conducive to individual self-perfection. He rejected laws of exchange equivalence for wage contracts and an a priori natural law of private property in favor of a broader consideration of consequences conducive

---

224. Ryan and Boland, *Catholic Principles*, 3, citing Joseph Rickaby.
225. John A. Ryan, *Social Reconstruction* (New York: Macmillan, 1920), 69.
226. Ryan, *A Living Wage*, 79.
227. Ryan and Hillquit, *Socialism*, 58.
228. Ryan, "The Method of Teleology," 429.
229. Ryan and Boland, *Catholic Principles*, 7–8.

to self-development. Ryan did not view the divine natural order as a governance by rigid and detailed laws. This natural order, nevertheless, establishes harmony between economic realities and individual self-perfection. Justice may have to adjust to economic realities, but a just economic order can accommodate the legitimate natural (and ultimate) interests of every person.

Ryan's theological differences with Rauschenbusch are ethically significant. Whereas Rauschenbusch perceived an evolving natural order of God through the redemptive influence of Christ in history, Ryan perceived an established divine order of nature. It follows from Rauschenbusch's conception of divine ordering that the struggle toward an emerging order justifies sacrifices of legitimate individual interests. For Ryan, by contrast, the established order of nature permits the satisfaction of most individual rights, especially those absolute rights essential for self-development. Ryan's conception of justice leaves little room to sacrifice legitimate individual interests for the sake of a future common good.

Ryan and Rauschenbusch agree, however, in affirming a divine ordering of nature that justifies a natural human interest in self-development. In this respect, they both differ from Niebuhr. Niebuhr refused to identify God's purpose with either an order or an ordering of nature. He conceived of God's end for humans as transcending all natural self-interest. According to Niebuhr, God's grace, by which this transcendent goal is achieved, necessarily conflicts with every conception of justice, because justice legitimates some human interests against others.

God's Order Can Be Known by Reason

Ryan's belief in a flexible but relatively static divinely appointed natural order also bears on his view that rational agents are capable of knowing what justice requires. Because the end and laws of human rational nature are in established harmony with humans' eternal end in union with God, knowledge of God's natural law is possible without the revealed knowledge required for attaining one's supernatural end. Rational agents are able to know the natural law of justice apart from the revealed law in scripture and without looking to Christ's redemption of the evolving natural order. Agents do not have to be converted or believe "religious doctrines" (i.e., revealed Christian doctrines) in order to know the norm of morality in nature and reason.[230] (We must keep in mind that this assertion of a natural morality accessible to all

---

230. Ryan, *The Norm of Morality,* 6.

rational agents is based on Ryan's doctrine of God. It is theologically grounded. Ryan does not assert a natural morality independently of a belief that God has ordered nature for the self-perfection of all individuals.) In this respect, Ryan differed from Rauschenbusch, for whom knowledge of God's natural ordering for justice is contingent upon faithfulness to the redemptive work of Christ in history. He also differed from Niebuhr, for whom discerning the requirements of justice depends upon experiencing in history God's grace, which transcends the natural order.[231]

Ryan's moral epistemology impinged on the content of his conception of justice in two ways. First, unlike Rauschenbusch and Niebuhr, Ryan's strategy for achieving justice did not rely on mobilizing powerful class interests to confront and defeat individual or collective agents blinded to rational argument by their sinful interests. If God's natural order can be known by rational agents, a rationally justified conception of justice is in itself the best way to achieve justice. As we have seen from Ryan's understanding of moral agency, there is no reason to endorse self-interested labor or social movements simply because they will transform the present distribution of power. The use of power is justified, not by its consequences for justice as a future goal, but only if power is itself just. Second, Ryan, unlike Niebuhr, was confident that rational principles of justice reflect God's will. The natural law is "imposed by God as the Author of nature."[232] Consequently, there is no reason for contrition or reluctance in enforcing the principles of justice upon those who defy the natural law. For Ryan, divine judgment accords with the rationally knowable natural order.

On this view of a divine natural order apprehendable by rational agents, Ryan was able to formulate principles to serve as the primary criteria for judging the justice of actions, policies, and institutions. We now turn to what Ryan called the canons of distributive justice.

CANONS OF DISTRIBUTIVE JUSTICE

Of our three authors, only Ryan set forth a conception of justice explicitly distinct from the other three base points that comprise his theory of justice. In the context of treating the morality of profits in

---

231. Note that Ryan's belief in an established divine natural order coheres with the relative unimportance of history in his analysis of the circumstances of justice. For both Rauschenbusch and Niebuhr, though in sharply different ways, historical studies bear heavily on the conception of justice.
232. Ryan, *The Norm of Morality*, 27.

Distributive Justice, Ryan devoted a brief chapter to the six "principal canons of distributive justice": equality, needs, efforts and sacrifice, productivity, scarcity, and human welfare.[233] Ryan suggested that these canons of justice govern only profits and wages as remuneration for human activity,[234] but we have seen that he also utilized them, especially human welfare, in his judgments about rents and interest.[235] Although Ryan did not explicate these principles in his earlier work, he mentioned a similar list of canons in two places in *A Living Wage.*[236] We see then that these canons of justice were actually present in his earlier thinking and were applied broadly to economic policies and institutions. Clearly, Ryan, more than either Rauschenbusch or Niebuhr, understood practical moral reasoning about justice to proceed from principles independently of beliefs that shape the perspective, attitudes, and disposition of moral agents. These principles guide his deliberations somewhat independently of his beliefs justifying them.

There is, however, reason to doubt that Ryan expected that agents could apply these principles of justice accurately without sharing his beliefs about human dignity, the relevant circumstances of justice, and God's natural order. Ryan prefaced his explication of these canons stating that they "will be helpful, if not necessary" in determining the morality of profits and wages.[237] He correctly did not claim that they would be sufficient.

First, those who do not share Ryan's view of human rational nature as a hierarchical ordering of sense and rational faculties subordinated to a spiritual end cannot fully comprehend the rights he associated with the canon of needs. For examples: The itemized account Ryan offered to determine his estimate of a living wage reflects his understanding of the proximate end of human nature. It includes line items for religion, charity, books and newspapers (separate from amusements), and labor and other organizations.[238] In Chapter 5, we will see how Ryan called for industrial democracy on the grounds that it would supply opportunities persons need to develop their "creative and directive faculties." Ryan's

---

233. Ryan, *Distributive Justice,* 243–253. Although all of these canons pertain to how society distributes the benefits and burdens of cooperation, only the canons of equality and needs refer to Ryan's own narrow definition of distributive justice. Distributive justice in this chapter includes human welfare or social justice, which he distinguished from distributive justice in other contexts.

234. Ibid., 243.

235. See also Krueger, "The Economic Ethics of John A. Ryan and Gustavo Gutierrez," 99.

236. Ryan, *A Living Wage,* 77–78, 326–327.

237. Ryan, *Distributive Justice,* 243.

238. Ryan, *A Living Wage,* 145.

application of the canon of need was informed by his beliefs about the constitution and proximate end of human nature.

Second, this canon of need can conflict, in the short run, with the canons of productivity and scarcity, based on economic efficiency. Ryan intended the canon of human welfare to unite the first five canons, but it does not stipulate a precise weighting among the other canons. Although Ryan claimed that human welfare stipulates a distribution that produces the greatest product at the lowest cost after the vital needs of individuals have been met,[239] he nowhere used that formula. His canon of human welfare (social justice) functions more to provide a perspective for analyzing circumstances than to stipulate a distributive pattern. We have seen how it widens the horizon of relevant circumstances to include the consequences of economic efficiency and stability and of social institutions. Thus, the canon of human welfare actually functions to require that the other canons, which stipulate a pattern of distribution, take account of the consequences of economic policies that bear on the long run satisfaction of the rights associated with individual dignity. Moreover, Ryan's application of this canon of human welfare depended heavily upon his belief that God has ordered the universe so that the dignity of each individual can be safeguarded if justice considers a broad range of consequences in applying natural laws. Ryan's analysis of the circumstances of justice and his beliefs about God impinged on his application of the canon of human welfare. He did not apply it independently of his interpretations of these other base points in his ethics.

It is not surprising, then, that Ryan concluded *Distributive Justice* admitting that his application of the rules of justice must seem complex and indefinite.[240] It was complex and indefinite because Ryan's application of the principles of justice was informed by his other base points. His moral reasoning did not proceed from his canons of justice alone. It drew on his beliefs about human dignity and how human dignity is respected only when moral reasoning about justice considers whether the consequences of economic policies are conducive to the divinely appointed end of human rational nature. Justice cannot be determined by a rigid application of principles. Thus, Ryan's canons of justice do not provide a full account of moral reasoning as he practiced it. They are, however, his only explicit account of the criteria for deliberations about justice, and they do provide "helpful" guides for determining justice as Ryan conceived it.

Ryan's canons of justice combined his theory of rights, based upon

---

239. Ryan, *Distributive Justice*, 252.
240. Ibid., 432.

human dignity, with his concern for consequences, based on economic analysis in light of the divine order of life. With this combination in mind, we can fairly summarize Ryan's first five canons in two principles: (1) needs requisite to every person's self-perfection and (2) deserts based upon superior development of the personality and/or contributions to economic welfare that are necessary for human welfare. This second sense of desert is not associated with personal moral achievement in fulfilling one's duty for self-perfection but with what a person deserves for amoral contributions to the economy. These contributions are morally relevant because they have positive consequences for the welfare of others.

Needs

Ryan listed the canon of equality prior to needs, but his canon of equality only affirms that each person has an equal right to what she or he needs for self-development. Consistent with his teleological conception of rights, Ryan construed equality to mean persons' "claims to equal degrees of welfare, not to equal amounts of external goods. . . . [E]xternal goods are not welfare; they must be determined by their bearing upon the welfare of the individual."[241] Thus, the canon of equality does not in itself stipulate a pattern of distribution; the pattern of distribution to which persons have an equal right is determined by what they need for self-perfection. Needs, not equality, is Ryan's primary distributive principle.

"Human needs," wrote Ryan, "constitute the primary title or claim to material goods."[242] In this respect, Ryan differed from Rauschenbusch, for whom equality in accord with service to the community was fundamental. For Rauschenbusch, development of the personality in the community requires the abolition of privileges that promote inequalities and set classes apart. He simply assumed that individual needs will be met by an egalitarian distribution. For Ryan, an economic system that treats persons equally in meeting their specific needs for self-development can permit inequalities of income and wealth, especially inequalities justified by the other canons of justice. This difference in their conceptions of justice helps to explain variations in Rauschenbusch's and Ryan's judgments about the justice of profits, rents, and interest.

The canon of needs also subsumes individuals' right to liberty. As we

---

241. Ibid., 244.
242. Ibid., 357.

have seen, individuals have no claims to liberties that are inessential for their self-perfection. For this reason, liberty is conspicuously absent from Ryan's list of canons. Unlike Niebuhr, who considered liberty and equality the two primary but conflicting principles of justice, Ryan perceived no conflict between legitimate claims to liberty and his primary principle of needs.

Ryan's canon of needs has two distinct aspects. First, it requires that all persons be treated as "beings endowed with the dignity and the potencies of personality."[243] All persons have a right to whatever they need to achieve the proximate end of their rational nature. Satisfying this aspect of the canon of needs demands near equality in the distribution of a minimum level of "external goods," because all persons have equal needs for a decent livelihood, rational liberties, education, and so forth. There are, however, some special needs that justify inequalities in the way these equal rights are satisfied; for example, women and children need to be protected from onerous labor, and persons living in an area that has a high cost of living need more income for a decent living. Unless these requisites for normal self-development are satisfied, the intrinsic and equal dignity of individuals is undermined. Consequently, all other titles to goods are subordinate to this aspect of needs.[244] Other titles are justified only insofar as they serve to secure these basic needs for all persons or after these basic needs are supplied. Ryan asserted, for example, that no workers are entitled to anything in excess of living wages until all others have received a living wage.[245]

Once these elementary needs of life are met for all persons, the second aspect of needs becomes relevant. At this point, distribution is proportional to "the varying needs and capacities of men to develop their faculties beyond the minimum reasonable degree."[246] Ryan calls these needs "nonessential" and concludes that this aspect of the canon of needs is inapplicable to the distribution of income for two reasons. First, these needs cannot be accurately determined, and second, they do not consider how distribution affects production. In order to account for how production affects human welfare, the other canons of justice must be considered.[247] Despite the practical inapplicability of this second aspect of needs, it provides a moral justification for inequalities. This justification allowed Ryan to view his more economic reasons for unequal distribution as morally permitted. In this way, Ryan's primary canon of

---

243. Ibid., 244.
244. Ibid., 357–358.
245. Ibid., 381.
246. Ibid., 382.
247. Ibid., 245–246, 382.

needs supports a more unequal distribution of goods than Rauschenbusch's first principle of equality according to contributions to the
community.

Deserts

The canons of efforts and sacrifices, productivity, and scarcity are all to
some extent based upon Ryan's analysis of the economic circumstances
of justice. Human welfare requires that these canons be considered for
the sake of long-run provision for needs. If we construe desert broadly to
include what persons deserve for contributions to the common good,
even when their actions are not morally meritorious, all these canons can
be viewed as distinct elements of a principle of desert.

The canon of efforts and sacrifices justifies unequal distributions in
proportion to unusual exertion and to especially burdensome training or
disagreeable work. This canon differs from the second aspect of needs in
that it measures, not potential for self-development, but contributions to
the making of a product that constitute actual "moral desert."[248] Inasmuch as efforts and sacrifices are ingredients in developing one's personality, they are claims based on the duty for self-perfection and not merely
the privilege of self-perfection. Because they measure moral merit,
efforts and sacrifices are like the canon of needs in that they are based
upon "the dignity and claims of the personality." They manifest ethical
worth and not merely economic worth.[249]

Yet special efforts and sacrifices also usually contribute to economic
efficiency. In this respect, they, like the canons of productivity and
scarcity, justify extra benefits in proportion to contributions to economic
welfare. Efforts and sacrifices differ from the latter canons in two
respects. First, they indicate moral merit. Second, mere effort and
sacrifice, absent talent for economic productivity, do not necessarily
produce superior economic results.[250]

The canons of productivity and scarcity are necessary only because
satisfying them contributes to the level of general economic welfare that
is required to meet persons' needs for self-development. Unlike unequal
rewards based on superior efforts or exceptional sacrifices, unequal
benefits received due to natural talents for economic efficiency or to
skills that are valuable merely because they are scarce are deserved for
their economic value alone.[251] These titles to goods are justified primar-

248. Ibid., 245.
249. Ibid., 382.
250. Ibid., 247–248, 383.
251. Ibid., 247–248.

ily on the basis of Ryan's analysis of the consequences of economic policies for safeguarding individual dignity. They are among those titles (effort and sacrifice are also included) to goods about which Ryan says they are methods by which "needs may be conveniently supplied."[252] "[T]he title of productivity must give way to that of needs, which is the end to which all other titles are but means."[253] Claims to deserts based on these economic contributions are valid only insofar as they are instruments to secure individual needs. In this way, they are linked to ethical value from the perspective of human welfare.

Human Welfare

Ryan included human welfare as a canon of justice, though it is more a perspective for linking economic efficiency that benefits social welfare with a concern for individual needs than it is a criterion for stipulating a just distribution. Ryan's elucidation of this canon in *Distributive Justice* did not express this connection between economic consequences and individual needs for self-development as clearly as did his later discussions of social justice. He did observe, in *Distributive Justice,* that human welfare "includes and summarises all that is ethically and socially feasible" in the other five canons.[254] Yet his statement that human welfare is a principle of "maximum net results" for economic welfare, once vital individual needs have been met, does not clearly indicate his view that social or economic welfare is never valued independently of its long-run relevance for safeguarding human dignity.

We have seen, however, that his application of human welfare to rent and interest and to private property links the consequences of economic efficiency, stability, and institutions to his conception of individual dignity. Further, his incidental comments about human welfare and his later discussion of social justice make explicit his contention that the determination of just policies always considers the common good in terms of how it provides for the means to individual self-perfection. We will see, in Chapter 5, that his later proposals for economic redistribution, for industrial democracy, and for the occupational group system were also based on how the common good serves individual development.

In light of this connection between social welfare and protecting individual dignity, the role of human welfare among Ryan's canons of

---

252. Ibid., 357–358.
253. Ryan, *A Living Wage,* 249.
254. Ryan, *Distributive Justice,* 252.

justice is clear. It shows how the conflicts between the canon of needs and the canons based on economic value, especially productivity and scarcity, are ultimately harmonized. Ryan acknowledged that all of these canons are somewhat vague and only approximate measures of what is due individuals.[255] He also observed that they sometimes conflict. The differences between needs and productivity are, for example, "so great that distribution based solely upon productivity would fall far short of satisfying the demands of needs."[256] Obversely, distribution based on needs alone is inadequate because it does not "give due consideration to the moral claims of the producer as such."[257]

Justice cannot be adequately determined by natural moral laws (e.g., laws of exchange equivalence in contracts, an a priori law of private property, or even a law of distribution proportional to need) without considering economic consequences. God has ordered the universe so that conformity to the natural law is best achieved by what is "conducive" to the proximate end of human rational nature. Nor can justice be achieved by the strict application of the purportedly scientific laws of productivity claimed by "orthodox" economics. For Ryan, there must be some flexibility and creativity in uniting moral theory and economic analysis for the purpose of securing human dignity.

The first five canons of justice do not provide a precise nor even a fully coherent determination of what level of wages, profits, and so forth, is just. The canon of human welfare provides a perspective from which the canons pertaining directly to individual dignity can be combined with the canons that account for economic consequences in an approximate determination of distributive justice that secures every individual the means for self-perfection. It does not resolve all conflicts between distribution proportional to needs and distribution designed to maintain productive efficiency. It does, however, balance a concern for economic welfare with the fundamental purpose of justice to provide for needs. For example, in justifying indefinitely large profits after the needs of wage earners have been met, human welfare accounts for both the needs of laborers and most persons in business while simultaneously encouraging a "maximum social product." On the basis of this balance, Ryan wrote: "In the field of profits the canon of human welfare is not only ethically sound but expedient socially."[258] Human welfare thus reflects Ryan's confidence that the divine natural order unites economic realities with God's intention that every individual should have opportunities to

---

255. Ibid., 245–246, 49–50, 385.
256. Ibid., 247.
257. Ibid., 244–245.
258. Ibid., 255–257.

develop his or her rational nature toward the supernatural end of eternal goodness and happiness.

In sum, Ryan's first five canons of justice, united by the perspective of human welfare, specify the criteria for making judgments about the distribution of economic benefits and burdens. This distribution, he believed, could safeguard human dignity in light of his economic analysis. The primacy of needs assures every individual equal access to the minimum level of goods required for self-development. Its second aspect also permits the significant inequalities indicated by the three canons of desert grounded in Ryan's economic analysis. (The canon of efforts and sacrifices draws on both his moral theory of human dignity and his concern for economic efficiency.)

On this conception of justice, we should expect the economic policies Ryan advocated to reflect a concern for character development similar to Rauschenbusch but to focus on minimal needs rather than on equality and "socializing" the economic process. The issues we have already considered to illustrate Ryan's theory of justice manifested these similarities and differences from Rauschenbusch. A brief explication of how these and other policies cohered in Ryan's program for economic justice, during the first two decades of this century, will demonstrate, even more vividly, his similarities to and differences from Rauschenbusch.

RYAN'S EARLY PROGRAM FOR ECONOMIC JUSTICE

Ryan, like Rauschenbusch, claimed that economic institutions should distribute the benefits and burdens of cooperation so as to enable persons to develop their capacities in accord with an ideal for perfecting their created nature. Yet Ryan's focus on safeguarding individual dignity, by providing what every person needs for self-development, led him to adopt a program for reform that differed somewhat from Rauschenbusch's. It differed primarily in the reforms that were emphasized and in the strategy for obtaining justice. To a lesser extent, it differed in the substance of policies advocated. The most prominent example of a difference in emphasis was the centrality of a family living wage in Ryan's program.

A Family Living Wage

We have reviewed how Ryan justified a living wage. We are now prepared to specify its content and to comprehend its paramount importance in his struggle against injustice.

Because the right to a living wage is based on what individuals need to attain the end of their rational nature, it "demands not merely the conditions of reasonable physical existence, but the opportunity of pursuing self perfection through the harmonious development of all the faculties."[259] For adult males, normal development includes provision for a family with four to five children; therefore, for the sake of the adult male worker's development, a living wage must be sufficient to support his family.[260] On this method of determining what adult males need to safeguard their dignity, Ryan could and did specify the content of the right to a living wage in a dollar amount. In 1906, Ryan calculated the minimum expenses of a "workingman's" family outside of major cities to be $601.03.[261] (Lest we overemphasize his willingness to specify rights quantitatively, please note that he rounds this figure to $600 in the discussion that follows.) In 1916, he set the figure at $750.[262] By 1920, after the war, he raised the living wage to $1400–1500.[263]

By comparing the specific wages to which workers have a right with wages actually received, Ryan noted the extent to which this right fundamental for human dignity remained unsatisfied. In *A Living Wage,* Ryan concluded that 60 percent of the adult males in cities of the United States were receiving less than a decent livelihood. Among the rights crucial for self-development, a living wage was the least widely satisfied. Given his conception of justice, in which specific needs for self-development were primary, Ryan's economic analysis led him to assert:

> [T]he remuneration of the laborer is the most important single question in any scheme of social reform. . . . [T]he industrial question in so far as it relates to the less prosperous classes, is a question of wages almost entirely. If the working people have sufficient income, they will be able themselves to meet many of the problems for which reformers are trying to find remedies.[264]

No single issue consumed more space in Ryan's writings or more of the time and energy he devoted to the politics of reform than his struggle for

---

259. Ibid., 361.

260. Ryan, *A Living Wage,* 117–122; idem, *Distributive Justice,* 373–375. We have observed that Ryan considered women to have special needs requiring legislation to protect them from onerous labor. He also viewed support for the family as the special responsibility of the husband and father; consequently, only the adult male has a need for and a commensurate right to a living wage sufficient to support a family. In Ryan's defense, he did claim for women, not merely a "woman's Living Wage," but the same remuneration as that of equally competent male workers. See Ryan, *A Living Wage,* 108.

261. Ibid., 145.

262. Ryan, *Distributive Justice,* 379.

263. Ryan, *Social Reconstruction,* 66.

264. Ibid., 62–63.

legislation requiring employers to pay a living wage. In his autobiography, Ryan noted with satisfaction that the Fair Labor Standards Act of 1938 had established a minimum wage for both males and females approaching the legal living wage he had been advocating for thirty-six years. Still, he maintained that the $800 minimum wage that had been enacted was inadequate, and in his last revision of *Distributive Justice,* Ryan reaffirmed a claim he had made in the first edition that a legal minimum wage is the "most desirable single measure of industrial reform."[265]

Ryan also sought legislation for measures that would complement the living wage in his struggle to secure the right to a decent livelihood for families. He called for legislation regulating child and female labor and for regulating maximum hours for all workers. These proposals were justified in their own right by the specific needs they satisfied, but Ryan also advocated them in order to decrease the supply of labor and thus raise the wages of adult males to a decent livelihood.[266] In addition, Ryan thought compulsory insurance programs against sickness, accidents, old age, and unemployment[267] and government assistance in providing adequate housing would be necessary until wages were sufficiently high that workers could provide for these needs from their own resources.[268] Ryan considered all of these proposals secondary to a legal living wage. They were apparently intended as temporary measures until a living wage could be achieved. In *Distributive Justice,* he wrote that if the state could establish a legal living wage and provide vocational and industrial education, the laboring class would have sufficient power to secure substantially all that was due by any of the canons of distributive justice.[269] He did not repeat this remarkable claim in the third edition.

The importance of a legal living wage in Ryan's program for reform follows from the primacy of needs in his conception of justice and from

---

265. Ryan, *Social Doctrine in Action,* 259–260; idem, *Distributive Justice,* 3d ed., 303, 323.

266. E.g., Ryan, *A Living Wage,* 108–109, 319; Ryan and Hillquit, *Socialism,* 40.

267. Despite occasional statements supporting unemployment insurance, Ryan was, in these early years, curiously uninterested in the problem of unemployment. He did not argue for a right to employment or consistently for public programs to employ persons out of work. He even allowed that if some persons are thrown out of work by a legal living wage, the magnitude of evil would be reduced because many more workers would be raised to a decent income. See Ryan, *Distributive Justice,* 408, 411; idem, *The Church and Socialism,* 93. In *The Church and Socialism,* Ryan advocated state action, including public employment as a last resort, to deal with the problem of unemployment (ibid., 95, 97), but he did not consider unemployment a crucial issue until the thirties.

268. Ryan and Hillquit, *Socialism,* 40; Ryan, *Social Reconstruction,* 81–82ff; idem, *A Living Wage,* 320–322.

269. Ryan, *Distributive Justice,* 416–417.

his comparatively narrow focus on the economic circumstances of justice. Providing a decent livelihood for individuals did not require the grand evolutionary scheme of reform that Rauschenbusch envisioned. It required a specific, though highly controversial, reform in the market system. Rauschenbusch also favored most of these proposals, but they were secondary components in a grander program to remove special privileges, especially privileges of land ownership, in order to secure equality and solidarity among the classes. Ryan's program also went beyond the need for a living wage. It included changes in the pattern of income and wealth distribution and revisions of rights associated with private productive property, but these reforms were of secondary importance in Ryan's total program, especially before the thirties.

Complete Distributive Justice

It was not mere coincidence that Ryan's first book was *A Living Wage,* or that he did not offer his complete system of distributive justice until ten years later. Even in *Distributive Justice,* his justifications for a total system of distribution remained tentative and secondary to his argument for a living wage. Ryan's justifications for rents, interest, profits, and wages beyond a minimum living wage are based primarily on those canons (productivity, scarcity, and human welfare) that promote economic efficiency for the sake of securing human dignity in the long run. They are not based directly on human dignity. Thus, these distributions in excess of a decent livelihood are only presumptively justified. They do not have the same importance as the right to a living wage. Ryan was emphatic that, wherever it is feasible, a decent livelihood should be paid to all before excess income is received by anyone, whether it be through rents, interest, profits, or wages.[270] Furthermore, Ryan noted, with regard to complete justice for wages, that it is "devoid of practical interest" because the more immediate problem is to secure a living wage for all.[271] Undoubtedly, this observation applies to complete justice in the distribution of profits, interest, and rents as well.

In this matter of complete distributive justice, the primacy of Ryan's canon of needs and his analysis of the circumstances focusing on the four factors of production led to differences of both emphasis and content with Rauschenbusch's policies based upon equality. We have already seen that Ryan opposed the single tax on landowners, allowed interest as

---

270. Ibid., 367–369, 381–382, 388; idem, *A Living Wage,* 253–261. The passages cited refer only to wages, profits, dividends, and interest, but because rent has the same justification as interest, we can presume Ryan's point applies to rent as well, ibid., 263.

271. Ryan, *Distributive Justice,* 399.

a payment for the use of capital as well as for risking capital,[272] and permitted unlimited profits gained from competitive markets after a living wage is paid. In regard to wages higher than the "equitable minimum," Ryan permitted laborers to bargain for them. He added, however, that the workers have no "strict right" to profits generated in conditions of competition or to wages that cause a reduction in the competitive rate of interest.[273] He thought no clear judgments were possible regarding the distribution of the proceeds of business that exceed what is needed for a decent livelihood. Thus, we do not find Ryan either as vehement or as thoroughgoing as Rauschenbusch about eliminating the privileges of business that create inequalities of income and wealth.

We must not, however, overestimate their differences. Ryan's justifications for inequalities in the distribution of income and wealth were mostly on tentative economic grounds. Although greater needs and capacities justified some inequalities and equality was not itself a goal, Ryan had no moral reason to defend large incomes and accumulations of wealth. At price levels in 1916, Ryan considered five to ten thousand dollars the maximum income required by the "true welfare" of any family.[274] Further, he considered some unequal distributions of income questionable, or at least unnecessary, on economic grounds. Thus, Ryan was never entirely comfortable with the inequalities that existed. In his interpretation of the Bishops' Program of Social Reconstruction (a document Ryan wrote), Ryan noted that the bishops considered the excessive incomes of a small minority of privileged capitalists as one of the main evils of the present economic system.[275]

Consequently, Ryan favored policies that would promote equality as long as they were consistent with economic expediency. Despite opposing the single tax, Ryan favored taxing some of the incremental gains on land sales, shifting taxes from personal property and improvements to taxes on land, and taxes on large landholdings. Despite his justifications for interest, Ryan favored cooperatives and co-partnerships[276] as means to equalize the distribution of capital and of interest payments. By 1913, in his debate with Hillquit, Ryan was saying that ways must be found to

---

272. Ibid., 138–141. Rauschenbusch also appears to have condoned the payment of interest as long as industry remains privately owned, but his distinctions between interest, profits, dividends, and salaries are less refined than Ryan's. See Rauschenbusch, *Christianizing the Social Order*, 223–226.

273. Ryan, *Distributive Justice*, 388–393.

274. Ibid., 316–318.

275. Ryan, *Social Reconstruction*, 182–183.

276. Co-partnerships differ from cooperatives in that in the former workers do not have total control of management and capital. See Ryan, *Social Reconstruction*, 161–162.

make the majority of workers owners of the instruments of production in order to abolish the excessive gains on privileged capital.[277] Despite his justification for unlimited profits under competitive conditions, Ryan favored progressive income and inheritance taxes as a means to limit large fortunes.[278] By 1920, he was calling for labor sharing in profits,[279] and in 1923 he was calling for state action to exclude stockholders from the recipients of profits.[280] Finally, Ryan defended wages somewhat higher than a decent minimum as both economically and morally justified,[281] and he approved of collective bargaining and strikes as legitimate means to obtain these higher wages.

Ryan favored these policies in part for the purpose of redistributing income and wealth in ways consistent with economic expediency. Combined, they approach Rauschenbusch's goal to remove all the privileges that create inequalities, but Ryan did not see them as as urgent as his struggle for a legal living wage. He consistently qualified their egalitarian thrust. The goal of progressive taxes, for example, was to equalize sacrifices and not to achieve equality. Taxes should never be so progressive as to discourage socially useful activity or deny rewards for productive efficiency.[282] Even though profit sharing may be justified on grounds of increasing the workers' efficiency, the workers have no right to anything more than a fair wage.[283] Ryan praised Henry Ford's highly publicized moves to raise wages and lower prices as generous acts of equity by a highly efficient businessman. They were not required by justice.[284] These qualifications on efforts at redistribution fit Ryan's canon of needs, which required proportional justice, not equality. He certainly did not share Rauschenbusch's view that significant inequalities of income and wealth indicate unjust privileges that must be abolished.

In response to unemployment during the Depression, Ryan would make greater use of Hobson's theory of underconsumption to argue for a redistribution of income as the means to achieve economic stability. The themes of workers sharing in profits and ownership would become part of a coherent program for industrial democracy in all enterprises, and Ryan would adopt other policies intended to put more money in the hands of consumers. In the first two decades of his career, however, the primacy of basic needs and a concern for productivity made the policies

---

277. Ryan and Hillquit, *Socialism,* 249.
278. Ryan, *Distributive Justice,* 296–299; idem, *Social Reconstruction,* 197–198.
279. Ibid., 156–157.
280. Ryan, *The Christian Doctrine of Property,* 18–30.
281. Ryan, *Social Reconstruction,* 51–54.
282. Ryan, *Distributive Justice,* 297, 300; idem, *Social Reconstruction,* 198–199.
283. Ibid., 157–158.
284. Ryan, *Distributive Justice,* 256; idem, *Social Reconstruction,* 193–195.

Ryan advocated for the sake of equality tentative, qualified, and a secondary part of his program for reform.

Private Ownership of Productive Property

As we have noted, Ryan's canon of human welfare provided a perspective for reconsidering the justice of private property, both with regard to its influence on economic efficiency and with regard to its provision for needs necessary for self-development.

Ryan obviously did not reject the right to private productive property. Using both of the measures above (i.e., efficiency and needs), Ryan devoted a significant proportion of his writings to opposing socialism. Even if it entails no more than public ownership of all industrial property, socialism, Ryan contended, is both economically inexpedient and a threat to liberty and the other needs required for self-development.[285] Inasmuch as private ownership of productive property, apart from its consequences for economic efficiency, provides essential support for self-development, it is a natural right (i.e., not contingent on its benefits for economic welfare). Ryan's program for social reform preserved elements of private property as among those specific rights required to safeguard human dignity. He, therefore, persistently rejected the socialist label, which Rauschenbusch accepted.

Ryan's reconsideration of private property nevertheless led him to adopt policies that raised the ire of more doctrinaire Catholic opponents of socialism. A comparison that stops at saying that Ryan was opposed to socialism and Rauschenbusch was a socialist is highly misleading. To be sure, Ryan's understanding of private property as a natural right meant that he could not imagine circumstances in which public ownership of all property could be just. Nevertheless, his justification of that right from the perspective of human welfare enabled him to limit the extent of the right on the basis of its consequences for the development of individuals. "[A]ll property rights are but means to the satisfaction of human needs."[286] The extent of the right of individuals to control property is dependent upon empirical analyses of how the right bears on the needs of all persons affected.

Thus, we have already seen that Ryan was quite willing to limit the capitalist's right to enter into wage contracts that deny workers a decent livelihood. We have also noted that he advocated other policies limiting the income and wealth justly allowed through the ownership of property.

---

285. See, e.g., Ryan and Hillquit, *Socialism*, 48–69.
286. Ryan, *Distributive Justice*, 367.

Beyond these limitations of property rights, Ryan advocated public ownership of natural monopolies. Like Rauschenbusch, he did not think public
regulation of these monopolies would be sufficient, though he softened
this position in later years.[287] He also favored retention of timber, mineral,
gas, oil, and water power lands presently owned by the government, and
he thought large cities should buy land to provide for housing.[288] In
addition, Ryan argued that the best way to prevent collusion to fix prices in
some industries may be for the government to own significant elements of
the industry in order to compete with privately owned oligopolies.[289] In
one case, the anthracite coal industry, Ryan advocated government ownership of the entire industry.[290] Finally, Ryan looked favorably upon plans
to establish a form of productive cooperative through government ownership of industries that would be managed by workers.[291] We need not
wonder why Ryan found himself constantly defending his program against
the charge that it was socialist.

Despite their differences regarding the socialist label, it is not easy to
distinguish Ryan's policies regarding public ownership of productive property from the practical measures Rauschenbusch proposed. There was a
difference in their senses of urgency (e.g., Ryan thought natural monopolies would *probably at some time* have to be publicly owned)[292] and a substantive difference in their views regarding artificial monopolies. Whereas
Rauschenbusch favored government ownership of artificial monopolies
because antitrust action would reaffirm excessive competition, Ryan
favored the breakup of artificial monopolies in order to regain the efficiencies of competition.[293] Ryan differed a little more sharply with Rauschenbusch's long-run vision for "socializing" the economy. Rauschenbusch
placed no limits upon public ownership of industrial property. Ryan, in an
essay distinguishing "public ownership" from "socialism," asserted that
public ownership of productive property should stop short of violating the
"right of private property." He suggested that the proper criterion might
be that nationalization should never proceed so far as to deprive individuals of opportunities to invest their money.[294]

287. Ryan, *Social Doctrine in Action,* 108–109; see also idem, "A Programme of Social
Reform by Legislation," *Catholic World* 89 (July–August 1901): 609.
288. Ryan, *Distributive Justice,* 95–97, 98–100; idem, "A Programme of Social Reform," 609.
289. Ryan, *Social Reconstruction,* 190–191.
290. Ryan, *Declining Liberty,* 281–291, esp. 289–290.
291. Ryan, *Social Reconstruction,* 171–175; idem, *Industrial Democracy from a Catholic
Viewpoint* (Washington, D.C.: The Rossi-Bryn Co., 1925), 8–10.
292. Ryan, *Distributive Justice,* 275; idem, *Social Reconstruction,* 192.
293. Ryan, *Distributive Justice,* 276–278; idem, 184–185.
294. Ryan, *Declining Liberty,* 263.

How could a defender of a natural right to private property go so far in advocating policies that limit this right? The answer is that Ryan justified the right to private property, not as an a priori right of individuals, but only indirectly. Private property is a natural right because as a social institution it has positive consequences for economic productivity (by encouraging individual incentives and ambition) and for self-development (by providing for liberties, self-respect, etc.). Ryan and Rauschenbusch were both asking what organization of property would provide the best opportunities for individuals to develop their natural interests toward an ideal character.

Their differences regarding private property are attributable to Ryan's greater concern for economic productivity in his analysis of the circumstances of justice and to his being less sanguine about institutions altering the natural inclinations of agents. These differences diminished when Ryan developed proposals for industrial democracy and the occupational group system in the thirties. These proposals further qualified the property rights of capitalists in the direction of wider worker participation and of cooperation, which were prominent reasons behind Rauschenbusch's proposals for "socializing" industry.

Despite their being on opposite sides of the socialist label, Ryan's total program of economic reforms differed most acutely from Rauschenbusch's in that Ryan emphasized the salutary effects of a legal minimum wage and de-emphasized the importance of removing the privileges that generate inequality. There were also differences in policy—namely, Ryan opposed the single tax and public ownership of all industrial property—but these differences were more radical in appearance than in reality. The most important contrast between Ryan's and Rauschenbusch's programs for reform was probably in their strategies for obtaining justice.

Strategy: Justice Through Rational Action by the State

Unlike Rauschenbusch and Niebuhr, Ryan did not include criteria for strategies to obtain justice within his conception of justice. He did not need them. A reasonable application of the canons of justice was itself the principal means for obtaining just reforms. He was less concerned with strategies for redressing inequalities in power among the classes and molding individual character than with developing arguments to persuade rational agents to adopt his proposed reforms. There were limits to the power of moral arguments. Ryan did not expect that many individual employers could be persuaded to pay a living wage or that monopolists would voluntarily restrain their power to charge extortionate prices. He did, however, expect the democratic state, as it was constituted, to enact just policies in response to rational moral arguments.

Ryan did not entertain the possibility that democratic politics could be controlled by capitalist interests. He saw no need, as Rauschenbusch did, to make the government more democratic as a means for attaining economic democracy.[295] He certainly never considered, as Niebuhr did in the thirties, that economic reforms would require partial subversion of constitutional democracies. Moreover, Ryan did not place his hope for reform in powerful social movements such as labor, socialism, or the church.

The Labor Movement

Ryan did not condemn the labor movement. He went at least as far as Rauschenbusch in justifying the right of labor to organize and use the methods available for protecting its interests. Using various aspects of just-war principles adapted to apply to unions as "fighting organizations," Ryan justified (within the limits of his principles) strikes, sympathetic strikes and boycotts against an unjust employer, bargaining for a closed shop, and union limitations on output and apprentices.[296] He concluded: "[T]he aims of the union are substantially right, and . . . of its methods, only violence, tyranny and the tendency to excessive demands are in all circumstances unjustifiable."[297] Although Ryan was much more precise about what union methods are justified, his differences with Rauschenbusch were not at the level of specific labor policies.

The differences occur at the level of a general endorsement of the labor movement as the principal instrument for obtaining justice. First, Rauschenbusch thought a general endorsement of working class interests, without careful scrutiny of their justice in each case, was necessary to redress the imbalance of economic power. Ryan insisted that each union activity should be judged according to its reasonableness.[298] In a lecture on labor unions in *Social Reconstruction,* Ryan criticized Samuel Gompers for Gompers' general endorsement of labor interests that presumed labor is always right. Ryan maintained that specific labor strikes should be judged by an impartial application of his adaptation of

---

295. In a 1936 essay on democracy, Ryan favored some of the same policies for democratic politics that Rauschenbusch advocated, namely, the initiative, referendum, recall, and proportional representation. Ryan, however, did not consider these changes crucial for safeguarding political or economic justice. See Ryan, *Seven Troubled Years,* 228–229.

296. Ryan, *The Church and Socialism,* 100–130.

297. Ibid., 149–150.

298. E.g., ibid., 150.

just-war principles.[299] Though he thought union power had positive consequences for justice, Ryan's endorsement of the labor movement was qualified by an insistence that each assertion of labor interest should be judged by reasonable canons of justice.

Second, Ryan thought achievement of reforms (especially a living wage) was beyond the capacity of unions alone. It depended upon legislation. He chided certain labor leaders who relied upon organization and bargaining exclusive of legislation. Ryan believed unions could and did play a role in securing helpful legislation,[300] but his own campaign for a legal living wage and other labor legislation was not coordinated through the labor movement. Ryan, observed Francis Broderick, was never close to the labor movement. Sometimes his distance occurred because labor leaders were not radical enough in their demands.[301] The point is not that Ryan was in every case critical of labor militancy, but that he was, more than Rauschenbusch, detached from the labor movement. He placed his hope for justice more in principled appeals for legislative action than in the labor movement as a redemptive force in society.

The Socialist Movement

Ryan's attitude toward the socialist movement was not one of detached approval of most of its goals and methods; it was vehement opposition. He made an explicit distinction between the socialist economic program and socialism as a movement with distinct philosophical underpinnings.[302] Rauschenbusch operated with a similar distinction, though he never explicitly articulated it, between the socialist movement and the policies it advocated. This distinction enabled Rauschenbusch to praise the socialist movement while criticizing specific socialist ideas, strategies, and policies. Ryan used his distinction to approve of some socialist economic policies while maintaining a gulf between himself and the social movement. We have seen how Ryan's approval of specific socialist economic policies left him with a program for reform reasonably close to Rauschenbusch's, but Ryan saw no basis for even a partial alliance between the socialist movement and the Catholic Church.[303] The posi-

---

299. Ryan, *Social Reconstruction*, 134–138.
300. Ryan, *Distributive Justice*, 420–423; idem, *Social Reconstruction*, 127.
301. Broderick, *Right Reverend New Dealer*, 129–131.
302. Ryan and Hillquit, *Socialism*, 13, 245–246.
303. Ibid., 265. Ironically, one of Ryan's rare references to Rauschenbusch cited passages from *Christianizing the Social Order* out of context in order to back Ryan's contention that Christianity and the socialist movement are totally antagonistic, ibid., 194–195.

tion of the Catholic Church, he wrote, is rightly one of "vigilant and ceaseless opposition to the concrete, living institution called the socialist movement."[304] Ryan mitigated this vehemence in the thirties in light of *Quadragesimo Anno* and changes in the socialist program, but he repeatedly cited a statement by Pope Pius XI that claimed harmonizing Catholicism and socialism was impossible.[305] Ryan had no sympathy for Rauschenbusch's view that the socialist movement was a part of God's redemptive work, or with Niebuhr's view, in the thirties, that the proletarian mission was necessary to achieve a balance of power that approximates justice. For Ryan, justice could not be achieved through a flawed socialist movement as part of God's work in redeeming an evolving natural order (Rauschenbusch) or by endorsing the partially corrupted proletarian mission in order to produce a more equitable balance of power (Niebuhr). The task was to teach the principles of the established divine natural order in their application to modern economic circumstances.

The Church

This understanding of the mission for social reform as didactic also applied to the church. Ryan's criticisms of some Protestants for their view that the church's mission is to reorganize society as the kingdom of God was evidently aimed explicitly at Rauschenbusch.[306] Ryan's criticism undoubtedly suffered from an inadequate comprehension of what Rauschenbusch meant by the kingdom of God and the social mission of church, but there are real differences in their views of the church's role in securing justice. Ryan conceived of the church's positive role in reform primarily as that of a teacher and example of the natural law rather than as an evangelizing and redemptive social force.[307] He did not understand the church, sociologically, as the primary mediator of Christ's redemptive influence in an evolving natural order. He understood it as the authoritative interpreter and teacher of the established divine and natural order. The church has to adjust the application of the natural laws of industrial ethics to the consequences of changing economic institutions, but its mission in this regard is to teach individuals and the state. Its

---

304. Ryan, *The Church and Socialism*, 14.
305. E.g., Ryan, *Seven Troubled Years*, 47; idem, *A Better Economic Order* (New York: Harper & Brothers, 1935), 135–136.
306. Broderick, *Right Reverend New Dealer*, 74.
307. See, e.g., Ryan, *The Church and Socialism*, 153; idem, *Social Reform on Catholic Lines*, 18–21; idem, *The Christian Doctrine of Property*, 31–36; idem, *Declining Liberty*, 181.

mission is not to become a social force for redeeming the social order by aligning itself with redemptive social movements. Ryan had no visions of church and labor leaders marching together in Labor Day parades, and he did not write about using churches as labor temples.[308]

The State

According to the church's teaching, the state has a fairly well-defined role within the natural order. Against what he called the individualistic theories of the state emanating from Kant and Herbert Spencer, Ryan argued that the legitimate functions of the state are not limited by voluntary agreements among individuals. The functions of the state are natural and necessary "means to right living and human progress."[309] Its natural functions are two: to protect the natural rights of individuals and to promote the general welfare.[310] As we would expect from Ryan's canon of human welfare, the first function is primary, and the state's proper care for the general welfare is directed to the welfare (self-development) of individuals.[311] Thus, the principal function and obligation of the state is to do what it can and must to provide "opportunities and immunities which the individual requires in order to attain the end of his nature, to live a reasonable life."[312]

Two points follow that bear on Ryan's view of how justice can be achieved. First, Ryan clearly considered the state a major player in the effort to secure justice. The relatively broad scope that he gave to state action does not, however, distinguish Ryan's strategy from Rauschenbusch's. Indeed, Ryan gave less scope for state intervention than Rauschenbusch did. The natural law, which justifies state action in the economy, also limits the scope of the state's activity. Ryan insisted that the state should limit its functions to those needs that private associations cannot provide.[313] He considered socialist proposals for public ownership as among those policies in which the interests of the state are so invasive that they interfere with individual self-development.[314]

The second point does distinguish Ryan's strategy from Rauschenbusch's. The state's function to enforce a living wage, and other policies to achieve justice, can be known by and taught to rational agents

308. Rauschenbusch, *Christianizing the Social Order*, 12, 456.
309. Ryan and Millar, *The State and the Church*, 208–217, esp. 212–213.
310. Ibid., 224; Ryan, *Social Reconstruction*, 201.
311. Ryan and Millar, *The State and the Church*, 204.
312. Ibid., 225.
313. Ibid., 196; Ryan, *Social Reconstruction*, 202.
314. Ryan and Millar, *The State and the Church*, 217–218.

capable of comprehending and acting on the laws of the established natural order. Moreover, the democratic tradition in the United States fits within Catholic teaching on the natural law.[315] Thus, the presently constituted government is capable of responding to well-reasoned appeals to natural rights and the canons of justice. There is no need for social movements to transform individuals and institutions before the program for reform can be achieved. The task is to teach Catholics and others that the principles of justice require legislative action to provide for individuals' natural rights.

It is not surprising that Ryan can be characterized as an "ethicist to the politicians" or that two of his first essays on policies were entitled "A Programme of Social Reform by Legislation." In *Social Doctrine in Action,* Ryan recollected that in his first reading of *Rerum Novarum* he was most impressed, not by the pope's teaching on a living wage, unions, property rights, or socialism, but by "the very large scope that [the pope] assigned to legislation as an instrument of social reform."[316] In the last chapter of this autobiography, Ryan noted with pride that three Supreme Court justices, two cabinet secretaries, and a senator sat at the speaker's table during the celebration of his seventieth birthday. The guests also "included a *large number* of labor union officials" and "some *thirty-five or forty* members of the Senate and House of Representatives."[317] (If any socialist leaders attended, Ryan does not classify them as such.) This account reflects accurately Ryan's career-long strategy of achieving justice through moral arguments for legislative action to secure natural rights.

Some Comparisons

In sum, Ryan sought to advance justice by teaching the natural law for industrial ethics in an effort to garner political support for legislative reforms. Whereas Rauschenbusch envisioned and encouraged social movements that could transform an evolving natural and social order (including church, state, and economic institutions), Ryan sought legislative reforms to bring economic institutions into line with an established and knowable natural order. Again, the differences can be overdrawn. We have seen that Rauschenbusch criticized dogmatic socialists for refusing to support piecemeal legislative reforms, and Ryan believed a full realization of justice awaited changes in religious and moral values.

---

315. See Curran, *American Catholic Social Ethics,* 70–71; McShane, *"Sufficiently Radical,"* 7–56 passim.
316. Ryan, *Social Doctrine in Action,* 44.
317. Ibid., 277–278 (my emphasis).

we cannot imagine Ryan addressing the church about how a "new ¿gelism" or relatively indiscriminate church support for the labor ¿ovement and the socialist movement could be a social force for justice. Nor can we imagine Rauschenbusch writing essays in detailed response to specific government policies: the Supreme Court's legal argument against the constitutionality of minimum wage laws, recommendations regarding the bituminous and anthracite coal industries, or the investment valuations upon which public utility rates are set.[318]

Differences on how benefits and burdens should be distributed inevitably accompanied these differences in strategy. As we have noted, Ryan was much less willing to countenance the "excesses" of social movements that sacrifice individual rights for the sake of future justice. He, for example, after conceding that socialist proposals for public ownership of some capital presently held privately are valid, criticized socialists for unjustly permitting the confiscation of capital without compensation.[319]

CONCLUSION

There were significant differences in the policies Ryan and Rauschenbusch advocated, reflecting differences in their theories and conceptions of justice. Ryan's program for reform, based on individual needs, was organized around his proposal for a legal minimum wage, was less egalitarian, and was more reticent to sacrifice individual rights for the sake of a future common good. More remarkable, however, are the similarities between this Roman Catholic opposed to socialism and the Protestant who considered himself a Christian socialist. The similarity runs much deeper than their common concern for justice for the working class. In that, Niebuhr and many others joined them.

At a deeper level, they shared a view of justice that committed them to economic institutions and policies that provide opportunities for individuals to develop their natural interests and desires toward an ideal for the perfection of the human personality. Both envisioned a just economic order in which natural individual interests and claims upon goods could be respected without leaving persons free to pursue whatever ends they prefer. Ryan did not fully develop his proposals for the structure of economic relations until the thirties, but even in these earlier writings he

318. Ryan, *The Supreme Court and the Minimum Wage;* idem, "The Senate Bill of the Regulation for the Soft Coal Industry," *Catholic Charities Review* 13 (June 1929): 184–186; idem, *Declining Liberty,* 268–280.
319. Ryan and Hillquit, *Socialism,* 52–55.

shared Rauschenbusch's concern to construct and limit property rights in order to enable the fullest development of the personality. In formulating principles of justice and economic policies with the intent of supporting the development of individuals' natural interests and desires toward a high moral character, Ryan and Rauschenbusch shared a view of justice in sharp contrast with Niebuhr's.

4

JUSTICE: A STRATEGY FOR APPROXIMATING LOVE

Reinhold Niebuhr did not inherit the theological or ethical resources that he applied to issues of economic justice from his family and community or from the German Protestant religious tradition in which he grew up. In this respect he was more like Rauschenbusch than Ryan. Like Rauschenbusch, Niebuhr came to an organizing perspective for his social ethics only after revising his inherited religious and moral views through the experiences of more than a decade in the parish ministry.

The first part of this chapter is the story of how Niebuhr came to the organizing perspective for his social ethics. Taking my cue from James Gustafson, I will show how the "overarching moral frame of reference" in Niebuhr's theological ethics was "the tension between the ideal and the actual."[1] Gustafson believes Niebuhr inherited this tension from the social gospel tradition.[2] Gustafson is probably correct in the general sense that Niebuhr, throughout his life, thought about ethics in terms of the relation between perfect love embodied in Jesus and the actual conditions of human relations. We should not, however, take this indebtedness to the social gospel to mean that the early Niebuhr adopted

---

1. Gustafson, "Theology in the Service of Ethics," 38; see also Stone, *Reinhold Niebuhr,* 49.
2. Gustafson, "Theology in the Service of Ethics," 34.

Rauschenbusch's social gospel perspective, which he then rejected as he developed his Christian realism in the early thirties. This way of reading Niebuhr in relation to Rauschenbusch has, I believe, led to considerable confusion. I am unaware of any evidence that Niebuhr ever carefully read or completely understood Rauschenbusch.[3] He certainly never fully endorsed Rauschenbusch's social ethics. Niebuhr's conception of the ideal, the actual, and the tension between them never closely paralleled Rauschenbusch's understanding of the kingdom of God in history. Nevertheless, the tension between the ideal and the actual was already central in Niebuhr's writings during his ministry in the twenties. It continued, in a radically modified form, to be the orienting perspective for his ethics after he became a Christian realist in the early thirties.

This chapter begins with an account of Niebuhr's understanding of the tension between the ideal and actual in the late twenties. In light of that background, I then analyze Niebuhr's revised understanding of that tension in the early thirties. This radical modification in his moral frame of reference shaped Niebuhr's Christian realism, which justified his earliest conception of justice. Gustafson properly observes that Niebuhr never explicitly developed a theory of justice nor explicated his criteria of justice in relation to classical or contemporary conceptions of justice.[4] (We will note later why an attempt to compare his criteria for justice with the ideal principles of philosophical conceptions would have been antithetical to his conception of justice.) Nevertheless, I believe we can ferret out of Niebuhr writings, even during the thirties, a set of working standards by which he assessed the distribution of benefits and burdens by the major structures of society. In this sense, Niebuhr's writings contain what Rawls calls a conception of justice. Hence, this chapter includes an account of the conception of justice Niebuhr held during the thirties followed by an interpretation of Niebuhr's application of that conception to what he considered the major policy issues: ownership of productive property, democratic government, and support for the Marx-

---

3. Christopher Lasch observes that Niebuhr bypassed analysis of Rauschenbusch in Niebuhr's criticism of the social gospel. Lasch considers it especially remarkable that Niebuhr "disingenuously" excused himself from close analysis of Rauschenbusch on the occasion of delivering the Rauschenbusch lectures in Rochester in 1934. See Christopher Lasch, "Religious Contributions to Social Movements: Walter Rauschenbusch, the Social Gospel, and Its Critics," *The Journal of Religious Ethics* 18, no. 1 (Spring 1990): 13 n. 5. I previously commented on how Niebuhr, in one of his rare interpretations of Rauschenbusch, wrongly charged that Rauschenbusch had no conception of the class struggle and thought a just society could be achieved by educational and purely moral means (*supra*, Introduction, 18; see Niebuhr: "Is Peace or Justice the Goal?" 276). The description fit Niebuhr's views in the twenties more closely than it did Rauschenbusch's.

4. Gustafson, "Theology in the Service of Ethics," 33.

ist proletarian movement. The chapter concludes with developments in Niebuhr's thought that led to his more focused theological investigations in the late thirties.

I contend that the Christian realism Niebuhr developed in the early thirties led him to conceive of justice as a strategy for approximating the social ideal entailed by Christian love under the actual conditions in which the ideal transcends all historical possibilities. I further believe that after *Moral Man and Immoral Society* in 1932, there was no fundamental change in this realist theory or in this general conception of justice. Why not, then, treat Niebuhr's writings after 1932 as a unified whole, as I did Rauschenbusch's writings? There are two reasons.

First, Niebuhr provided no sustained theological support for his early Christian realism. He did not offer a highly developed theological backing for his realism until he delivered the Gifford Lectures in 1939, later published in two volumes as *The Nature and Destiny of Man*. Niebuhr, even more so than Rauschenbusch, formulated a revision of his received theology after having set forth his social ethics. He did not turn to a concentrated study of theology until a crisis in his thinking about justice precipitated the need to rethink the theology he had received in his formal education. We must not take this point to mean Niebuhr's early writings were bereft of theology. I concur with Paul Merkley's judgment that Niebuhr's "politics cannot at any point be disengaged . . . from his theology,"[5] even during his idealist period in the twenties.[6] Indeed, we will see (in the conclusion of this chapter) that conflict between his inchoate theological anthropology and interpretation of history and his Marxist politics in *Moral Man and Immoral Society* led him naturally, if not inevitably, to a more systematic study of theology. Nevertheless, we will be truer to the development of Niebuhr's thought if we treat the theological bases of his Christian realist theory of justice in connection with the deepening and refinement of his theology in the late thirties and forties.

Second, even casual students of Niebuhr know that he changed his views regarding Marxism, democracy, and public ownership of property during the forties. Niebuhr also developed a new interest in narrower policy questions, issues that did not involve changes in the fundamental political and economic structures of society. This shift in the policies Niebuhr advocated was more dramatic than changes that took place in Ryan's thinking about policies, which we will examine in the next

---

5. Paul Merkley, *Reinhold Niebuhr: A Political Account* (Montreal: McGill-Queen's University Press, 1975), viii.
6. Ibid., 22.

chapter. The new policies Ryan advocated were merely an extended application of his conception of justice in the context of new circumstances. Niebuhr altered his position on fundamental policy issues on the basis of changes in his working standards of justice, particularly a de-emphasis on equality as the goal for justice. These changes in policies and the working standards of justice were, however, still based on Niebuhr's Christian realist strategy to approximate the social ideal of love under the actual conditions of history. I will explain this shift in Niebuhr's thinking in terms of the theological deepening and refinement of his overarching frame of reference and of his interpretation of unfolding political and economic events in the United States and Europe, especially the Soviet Union. Despite the constancy of the tension between the ideal and the actual as Niebuhr's orienting perspective, the revisions in his thinking are sufficient to demand separate chapters and a lengthier analysis of Niebuhr's thought than either Rauschenbusch or Ryan require.

For these two reasons, I have separated my analysis of Niebuhr into three chapters. The present chapter, dealing with his theory and conception of justice in the early thirties, does not offer a distinct explication of Niebuhr's ethics in terms of Gustafson's first three base points. Chapter 6 will examine the interpretations of human nature and agency, of history, and of God that Niebuhr developed in the late thirties and early forties. His interpretations of these three base points constitute his Christian realist justification for a conception of justice. Chapter 6 concludes with a brief revisit to Niebuhr's understanding of the tension between the ideal and the actual. Chapter 7 considers Niebuhr's modification in his earlier realist strategy for approximating love. It treats Niebuhr's revision of his working standards of justice, that is, Gustafson's fourth base point, and the policies Niebuhr advocated in the forties and fifties.

THE IDEAL AND THE ACTUAL—I: THE IDEAL IS REAL

Niebuhr, like Rauschenbusch, grew up in the home of a German immigrant minister and decided to follow his father into the ministry. After attending German Evangelical Synod schools in preparation for his ministry—he received a B.D. from Eden Theological Seminary in 1913—Niebuhr entered the recently rejuvenated Divinity School at Yale, from which he received an M.A. in 1915. From this combination of formative influences, Niebuhr, at age 23, entered the ministry in Detroit with decidedly different attitudes from those Rauschenbusch brought to the Second German Baptist Church in New York. Niebuhr was a self-described liberal[7] imbued with what he would later remember as "the mild moralistic idealism, which I had identified with the Christian faith."[8] Niebuhr did not come to Detroit to save souls. He was not averse to applying religion to social issues. Even before entering Yale, Niebuhr had preached that the ethic of Jesus requires capitalists to " 'voluntarily release some of their fat profits . . . to lose themselves for their employees.' "[9] The Niebuhr who came to Bethel Church in Detroit was clearly like neither the young Rauschenbusch before Hell's Kitchen nor the mature Rauschenbusch who sided with the interests of the social movement.

Neither was Bethel an impoverished church in which Niebuhr would be shaken by ministering to the unemployed and families of children dying due to unhealthy conditions. It was a small middle-class congregation, which increased in size as Detroit grew. Its German-oriented congregation became more integrated into American culture and somewhat more oriented to reform under Niebuhr's tutelage. Unlike Rauschenbusch, Niebuhr did not need a first-hand engagement with poverty to evoke a passion for social reform. He was already convinced of the need for reform. The question was what kind of reform and how it could be achieved. What Niebuhr gained from his Detroit ministry was time to read, opportunities to write and travel in order to learn from some of the leading social reformers of the period, and the experience of observing industrial relations in one of the most important manufacturing cities in the United States. Richard Fox puts it nicely: "There was no better laboratory than Detroit for observing the industrial conflicts of modern America."[10] Niebuhr's thirteen-year parish ministry provided a laboratory for making observations, not a crucible for a sensitizing encounter with poverty. His observations soon convinced him that the "mild moral idealism" of his more youthful liberalism was not sufficient to realize the reform of industrial relations in America. Reform would require a new social and economic order, and Niebuhr became increasingly disillusioned about achieving the new order through the liberalism that he believed characterized the Protestant theology of his day.

Already in 1920 he was criticizing churches for depending upon the

---

7. Richard Wightman Fox, *Reinhold Niebuhr: A Biography* (New York: Pantheon Books, 1985), 39.

8. Reinhold Niebuhr, "Intellectual Autobiography," in *Reinhold Niebuhr: His Religious, Social, and Political Thought,* ed. Charles W. Kegley (New York: Pilgrim Press, 1984), 6.

9. Fox, *Reinhold Niebuhr,* 23, citing Reinhold Niebuhr, "Sermon at Union Services," typescript of sermon delivered in Lincoln, Illinois, August 17, 1913.

10. Ibid., 85.

conversion of individuals to bring democracy to business. Democracy in industry, he argued, "must be written into the very constitution of civilization" and will involve "some degree of socialization of property." "Our economic order needs reconstruction," he asserted.[11] In 1922, he helped establish the Detroit chapter of the Fellowship for a Christian Social Order, an educational organization considering ways to reform industrial capitalism for the benefit of labor.[12] By 1922, Niebuhr chided the middle class in the church for remaining neutral in the struggle between labor and capital and for supporting strikes in theory but never in practice.[13] In 1923, he asserted that Christianity ought to disassociate itself from "the organization of industrial civilization."[14] Niebuhr was clearly on record for the need to reform the economic order before his celebrated attacks on Henry Ford's claim to have made industry humane through management practices.[15]

Simultaneously, he was criticizing both secular and religious liberalism for lacking the resources required for the task of reform. Already in 1919, Niebuhr wrote to the *New Republic* about his disillusionment with secular liberalism. He concluded a letter criticizing the Treaty of Versailles: "We need something less circumspect than liberalism to save the world."[16] By 1923, Niebuhr was expressing disenchantment with the capacity of naturalistic liberal theology to muster a prophetic stance toward the old order.[17]

We should not take these early criticisms of liberalism to mean that Niebuhr was beginning to doubt the effectiveness of applying the ideal to actual human conditions or that he was pessimistic about progress. The

---

11. Reinhold Niebuhr, "The Church and the Industrial Crisis," *The Biblical World* 54, no. 6 (November 1920): 590–592.

12. Fox, *Reinhold Niebuhr*, 75–76.

13. Reinhold Niebuhr, "The Church and the Middle Class," *The Christian Century* 39, no. 49 (December 7, 1922): 1513–1515.

14. Reinhold Niebuhr, "Wanted: A Christian Morality," *The Christian Century* 40, no. 7 (February 15, 1923): 202; see also Fox, *Reinhold Niebuhr*, 77.

15. Niebuhr's articles attacking Ford appeared in *The Christian Century* in 1926. We should probably not make too much of the contrast with Ryan's praise for Ford in the first edition of *Distributive Justice* in 1916 and in *Social Reconstruction* in 1920 (see *supra*, chapter three, 178). Richard Fox points out that Niebuhr did not criticize Ford until other attacks on Ford's policies had made such criticism acceptable. It was more daring to criticize Ford in the early twenties. See Fox, *Reinhold Niebuhr*, 94–95. Ryan retained his praise for Ford in the 1927 edition of *Distributive Justice* but excluded it from the 1942 revision. See John A. Ryan, *Distributive Justice: The Right and Wrong of the Present Distribution of Wealth*, 2d ed. (New York: Macmillan, 1927), 225; idem, *Distributive Justice*, 3d ed., 191.

16. Reinhold Niebuhr, "The Twilight of Liberalism," *The New Republic* 19, no. 241 (June 14, 1919): 218.

17. See Niebuhr, "Wanted: A Christian Morality," 201–203; Fox, *Reinhold Niebuhr*, 83–84.

essential contribution religion has to make to the attainment of the "ideal of human brotherhood," Niebuhr maintained, is found "in the gospel of Jesus."[18] Early criticisms of liberalism also appeared in Niebuhr's diary, published in 1929 as *Leaves from the Notebook of a Tamed Cynic*. In a 1925 entry he wrote:

> It seems pathetic that liberalism has too little appreciation of the tragedy of life to understand the cross. . . . [L]ove pays such a high price for its objectives and sets its objectives so high that they can never be attained. There is therefore always a foolish and a futile aspect to love's quest which give [*sic*] it the note of tragedy.[19]

Here again Niebuhr's criticism was that liberalism failed to appreciate the difficulty of the task of social reform rather than a questioning of liberals' commitment to ideals or to optimism about progress. In the paragraph following this passage, Niebuhr wrote: "What makes this tragedy redemptive is that the foolishness of love is revealed as wisdom in the end and its futility becomes the occasion for new moral striving."[20] In a slightly later entry, Niebuhr commented: "Love conquers the world, but its victory is not an easy one. The price of all creativity and redemption is pain."[21]

The initial changes that Niebuhr's Detroit parish experience wrought in the simple liberal idealism that he brought with him from Yale are summarized in his first book. According to Fox, *Does Civilization Need Religion?*, written from 1923 to 1927, collates Niebuhr's religious and ethical views as they developed during the midtwenties. It reveals little of his positions on political and economic policies. "It was a general moral stance, a proclamation of radical intent."[22] But it does set out the religio-moral frame of reference by which Niebuhr addressed the social problem.

In that volume, Niebuhr posed the moral problem in the general terms he inherited from the social gospel: How can the religious ideal be realized in history where the forces of nature seem to resist it? Niebuhr, however, understood the ideal and the actual and their relation differently from Rauschenbusch, for whom the relation between Jesus' ethic of love and the actual human condition was understood in the context of evolutionary social science. Thus, the way in which Niebuhr under-

---

18. Niebuhr, "Wanted: A Christian Morality," 203.
19. Reinhold Niebuhr, *Leaves from the Notebook of a Tamed Cynic* (New York: Richard R. Smith, 1929; repr. ed., Louisville, Ky.: Westminster/John Knox Press, 1990), 85–86.
20. Ibid., 86.
21. Ibid., 102.
22. Fox, *Reinhold Niebuhr*, 101–102.

stood the question and his subsequent answer differed markedly from Rauschenbusch's.

For Niebuhr, the religious ideal asserts the dignity and the worth of the human personality in harmony with itself, nature, and other humans. These harmonious relations occur where Jesus' love reigns. In modern society, this ideal is threatened on two fronts: (1) intellectually, because the naturalism encouraged by science threatens the idea of a personal God who values the human personality; and (2) ethically, because the impersonality of mechanized relationships in civilization threatens to destroy care for the worth of each person.[23] Liberal theology, Niebuhr believed, had dealt primarily with the first problem in an effort to compensate for the inadequacies of traditional religion in the face of modern science.[24] This focus had failed to make civilization ethical, and the failure had resulted in indifference and hostility toward religion by the industrial workers, who suffer most from the impersonality of civilization.[25]

For Niebuhr, the ethical problem was paramount. The primary test of religious ideas is in the moral fruits they bear, not in their intellectual consistency.[26] Religion must be made useful for resolving the social problem. Liberal theology had not been useful because it relaxed the tension between the ideal and the actual situation of civilization. "[I]t compounds the pure idealism of Jesus with the calculated practicalities of the age and attempts to give the resultant compromise the prestige of absolute authority."[27] The consequence was a religious sanctification of prudence within the social order, a prudence that hindered the ethical reconstruction of society.[28] The religious ideal must be detached from and challenge the actual; only then will it be vital enough to provide enthusiasm for a moral adventure or quest to save civilization from its disregard for the dignity of the personality.

The actual is a formidable foe. It is strengthened by the complexities of the modern impersonal economic order, but its roots are deeper. The roots of the actual are in the conflicts of interest that arise from the unqualified natural will-to-live. This unqualified will-to-live manifests itself most forcefully in the predatory nature of collectivities like nations and classes. Niebuhr did not believe that the problem was based in the

---

23. Reinhold Niebuhr, *Does Civilization Need Religion?* (New York: Macmillan, 1927), 1–18.

24. Ibid., 7–12; idem, "Impotent Liberalism," *The Christian Century* 43, no. 6 (February 11, 1926): 167.

25. Niebuhr, *Does Civilization Need Religion?* 12–16; idem, "Impotent Liberalism," 167.

26. Niebuhr, *Does Civilization Need Religion?* 210, 31.

27. Ibid., 78.

28. Ibid., 76.

inevitably sinful nature of humans. He casually rejected the notion of original sin[29] and declared that humans are neither totally good nor bad.[30] Niebuhr did not understand the actual as a persistent human tendency to sin. He understood it as a capitulation to natural human inclinations. "[M]en have suffered longer from the sins of nature than from the sins of man."[31] The roots of the conflict that crush the personality are two: the natural animal instincts that must be qualified if humans are to live together in harmony, and the unwillingness or inability to transcend and qualify natural desires and interests. The foe is ultimately the natural inclinations of humans. Sin, Niebuhr thought, is the failure to understand this foe as it is manifest in political and economic relations and the consequent lack of enthusiasm for a moral fight with it. The human personality cannot be developed without lifting "life above the level of nature."[32] Religious idealism must contend with the forces of nature.[33] The naturalistic and pantheistic elements that have crept into liberal theology make it ill-suited for the battle. By identifying God "with automatic processes," it hallows "the necessary [as perceived by naturalism?] limitations of life" rather than "seeking to overcome them."[34] Thus, liberalism sanctifies the foe, making it more powerful.

Despite the power of these natural individual and collective interests, they can, Niebuhr contended, be defeated. But victory will be won only through a vital religious idealism that inspires persons and groups to sacrifice their natural interests and trust others to do the same. Niebuhr's answer to the inadequacies of his earlier mild moral idealism seems to have been "robust moral idealism."[35] He called persons to a quest, albeit self-critical, for absolute standards[36] and to trust in the absolute values of the religious ideal.[37] Such idealism appears absurd in the present order. It will, however, be self-verifying as it creates an atmosphere of mutual trust in which human action becomes trustworthy.[38] Faith "tends to create what it assumes."[39] Niebuhr's method for dealing with the epistemological problem that had occupied liberalism and forced it into con-

29. Ibid., 206.
30. Ibid., 109.
31. Ibid., 25–26.
32. Ibid., 239.
33. Ibid., 240.
34. Reinhold Niebuhr, "Our Secularized Civilization," *The Christian Century* 43, no. 16 (April 16, 1926): 509.
35. Niebuhr, *Does Civilization Need Religion?* 223.
36. Ibid., 223–224.
37. Niebuhr, "Our Secularized Civilization," 508.
38. Niebuhr, *Does Civilization Need Religion?* 152.
39. Reinhold Niebuhr, "The Use of Force," in *Pacifism in the Modern World,* ed. Devere Allen (New York: Garland Publishing, 1971), 24. First published in 1929.

cessions to naturalism was to assert that the moral fruits of idealism would prove its understanding of God. In 1929–30, he was still arguing that belief in God, the spiritual harmony of the world, and the ultimate law of love are derived from a "moral and spiritual adventure" that proceeds on these assumptions rather than from treating the understanding of God as an intellectual problem. Moral experience shaped by this adventure, Niebuhr thought, would create its own proof.[40]

To be sure, Niebuhr admitted, religious idealism must be combined with "social intelligence." Social intelligence comprehends the complexities of modern economic and political life and produces awareness that the roots of the social problem lie in conflicting economic and collective interests that defy easy resolution. It prevents idealism from degenerating into a sentimentality that does not understand the formidable actual situation it is challenging.[41] This criticism of the sentimentalism of unintelligent idealism reflected Niebuhr's growing doubts about the power of love to forge a new order. Niebuhr recognized that love that qualifies self-assertion also curtails the use of political force and conflict required by social intelligence, but his doubts about the effectiveness of love were veiled by replacing sentimentalism with "robust" love.[42] Only robust idealism, which envisions a new order of mutual trust, can defeat the cynicism of mere social intelligence,[43] for example, the cynicism of the Marxist strategy of class struggle as the way to a new order.[44]

For the Niebuhr of the twenties, a radical tension between the ideal and the actual was the key to providing the religious resources to achieve a new social order in which the dignity of each personality is affirmed in harmony and mutual trust. A religious ideal, which transcends and contends with natural human inclinations and present realities, can be realized in history. Sin can be overcome. The religious ideal can be victorious. It needs only a social strategy based on the "robust love" that qualifies self-assertion and forgives as Jesus taught his disciples to forgive. This love could "overcome momentary disappointments" and subdue "evil by its unswerving confidence in the good."[45]

A Niebuhr confident of the adequacy of religious resources for dealing with the social problem could write:

---

40. Reinhold Niebuhr, "Religion and Moral Experience," in *What Religion Means to Me,* ed. Reinhold Niebuhr et al. (Garden City, N.Y.: Doubleday, Doran, & Co., 1929), 57; idem, "Christian Faith in the Modern World," in *Ventures in Belief,* ed. Henry P. Van Dusen (New York: Charles Scribner's Sons), 5–22, especially 16, 21–22.
41. Niebuhr, *Does Civilization Need Religion?* 161.
42. Fox, *Reinhold Niebuhr,* 100, 103.
43. Niebuhr, *Does Civilization Need Religion?* 162.
44. Ibid., 144–148.
45. Ibid., 42.

Only the foolishness of faith knows how to assume the brotherhood of man and to create it by the help of the assumption. A religious ideal is always a little absurd because it insists on the truth of what ought to be true but is only partly true; it is however the ultimate wisdom, because reality slowly approaches the ideals which are implicit in its life. . . . The creative and redemptive force is a faith which *defies the real in the name of the ideal, and subdues it.* . . . The religious interpretation of the world is essentially an insistence that the *ideal is real* and that *the real can be understood only in the light of the ideal.*[46]

This is a religious idealism that Rauschenbusch never contemplated.[47] Interpreters of Niebuhr often liken this period of Niebuhr's thought to the social gospel.[48] They are mistaken, at least insofar as they have Rauschenbusch in mind. Fox says that the Niebuhr of the midtwenties is distinguishable from Rauschenbusch only by the stridency of Niebuhr's prose.[49] The differences were more substantial. Rauschenbusch never believed that Jesus' ethic of love was in a battle with the best of modern science or that it could raise humans above their natural interests. Rauschenbusch believed that just criteria are required to discriminate between excessive acquisitive interests and morally healthy interests in acquisition for the sake of self-preservation and development. Niebuhr, during the twenties, could not have consistently formulated such criteria. Justice discriminates among conflicting interests. Niebuhr still believed robust love could eliminate conflicting interests.

These assertions of similarities between Niebuhr and the social gospel do, however, reveal something about Niebuhr's criticism of liberalism in the twenties. Part of the intent of such comparisons seems to be to show that Niebuhr, despite his attacks on liberalism, had not gone beyond salient aspects of liberalism that he would reject in his later realist stage. *Does Civilization Need Religion?* accepted the liberal assumptions that the ideal is applicable to the actual human condition and that a forceful application of the ideal will produce moral progress. In religious terms, the ethic of Jesus' love is applicable to the social order, and hope for the kingdom of God in history is justified, not an illusion. Niebuhr did not fault religious liberalism for applying the ethic of Jesus to issues that required a realist conception of justice. He chastised it for failing to develop "any real fervor for the advanced ethical positions of Jesus."[50] The failure of

---

46. Ibid., 44–46, my emphasis.
47. See *supra*, chapter one, 37.
48. Fox, *Reinhold Niebuhr,* 90; Merkley, *Reinhold Niebuhr,* 28–29; Stone, *Reinhold Niebuhr,* 44.
49. Fox, *Reinhold Niebuhr,* 90.
50. Niebuhr, "Impotent Liberalism," 167.

liberalism, Niebuhr thought, was not its illusions about what idealism could achieve but its blurring of the tension between the ideal and the actual. This blurring robbed idealism of its vitality and robustness. Thus, liberalism was impotent to achieve the goal for which it legitimately hoped.

The writings on religion and social reform that emerged from Niebuhr's experience in Detroit do not constitute a major contribution to American theological thinking about justice. They are not the writings for which he is justifiably respected. I have treated them at some length for two reasons. First, Niebuhr's understanding of the tension between the ideal and the actual in the twenties clearly shows that he was never aligned with Rauschenbusch's theological ethics. When, in the early thirties, Niebuhr's realism went beyond his own earlier "robust idealism," he was not, his own later perceptions notwithstanding, rejecting Rauschenbusch's social gospel. He had never accepted it. I doubt we will be able to understand fully Rauschenbusch or Niebuhr until we get beyond the notion that Niebuhr's realist refutation of his own earlier liberal idealism explains simultaneously his differences from Rauschenbusch. That notion is mistaken. Second, the increasing tension between the ideal and the actual that characterizes the development in Niebuhr's social thought during the twenties sets the stage for understanding his Christian realism. I will explain his Christian realism as a tightening of this increasing tension to the point that the ideal is no longer realizable or directly relevant to social relations in history. The tension between the ideal and the actual was the organizing perspective for Niebuhr's social thought in the twenties. In radically revised form, it remained the organizing perspective for the theological ethics of his Christian realism. "The polarity between the ideal and the real was contained within his thought by 1927," Ronald Stone observes, "but the tension between the two required further development before the mature political philosophy of Reinhold Niebuhr would appear."[51] We turn now to that development.

THE IDEAL AND THE ACTUAL—II: CHRISTIAN REALISM

Fox argues that by the time *Does Civilization Need Religion?* was published Niebuhr's confidence in religious idealism was beginning to crack.[52] The crack slowly developed into a ravine that could not be bridged by adding robustness to love. In 1931, Niebuhr was still writing

---

51. Stone, *Reinhold Niebuhr*, 51.
52. Fox, *Reinhold Niebuhr*, 90, 103–104.

about "a heroic defiance of the forces of nature" and "vigorous action which reveals the potency and the potentialities of the moral will," but these were more hollow assertions than confident convictions. "It is not easy," he wrote, "to maintain this antithesis [no longer merely tension between the ideal and the real] without losing confidence in the *possibility of realizing the ideal,* or to restore that confidence without effacing the distinction between the two."[53]

Between the publication of *Does Civilization Need Religion?* and this last gasp of his "robust idealism," Niebuhr moved from Detroit to become associate professor of Christian ethics at Union Theological Seminary in New York, and the Depression began. Because observations in Detroit had already begun to undermine his confidence in idealism, these events, though significant, do not account for the shift that occurred in Niebuhr's understanding of the tension between the ideal and the actual. Although his location in New York put Niebuhr in closer contact with a variety of Protestant socialists, Fox perceptively observes that the chief theme in *Moral Man and Immoral Society* went beyond the unifying commitment of all of these colleagues. That theme was not Niebuhr's cautious acceptance of selective violence nor his support for the proletarian mission. It was his repudiation, "in the name of Protestantism itself, of the historic liberal Protestant quest for the Kingdom of God."[54] Niebuhr's location at Union no doubt gave this shift in his thinking more exposure. But I doubt that the influence of Union nor any combination of influences can adequately explain the change.[55] The creative genius of Niebuhr himself must be part of the explanation.

Whatever its sources, the publication of *Moral Man and Immoral Society* in 1932 was the watershed event for Niebuhr's Christian realism. He gave up *"the possibility of realizing the ideal"* and abandoned his hope that the ethical resources of religion are sufficient for the task of addressing the social problem. The tension between the ideal and the actual remained his moral frame of reference, but he changed his understanding of the content of the ideal and of the actual so that the tension became irresolvable in history. The religious ideal was still a

---

53. Reinhold Niebuhr, "Let the Liberal Churches Stop Fooling Themselves!" *The Christian Century* 48, no. 12 (March 25, 1931): 403–404, my emphasis.

54. Fox, *Reinhold Niebuhr,* 140.

55. Niebuhr's position at Union was obviously more important in offering opportunities to cultivate his increasing interest in theology that culminated in the publication of *The Nature and Destiny of Man.* (Detroit ministers are unlikely to receive an invitation to deliver the Gifford Lectures.) Both Fox and Merkley, who offer incompatible accounts of the principal sources for Niebuhr's Christian realism, note Niebuhr's increasing contact with European theologians after his move to Union. See ibid., 123–128, 160–161; Merkley, *Reinhold Niebuhr,* 65–81.

resource for social ethics, but it was now considered inadequate to cope with the intractable realities of power and conflict, even as supplemented by social intelligence. The ideal of Christian love embodied in the ethic of Jesus is an impossibility in history; it is no longer directly applicable to the social problem. This new understanding of the tension between the ideal and actual constituted Niebuhr's Christian realism. Because it presumed the persistence of conflicting interests, it required a theory and conception of justice.

The Ideal

Niebuhr might have responded to his growing discovery that actual experience is intractable to love by reassessing his understanding of God and the ultimate law of love. He did not. He asserted the reality of love by pushing it beyond possibility in moral experience. Christian love was the ideal for Niebuhr before 1932 and remained so thereafter. His earlier references to sacrificing individual and collective interests, to qualifying the will-to-live and self-assertion, and to unqualified forgiveness were extended to require total disinterestedness. Niebuhr heightened the conception of love beyond all possibility of achievement in collective human relations.[56]

Love, he said in *Moral Man and Immoral Society,* absolutizes the principle of disinterestedness and imparts transcendent worth to the lives of others.[57] Disinterestedness is not just a negation of interest in one's own welfare nor avoiding the prejudice of preferring one person's welfare to another's. (It is neither altruism nor impartiality.) It prohibits all assertions of the self that resist any, including unjust, interests of others. Even assertions on the behalf of others are prohibited. Love is interested in the well-being of others, but it cannot assert itself on behalf of their interests. "It submits to any demands, however unjust, and yields to any claims, however inordinate, rather than assert self-interest against another."[58] By "self-interest" Niebuhr means any assertion of interests whether it be for one's own rights or for another's, as is evidenced by his criticism of Gandhi for failing to recognize that even "soul-force" is a form of resistance that falls short of the ethic of Jesus.[59]

---

56. Niebuhr's later observation that the social gospel did not understand the height of the pinnacle of love (Niebuhr, "Walter Rauschenbusch in Historical Perspective," 38) was reflected in the content of his conception of love in 1932.

57. Niebuhr, *Moral Man and Immoral Society* (New York: Charles Scribner's Sons, 1932), 71.

58. Ibid., 264.

59. Ibid., 241–246.

Within history, this love is self-contradictory. As disinterestedness, love transcends justice. Justice requires discriminating among the competing interests of different groups, resisting some interests and promoting others. But as a commitment to the transcendent worth of each individual, love also impels the Christian to secure justice for others. Love safeguarding the worth of individuals amidst the conflicts of history requires justice. But disinterested love prohibits actions that are required to protect the worth of individuals against others who would destroy it. Love both requires justice and prohibits actions to secure it.

Love continued to motivate Niebuhr's passion for justice, but it was no longer an effective means for achieving justice. Niebuhr, therefore, dropped his former references to the dignity and worth of the personality as a basis for social ethics. He now referred to this notion as an attenuated symbol of liberalism.[60] Presumably, affirming the worth of the individual is only a transcendent possibility beyond all possibilities in history.

Love is not intrinsically confined to relations between individuals. It entails a social ideal. In a 1932 essay, "The Ethic of Jesus and the Social Problem," Niebuhr defined that social ideal as a combination of anarchism and communism. Perfect love, he said, would obviate the need for coercion because persons would not transgress their neighbors' rights (i.e., anarchism). Differences in privilege and the distinction between thine and mine would disappear in communism.[61] This ideal contains three elements, namely, the perfect harmony of all life (by eliminating conflict and the need for coercion), absolute freedom (anarchy), and absolute equality (communism). These three elements became constitutive for the understanding of original perfection in creation that Niebuhr developed in *The Nature and Destiny of Man*.[62] (These elements were also crucial for Niebuhr's later formulation of the twin transcendent principles of freedom and equality[63] and still later the third principle of order as peace.)[64] This social ideal relates Christian love to social relations, but it is even less attainable for a social order in history than love is for individuals.

---

60. Reinhold Niebuhr, "Christianity Today," *New York Herald Tribune*, 17 Sept. 1933, sec. 7, 18.

61. Reinhold Niebuhr, "The Ethic of Jesus and the Social Problem," in *Love and Justice*, ed. D. B. Robertson (Cleveland: World Publishing Co., 1957; repr., Gloucester, Mass.: Peter Smith, 1976), 32. First published in 1932.

62. Reinhold Niebuhr, *The Nature and Destiny of Man*, vol. 1: *Human Nature* (New York: Charles Scribner's Sons, 1942), 280–300.

63. Niebuhr, *An Interpretation*, 134–135; idem, *The Nature and Destiny*, vol. 2, 254.

64. Reinhold Niebuhr, "The Problem of a Protestant Social Ethic," *Union Seminary Quarterly Review* 15 (November 1959): 10.

The Actual

Niebuhr's understanding of love and the social ideal it entails did as much to sever the close link between love and justice in the social gospel as his view of the actual did. It made all assertions of interests to resist injustice a form of sin. This heightened view of love partially explains Niebuhr's increasing emphasis on sin. On this understanding of love, all natural interests contain an element of sin. But Niebuhr also changed his understanding of human nature in a way that makes actual social relations intractable to the direct application of love.

The change was not primarily in his emphasis on collective egoism, which has received so much attention. Collective egoism is obviously the most prominent theme in Niebuhr's interpretation of the actual in *Moral Man and Immoral Society,* but it was already significant in his previous writings.[65] More important for the development in his thought, he no longer understood the human selfish drive as limited to a natural impulse for "self-preservation" through the will-to-live. The human will-to-live is easily transmuted into "self-aggrandizement" through the "will-to-power."[66] In *Reflections on the End of an Era,* Niebuhr described the origins of this will-to-power in the threat that competing systems of thought and life pose to the precarious existence of a group's particular "form of life." Attempting to ward off this threat, a nation or class seeks to universalize its particular form of life by subjecting all competing forms to it.[67] When reason alone fails to convince others that the threatened group's values are universal, it endorses coercion and power over others as the means for preserving its way of life. "Thus," Niebuhr concluded in *Moral Man and Immoral Society,* "nature's harmless and justifiable strategies for preserving life, [*sic*] are transmuted in the human spirit into imperial purposes and policies."[68]

Sin rooted in the will-to-power cannot be overcome by taming humans' selfish animal impulses. Reason transmutes humans' animal impulse for self-preservation into a will to destroy or enslave others who challenge their form of life. Unlike the beasts of prey whose conquests cease when their maws are crammed, humans, in their protest against finiteness (i.e., the inevitable end of their group's form of life) give a

---

65. In addition to the previously noted appearance of this theme in *Does Civilization Need Religion?,* a 1926 entry in *Leaves* states: "Men are not very lovely in the mass. One can maintain confidence in them only by viewing them at close range." See Niebuhr, *Leaves from the Notebook,* 95.

66. Niebuhr, *Moral Man and Immoral Society,* 41–42.

67. Reinhold Niebuhr, *Reflections on the End of an Era* (New York: Charles Scribner's Sons, 1934), 6–8.

68. Niebuhr, *Moral Man and Immoral Society,* 41–44.

universal character to their imperial dreams.[69] The human appetite for power and dominion over others is insatiable.

A religious quest to realize the absolute in history is no longer a remedy for sin when sin is rooted in this will-to-power. When religion restrains the natural interests in self-preservation, they are only sublimated into more dangerous collective assertions of the will-to-power in the name of the absolute.[70] Sin is no longer a lack of enthusiasm for contending with the forces of nature. Sin inevitably appears in all efforts to subdue the actual. Here, as Langdon Gilkey observes, we have the seeds of the theological anthropology and doctrine of sin that Niebuhr developed on the basis of biblical symbols in *The Nature and Destiny of Man*.[71]

Niebuhr now joined this altered understanding of human nature to his previously developed theme of collective egoism. Consequently, conflicting collective interests can no longer be reconciled by applying the religious ideal. The stated thesis of *Moral Man and Immoral Society* is that collective egoism is more intransigent to moral and religious correction than individual egoism.[72] The will-to-power is a characteristic of individuals and not merely of social structures, such as private property or national identity, but it is manifest most vigorously in collective behavior. Niebuhr believed that rational and especially religious resources could restrain or even totally sublimate the egoism of individuals, but these sublimated interests will then manifest themselves in class or national assertions.[73] Consequently, the moral principles and religious ideals that apply to individual relations are not similarly applicable to social justice.

The Tension

These two elements of sin—the human will-to-power and its collective manifestations—which both secular and religious liberalism neglected, drove deeper the wedge between the ideal and the actual condition of man. Earlier, Niebuhr had faulted liberalism for sanctioning the present order by failing to distinguish clearly the ideal from the actual. A clear distinction would have allowed the ideal to be a resource for transforming the actual. Now that Niebuhr had heightened the tension between

---

69. Ibid., 44.

70. Ibid., 63–66.

71. Langdon Gilkey, "Reinhold Niebuhr as Political Theologian," in *Reinhold Niebuhr and the Issues of Our Time,* 161, 166–167.

72. Niebuhr, *Moral Man and Immoral Society,* xi.

73. Ibid., 40–41, 63–66.

the ideal and the actual (between love and egoism, spirit and nature), he no longer thought the ideal could be directly normative for political and economic structures. Because he had separated love from human natural capacities more sharply than did Rauschenbusch, this criticism of liberalism applied both to Rauschenbusch and to the Niebuhr of the midtwenties, albeit in different ways. It also applied to secular liberals who attempt to achieve justice through the application of rational principles. Niebuhr's ideal now transcended all possibilities *in* history. But justice had to deal with powerful interests intransigent to both rational and religious ethics. Neither rational principles of justice nor Jesus' ethic of love was directly applicable for assessing the structures of distribution.

Secular Liberalism: Rational Principles Applied

Rational principles are, Niebuhr believed, the means by which reason extends benevolent natural impulses and limits selfish ones. They attempt to specify a general distribution of benefits and burdens in a universal harmonious order of relations between selves. They fail, Niebuhr contended, because they end up in the service of powerful groups and because they do not account for the need for coercion.

Reason offers humans the capacity to transcend their natural impulses, but it then becomes subject to abuse by the will-to-power. It becomes an instrument for justifying egoism, especially in its collective manifestations.[74] The privileged classes formulate specious principles intended to justify inequalities on the basis of superior contributions to society,[75] moral superiority,[76] or peace and order.[77] These universal principles veil, with hypocritical moral illusions or even dishonest pretensions, the privileged classes' real interests in power.[78] Measured against the transcendent social ideal of communism, all inequalities are specious. Rationales for inequality can be explained only by the hypocritical self-deception or the outright lies of the intellectual servants of power. In history, where the ideal is in tension with the possibilities of the actual, Niebuhr admitted, some inequalities are justified on the basis of their social utility, but the inequalities that most rational principles attempt to justify are "clearly afterthoughts."[79] They are contrived to place a moral veneer over the ugly reality of a group's will-to-power.

---

74. Ibid., 40–41.
75. Ibid., 117–122.
76. Ibid., 122–128.
77. Ibid., 129–136.
78. Ibid., 136.
79. Ibid., 8.

Even if a rational conception of justice were possible, the ethical alone is not able to deal adequately with the coercive elements in all structures. Consequently, the relations between groups are always factors of power,[80] and the movement for justice must employ power, even though such assertions of interest fall short of what the ethical ideal demands.

Religious Liberalism: Love Applied

The religious ideal of love is purer than the rational conception of justice.[81] It rules out all assertions of interests,[82] including the will-to-live.[83] It is even harder to achieve than the rational ideal of justice.[84] Moreover, where it is approximated by some individuals, the religious ideal of love, by restraining all self-assertion, "makes for injustice by encouraging and permitting undue self-assertion in others."[85] Attempts to apply the ideal of love directly to the structures of justice can have only disastrous consequences. It does not account for conflicts of power, which can be controlled only by coercion. Protestant liberalism, however, attempts to apply love to conflicts of power. It makes the kingdom of God a goal *in* history,[86] thereby relaxing the tension between the ideal and the actual. This sentimental moralism is always an illusion, and when promulgated by Protestants of the privileged classes, it is hypocritical as well. It obscures the cruelties of economic and political life from which the privileged classes benefit.[87]

Niebuhr, in the early thirties, opposed all liberal efforts to apply a rational moral ideal or the religious ideal directly to issues of justice. All such attempts misconstrue, in one way or another, the relation between the ideal and the actual. But he also criticized two other Christian traditions that he thought dissolved the tension between the ideal and the actual by separating them entirely.

Protestant Sectarianism: Love Withdrawn

First, the Protestant sects take seriously the religious ideal as a transcendent standard for their moral lives by refusing "to be involved in the

---

80. Ibid., xxiii.
81. Ibid., 57.
82. Ibid., 60.
83. Ibid., 56.
84. Ibid., 75.
85. Ibid., 262.
86. Ibid., 82.
87. Ibid., 80.

coercion and the inequalities of the political and economic order."[88] But this way of life "does not concern itself with the social problem." Following Jesus, it ignores the social consequences of making the ideal of love normative for political and economic relations.[89] These sectarians are honest. They reject participation in the processes of history and have no expectation that they will be agents of the triumph of love in history.[90] They do not locate the ideal in the future history of civilization, but neither do they place it in tension with actual economic and political conditions. For Niebuhr, this meant that sectarians are uninterested in justice.

Christian Orthodoxy: Love Above

Second, Catholic and Protestant orthodoxy (he later treated Catholicism separately in terms of the medieval synthesis of the ideal and actual)[91] and the neo-orthodox reaction against liberalism recognize the ongoing tension between the ideal and actual without retreating from public life. They, however, dissolve the tension in public life by relegating the meaning of love to the transhistorical religious realm. Consequently, the ideal of love becomes totally irrelevant to issues of justice. There is "little disposition to challenge the basic social customs and relationships in the name of the Christian ideal." Niebuhr called the accompanying attitude toward justice "defeatism."[92]

Christian Realism: Love in Tension

In sum, Niebuhr rejected secular and religious liberalism for relaxing the tension between the ideal and the actual, and Protestant sectarianism and Christian orthodoxy for removing the tension from the political and economic arenas. The sectarians keep it vital for their lives together but remove it from the wider society. Orthodoxy permits participation in the wider society but locates the meaning of the ideal completely beyond history.

Throughout the early thirties, Niebuhr attempted to (1) maintain this tension between the ideal and the actual and (2) maintain it within the

---

88. Niebuhr, *Reflections on the End of an Era*, 112.
89. Niebuhr, *Moral Man and Immoral Society*, 263–264.
90. Niebuhr, *Reflections on the End of an Era*, 134.
91. Niebuhr, *The Nature and Destiny*, vol. 2, 134–148.
92. Niebuhr, *Moral Man and Immoral Society*, 76–78; see also idem, "Is Peace or Justice the Goal?" 275.

realm of political and economic relations. The ideal remained relevant, though not directly applicable, to issues of justice. On the one hand, the ideal ought not be "in-principled" as a standard for assessing the structures of justice[93] or be a goal within history. "The tension between spirit and nature," wrote Niebuhr, "must remain to the end of history lest the impulses of nature clothe themselves with the moral prestige of the spiritual."[94] On the other hand, the tension should not be heightened to the point that it is dissolved within history by pushing the ideal entirely beyond political and moral relations. "[V]ital religion," said Niebuhr, "catches glimpses of ultimate perfection in the very imperfections of man and history." It does not relegate "perfection completely to another world of pure transcendence."[95] Writing in response to his brother, H. Richard, he asserted that the forces of nature (realistic politics) can be used in the service of the ideal because "the world of man remains a place where nature and God, the real and the ideal, meet."[96] By maintaining the ethical tension within history, vital religion can provide a moral vigor that is relevant to the urgent moral problems of the day.[97]

I conclude, therefore, that this understanding of the tension between the ideal and the actual provided the overarching moral frame of reference that was central to Niebuhr's thought beginning in the early thirties. It was the core (which he later elaborated and refined in more explicit theological formulations of the base points) of his theory of justice. It also constituted the essentials of his Christian realism.

Christian realism was not simply, or even primarily, based on Niebuhr's rediscovery of sin. It included his ideal of love and its accompanying social ideal in tension with his increasing emphasis upon humans' sinful nature. Dennis McCann states this point well when he portrays Christian realism as a "creative tension" between two difficult truths: "an unflinching realism about human nature ultimately inspired by a religious awareness of its limits and possibilities, and an uncompromising loyalty to the absolute moral demands of Jesus."[98]

---

93. See Gustafson, "Theology in the Service of Ethics," 32–33.

94. Niebuhr, *Reflections on the End of an Era*, 136.

95. Ibid., 286.

96. Reinhold Niebuhr, "Must We Do Nothing?" *The Christian Century* 49, no. 13 (March 30, 1932): 417.

97. Niebuhr, *Reflections on the End of an Era*, 292.

98. Dennis P. McCann, *Christian Realism and Liberation Theology: Practical Theologies in Conflict* (Maryknoll, N.Y.: Orbis Books, 1981), 44. I am clearly not adopting McCann's views that this Christian realism emerged as decisive only in 1934 (ibid., 32), and that it developed out of his disenchantment with socialism and appreciation for the pragmatic style of the New Deal, ibid., 17.

THE CONCEPTION OF JUSTICE

The social ideal Niebuhr extracted from the ethic of Jesus provided direction for his conception of justice. It is not a realistic goal because it can never be fulfilled. To make this ideal directly applicable to the social order is an illusion detrimental to approximating it. It is, however, "possible of approximation . . . in actual history."[99] It is not a true possibility in actual history, but it "ought to be true" and "may be partially realised" by those who believe it to be true and "can be approximated only by those who do not regard it as impossible."[100] Niebuhr abandoned his earlier claim that the ideal of love can be realized. But if we make the "forces of nature . . . instruments of the moral ideal, a progressively higher justice and more stable peace can be achieved."[101] The recurring point is that the ideal, which remains in proper tension with the actual in Niebuhr's Christian realism, offers the direction in which a conception of justice must point. It ought to be approximated as nearly as possible.

The similarities to and differences from Rauschenbusch are instructive. Neither believed the kingdom of God is realizable within history. Both believed progress toward it is possible, though Niebuhr severely limited the prospects for long-term progress. They disagreed, however, on two crucial points. Rauschenbusch never envisioned a social ideal of perfect harmony, freedom, equality, but he did believe that the kingdom of God, as he understood it, is a goal that need not be thoroughly and permanently compromised in order to approximate it. Niebuhr, the realist, thought, no doubt rightly, that an uncompromised application of his social ideal would exacerbate injustice.

A General Principle of Justice

Niebuhr's Christian realist tension between the ideal of love and the actual human condition led him to adopt a general principle of justice that can be fairly summarized as follows: Utilize whatever intellectual, moral, religious, and political resources will produce the best consequences for approximating the social ideal entailed by Jesus' ethic of love. Justice is then a *strategy for approximating the social ideal of love*. This principle was operative in Niebuhr's thought throughout the remainder of his life.

The question of what specific standards should be used to assess the

---

99. Niebuhr, *Moral Man and Immoral Society*, 22.
100. Ibid., 81.
101. Ibid., 256.

basic structure of society now became, What standards (for actions, attitudes, dispositions, etc.) are the best instruments for approximating the social ideal? Unlike most conceptions of justice, including Rauschenbusch's and Ryan's, the purpose of Niebuhr's criteria for justice was not to determine what pattern of distribution of benefits and burdens would be ideally just. All such criteria assume a discrimination among conflicting interests of individuals and groups that could be called ideally just. The social ideal of love admits no such a discrimination among conflicting interests. It is a perfect harmony of interests in absolute freedom and absolute equality. Thus, no criterion or combination of criteria such as needs, earned income, economic contributions, liberty, and so forth, can determine what would be an ideally just distribution.[102] "Niebuhr gives no criteria," Karen Lebacqz concludes, "by which we can be assured that 'justice' has been done. . . . [E]very historical enactment [she could have said formulation] of justice is also an enactment [formulation] of injustice."[103] What we need, Niebuhr thought, is not criteria for determining what is just but criteria for determining what policies and structures are most likely to approximate the ideal of absolute freedom and absolute equality in the midst of the actual conditions of history. Hence, Niebuhr set forth working standards of justice to specify the strategy (for approximating love) dictated by his general principle of justice. These working standards should be viewed as instruments of his general strategy rather than as principles for determining what is just. (Unlike his general principle of justice, the working standards that constituted Niebuhr's conception of justice in the thirties changed significantly as he elaborated the theological basis for his

---

102. Niebuhr does use some of these traditional norms for determining what is due to whom at various points in his writings. Merle Longwood has shown how Niebuhr's application of the transcendent principle (i.e., social ideal) of equality to actual situations in history admits inequalities of distribution based on inequalities of function, needs, and work performed. Longwood has combed Niebuhr's writings for such criteria that would place him on a map delineated by canons drawn from philosophical theories of justice. Longwood observes that Niebuhr did not emphasize or develop these canons of justice. See Longwood, "Niebuhr and A Theory of Justice," 253–262. According to my interpretation of Niebuhr, a full explication of these norms of justice in relation to philosophical conceptions of justice would have been inconsistent. Although Niebuhr could countenance inequalities based on social function, and so forth, such norms were merely part of a strategy to approximate the social ideal under actual human conditions. Consequently, Niebuhr's use of such norms remained instrumental and peripheral to this primary aim of justice. They were never intended to specify what is truly just, and they could not be the basis for comparing Niebuhr's conception of justice to philosophical conceptions of an ideal distribution of goods. This peripheral use of the ordinary norms of justice also explains Gustafson's observation that Niebuhr did not develop his understanding of justice in relation to classical and contemporary philosophers. See Gustafson, "A Theology in the Service of Ethics," 33–34; see also *supra*, Introduction, 16.

103. Lebacqz, *Six Theories of Justice*, 98–99.

Christian realism and took account of historical developments in the late thirties and forties.)

Working Standards of Justice

Once he pointed out why neither rational morality nor the religious ideal of love could establish standards for assessing the structures of justice, Niebuhr reintroduced them as instruments of his strategy of justice. The relevance of these resources prevents a total capitulation to political and economic forces.

Equal Justice as the Goal

Both rationality and the religious ideal support equality as the goal of justice in history. Rationality leads to the correct conclusion that equality or equal justice is the ultimate objective for society.[104] (As a goal in history, justice can countenance functional inequalities based on technical skills that serve the whole society.[105] On this basis, Niebuhr made a theoretical distinction between equality and equal justice, which admits some inequalities, but there was no practical difference because all present inequalities are unjustified.)

Because reason is incapable of comprehending the religious social ideal, we must not interpret Niebuhr as claiming that equal justice is identical with the religious ideal. Equal justice is not an absolute value. Niebuhr, as a Christian realist, had no place for absolute values in history. In a 1933 essay responding to critics of *Moral Man and Immoral Society,* he argued that there are no absolute values. "There are merely competing values. Social justice is such a value."[106] (There is, of course, an absolute value, but it is the religious ideal, which transcends history.) Niebuhr explicitly distinguished the rational "social goal" or "ideal for society" and the Marxist transcendent ideal of from each according to ability and to each according to need. The Marxist ideal, like Christian love, is the ideal beyond history toward which a rational society must move.[107] Merle Longwood observes that Marx understood this formula as a description of the way benefits and burdens would be distributed in the communist millennium rather than as a principle of what is due

---

104. Niebuhr, *Moral Man and Immoral Society,* 159, 234.

105. E.g., ibid., 8, 159; idem, *Reflections on the End of an Era,* 157.

106. Reinhold Niebuhr, "Optimism and Utopianism," *The World Tomorrow* 16, no. 8 (February 1933): 180.

107. Niebuhr, *Moral Man and Immoral Society,* 159–160.

persons in the present state of history.[108] It describes what persons will freely give rather than prescribing a just arbitration of conflicting interests. This was also Niebuhr's understanding of the formula. In *The Nature and Destiny of Man*, he continued to associate it with the fully free and harmonious relations envisioned by the transcendent ideal of love. The goal of equality or equal justice, by contrast, prescribes whose interests are to be constrained in order to satisfy other interests. Despite Niebuhr's confusing language about equal justice being an "ultimate objective" or an "ideal for society," his point was not that equal justice is the social ideal. It was the goal *in* history that will bring about the best consequences for approximating the transcendent social ideal.

Niebuhr did not establish the goal of equal justice on the basis of rationality alone. In an argument for Christians to endorse socialism, he asserted that the ideal of love and brotherhood also supports the ultimate aim of equal justice. Even though love goes beyond justice, it should not stand for something that is less than just. He admitted that the "absolute ideal" can be used to criticize the class conflict required to obtain equal justice, but he thought such criticism commits love to social programs that fall short of justice.[109] The clear implication of Niebuhr's argument is that the ideal of love supports equality as the ultimate aim of social policy because any lower regard for equality permits economic structures that less closely approximate the ideal of love.

Niebuhr was aware that equal justice conflicts with the disinterestedness (nonassertion) and the freedom that were part of his transcendent social ideal. Nonetheless, he asserted that "equality is a higher social goal than peace"[110] and that the value of freedom is measured in relation to the social purpose it serves.[111] Because equal justice is the goal, judgments about policies that involve coercion and violence, which disrupt peace and restrict freedom, should be determined by whether they serve as realistic means to equality. In attributing this dominance to equal justice, Niebuhr came close to making it the end, and all other values merely means to this end. To be sure, he denied there are any intrinsic values, except for good will,[112] or any absolute values, and he asserted the need to view values as "inclusive ends," some subordinated to others.[113] Presumably equality was only one, though the dominant one, of those values, yet he simultaneously

108. Longwood, "Niebuhr and A Theory of Justice," 261.
109. Reinhold Niebuhr, "Socialism and Christianity," *The Christian Century* 48, no. 13 (August 19, 1931): 1039.
110. Niebuhr, *Moral Man and Immoral Society*, 235.
111. Ibid., 246.
112. Ibid., 170.
113. Ibid., 174.

maintained that "each action is judged with reference to its relation to the ultimate goal," which was equal justice.[114]

In order for his claim that equality is the goal of justice to cohere with his transcendent social ideal (which includes freedom and harmony), we must interpret him as intending to make equal justice the strategic goal or end under the economic circumstances that existed at the time. Thus, equal justice as the goal in history was instrumental to fulfilling the other values (freedom and peace) in the transcendent ideal, as well as the presently dominant value, if societies were to approximate that ideal. Obversely, peace and freedom are intrinsic values insofar as they are constitutive of the social ideal but merely means for approximating the ideal in history. Under the circumstances that existed at the time, Niebuhr viewed peace and justice primarily as means to remedy gross inequalities. They should not be viewed as goals in history. They are valued primarily insofar as they are means to the goal of equality. Niebuhr was clearer about this relationship among values in 1935 when he wrote that every value is only "*partly* intrinsic." Each value is also "partly instrumental, in the sense that its worth must be estimated in terms of its support of other values." Equal justice remained dominant in 1935, but freedom was "a high value which ought not be too readily or completely sacrificed for other values."[115]

If we interpret Niebuhr's singular goal of equal justice in this way, it functioned similarly to what he later called a "regulative principle" in a Christian realist strategy for approximating the social ideal. It was not an absolute goal of justice, but it was of singular strategic importance for approximating the social ideal. It is, then, easy to see how, in light of a different interpretation of circumstances, Niebuhr later gave freedom and a peaceful order equal status with equality without altering his Christian realist theory or his general principle of justice. Under different circumstances, freedom and peace could become more important as means for approximating the ideal of absolute equality, freedom, and harmony. During the early thirties, however, equality or equal justice was the goal that determined Niebuhr's judgments about the justice of intellectual movements and political and economic policies.

Useful Attitudes Engendered by Love

In addition to providing the social ideal that justice aims to approximate and supporting equality as the goal of justice in history, Christian love

---

114. Ibid., 170–171.
115. Niebuhr, *An Interpretation*, 174–176, my emphasis.

was an instrument in Niebuhr's strategy of justice. Love is a useful resource for justice when the attitudes it engenders encourage actions that have good consequences. In this way, love is relevant for determining what policies are just. It is not directly applicable as a principle or norm to determine what is right, but it is relevant when its fruits contribute to the strategy of justice. Although the religious ideal as a goal in history will always be an illusion, it may be a useful illusion if it inspires an attitude of hope for a just society.[116] Further, only the religious imagination can create "attitudes of repentance which recognize that the evils in the foe are also in the self" and attitudes of "kinship with all men in spite of social conflict." These attitudes can mitigate the cruelties of the necessary social struggle.[117]

The question is, What consequences do these influences of love have for approximating the social ideal? They may be detrimental to justice. They may, for example, discourage participation in social conflict. On the other hand, they sometimes have "redemptive social consequences" and are "socially useful," as when these attitudes inspire an individual to withdraw support from his or her particularly evil group.[118] Applied to the social problem under this criterion of usefulness, love aids the struggle for equal justice. It can open the most dogmatic supporters of equal justice to aid from parties less dedicated to their cause, and it can mitigate the cruelties that pursuit of equal justice in a spirit of vengeance inevitably produces.[119] If the pursuit of equal justice as a political and moral goal is not tempered by these religious resources, the structure of justice will not approximate the social ideal as nearly as possible.

Balance of Power

In addition to the goal of equal justice and the socially useful attitudes of love, the working standards for Niebuhr's strategy of justice included using coercive means to create a balance of power. Because the will-to-power subverts the moral and religious intentions of the privileged classes into serving their self-aggrandizement, moral and religious resources alone are unable to obtain equal justice. On the basis of this assessment of human nature, Niebuhr concluded that relations among groups must "be determined by the proportion of power which each group possesses at least as much as by any rational and moral appraisal."[120] The strategy for approxi-

---

116. Niebuhr, *Moral Man and Immoral Society*, 81.
117. Ibid., 255.
118. Ibid., 273, 264.
119. Niebuhr, *Reflections on the End of an Era*, 165–189.
120. Niebuhr, *Moral Man and Immoral Society*, xxiii.

mating the ideal necessarily requires a "balance of power" in which the "contending forces are fairly evenly matched."[121]

Niebuhr's realism dictated that success in the struggle for justice was political and not purely moral or religious. But neither was a political balance of power sufficient apart from the other two working standards. It was restricted as well as justified by Niebuhr's overall strategy of justice. He believed a "too consistent political realism" would have "unhappy consequences."[122] Realism needs to be tempered by the moral goal of equality and by the attitudes engendered by love.

Thus, a full understanding of this political standard incorporated an appreciation for the relevance of rational and religious resources. Even though rationality is an inadequate foundation for discerning what is just, social intelligence tends to withdraw support from inequalities of privilege. Insofar as the power of the privileged classes depends on rational support, "reason itself tends to establish a more even balance of power."[123] Principles of justice do not determine what is just, but to the extent that their consequences promote equality, they are instruments in the strategy of justice. In asserting the need for a politically established balance of power, Niebuhr argued that preserving and improving upon a mere balance of power required rational and religious resources. "The realists who have recognized the limits of politics in the establishment of justice [those who keep the ideal in tension with the actual] will be encouraged to supplement pure politics . . . with the refinements of rational justice and imaginative altruism."[124] Niebuhr was never just a realist; he was a Christian realist.

Conclusions

In sum, Niebuhr used rational and religious resources to establish the goal of equal justice, the socially useful attitudes of love, and the rule to balance powers as the working standards for determining what political and economic structures are most just. These standards are obviously different from the principles developed by most philosophical conceptions of justice. Niebuhr's standards are not intended to determine the right distribution of benefits and burdens independently of its consequences for the good, as some neo-Kantians do. Yet the highest good in history entails an egalitarian distribution of power, privileges, income,

---

121. Niebuhr, *Reflections on the End of an Era*, 243.
122. Niebuhr, *Moral Man and Immoral Society*, 131–132.
123. Ibid., 237.
124. Niebuhr, *Reflections on the End of an Era*, 248; see also Reinhold Niebuhr, "Marxism and Religion," *The World Tomorrow* 16, no. 11 (March 1933): 255.

and wealth. It is not an aggregate good[125] to be maximized by a utilitarian calculus. Niebuhr's conception is consequentialist, but it is not utilitarian. Nor is the highest good in history, as Niebuhr conceived it, maximum opportunities for individuals to develop their personality. The good for which justice aims is an egalitarian distributive pattern without regard for its impact on character development. From his realist perspective, Niebuhr did not consider how economic and political structures facilitate the development of virtues or excellences, as Rauschenbusch, Ryan, and some neo-Aristotelians do.

Niebuhr's working standards were intended to indicate what consequences are most likely to approximate the social ideal. They leave considerable room for intuitive judgments (informed by historical and social facts) about which policies produce the desired consequences. They are, however, guides for assessing which basic structures (e.g., system of government or of property ownership) will produce consequences that most nearly approximate the Christian social ideal. In that sense, they constitute what Rawls calls a conception of justice and provide an interpretation of how persons ought to judge a state of affairs, as required by Gustafson's fourth base point.

Because this conception is a strategy presuming that greater justice must always emerge out of injustice, Niebuhr's standards of justice are means for social change as well as guides for the distributive aspects of society. As previously noted, attempts to establish principles for a perfectly just order, such as Rauschenbusch's or Ryan's, wrongly locate the ideal within history. Christian realism presumes the constancy of what Rawls calls partial compliance theory. The standards of justice deal only with structures that fall short of perfect justice.

I believe this is a fair representation of the operative, though not systematically formulated, conception of justice that informed Niebuhr's judgments about the basic structure of society. We turn now to Niebuhr's application of this conception of justice to judgments about property ownership, democracy, and Marxism as an intellectual and political movement. That these issues were the most crucial for Niebuhr reflects his working standards of justice (viz., the single goal of equal justice and the balance of power).

Narrower issues (e.g., a living wage, union rights, unemployment, and taxes) that occupied the attention of Rauschenbusch and Ryan did not, from Niebuhr's realist perspective, address the inequalities of power that impeded progress toward equal justice. Reforms with this narrow scope would be either made trivial or prevented by those with economic

---

125. Longwood, "Niebuhr and A Theory of Justice," 254.

power. Such reforms were incapable of correcting the more systemic problem of inequalities of power in an economy based on private ownership of productive property. In a 1936 editorial on inheritance taxes, for example, Niebuhr concluded: "A capitalist society heaps up inequalities faster than even a fairly vigorous tax policy can equalize."[126] Niebuhr did not agree with those who opposed these ameliorative reforms, such as progressive taxation, in order to harden radical movements and hasten revolution. He considered it a "romantic hope" to believe "that a better social order must inevitably spring out of the chaos of a ruined one."[127] Niebuhr even lamented that efforts at piecemeal reforms were constantly thwarted by the economic and political power of property owners. His point was that focusing on these reforming efforts would prove ineffective as long as private productive property existed. Later, as his goal of equal justice gave way to the regulative principles of equality and freedom, Niebuhr would give more attention to these narrower issues.

JUSTICE APPLIED
Ownership of Productive Property

Despite the fact that Niebuhr later remembered himself as a socialist of sorts during the twenties,[128] he did not advocate broad-scale public ownership of productive property until the mid to late twenties. Even then he argued only for a "step by step" move toward socialism. Socialism was needed, Niebuhr thought, in order to obtain the cooperation required for efficiency in modern industry and in order to distribute profits with a degree of fairness. During this period, Niebuhr believed socialism was required to provide a structure for an equitable distribution of economic resources. The structure of capitalism provided unwarranted income and wealth to the owners. He did not yet believe that inequalities of power necessarily prevented a "step by step" move to socialism and equal distribution.[129]

Niebuhr did not join the Socialist Party until 1929. Then in the winter of 1930–31, Niebuhr, Sherwood Eddy, and Kirby Page led a transforma-

---

126. Reinhold Niebuhr, "Taxation and Equality," *Radical Religion* 1, no. 3 (Spring 1936): 5.

127. Reinhold Niebuhr, "Catastrophe or Social Control," *Harper's Monthly Magazine* 165, no. 6 (June 1932): 118.

128. Merkley, *Reinhold Niebuhr*, 51; June Bingham, *Courage to Change* (New York: Charles Scribner's Sons, 1961), 134.

129. Reinhold Niebuhr, "Why We Need a New Economic Order," *The World Tomorrow* 11, no. 10 (October 1929): 395–398.

tion of the Fellowship for a Christian Social Order into the Fellowship of Socialist Christians (FSC). The FSC was premised on the belief that property had to be brought under social control immediately.[130]

As his Christian realism developed, so did the urgency of Niebuhr's call for the public ownership of productive property. The connection is explicit. His argument no longer centered on the need for cooperation and efficiency or on the structures of distribution. It was now based on the inequalities of power private ownership inevitably produces. Those who hold this power use it to block attempts to equalize the distribution of income and wealth. In two 1931 essays on property, Niebuhr argued that "significant power derives from the ownership of property." Through this power, property owners control both political and economic affairs. Therefore, reforms that stop short of destroying property rights (e.g., regulation, taxation, minimum wage bills, strikes, and other "progressive abridgments of the rights of private property") have failed. Because the Christian ideal of love shares the goal of equal justice with the socialists, Christians who understand these realities of power should endorse the socialist intention to abolish the private ownership of productive property in order to move toward equality.[131]

His argument was based on the consequences of private property for the goal of equality. Private property is not intrinsically wrong. Nor was Niebuhr concerned, as were Rauschenbusch and Ryan, with the consequences of property rights and the relations of production for the possibilities of human fulfillment or for the development of the personality through work. Niebuhr demonstrated little interest in the Marxist idea of the workers' alienation from the work process or the product of their labor. He never developed an interest in democratizing the workplace, as Rauschenbusch and Ryan did. His primary concern was with consequences of private property for promoting equality. Property rights produce disparities of economic and political power that are not amenable to significant limitation by reforming the system. Thus, private productive property has uncorrectable deleterious consequences for the goal of equality. This argument was confirmed and hardened as Niebuhr's Christian realism developed. In *Reflections on the End of an Era,* he wrote: "Private ownership means social power; and the unequal distribution of social power leads automatically to inequality and injustice."[132]

This consequentialist argument also restrained Niebuhr's opposition to

---

130. Fox, *Reinhold Niebuhr,* 128–129.
131. Reinhold Niebuhr, "Property and the Ethical Life," *The World Tomorrow* 14, no. 1 (January 1931): 19–21; idem, "Socialism and Christianity," 1038–1040.
132. Niebuhr, *Reflections on the End of an Era,* 24.

private property. He thought Russian communist attempts to collectivize farming and small trade were unnecessary because the property owned by the peasants and small traders did not issue in inequalities of power.[133] Niebuhr thought this doctrinaire socialism issued from vindictiveness rather than realism. Whereas a spirit of vengeance can never be purged entirely from a realistic pursuit of justice, the attitudes engendered by love can mitigate vengeance and thereby restrain the kind of dogmatism to which it gives birth.[134] In this way, the attitudes engendered by the ideal of love played a role in Niebuhr's judgment against doctrinaire socialism.

Democracy

Niebuhr's criticism of democracy came later and was more ambivalent than his attack on private property. The change in Niebuhr's view of democracy came between 1931 and 1932 and reflected his deepening realism. In his 1931 judgment against private property, Niebuhr still hoped that the "moral insight and intelligence" of "disinterested observers" were instruments by which "schools and churches" could influence the middle class to support the reorganization of society.[135] In *Moral Man and Immoral Society,* he wrote:

> It would be pleasant to believe that the intelligence of the general community could be revised to such a height that the irrational injustices of society would be eliminated. But unfortunately there is no such general community. . . . [The middle class], living in comfort and security, is unable to recognise the urgency of the social problem; and . . . is unable to appreciate the consistency with which economic groups express themselves in terms of pure selfishness.[136]

Because the middle class (and the farmer) could not be counted on to support socialism, Niebuhr concluded that "winning a parliamentary majority for evolutionary socialism is fairly remote and may be entirely out of the question."[137] Here we see a clear distinction between Niebuhr's Christian realist emphasis on a balance of power and Rauschenbusch's emphasis upon democracy. Rauschenbusch's solution for business influence on the political process was more democracy.[138]

---

133. Ibid., 187, 238; Reinhold Niebuhr, "A New Strategy for Socialists," *The World Tomorrow* 16, no. 21 (August 1933): 490.
134. Niebuhr, *Reflections on the End of an Era,* 170–173, 178–179.
135. Niebuhr, "Property and the Ethical Life," 20–21.
136. Niebuhr, *Moral Man and Immoral Society,* 213–214.
137. Ibid., 219.
138. See *supra,* chapter two, 63, 95, 98–99.

Niebuhr never believed, not even in the early thirties, that economic interests were the sole source of a society's moral and political values. The will-to-power makes the insertion of collective interests into morality inevitable. But the will-to-power is more fundamental than economic interests, and it can manifest itself in a variety of collective interests. He did conclude, however, that the concentration of economic power during the industrial age made it, rather than military or political power, the "significant coercive force in modern society."[139] Consequently, he lost confidence that democracy could be the instrument for achieving equal justice. Democracy was, Niebuhr contended, already subject to a demagogic manipulation by property owners. Even within the democratic process, they used coercion to thwart the move toward justice, and the situation was likely to degenerate. Like most radicals of his day,[140] Niebuhr decided that capitalist property owners would almost inevitably turn to a fascist state in an attempt to maintain their power when democracy no longer served their interests. Thus, they would assure a revolutionary and bloody end to capitalism.[141]

This negative view of democracy never hardened in Niebuhr's thought. If it is certain that the enemies of labor will disavow democratic principles, labor ought to beat them to it, Niebuhr asserted. Still, democracy was a tool that should be used in the cause of justice.[142] Niebuhr consistently opposed absolute allegiance to democratic procedures and to "constitutionality." "[E]very legal system must be regarded as a rationalization of a given equilibrium of political and economic power and can therefore hardly be a perfect instrument for changing the equilibrium."[143] "[A] workers' movement can never make democracy an end in itself nor even go upon the assumption that it is a certain means to an ultimate end," but socialists ought not abandon party politics within a democratic system. The workers' movement "need not necessarily have a majority of votes [to establish the socialist order], but it will have to be the most powerful social will standing against the old order."[144] Even if, as is likely, the capitalists replace democracy with fascism, revolutionary violence may not be the only alternative. The final transfer of power, even from a fascist state, might come through a general strike or some

---

139. Ibid., 14–15.
140. Sidney Hook, *Out of Step* (New York: Harper & Row, 1987), 179.
141. Niebuhr, *Reflections on the End of an Era*, 51–61.
142. Reinhold Niebuhr, "Democracy in Crisis," review of *Democracy in Crisis*, by Harold Laski, in *The World Tomorrow* 16, no. 17 (May 1933): 404.
143. Niebuhr, "A New Strategy for Socialists," 491; idem, "After Capitalism—What?" *The World Tomorrow* 16, no. 9 (March 1933): 204.
144. Reinhold Niebuhr, "The Revolutionary Moment," *American Socialist Quarterly* (June 1935): 8–13.

similar technique.[145] Political consensus has instrumental (and perhaps some intrinsic) value even where democratic institutions are absent.

Niebuhr was certain that the transfer of economic power, upon which the goal of equality depended, could not be achieved by purely democratic means.[146] He was uncertain, however, about whether violent revolution would be necessary. He valued democratic means for achieving justice insofar as they could be made effective. Government depends upon consent as well as force, and democratic methods spare unnecessary conflict and chaos.[147] Furthermore, Niebuhr, presaging his later defense of democracy, saw value in preserving democratic procedures as an instrument for checking the concentrations of political power that would inevitably arise from the social ownership of property under the control of the proletariat.[148]

Niebuhr valued democracy primarily as a means to the goal of equal justice. It was not, as it was for Rauschenbusch, a principle for determining what is just. Niebuhr had only a little interest in the intrinsic values of freedom or consent of the governed that democracies claimed to protect. Equal justice was the goal, and his ambivalence toward democracy corresponded to his uncertainty about the prospects of eliminating the unequal power of property owners through parliamentary means. His reluctance to abandon it entirely issued from his fear that radicals who failed to recognize the limits of their revolutionary political strategy would subvert the fragile balance of power upon which the maintenance of equal justice depends. For that task, democracy is a "perennial necessity," but a necessity not likely to be perceived by those incapable of recognizing the inevitable selfishness in their own use of power.[149] Here again, the actual was held in tension with the ideal, and the usefulness of the attitude of repentance was present just beneath the surface of Niebuhr's political realism.

Marxism and the Proletarian Movement

Niebuhr's depreciation of the value of democracy coincided with his growing appreciation for Marxism. The commonplace observation that Niebuhr was a quasi Marxist during this period does not, however, adequately explain why he gave Marxism a qualified endorsement. Niebuhr never believed Marxist thought was true. Marxism (along with

145. Niebuhr, "After Capitalism—What?" 204.
146. Niebuhr, Reflections on the End of an Era, 157.
147. Ibid., 152–153, 157.
148. Ibid., 243–244.
149. Ibid., 244.

what he called classical or orthodox Christianity and his study of the history of the industrial age) contributed to his formulation of Christian realism. But Niebuhr's view of the actual human condition was grounded in the self-conscious assertion of the will-to-power, not in economic relations. To be sure the will-to-power manifests itself in conflicting economic interests that will lead to the inevitable doom of capitalism,[150] but most Marxists fail to understand that the seeds of injustice will remain in human nature after the economic inequalities of capitalism are destroyed.[151]

The Marxist ideal, in which each person will voluntarily give according to ability and take freely according to needs,[152] is also close to Niebuhr's Christian social ideal of communism and anarchy.[153] The Marxists, however, associate equal justice, as a goal in history, with this transcendent ideal. They wrongly believe that the equality that is the goal of revolutionary socialism will be identical with the ideal of voluntary communism. Niebuhr thought the proletarian movement had possibilities for almost achieving equal justice, but he never thought it could produce the conditions in which each person would freely give according to ability and receive according to needs. Because it considers this ideal attainable, "Marxism betrays the ethical enterprise into an illusion, akin to the liberal illusion; for it believes that a kingdom of pure love can be established in history and that its vindictive justice will be transmuted into pure justice."[154]

Marxism clearly fails to comprehend the creative tension between the ideal and actual; therefore, it cannot fully comprehend the working standards of justice. Though Marxists pursue equality by realistic means, they do not combine this goal and means with attitudes of kinship for all and of repentance, which only the transcendent ideal of love can engender. "The trouble with communism," Niebuhr contended, "is not its doctrine of violence but its spirit of vindictiveness."[155] Without the useful attitudes of love, equal justice and realism are both distorted. First, the Marxist pursuit of equal justice risks a fanaticism that could lead to unjust tyrannies and cruelties that shut "the gates of mercy on mankind."[156] It risks subverting its own goal of equality. Second, its dogmatism closes it to seeing the possibility and need for support from

150. Ibid., 23–25.
151. Niebuhr, *Moral Man and Immoral Society*, 192–199.
152. Ibid., 194.
153. Ibid., 159–160.
154. Niebuhr, *Reflections on the End of an Era*, 136.
155. Reinhold Niebuhr, "Making Radicalism Effective," *The World Tomorrow* 16, no. 29 (December 1933): 683.
156. Niebuhr, *Moral Man and Immoral Society*, 199.

agrarian, nationalistic, and religious allies in the cause of the proletariat.[157] Niebuhr always thought realism required bringing farmers and the lower middle class into a coalition with the proletariat. Communism's dogmatic vindictiveness barred such cooperation. To that extent, it was unrealistic about the means available for constructing a balance of power.

Despite these substantial criticisms of Marxist theory and its operative conception of justice, Niebuhr's Christian realist theory could not be satisfied merely by establishing the truest theory of justice. As a consequentialist, he was committed to endorsing whatever extant intellectual and political movement was the best instrument for approximating justice. From Niebuhr's realist perspective, no other religious or political movement in the thirties offered a viable alternative to the Marxist proletariat.

In 1924, Niebuhr had thought that the ideals of the middle class could be awakened and enlisted "to support a program of thoroughgoing political and economic reconstruction." It was "realistic" to hope that "a Christian political party could be created if the church really took the social implications of its gospel seriously."[158] By 1932, he had abandoned that hope. He expected neither liberal nor orthodox Christian churches and seminaries to be effective instruments for the cause of equal justice.

Nor did Niebuhr expect the Democratic Party to be an instrument for equal justice. For someone who saw social ownership of property as "a primary requisite of social health in a technical age," as Niebuhr did as late as 1938,[159] the New Deal restrictions on the power of business were not regarded as a "permanent gain in the direction of a socialized state."[160] Niebuhr perceived that the base of Roosevelt's economic reforms was in Western agrarianism. The features of the NRA designed to benefit labor were mere "gratuitous contributions" from radical agrarianism. The New Deal was not fascist, but Niebuhr believed that its semiradical policies would precipitate a fascist reaction.[161]

Even in the midtwenties, Niebuhr had lost confidence that the United States labor movement could effectively challenge capitalism without

---

157. Niebuhr, *Reflections on the End of an Era*, 180–189; idem, "A New Strategy for Socialists," 490–491; idem, "Making Radicalism Effective," 681–684.

158. Reinhold Niebuhr, "Christianity and Contemporary Politics," *The Christian Century* 41, no. 16 (April 17, 1924): 499, 501.

159. Reinhold Niebuhr, "Socialist Decision and Christian Conscience," *Radical Religion* 3, no. 2 (Spring 1968): 2.

160. Niebuhr, *Reflections on the End of an Era*, 81.

161. Ibid., 79–81.

guidance to make it more radical.[162] In the thirties, Niebuhr perceived American labor organizations to be too bound to the old political parties and by strictly economic weapons to be able to secure justice for the workers.[163] The American worker remained, he lamented, an exception to the radical attitudes of the proletarian class. The radicalization of American labor, Niebuhr predicted, awaits the material conditions that will emerge with the full maturity of American capitalism and the timely Marxist education of the workers.[164] The American labor movements failed to understand that justice requires a balance of economic powers that can be achieved only by eliminating private productive property through extrademocratic political means. They did not meet Niebuhr's criteria for realism.

Other movements may dream of equality, but Marxism was distinctive in that it alone understood that the destruction of power is a prerequisite for attaining equal justice.[165] The choice, said Niebuhr, is between "hypocrisy and vengeance."[166] Given this option, Niebuhr's conception of justice justified support for the proletarian political movement because of its "strategic importance" in the task of rebuilding society.[167] Despite the oversimplifications of Marxist theory, it was "potent in arousing those passions which are necessary for . . . the forces of history which destroy the old and construct the new. If a higher degree of objectivity should provide more discriminating judgments there is always the possibility that they will lame the nerve of action."[168] The pages following that statement are devoted to the liberal values of individual rights, universal suffrage, and humanitarian philanthropy, which Niebuhr feared Marxism would unnecessarily discredit.[169] But those were values that had to be risked until the work of rebuilding the economic order was done.

Niebuhr's realism did not permit Ryan's method of supporting justice by detached judgments about a movement's values and specific policies. Obversely, Ryan's reliance on principles of ideal justice did not admit

---

162. Merkley, *Reinhold Niebuhr,* 34–35.
163. Niebuhr, *Moral Man and Immoral Society,* 200–201.
164. Ibid., 144, 148. See Niebuhr's 1933 review of Trotsky's *History of the Russian Revolution* for appreciative comments on Trotsky's views on the relationship between the material conditions and timely education and leadership. Reinhold Niebuhr, "Trotsky's Classic," review of *History of the Russian Revolution,* vols. 2 and 3, by Leon Trotsky, in *The World Tomorrow* 16, no. 5 (February 1933): 116.
165. Niebuhr, *Moral Man and Immoral Society,* 163.
166. Niebuhr, *Reflections on the End of an Era,* 272.
167. Niebuhr, *Moral Man and Immoral Society,* 157.
168. Niebuhr, *Reflections on the End of an Era,* 88.
169. Ibid., 88–95.

such consequentialist endorsements of movements that were not fully just.[170] Rauschenbusch stood between Niebuhr and Ryan on this issue. His concern for a strategy to achieve justice allowed for an endorsement of the labor and social movements without close scrutiny of the precise justice of their interests, but his commitments to democracy and cooperation made him leery of the violent and catastrophic elements in dogmatic socialism.[171]

Niebuhr's consequentialist commitment to Marxist thought and the proletarian movement did not include the Communist Party, U.S.A. He viewed it as an arm of Soviet policy.[172] His respect for national differences and his patriotism convinced him that radical parties should have no more than consultative relations with similar parties in other nations.[173] Instead of allying himself with one of the Communist parties, Niebuhr remained with the Socialist Party. But he argued that socialists should stay within the range of policies required by the realism he shared with the Marxists. The proper strategy, he maintained, is "a Marxism which disavows revisionist and parliamentary optimism in the field of politics and economics," but is revisionist in dealing with the communist psychology of vengeance and its concomitant refusal to muster agrarian and nationalistic cultural forces in support of socialism.[174] He castigated socialist liberals who "underestimate the power and persistence of the reactionary impulse in society, to imagine that . . . privilege in any society can be subdued by compromises or by a parliamentary majority."[175] When a dispute arose in the midthirties between the Old Guard and the Militants within the Socialist Party, Niebuhr sided with the Militants, who were willing to deny "majority rights" and seek cooperation with the communists in the cause of equal justice. On the other hand, he opposed the "revolutionaries" within the Party for being unrealistic in their refusal to cooperate with the middle class and farmers.[176]

When asked how an intelligent person could belong to a political party that is dogmatic, Niebuhr answered that he was willing to sacrifice intellectual liberty for unity with a political group that is "facing in the

---

170. See *supra,* chapter three, 181–185.
171. See *supra,* chapter two, 97–98.
172. Merkley, *Reinhold Niebuhr,* 91.
173. Niebuhr, "A New Strategy for Socialists," 491.
174. Niebuhr, "Making Radicalism Effective," 682–684.
175. Niebuhr, "A New Strategy for Socialists," 491.
176. See Merkley, *Reinhold Niebuhr,* 96–101, for an account of this struggle. Fox, *Reinhold Niebuhr,* 157–158, emphasizes that Niebuhr did not participate directly in this intraparty struggle and cites it as evidence for a decreasing enthusiasm for direct political action.

right direction in the world."[177] His answer illumines the nature of his support for Marxism. As an academic, Niebuhr learned from Marxism but was never committed to it as true. As a consequentialist proponent of justice (Niebuhr was an academic and a proponent for justice simultaneously), he offered his qualified endorsement of Marxist thought and the proletarian political movement. That is why Niebuhr's view of Marxism is more important for understanding his application of justice than for understanding his theory of justice. It is also why he concluded *Moral Man and Immoral Society* with the widely cited assertion that the illusion that humankind can achieve perfect justice is a valuable illusion, even though it cannot withstand the scrutiny of reason.[178]

NEW WINDS OF CHANGE

Already in 1933, Niebuhr lamented that statement as "the greatest mistake in my book." He lamented it because illusions have dangerous as well as good consequences.[179] He longed for an intellectually mature age that could dispose of capitalism without the false hope that socialism would be a moral paradise.[180] From that time, Niebuhr ceased to advocate illusions as a part of his strategy of justice. He began to think of philosophies that give meaning to history not as illusions but as myths. Unlike illusions, which are false but can be useful, myths embody more or less religious truth. As a myth, Marxism did not compare favorably to Christianity, because a true myth makes the ideal a goal *of* history rather than a goal *in* history.[181] It maintains the creative tension between the ideal and the actual.

This new focus on myth was not a change in the substance of Niebuhr's

---

177. Merkley, *Reinhold Niebuhr,* 96; Reinhold Niebuhr, "When Virtues Are Vices," *The Christian Century* 48, no. 3 (January 31, 1931): 115.

178. Niebuhr, *Moral Man and Immoral Society,* 277. Niebuhr is notorious for using the same term to mean different things, and without explanation. In this context, reason can mean only the dialectical reason of Christian realism and not the reason of secular and religious liberalism, which he had previously criticized for concluding that the ideal can be achieved in history.

179. In 1935, writing in the Marxist periodical *The Modern Monthly,* Niebuhr said of Marxism: "I once thought such a faith to be a harmless illusion. But now I see that its net result is to endow a group of oligarchs with the religious sanctity which primitive priest-kings once held." See Reinhold Niebuhr, "Religion and Marxism," *The Modern Monthly* 8 (February 1935): 714. Niebuhr was never precise in describing his previous positions. He had previously viewed Marxism as a useful but risky (not harmless) illusion, but by 1935 he had evidently decided that there were more bad than good consequences in endorsing the illusions of Marxist religion.

180. Niebuhr, "Optimism and Utopianism," 180.

181. Niebuhr, *Reflections on the End of an Era,* 121–136, 193–205.

understanding of the tension between the ideal and the actual nor a new judgment about the truth of Marxism as a religion. He had judged it false before. Nor did it represent a decision to withdraw his consequentialist endorsement of Marxist political thought. As we have seen, Niebuhr continued to endorse Marxism in *Reflections on the End of an Era*. It was an effort to distinguish Marxist politics more clearly from Marxist religion in order to avoid the errors of Marxist religion without abandoning its politics. In a 1934 essay on "The Problem of Communist Religion," Niebuhr commented: "We may deny the Communist belief that the proletariat is a messianic class and still insist that [it is] a class with a very fateful mission." Niebuhr was aware that the "line between such a sense of mission and a religious belief . . . is not always clear." "Communism is not only a bad religion; but it is in some of its aspects blind politics."[182] How could the relation be perceived otherwise by someone whose religious, ethical, and political views were so deeply intertwined? Nevertheless, this distinction allowed Niebuhr to join "conservative religious convictions" with a "radical political orientation," the underlying conviction of *Reflections on the End of an Era,* according to his preface.[183] He no longer believed that he had to endorse the false illusions of Marxist religion in order to produce the best justice for the proletariat.

Reflections on the End of an Era was, however, a volume of loosely connected essays. It was not a comprehensive attempt to join traditional Christianity with radical politics. Niebuhr never claimed otherwise. In 1936, in his most exhaustive of a series of essays on Christianity, communism, and politics during this period, Niebuhr still saw Christianity as "a religion with an inadequate political strategy."[184] Marxism was, on the other hand, an inadequate religion with a political philosophy that rightly backs the "mission" of the proletariat, but wrongly transmutes it into a "demonic pretension."[185] Niebuhr saw "no reason why Christianity should not have a political ethic which inspires men to the attainment of justice without sacrificing the values of its love perfectionism." Justice, he asserted, is "the most significant approximation of the ideal of love in politics and economics."[186] To accomplish this task, the church would have to affirm many Marxist tenets regarding the depths of the political and economic realm while relating that realm to the heights of

---

182. Reinhold Niebuhr, "The Problem of Communist Religion," *The World Tomorrow* 17, no. 15 (July 1934): 379.

183. Niebuhr, *Reflections on the End of an Era,* ix.

184. Reinhold Niebuhr, "Christian Politics and Communist Religion," in *Christianity and the Social Revolution,* ed. John Lewis, Karl Polanyi, and Donald K. Kitchin (New York: Charles Scribner's Sons, 1936): 442.

185. Ibid., 466.

186. Ibid., 470.

pure religion.[187] This "Christian political ethic" would correct the Marxist illusion about achieving the ideal in history while providing resources to support "the fateful mission of [the industrial proletariat] in modern society."[188]

This call for a Christian political ethic was merely a summary of the Christian realism and strategy for justice Niebuhr had developed in 1932. His own inchoate theology and ethics already backed his radical politics. Two significant problems remained. First, the truth of his assertions about the transcendent ideal of love could not be verified by the fruits of morality as he imagined in the twenties, when he claimed that the ideal would conquer the actual creating its own proof. Second, despite his newfound appreciation for traditional Christianity, Niebuhr was not yet able to retrieve a theology from the Bible and tradition that could support his politics. The idea of myth was crucial to Niebuhr's resolution to both these problems. By understanding the biblical and traditional doctrines as myths that transcend rational and scientific capacities, Niebuhr thought he had discovered truths in these doctrines that confirmed his Christian realism.

His investigation into these theological myths, culminating in *The Nature and Destiny of Man,* provided a more comprehensive and more explicitly theological treatment of Gustafson's base points—an anthropology, an interpretation of history, and an understanding of God (though it was not comprehensive)—as a realist theory to justify his conception of justice. In the end, however, these theological investigations combined with changing political and economic events to lead Niebuhr away from Marxist politics and from support for the mission of the proletariat. Niebuhr came to view his age as mature enough to achieve relative justice without an illusory hope for moral paradise, but this judgment resulted from changes in his working standards of justice and in the policies he advocated rather than from the destruction of capitalism.

We will explore these developments in Niebuhr's theory and conception of justice after considering Ryan's response to the thirties and the New Deal, which was quite different from Niebuhr's. Ryan was not searching for a strategy to approximate the kingdom of God in a balance of power among conflicting class interests. He did, however, advocate what were for him new policies in an attempt to secure the opportunity of every individual to develop his or her personality.

---

187. Ibid., 471.
188. Ibid.

5

POLICIES FOR NEW TIMES

Ryan's views also changed during the late twenties and early thirties, but not at the fundamental level at which Niebuhr was working. While Niebuhr was creating a Christian realist framework that eventually forced him to revise much of his received Protestant liberal theology, Ryan expanded the application of his fully developed theory of justice to new problems and possibilities. While Niebuhr was abandoning any hope of reforming capitalism or reconciling economic classes and was questioning democracy, Ryan proposed policies that he believed could save capitalism as a system of private productive property. Ryan intended these policies to extend democracy and cooperation to industry. While Niebuhr was cynical about the "vague liberalism" of the Roosevelt administration offering any hope for "permanent gains in the direction of the socialized state,"[1] Ryan praised Roosevelt as the best hope for saving capitalism.[2]

---

1. Niebuhr, *Reflections on the End of an Era*, 80–81.
2. Ryan, *Seven Troubled Years*, 109. Ryan's relationships to capitalist and socialist ideas and to the Roosevelt administration during the thirties were more complex than one might expect from a person called the "Right Reverend New Dealer." They reveal both the pragmatism and openness of Ryan's theory of justice based on his "teleology of obligation" and his ultimate confidence in securing just policies by rational moral appeals to the politicians.

Ryan and Niebuhr shared a conviction that injustices to the laboring class required a dramatic remedy. In those days, however, leading Catholic and Protestant ethicists who shared such an important commitment could take very different directions without taking account of the other's work. As we have previously noted, Ryan and Niebuhr did just

---

Although Ryan steadfastly opposed the socialist movement, he was not, during the early years of the Depression, entirely certain that a system of private productive property, let alone other aspects of capitalism, could be saved. In 1931, Ryan repeated an earlier thought that the present industrial system may not be able to distribute a decent livelihood to every person. If it cannot, Ryan suggested, this information is something we should know. See Ryan, *Distributive Justice*, 415; idem, *Seven Troubled Years*, 21. (The essays in *Seven Troubled Years* were written between 1930 and 1936. Instead of citing individual essays, I indicate specific dates where it is necessary for understanding.) In neither passage does he indicate what other industrial system might replace the present one, but in his first essay praising Roosevelt, Ryan allowed that it may be too late for Roosevelt to save capitalism. "Possibly the government of the United States," he mused, "will have to take over and operate the essential industries," ibid., 109. Ryan continued to evaluate the morality of private productive property on the basis of its consequences for securing the rights necessary for each person's self-development. Despite repeated opposition to socialist thought and the socialist movement, Ryan was willing to adopt whatever socialist economic policies, including public ownership of industrial property, could effectively distribute a decent livelihood to every family.

Ryan's relationship to Roosevelt is equally revealing. Ryan was not an early Roosevelt supporter. As late as December 1932, Ryan—noting that many Catholics had, in "good faith," voted for Norman Thomas—rather meekly urged Catholics not to vote for Socialist Party candidates, but he took quite seriously the objection that neither of the two major parties was equal to the task of social justice. He even suggested that Catholics might have to organize a new political party, ibid., 89–91. By June of 1933, following Roosevelt's inaugural and initial legislative proposals, Ryan was prepared to write that Roosevelt's "guiding motive is social justice," ibid., 109. He never again wavered in that judgment. Following FDR's death, Ryan wrote: "Indeed, he did more for those who stood most in need of social justice than any other man who ever occupied the White House." See John A. Ryan, "Roosevelt and Social Justice," *The Review of Politics* (July 1945): 297.

Undoubtedly, the Roosevelt administration renewed Ryan's hope that social justice could be achieved by addressing rational moral arguments to the politicians. Ryan, reflecting aspects of the Protestant view that sin could undercut moral arguments for just political action, constantly feared that the greed of business might overcome the moral and economic policies of the New Deal (e.g., Ryan, *Seven Troubled Years*, 109–110). In his darkest moments, he even wondered in writing "whether there is sufficient honesty left in the American people to get out of the depression by any rational method," ibid., 154. Yet the fact that he only incidentally expressed these doubts confirms Ryan's commitment to his "rational method." From the spring of 1933 to the end of his career, Ryan based his strategy for justice upon ethical and economic arguments addressed to politicians in the administration and Congress and to their potential supporters.

Legends exaggerating Ryan's connections to the New Deal indicate the extent to which his strategy for justice depended upon an appeal to the politicians. Francis Broderick reports that in 1959 a priest, frustrated because phone service was discontinued during the night at the residence hall where Ryan had stayed, was told that the phones had been shut off during the Roosevelt years. According to the story, the White House was always calling in the middle of the night to consult with Ryan. See Broderick, *Right Reverend New Dealer*, 241. Patrick Gearty recounts the apocryphal story of Ryan's response to a

that.[3] They had quite different visions of the possibility for and substance of a just society and economy. Niebuhr sought a redress in the imbalance of power between labor and the privileged classes through the militancy of the proletariat mission. He hoped for an equality of power in a socialist economy that would be the closest realistic approximation of his ideal of love. Ryan sought to use the moral reason of Catholic natural law combined with economic analysis to achieve legislation (and Court approval) that would restructure the existing capitalist economy. His goal was not the ideal of perfect freedom, equality, and harmony, but to satisfy every person's natural interest in attaining his or her proximate end. He hoped for a reconstructed economic system that would, by cooperation in furthering the common good, secure the means for every individual to develop his or her personality.

The thirties brought no change in Ryan's theory of rights based on human dignity or in his canons of justice. Ryan did, however, redirect the focus of his economic analysis. He broadened the scope of relevant circumstances to emphasize the stability of the whole economy and the effects of economic institutions for self-development. As we will see, this change only strengthened his conviction that the world is ordered so that harmony exists between a Catholic teleological ethic and economic expediency. There were only minor changes in Ryan's theory of justice. There were, however, significant expansions in the policies he advo-

---

chiding remark that he was " 'following after everything Roosevelt and the New Deal does.' " Ryan was supposed to have retorted: " 'It's not so. Before the New Deal was, I am.' " See Gearty, *The Economic Thought of Monsignor Ryan*, 264–265.

In fact, Ryan only occasionally communicated with Roosevelt (see Broderick, *Right Reverend New Dealer*, 241), and as we will see, he maintained sufficient critical distance from the New Deal to criticize it and Roosevelt for not going far enough in efforts to redistribute wealth and restructure the economy. Ryan's most full-hearted endorsement of Roosevelt came during the 1936 election campaign. In response to Father Coughlin's stinging attacks upon Roosevelt, Ryan consented to an appeal by the Democratic Party that he defend Roosevelt in a radio speech, "Roosevelt Safeguards America," sponsored by the Democratic National Committee. See Ryan, *Seven Troubled Years*, 295–299, for the full text. It was this speech that elicited Coughlin's taunt that Ryan was the " 'Right Reverend spokesman for the New Deal.' " Broderick, *Right Reverend New Dealer*, 227. Ryan began the speech disclaiming that his talk was political. It was, he insisted, "a discussion of political events in light of the moral law." Ryan, *Seven Troubled Years*, 195. Ryan's discomfort with a purely political role illustrates his self-perception as an ethicist making moral arguments for just political policies. Although Ryan assisted the Roosevelt administration in a variety of small ways—the most important of which was his ten-month service on the Industrial Appeals Board of the National Recovery Administration—he was an "ethicist to the politicians," not a politician. Niebuhr had been more deeply involved in socialist politics than Ryan was in the New Deal. Unlike Niebuhr, however, Ryan's view of human agents grounded a confidence that the politicians, and particularly Roosevelt's people, would act on rational arguments for economic justice.

3. See *supra*, Introduction, 18.

cated. The struggle for a living wage remained the centerpiece of Ryan's reforming efforts, but he now began to emphasize the importance of a redistribution of income and wealth and of industrial democracy. He also developed earlier inchoate ideas for an industrial economy that would reestablish the cooperative spirit of medieval guilds. If a living wage was to be the foundation for a just economic order, the occupational group system Ryan proposed was to be its pinnacle.

These three proposals—that is, redistribution, the occupational groups system, and industrial democracy—were new applications of the theory of justice Ryan had developed by 1916. Ryan's emphasis on these proposals and his specific formulations of them were evoked by three events of the late twenties and early thirties. He was deeply influenced by the high level of unemployment beginning in 1928 and increasing during the Depression, by Pope Pius XI's encyclical, *Quadragesimo Anno,* issued in May of 1931, and by what he called the economics and ethics of Roosevelt's New Deal.[4]

My purpose in this chapter is to show how Ryan developed and emphasized these three economic proposals by applying his theory of justice in light of the changing times. After examining these interrelated proposals, we will be able to see that Ryan, during the thirties, moved closer to some of Rauschenbusch's emphases: equality, a broad interpretation of the circumstances of economic justice (including the effect economic institutions have upon opportunities for self-development), and cooperation rather than competition. They both stand in contrast to Niebuhr in contending that the purpose of a just society and economy is to provide opportunities for individuals in community to integrate their legitimate natural interests in a fully developed character.

REDISTRIBUTION OF INCOME AND WEALTH

In 1940, Ryan wrote that unemployment had become "our worst economic evil and our most baffling economic problem." He acknowledged that he had given little attention to unemployment in his writings until 1928. In that year, his focus had changed dramatically. Ryan observed that since 1929 he had produced more than thirty speeches and magazine articles dealing with unemployment.[5] In his 1941 autobiography, Ryan remarked that since 1929 no economic problem had consumed more of his attention than unemployment.[6] Ryan also offered a terse summary of

4. Ibid., 104–109.

5. John A. Ryan, *Can Unemployment Be Ended?* (Washington, D.C.: American Association for Economic Freedom, 1940), 3.

6. Ryan, *Social Doctrine in Action,* 233.

his position over the last decade: unemployment, he said, was caused by "bad distribution." The owners of capital receive more money than they can spend, and laborers obtain less than they would like to spend. The remedy for unemployment is for capital to receive less and labor to receive more.[7] During the thirties, Ryan became much more egalitarian regarding the distribution of income and wealth than he had been earlier. Yet there was little change in his conception of rights or his canons of justice. His position changed on the basis of his economic analysis of the causes of unemployment.

When Ryan first noticed the problem of unemployment, he was already attributing it to overproduction and underconsumption. In late 1928 and early 1929 before the October crash, Ryan wrote at least five articles addressing the growing unemployment problem. He blamed "chronic" unemployment on "a general and constant capacity for over-production" and criticized "traditional and theoretical economics" for its view that "[a] supply of any kind of goods . . . is a demand for other goods." The key to ending chronic unemployment was, Ryan insisted, an increase in consumer demand. Consumer demand, he conceded, could be produced by the invention of new luxury items that the rich would buy, but he found "two vital defects" in an economic policy that tried to increase demand by catering to the insatiable wants of the rich. First, it is not easy to invent such luxury items. Second, and more fundamentally, it would employ the working class, who would remain without "a reasonable amount of necessaries and comforts," to produce superfluous goods for the few.[8] Based on his concept of human dignity and his canon of needs, Ryan argued for a policy that would satisfy the "elementary and rational wants of the majority."[9] For Ryan, the only policy that properly combines good economics and ethics is to distribute purchasing power more widely. At the time, he emphasized paying higher wages in order to enhance consumer demand and restricting working hours in order to reduce overproduction.[10]

We can note several themes of Ryan's theory of justice behind this analysis and these recommendations. First, these policies to remedy unemployment comport with Ryan's canon of needs that limits liberty and other goods to those that may be reasonably used for the proximate end of life. Here Ryan went beyond limiting property rights and "free-dom" of contract by prescribing a living wage. He was now prepared to reduce the productive capacity of society by restricting the hours of labor

---

7. Ryan, *Can Unemployment Be Ended?* 3, 12.
8. Ryan, *Questions of the Day*, 192–195.
9. Ibid., 206.
10. Ibid., 196–208.

per worker. This policy, he thought, would have two effects. In addition to increasing employment, it would "retard the production of new luxuries." Ryan considered this limit on production ethically beneficial, because production is justified only insofar as it provides for rational consumption necessary for the good life (meaning morally good). "[T]he supply of useless and harmful luxuries should be kept down to a minimum." By meeting the "rational needs of the masses" and limiting the production of superfluous goods, the twin policies of increasing wages and reducing hours would "be an immense gain for the good life."[11] Throughout the thirties, Ryan cited a 1932 campaign speech in which Roosevelt maintained that "[o]ur industrial plant is built."[12] Ryan favored government policies to discourage investment in productive capacity for the economic reason that the existing productive capacity was underutilized. He also associated calls for unencumbered investment in production with the fallacious moral value of "economic progress as an end to be consciously sought."[13] Government policies that limit individual freedom for investment and for the consumption of luxury goods are fully consistent with Ryan's theory of justice based on a "teleology of the human person."

Second, Ryan's earlier emphasis upon economic analysis remained, but in the thirties he gave more attention to what Patrick Gearty calls the "equilibrium of the economy" as a whole. Except for the 1942 edition of *Distributive Justice,* Ryan's economic analysis was no longer organized around the factors of production in a particular firm, industry, or market. He moved beyond neoclassical economics and used more fully than before the then heterodox economics of John Hobson. In the thirties, he could also draw upon John Maynard Keynes and other macroeconomic theorists to analyze the causes of the Depression.[14] This shift was already apparent in Ryan's initial responses to unemployment; it was bolstered by Pius XI's use of the concept of social justice in *Quadragesimo Anno.* As we observed in Chapter 3, Ryan's earlier use of the concept of human welfare placed the same emphasis upon the common good as the concept of social justice, which he substituted for human welfare after the publication of *Quadragesimo Anno.* Both concepts impelled Ryan to broaden the circumstances relevant to justice to examine the whole economy and not just economic exchanges and distributions. No doubt the authority of a papal encyclical and the

---

11. Ibid., 204–205.
12. E.g., Ryan, *Seven Troubled Years,* 106; idem, *Can Unemployment Be Ended?* 6.
13. Ryan, *Seven Troubled Years,* 108, citing R. H. Tawney to criticize Herbert Hoover.
14. See Gearty, *The Economic Thought of Monsignor Ryan,* 171–200, esp. 185–186 and 200, also 312.

explicit clarity with which the concept of social justice linked a concern for the common good and "the good of each and every constituent element of the community"[15] encouraged Ryan's increasing focus on macroeconomic analysis. As Gearty observes, social justice is specifically concerned with the equilibrium of the economy as a whole.[16] Ryan, for example, claimed that the pope's principle of the common good had many implications for industrial recovery. He went on to illustrate, arguing that an increase in wages and decrease in profits and interest are necessary for increasing employment and are demanded by social justice.[17] In a later essay, Ryan averred that social justice demands "a far greater equality" of distribution in order to avoid excessive investment and encourage consumer demand.[18]

A third theme in Ryan's earlier writings also emerged with vigor in the thirties, that is, the harmony between economic expediency and ethics. Good economics is not only compatible with justice; injustice is also bad economics. In 1935, Ryan wrote that capitalism had been committing suicide over the last half century because no efforts were made to put purchasing power into the hands of those who would use it to buy what was being produced.[19] He repeatedly berated orthodox economists for failing to recognize the "kindergarten fact" that the Depression was caused by a lack of sufficient purchasing power in the control of laborers and farmers, who had a need to consume more.[20] He insisted that an unjust distribution both deprives the majority of a decent livelihood and compels industry to operate far below capacity, hence unemployment. The economic solution—distributing $2,000 in 1929 prices to every family to keep industry at full capacity—is also a just policy of providing a decent livelihood for all. "This fact," Ryan contended, "is a very striking illustration of the principle that in the long run and for the community as a whole, good ethics is in harmony with good business."[21]

As unemployment and papal backing for the concept of social justice moved Ryan toward a focus on the health of the whole economy, he became increasingly egalitarian. He had always been concerned to redistribute income to the extent required for providing every person a decent livelihood. Now Ryan had economic reasons for backing redistribution. He began to focus more attention on whatever politically attain-

15. Ryan, *Seven Troubled Years*, 175.
16. Gearty, *The Economic Thought of Monsignor Ryan*, 245.
17. Ryan, *Seven Troubled Years*, 112.
18. Ibid., 210.
19. Ryan, *A Better Economic Order*, 58.
20. E.g., Ryan, *Seven Troubled Years*, 259–263.
21. Ibid., 260, see also 58–59, 139, 158–161.

able economic policies would redistribute income and wealth to those who would spend it on consumption. After advocating higher wages and reduced hours in his initial essays on unemployment, the remainder of Ryan's essays during the Hoover administration focused more on massive increases in public works and unemployment insurance. Both were to be financed by higher taxes on large incomes and inheritances.[22] He continued to tout higher wages and reduced hours as the only adequate methods for preventing future unemployment, but he saw these policies as coming after the Depression.[23] Evidently Ryan, ever the pragmatist, had decided living wages and reduced hours were politically and economically infeasible during the Depression.[24]

After Roosevelt's election and the establishment of the National Recovery Administration, the situation changed. So did Ryan's response. He renewed his call for an immediate increase in wages and a reduction in hours. By October of 1933—Roosevelt had signed the National Industrial Recovery Act on June 16—Ryan was praising the NIRA for its support for organized labor and for its NRA codes that could set minimum wages and reduced hours.[25] Roosevelt's rhetoric and policies emboldened Ryan's support for redistributive policies. From 1933 until his last published essay eulogizing Roosevelt in July of 1945, Ryan emphasized Roosevelt's intentions and efforts to redistribute income.[26] During the New Deal, Ryan continued to advocate massive public works financed by progressive taxes and persistently argued for a shift of income from capitalists to labor and farmers through higher wages and lower interest and profits.

On each of these points, Ryan thought the New Deal should have gone further than it did. In 1934, he criticized the NRA for not increasing wages and decreasing interest and profits so that more of the product of business would go to labor.[27] Ryan believed this redistribution would have to be permanent in order to prevent future depressions.[28] In lectures on economics he gave at the University of Wisconsin in 1934, Ryan claimed that the current tax policies were the most inadequate of all the recovery measures. He contended that "the highest feasible taxes should be imposed upon inheritances and large incomes as a fundamental measure of permanent recovery."[29] These words were written prior

22. E.g., ibid., 26–33, 33–39, 49–52.
23. Ibid., 58–60.
24. Ibid., 39; idem, *Questions of the Day*, 214.
25. Ryan, *Seven Troubled Years*, 110–114, 114–116.
26. Ibid., 107, 109; idem, "Roosevelt and Social Justice," 300.
27. Ryan, *Seven Troubled Years*, 156–164.
28. Ibid., 156.
29. Ryan, *A Better Economic Order*, 107–108.

to Roosevelt's "soak the rich" tax proposal in 1935,[30] but Ryan later commented that the 1935 tax law was inadequate to achieve full proportional justice.[31] Finally, Ryan was constantly urging larger expenditures for public works.[32] In May of 1935, he went so far as to refer to the "great delusion" and "deplorable error" of the president in assuming that the small amount of money spent on Work Relief would put sufficient purchasing power in the hands of laborers to effect an economic recovery.[33]

Ryan was fervent in his belief that redistribution was the only economic solution for permanent prevention of depressions. He never became interested in countercyclical fiscal policy. Although he cited Keynes often and favorably, especially on the problem of underconsumption, and had read *The General Theory* by April of 1936 (soon after it was published), Ryan never advocated deficit spending as an effective means to avoid depressions. In the late thirties and early forties, Ryan wrote several essays rejecting "pump priming" as a permanent solution to unemployment. Only a redistribution of income from capital to labor will prevent unemployment, maintained Ryan. "[T]here is no need of increasing the national debt further." According to Ryan, unless capital receives less and labor more than under the present distribution, the industrial pump will not stay primed.[34]

During the thirties, redistribution of income and wealth from those who had no rational need for more consumption to those who needed to, or at least could, consume more for their reasonable development was the most persistent theme in Ryan's writings. This theme was compatible with his principal canon of need, yet it now took on an egalitarian cast for economic reasons. Sound economics required redistributing money into the hands of those who would spend it, whether or not they had crucial needs. Despite the encouragement the New Deal provided for sounding this note, Ryan never thought Roosevelt's policies went far enough in achieving redistribution. In a reflective mood at his seventieth birthday party in 1939, Ryan, after noting the progress toward social justice during the New Deal, announced that two "perplexing" economic problems remain to be solved. The first, he said, is unemployment, for which he continued to prescribe " 'a better distribution of purchasing

---

30. William Leuchtenburg, *Franklin D. Roosevelt and the New Deal: 1932–40* (New York: Harper & Row, 1963), 150–154.

31. Ryan, *Seven Troubled Years*, 203.

32. E.g., Ryan, *A Better Economic Order*, 98–100.

33. Ryan, *Seven Troubled Years*, 193.

34. John A. Ryan, "Can Capitalism Be Saved?" *Social Science* 13 (April 1938): 118–119; idem, *Can Unemployment Be Ended?* 9–10; idem, an address delivered at the American Catholic Sociological Convention on December 29, 1942, and printed in the Appendix to the *Congressional Record* (January 14, 1943): A154.

power.' "[35] Even in his final tribute to Roosevelt, Ryan continued to insist that "the farmers and the wage earners will have to gain considerably more at the expense of the receivers of interest, dividends, and profits before the distribution will fully accord with the requirements of social justice."[36]

Ryan, during the thirties, moved closer to the egalitarian emphases in Rauschenbusch's and the early Niebuhr's conceptions of justice. His reasons for redistribution were, however, quite different from theirs. For Ryan, economic equality was neither the goal of justice nor a necessity for balancing class power. Nor had Ryan accepted Rauschenbusch's view that a principle of earned income entailed a nearly equal distribution of income and wealth. He continued to point out that equality of rights does not mean equal amounts,[37] and he did not revise his canons of justice in the 1942 edition of *Distributive Justice*. It was a new economic analysis, elicited by the unemployment problem, focusing on the whole economy that compelled Ryan to advocate policies for a radical redistribution of income and wealth.

GUILDS FOR AN INDUSTRIAL ECONOMY

The second perplexing, unsolved economic problem to which Ryan referred at his seventieth birthday celebration was a reconstruction of the industrial order. He recommended adopting an "adaptation of the Guild System as outlined by Pope Pius XI in his recommendation concerning occupational groups."[38] *Quadragesimo Anno* and the New Deal influenced Ryan's development of this proposal even more directly than they did his policies for redistribution.

The idea of industrial guilds entered Ryan's mind as early as 1913.[39] He continued to refer to it infrequently in his writings prior to 1931.[40] This idea, however, remained unformed until Pope Pius XI affirmed the concept of social justice and occupational groups in *Quadragesimo Anno*. Ryan, in his first essay on *Quadragesimo Anno*, mentioned these ideas as among the new things in the encyclical, but he did not develop

35. Ryan, *Social Doctrine in Action*, 280.
36. Ryan, "Roosevelt and Social Justice," 301.
37. Ryan, *A Better Economic Order*, 149.
38. Ryan, *Social Doctrine in Action*, 280.
39. Ryan, *Social Reform on Catholic Lines*, 6–7.
40. E.g., Ryan, *Social Reconstruction*, 150–151; idem, "The Teaching of the Catholic Church," in *Industrial Relations and the Churches*, vol. 103: *The Annals of the American Academy of Political and Social Science*, ed. John A. Ryan and F. Ernst Johnson (Philadelphia: The American Academy of Political and Social Science, 1922), 79; idem, *Industrial Democracy from a Catholic Viewpoint*, 12.

them.[41] In next two years, he began to develop his proposal for the occupational group system in the American context, but he lacked a model in American experience until Roosevelt established the NRA in mid-1933. By February of 1934, Ryan was suggesting that the NRA provided a base upon which to restructure capitalism along the lines of Pope Pius's occupational group system.[42] Thereafter, Ryan's proposal to reconstruct the industrial order by modifying the NRA to incorporate occupational groups became a theme in his essays only slightly less prominent than his call for redistribution. Even after the NRA was declared unconstitutional by a 9–0 vote in the Schechter Case,[43] he called for its revival and amplification in order to reorganize the economy in accord with the occupational group system.[44] In his autobiography, Ryan reiterated his judgment that the NRA could have developed into the kind of industrial order recommended by Pope Pius.[45] Here again, Ryan tried valiantly to unite economic proposals coming from the church with those of the New Deal.

A brief description of Ryan's proposal will show how it extended the application of his theory of justice in ways that brought him closer to Rauschenbusch's emphases upon economic cooperation and institutional influences upon self-development. Ryan repeatedly quoted Pope Pius's call for "reestablishing" occupational groups. Ryan believed these groups would recapture the spirit of medieval guilds in which masters, journeymen, and apprentices in a particular trade united in cooperation rather than competing for the fruits of economic production. He envisioned the owners, managers, and laborers in part of an industry, such as railroads, uniting in occupational groups. These groups would be "empowered by law to fix wages, interest, dividends, and prices, to determine working conditions, to adjust industrial disputes, and to carry on whatever economic planning was thought feasible." Each occupational group would be federated into a national council for a whole industry, such as transportation. These national councils might also be united into a supreme council for all the industries of a nation. These hierarchically ordered planning councils would constitute what Ryan called the "genuine self-government in industry." The state would establish and supervise these occupational groups, but it would not exercise direct control over the planning.[46]

41. Ryan, *Seven Troubled Years*, 42, 45–46.
42. Ibid., 130, 132–133.
43. Leuchtenburg, *Franklin D. Roosevelt*, 145.
44. E.g., ibid., 222.
45. Ryan, *Social Doctrine in Action*, 249.
46. See Ryan, *A Better Economic Order*, 179–180; idem, *Seven Troubled Years*, 215–216, 308–309; Ryan, *Distributive Justice*, 3d ed., 340–341, for nearly identical descriptions of the occupational group system.

In the NRA codes fixing minimum wages and maximum hours for an industry, Ryan saw the beginnings of these occupational groups. But as with its efforts at redistribution, the New Deal did not go far enough. It did not restructure the capitalist organization of industry that separated economic classes. Ryan repeatedly argued that the major flaw of the NRA was its failure to include labor representation in the authorities that drew up and enforced industry codes. Without labor representation, the interests of the wage-earning class could not be protected and genuine self-government of industry would not be possible.[47] He also saw that government would have to impose codes—the NRA codes were voluntary, and General Hugh Johnson had to use jawboning and compromises to gain business consent[48]—and supervise the substantive provisions in those codes, for example, for minimum wages and maximum hours.[49] Despite these flaws, Ryan saw in NRA cooperative planning an opportunity to apply the Catholic principle of social justice. With modifications, the NRA could achieve an industrial system in the middle ground between capitalist individualism and socialist collectivism.[50]

Ryan understood his proposal for occupational groups to be more than a reform of distributive defects in capitalism. "Reform" is too weak, Ryan wrote, to characterize the "new social order" and "industrial organization" Pope Pius is proposing. "Restructuring" or "rebuilding" is more appropriate to describe this change in the economic arrangements that have existed in capitalism for the last one hundred and fifty years.[51] According to Ryan, "historical capitalism," by which he meant a spirit and a political, economic, ethical philosophy that encourages the unrestricted individual pursuit of selfish ends,[52] is "bankrupt" and "excluded by every important principle and proposal in *Quadragesimo Anno.*"[53] The occupational group system would retain the private ownership of productive property and a limited scope for the profit motive, and would avoid government control of industry. It would abolish unlimited competition and the unrestrained pursuit of profits and interest, which are now defended by disguising them as "free" contracts.[54] It would replace "historical capitalism."

The occupational group system was a new and radical proposal that distinguished Ryan's view of a just economic system more sharply from

---

47. E.g., Ryan, *A Better Economic Order,* 181; idem, *Seven Troubled Years,* 161.
48. Leuchtenburg, *Franklin D. Roosevelt,* 64–67.
49. Ryan, *A Better Economic Order,* 187; idem, *Seven Troubled Years,* 184.
50. Ibid., 161.
51. Ibid., 143.
52. Ibid., 121–127.
53. Ibid., 183.
54. Ibid., 183–184.

the extant capitalist economy than his earlier policies. We should not conclude, however, that it represents a departure from the theory of justice Ryan had developed by 1916.

First, human dignity, that is, the right of every individual to whatever means are required for development toward her or his proximate end, remained the foundation for justice. This new economic order, Ryan argued, "would provide all the freedom and opportunity that the individual needs in order to develop his personality."[55]

Second, Ryan merely extended his earlier application of human welfare focused on how the common good and social institutions provide necessary means for the individual's proper development. With backing from Pope Pius's stress on social justice, Ryan now claimed that a concern for the health and stability of the whole economy demands a reorganization of the productive process. Moreover, he extended his previous analysis of how private property as a "social institution" serves individual development to include the need for reorganized production. An exclusive focus on commutative justice or distributive justice, narrowly defined, is even more inadequate than before. In introducing the chapter that he added to the third edition of *Distributive Justice,* describing industrial democracy (which we will examine below) and the occupational group system, Ryan expressed his view that distributive justice alone is inadequate. "Neither the minimum wage nor labor unions, nor a better distribution, nor all of them together," Ryan claimed, "are capable of giving laborers satisfactory conditions, or society a stable industrial system."[56] Laborers need goods they can possess that are necessary for self-development (e.g., a decent livelihood), but they also need "social institutions" that promote a common good that "distributes" opportunities for individual development.[57] "[J]ustice must become truly effective through the establishment of a juridical and social order which will pervade and inform all economic activity." Changes in the industrial organization embodying these demands of social justice "would make the worker more interested in his work, induce him to turn out a larger and better product, [and] safeguard his dignity, indepen-

---

55. Ryan, *A Better Economic Order,* 183; idem, *Seven Troubled Years,* 184.

56. Ryan, *Distributive Justice,* 3d ed., 333.

57. Recall that social justice considers the common good in its distributive dimension (see *supra,* chapter three, 152–153). Ryan insisted that the pope's concept of social justice considers how the common good distributes what each individual has a right to for the sake of his or her self-perfection. See Ryan, *Seven Troubled Years,* 174–176. The occupational group system, he maintained, is "distributivism" and not "collectivism." Ryan, *A Better Economic Order,* 176–178. By "distributivism" he meant that it obligates persons to institutions that embody common values essential for individuals to perfect their rational nature.

dence and security," as well as bring him a higher standard of living.[58] In sum, the occupational group system (and industrial democracy) are, like private property, social institutions necessary if individuals are to have an opportunity to perfect their personalities.

Ryan thought the occupational group system would promote the common good in three important ways. The first way concerns the long-run stability of a just and prosperous economy. The second and third concern how social institutions promote common values that are necessary for individual self-development.

Ryan believed that occupational groups could redistribute income and wealth through their authority to set wages, hours, interest and dividend rates, and to distribute profits. Further, its federated national councils could adjust "output to probable and reasonable demand."[59] In short, occupational groups could function to stabilize the economy at full employment. Alternatively, this regulation of the economy could be performed by direct state action. Indeed, Ryan thought "effective action by the government" was the only immediate alternative to political and economic liberalism. Nevertheless, he held that occupational groups could perform this function better in the long run. The cooperative action of the people that the self-government of occupational groups could provide is, according to Ryan, "preferable to State action because it is always more conducive to human dignity and human development when men do things for themselves."[60] Ryan feared the "collectivism" and bureaucratic control that might result from direct government action if occupational groups did not govern economic planning.[61] One reason he pushed to transform the NRA codes to redistribute income to labor was that a failure of the NRA to perform this function would probably lead to government operation of essential industries.[62] In sum, Ryan thought the occupational group system was the only viable alternative to socialism for performing the tasks required for economic stability. In the long run, only economic regulation by the occupational group system could avoid both the dominating power of private industrialists and political and bureaucratic dictatorship. It would regulate business but keep control of the economy in the hands of the agents of production.[63]

This cooperation between business and labor in regulating the econ-

---

58. Ryan, *Seven Troubled Years*, 74–75.
59. Ibid., 76.
60. Ibid., 168.
61. Ryan, *A Better Economic Order*, 184–186; idem, *Seven Troubled Years*, 164.
62. Ryan, *Seven Troubled Years*, 164.
63. Ibid., 210–211.

omy points to the second way in which the occupational group system would enhance the common good. It would limit competition and class conflict by encouraging cooperation. Ryan often reiterated the point that the occupational group system was a practical scheme of cooperation that could eliminate class antagonism.[64] He declared this self-government of industry through the cooperation of interested economic parties superior to either capitalist rule or government rule.[65] The claim that occupational groups would encourage cooperation was a large part of Ryan's case for them.

Ryan had never been a champion of economic competition. In the thirties, he became a harsh critic of the competitive spirit encouraged by "historical capitalism." He no longer repeated his earlier willingness to give "competition a fair opportunity to prevent" monopolistic control.[66] In the third edition of *Distributive Justice,* Ryan still supported antitrust action to abolish complete monopolies,[67] but he omitted an earlier passage supporting a return to economic competition.[68] Praise for "unlimited freedom of enterprise and competition" is "perverted Americanism." Ryan associated this perversion with Herbert Hoover's notion of equal opportunity as the unrestrained freedom for individuals to pursue economic goals. Roosevelt, who understood opportunity, not as the "freedom to compete," but as a reasonable minimum of positive economic goods, was on the right track.[69] Yet as we have noted, a just distribution of economic goods is not sufficient to satisfy social justice. Social justice had led Ryan to emphasize the need for social institutions to promote common values that contribute to individual development. Thus, the occupational group system could contribute to self-development simply by replacing the disastrous principle of "free competition" with an arrangement of social life "imbued with the spirit of social justice . . . which will pervade and inform all economic activity."[70] By replacing the competitive spirit of historical capitalism with a cooperative concern for the common good, the occupational group system would advance individual development.

---

64. E.g., Ryan, *A Better Economic Order,* 178; idem, *Seven Troubled Years,* 144, 231, 308.

65. Ibid., 162.

66. Ryan, *Distributive Justice,* 278; see *supra,* chapter three, 180.

67. Ryan, *Distributive Justice,* 3d ed., 222.

68. Ryan no doubt expected occupational group codes to replace competition in performing the task of protecting consumers from the "extortionate" prices of monopolies. In addition to demanding labor representation on code authorities, though with considerable less persistence, Ryan called for consumer and small business participation. See Ryan, *Seven Troubled Years,* 161.

69. Ibid., 223–224.

70. Ibid., 75.

Ryan was well aware that these cooperative agreements, in establishing the distribution and production of economic goods, would limit some individual freedoms. But limitations on freedoms had never bothered Ryan. His question had always been whether freedom provides the opportunity for self-development. "Economic freedom presupposes the actual and proximate opportunity to obtain those goods which are essential to right living and the development of the personality." The freedom Hoover and other unreconstructed capitalists wanted to protect was the opportunity for powerful individuals and groups "to oppress and exploit the majority."[71] Of that freedom we need less, not more. "There is too much individual freedom for the strong, the cunning, and the unscrupulous." The occupational group system seeks to provide more of only "rational freedom." By establishing a graded hierarchical order of cooperating groups between individuals and the state, the occupational groups system avoids both excessive individual freedoms and a powerful state that would threaten the "rational freedoms" individuals need to develop.[72]

For Ryan, the key to economic justice remained what it had been in 1916: safeguarding individual dignity by providing each individual what one needs for moving toward the proximate end of one's rational nature. On the basis of social justice, Ryan had now expanded those needs to include an industrial organization that encouraged individuals and classes to cooperate in promoting a common good that furthers individual development.

There is a third way in which the occupational group system could contribute to the common good. Industrywide cooperation between business and labor could easily develop industrial democracy in each firm.[73] Ryan had been promoting his version of industrial democracy since *Social Reconstruction*, his commentary on the Bishops' Program of 1919. In the thirties, as he came to view the occupational group system as the best method for introducing industrial democracy, Ryan treated the latter as a second part of his proposal for restructuring the economic order of historical capitalism. Like the occupational group system, industrial democracy is a restructuring of capitalism. These two proposals share the purpose of promoting common values that are required for individual development, but industrial democracy was a separate proposal with its own distinct contributions to human dignity. It deserves examination in its own right.

---

71. Ibid., 275.
72. Ryan, *A Better Economic Order*, 178; idem, *Seven Troubled Years*, 134, 231.
73. E.g., Ryan, *A Better Economic Order*, 186–187; idem, *Seven Troubled Years*, 144.

Labor Sharing in Management, Profits, and Ownership

Unlike his emphasis upon redistribution and his proposal for the occupational group system, Ryan's vision for a democratic organization of firms was not initially a response to events in the thirties. Ryan recalled that he first proposed labor sharing in management, profits, and ownership in his 1913 debate with Morris Hillquit.[74] Actually, he advocated only a wider distribution of ownership in that debate. In 1916, *Distributive Justice* proposed an expansion in consumer and productive cooperatives, which Ryan thought would foster the same qualities among workers that he later associated with industrial democracy.[75] Then in 1920, Ryan began to call for labor sharing in management and profits independently of expansions of the cooperative movement.[76] During the twenties, he wrote several essays supporting the gradual reorganization of corporations to include workers' sharing in management, profits, and ownership.[77]

Patrick Gearty notes that during this period Ryan was promoting his version of industrial democracy without explicit approval from Catholic social teachings.[78] Furthermore, other than urging labor unions to change their goals and seek cooperation with management in a more democratic organization of firms,[79] Ryan had been vague about how industrial democracy might come about. *Quadragesimo Anno* changed that situation. Pope Pius deemed it advisable for the wage contract to be modified so that "workers and executives [could] become sharers in the ownership or management, or else participate in some way in the profits."[80] Ryan, as he subtly observed in his first essay on *Quadragesimo Anno,* now had a papal imprimatur for his version of industrial democracy.[81] Pius's proposal for occupational groups, and then the NRA, also provided a means by which the state could bring about conditions of cooperation that would encourage labor and corporations to adopt various features of industrial democracy. Thereafter, Ryan

---

74. Ryan, *Social Doctrine in Action,* 228.
75. See *supra,* chapter three, 157; Ryan, *Distributive Justice,* 210–234.
76. Ryan, *Social Reconstruction,* 141–160.
77. Ryan, *Industrial Democracy from a Catholic Viewpoint,* 1–12; idem, "Social Objectives of Catholics," *Catholic Charities Review* 13 (April 1929): 114–116; idem, *Declining Liberty,* 213–223, 224–238.
78. Gearty, *The Economic Thought of Monsignor Ryan,* 286.
79. Ryan, *Declining Liberty,* 213–223.
80. Pope Pius XI, *Quadragesimo Anno,* in *Seven Great Encyclicals* (New York: Paulist Press, 1939), 144, sec. 65; see also Gearty, *The Economic Thought of Monsignor Ryan,* 286–287.
81. Ryan, *Seven Troubled Years,* 44–45.

incorporated discussions of industrial democracy into his arguments for occupational groups.[82]

Because industrial democracy became a part of Ryan's proposals for a new industrial organization to replace historical capitalism, it is appropriate that we treat it among those policies he endorsed in the thirties. As with the occupational group system, Ryan grounded this proposal in Pope Pius's concept of social justice, namely, how the common values fostered by social institutions are essential for individual development. That Ryan had formulated most aspects of his version of industrial democracy before 1931 confirms that Ryan's concern for the common good was already largely incorporated into his earlier concept of human welfare.[83] It demonstrates continuity in Ryan's theory of justice.

As Ryan recognized, "industrial democracy" was an umbrella concept during the twenties and thirties. It referred to ideas ranging from collective bargaining to socialism. Ryan, of course, rejected socialism, but he did not think "trade unionism" or collective bargaining went far enough in reorganizing employer-employee relations. It continues a conflictual relationship and provides no basis for laborers to have an interest in their work.[84] Ryan believed that his proposals for labor sharing in management, profits, and ownership were much more radical, but he also recognized why trade unionists were often critical of programs under the guise of these names. Cooperative arrangements could be used by management to co-opt the labor movement. Labor sharing in management could, for example, be used to describe arrangements in which owners dominated laborers in a "company union."[85] It is important, therefore, to describe the crucial features of each of the three aspects of Ryan's proposal for industrial democracy. Ryan considered each of these plans for sharing to be relatively distinct from the others. It is possible to have labor sharing in management without sharing in profits and sharing in management and profits without sharing in ownership.[86]

These three proposals do, however, have something in common. Ryan considered them a necessary addition to the just distribution of wages if individuals were to have an opportunity to develop. "An economic society which entirely ignores these three objectives will fail to provide individuals with the necessary means of developing some of their very important faculties."[87] Thus, these objectives are required so that "the

---

82. E.g., ibid., 74.
83. See *supra,* chapter three, 152–153.
84. Ryan, *Industrial Democracy from a Catholic Viewpoint,* 1–3.
85. Ryan, *Declining Liberty,* 218.
86. Ryan, *A Better Economic Order,* 161.
87. Ryan, "Social Objectives of Catholics," 115.

human dignity of the laborer will be adequately safeguarded."[88] Ryan explained how each of these reorganizations of a firm serves as a means to self-development.

Ryan believed laborers should share in management because it would provide the majority of persons "the opportunity to exercise their directive [and creative] faculties, as well as their obedient faculties, and to become something more than instruments of production." Sharing in management would offer laborers opportunities to exercise the "higher faculties" that are part of human rational nature.[89] Ryan did not expect the wage earner, at least in the short run, to participate in management decisions about the commercial or financial operations of a firm. On the other hand, laborers have a direct interest in and are capable of all management decisions that bear on production in the workplace. They should not be limited, as collective bargaining is, to participation in the determination of wages, hours, and working conditions.[90] In order to protect union interests from being co-opted by this cooperative management, Ryan proposed that the labor members on joint committees be elected by shop unions.[91] Ryan conceived a program for labor sharing in management that he believed would permit workers to develop their rational faculties without sacrificing managerial efficiency or undermining unions' capacity to represent labor's interest.

Ryan's justification for laborers' sharing in profits focused more on inducing initiative and expenditures of energy that would serve economic welfare than on expanding opportunities for individuals to develop. It would, said Ryan, extend to laborers the opportunity for indefinite gains as a reward for efficiency and success.[92] Again, Ryan warned against profit-sharing plans that undermine labor interests. He rejected profit sharing designed to keep workers out of labor unions or that substitute profit sharing for reasonable wages.[93] His profit-sharing plan would distribute profits, in excess of what is required to pay a dividend sufficient to attract capital, to wage earners and salaried employees in proportion to their contracted wages or salaries. Stockholders would be paid at a set rate like bondholders rather than receive a share of

---

88. Ryan, *A Better Economic Order*, 161.

89. Ryan, *Declining Liberty*, 231; see also idem, *Social Reconstruction*, 141–144; idem, *A Better Economic Order*, 163; idem, *Seven Troubled Years*, 229; idem, *Distributive Justice*, 3d ed., 335.

90. Ryan, *Social Reconstruction*, 148–149; idem, *Declining Liberty*, 231; idem, *A Better Economic Order*, 162–163; idem, *Seven Troubled Years*, 229–230.

91. Ryan, *Declining Liberty*, 218; idem, *Distributive Justice*, 3d ed., 335.

92. Ryan, *Declining Liberty*, 231–232; idem, *A Better Economic Order*, 167–168; idem, *Seven Troubled Years*, 230; Ryan, *Distributive Justice*, 3d ed., 336.

93. Ryan, *Declining Liberty*, 233.

the profits. Profits, Ryan argued, should "go to those who create them, and who require them as stimulus to increase production." He opposed the existing practice of basing dividends on profits because it "rewards idle ownership at the expense of labor." It does not encourage productivity.[94] Ryan could have argued for this profit-sharing plan on the basis of his canon of efforts and sacrifices.[95] In accord with that canon, it rewards achievements in self-development that are simultaneously contributions to economic welfare. Ryan intended profit sharing both as an inducement for proper individual development and as economically expedient.

Ryan associated labor sharing in ownership with "consciousness of independence, security, self-respect, and the possession of a degree of social and political power."[96] Labor sharing in ownership would benefit persons in much the same way as the institution of private property does. It would expand the benefits of private property to more persons in an industrial economy in which few persons can own their own productive property. Again, Ryan warned that most plans for employees to participate in stock ownership are inadequate shams instead of real sharing in ownership. Mere proprietorship of securities fails to give the workers control. Such programs may provide greater security and a better distribution of income, but they do not confer power on the workers.[97] For sharing in ownership of corporations to aid individual self-development maximally, worker ownership would have to confer greater independence, self-respect, and power, just as ownership of private property in agriculture does.[98] To confer these benefits, programs for labor ownership in corporations must include labor participation in the control of corporate policies. The worker needs more than a better distribution; social justice demands a new status for the worker.

From the beginning, Ryan understood this vision for industrial democracy as a scheme of cooperation for cultivating the common interests between labor and capital.[99] Long before he proposed the occupational group system, Ryan considered industrial democracy to be in harmony with the spirit of the medieval guilds.[100] He intended it to eclipse the spirit of class antagonism and competition and the industrial autocracy that characterized historical capitalism. By mitigating class conflict, it

---

94. Ryan, *A Better Economic Order*, 166–169; idem, *Seven Troubled Years*, 230; idem, *Distributive Justice*, 3d ed., 337.
95. See *supra*, chapter three, 170–171.
96. Ryan, *Declining Liberty*, 230, 234.
97. Ryan, *A Better Economic Order*, 170–171; idem, *Distributive Justice*, 3d ed., 338.
98. Ryan, *Declining Liberty*, 236–237.
99. Ibid., 229–230.
100. Ryan, *Industrial Democracy from a Catholic Viewpoint*, 12.

was also intended to avert the threat of socialism.[101] Ryan's version of industrial democracy retained the profit motive and private ownership of productive property as positive forces for individual development. His purpose was to open these opportunities to all persons by a scheme of cooperation that would make the advantages of seeking profits and ownership available to the majority of laborers.

Together, industrial democracy and the occupational group system were to form a hierarchical system of economic and political cooperation that Ryan believed would comply with God's teleological ordering of the universe, an order in which each individual could develop toward his or her proper end. In an essay written during the period in which he was advocating these proposals for a new industrial order, Ryan criticized socialism for proposing economic policies incompatible with the Catholic view that the economic order should serve as a means for humans to attain their end in God. Ryan wrote: "[T]he Catholic conception of society is organic, implying a hierarchical order of social functions, subordination of the whole to God and public authority derived from and representing the authority of God." This ordered society is a necessary "means of fulfilling one's duties, following one's vocation, developing one's faculties, living a rational life and attaining one's final end in compliance with the purpose of God."[102] Ryan could have employed these same passages in criticism of capitalism. The point is that Ryan conceived of the new economic order he proposed in the thirties as a means for individuals to develop toward the proximate end established for them by God's eternal law.

This conception of a divinely ordered economic life was a continuation of Ryan's previously formulated theory of justice. It was also continuous with the primacy of the canon of needs correlative to the necessary means for self-development. Moreover, those needs include a common good in the form of social institutions that create opportunities for developing all one's faculties. What is new is an extended application of the concept of human welfare, now social justice, to include an industrial organization that safeguards human dignity by facilitating individual development through cooperation. Ryan did not abandon his earlier concern for distribution of the goods each individual needs for self-development. Political action to secure a living wage for every family remained the foundation of his proposals for justice. Nevertheless, in the thirties Ryan gave more attention to the common good required by social justice. His arguments for a more egalitarian distribution were based on

---

101. Ryan, *Declining Liberty*, 229.
102. Ryan, *Seven Troubled Years*, 89.

the need for a stable economy to prevent unemployment. His arguments for the occupational group system and industrial democracy were based almost exclusively upon social justice. They were concerned with distributive justice only in the sense that the "distributive" side of social justice considers how social institutions and the common good "distribute" the means for individuals to perfect their rational nature.

SOME COMPARISONS AND CONTRASTS

The differences from Niebuhr and the increasing similarities to Rauschenbusch are apparent. At the level of policy, Ryan never accepted the public ownership of all essential industries nor a strategy of achieving justice by backing the militancy of the proletarian mission. He was not dogmatic in opposition to state ownership of industry. Ryan was not afraid to incorporate "socialist" policies of state ownership and regulation of industry into his economic program. Nevertheless, his proposals for restructuring of industry retained private ownership of corporations and a wider, albeit restricted, application of the profit motive. He wanted the profit motive applied to laborers and management but not to shareholders. Instead of trying to achieve justice through a proletarian confrontation with capitalism and its democratic support, Ryan favored ethical arguments addressed to New Deal politicians in order to obtain state action to bring about economic cooperation. As Niebuhr was seeking a balance of power to remedy injustice to the laboring class, Ryan sought to enhance the power of workers via economic arrangements that would make them partners in cooperation.

These policy differences reflect more fundamental differences in Ryan's and Niebuhr's theories of justice. Theological and ethical differences underlay differences in the policies Niebuhr and Ryan advocated during the thirties. They also explain why Ryan's proposals for industrial democracy and the occupational group system were a more radical challenge to historical capitalism than the policies Niebuhr would favor during the forties and fifties. For Ryan, there was neither an inevitable conflict between the ideal and the actual nor a need to maintain a creative tension between them. Ryan's vision for justice to safeguard human dignity was not as high an ideal as Niebuhr's, nor was his view of the human capacity for justice as pessimistic. We will consider each point in turn.

First, Ryan did not consider perfect justice an embodiment of the social ideal of disinterested love in which persons would live in a perfect harmony of absolute equality and freedom. For Ryan, divine love does not transcend all natural interests. God is the ultimate end of a divine and natural order in which individuals have a natural and proper interest in developing their rational nature in a way conducive to attaining their ultimate end in God. The question of justice, then, "becomes the question of the kind of life which is desirable for the individual." "According to the Catholic view, organized society and all forms of social organization exist for the welfare [i.e., perfecting rational nature] of the individual members."[103] The aim of justice is to provide every person with the goods and social institutions one needs to develop one's rational nature. Justice is relatively independent of love, but it is not in conflict with love. The function of justice, even perfect justice, is to discriminate between the rightful interests of persons in the means to develop their rational nature and their interests that impede the opportunities for others to develop. Thus, Ryan considered the occupational group system and industrial democracy fully compatible with divine justice and love. The fact that these ways of organizing industry would restrict some freedoms, permit some inequalities, and assert the right of each individual to the freedoms and other goods required for self-development does not make them less than ideal. Such discriminations among interests are the task of justice, even divine justice. These discriminations comply with the divine ordering of nature that affords all persons the opportunity to develop. They are required to correct deficiencies in historical capitalism—for example, "free" contracts and unfettered competitive markets—that diminish human dignity.

Second, Ryan believed that his canons of justice could be applied to policies without having to compromise them in order to take sin into account. Ryan did not ignore sin. In the thirties, he repeatedly held that the sin of greed was the major obstacle to New Deal reforms and to a new economic order.[104] As with Niebuhr, this greed includes greed for power as well as for profits, and it threatened Ryan's confidence in getting out of the Depression by any rational method.[105] Ryan certainly viewed achieving justice as a struggle against sin, and he did not think greed could be eliminated by a just economic system.[106] What we do not find in Ryan's writings, however, is a view of sin as a universal and insatiable will-to-power that distorts all reasoning about justice. Even those whose greed impedes justice can be persuaded by sound moral arguments. The most important contribution to a new economic order

103. Ryan, "Social Objectives of Catholics," 114.
104. Ryan, A Better Economic Order, 189–190; idem, Seven Troubled Years, 109–110, 130, 146.
105. Ibid., 154.
106. Ibid., 109.

would be "an increase of ethical instruction and a lifting of ethical standards."[107]

Ryan believed the persistent reality of sin made the progress toward a better economic system gradual and arduous. He was willing to settle for immediate gains, delaying the implementation of his proposals for restructuring the economy. But Ryan, unlike Niebuhr, did not modify his standards of justice to deal with the inevitability of sin. Ryan had more confidence in the rational resources for social ethics. Niebuhr, had he commented on Ryan's theory of justice, would have criticized it for the naivety and rigidity characteristic of Catholic natural law. Ryan did not seek a balance of power that would approximate justice, but an industrial organization that encouraged cooperation in securing just opportunities for all individuals. Cooperation could not eliminate sin or the need for sanctions against unjust behavior, but it could eliminate the conflict and spirit of competition that undercut opportunities for self-development in historical capitalism. Ryan, with his hope for cooperation, could not have countenanced either Niebuhr's strategies for achieving a balance of power in the thirties or Niebuhr's later view that Roosevelt's policies adjusted the balance of power within capitalism to achieve a tolerable justice. Despite his plaudits for Roosevelt, Ryan ended his career saying that Roosevelt had not gone far enough either in redistribution or in restructuring the economic order. Ryan's understanding of sin could not have given him reason to accept the justice of any economic system that was not based on cooperation in safeguarding the dignity of every individual.

As we have discovered, Ryan and Rauschenbusch shared the view, contrary to Niebuhr's social ideal, that justice requires securing persons an opportunity to develop their best natural interests. Rauschenbusch's insistence on the interconnectedness of love and justice and on a broad socio-historical analysis of economic institutions led him to emphasize cooperation and equality more than Ryan. But Ryan's response to events in the thirties, although not dissolving these differences, closed the gap. The increasing attention he gave to the stability and efficiency of the whole economy led Ryan to emphasize redistribution. His increasing concern for how social institutions shape opportunities for character development led Ryan to push proposals for the occupational group system and industrial democracy. These changes in industrial organization were intended to encourage cooperation and other common values by which laborers could perfect their character.

To be sure, Ryan's economic analysis based on the theory of under-

---

107. Ryan, *A Better Economic Order,* 185.

consumption and overproduction never persuaded him to include an egalitarian principle in his canons of justice. Nor did his call for economic institutions that encourage cooperation go so far as Rauschenbusch's "socializing" the economy. For Ryan, justice, even social justice, differs from love in that it "considers human persons as mutually independent and as possessing individual rights."[108] Justice requires cooperation in promoting a common good that will safeguard individual dignity, but it does not require institutions that will engender love and solidarity for the sake of self-development. How far Ryan might have gone in uniting his economic analysis and moral theory in a conception of justice that emphasized equality and cooperation is not easy to discern. His 1942 edition of *Distributive Justice* was still organized around the four factors of production and offered no substantive revision of his canons of justice, but in the preface, Ryan conceded the need for a sweeping reorganization of the entire project. After the war, he observed, capitalism will be replaced by "some form of collectivism" in which the "instruments of production will be owned and operated by the state." "[A] discussion of just distribution in terms of the landowner, the capitalist, the businessman and laborer, [*sic*] will be outmoded and outdated." The "*principles* of justice will remain unchanged," but "their *application* to . . . the new economic order will call for a vast amount of argument and discussion which are not found in this volume." Much of this volume, Ryan conceded, "will become superfluous and useless."[109] What Ryan had in mind is intriguing and ambiguous.[110] He certainly was prepared to go further in the directions his thinking had moved in the thirties.

On the matter of sin and redemption from it, Ryan remained distant from Rauschenbusch. Neither of them took Niebuhr's tack of adjusting the standards of justice to sin, but Rauschenbusch looked to social movements and changing social institutions to redeem persons from

---

108. Ryan, *The Norm of Morality*, 53.

109. Ryan, *Distributive Justice*, 3d ed., v–vi.

110. Ryan's analysis of the circumstances of justice in terms of the whole economy and the effects of economic institutions on character development had apparently convinced him to doubt the usefulness of his earlier attention to productivity within a firm. Ryan's expanded application of the concept of social justice had apparently led him to see a need for reformulating his theory of justice. Ryan was too old for such a mammoth project, and there is no indication in *The Norm of Morality*, published in 1944, of fundamental changes in his moral theory. Nevertheless, one wonders what direction Ryan's thought might have taken had he been younger. There is no reason to believe that changes in analysis would have forced Ryan to alter the primacy of his canon of needs, but would a reorganization of *Distributive Justice* have required him to incorporate equality and cooperation into his canons? What form of "collectivism" did he expect? Was he really prepared to move further in the direction of socialism?

selfishness and corrupted moral reasoning inculcated by institutional influences. We do see some shades of Rauschenbusch in Ryan as he expanded his analysis of the relation between economic institutions and opportunities for self-development. In the thirties, Ryan observed that the "hearts and minds" of the "heads of corporations" "have been corrupted by a long tradition of immoral business practices, unlimited economic domination, unjust legislative favoritism and ethically unsound decisions by the courts."[111] In another essay, he called for "more favorable economic institutions" to counter an economic system that "makes it almost morally impossible . . . to resist the temptations to greed."[112] Ryan, however, never viewed social movements or social institutions as means of grace to redeem persons from corrupted reasoning about justice. He thought in terms of a supernatural order distinct from the natural order. Francis Broderick cites a letter, written in 1935, in which Ryan confesses "the assumption of no connection between the two [supernatural and natural orders] except by elevator."[113] Rauschenbusch's hope for social redemption through the new evangelism of the church, the labor movement, and the socialist movement was alien to Ryan. If the occupational groups system and industrial democracy were to have a role in improving the moral character of persons, they would have to be brought into existence by interpreting the natural law for morally sensitive politicians and judges who would enact and enforce just policies. At the end, Ryan's hope for social justice lay with the New Deal culminating the reforms it had initiated in the early thirties.

---

111. Ryan, *Seven Troubled Years*, 137.
112. Ibid., 113.
113. Broderick, *Right Reverend New Dealer*, 242.

6

RETRIEVING CHRISTIAN THEOLOGY TO BACK A REALIST STRATEGY

In the end, Niebuhr too would come to view the New Deal as an instrument of justice, but in the late thirties and early forties, he was still working at a more fundamental level. He was seeking a Christian theology to back and clarify his realist strategy for justice.

Niebuhr's attempt to combine traditional theology with a political ethic culminated in the publication of *The Nature and Destiny of Man* in the early forties. The concept of myth, which he introduced in *Reflections on the End of an Era,* enabled him to appropriate traditional Christian doctrines in ways that supported his Christian realism. This retrieval in turn allowed Niebuhr to offer more theological and more comprehensive interpretations of human nature, history, and God to back the creative tension between the ideal and the actual as his overarching frame of reference for justice. These theological investigations, coupled with the momentous political and economic events of the late thirties and forties, led to changes in Niebuhr's working standards of justice and their application.

This chapter is the story of these developments in Niebuhr's thought. It begins with an account of how his concept of myth functioned. First, it served hermeneutically to correct defects in a simple appropriation of traditional Christian doctrines. Second, it lent credibility to the paradoxical truths in those doctrines. I then consider Niebuhr's understanding of the first three base points as he interpreted them through the retrieval of traditional Christian doctrines understood as myth. This chapter concludes with a brief revisit to the tension between the ideal and the actual in light of these theological developments and Niebuhr's interpretation of political and economic events. In the seventh chapter, we will examine his modified strategy of justice and its application to democracy, property, and other narrower issues. In the forties and fifties, narrower issues took on new importance for Niebuhr.

My thesis is that Niebuhr's overarching frame of reference in Christian realism and his general principle of justice changed very little, while changes in his working standards of justice led him to alter his policy judgments.

THE FUNCTION OF MYTH

As noted at the end of Chapter 4, Niebuhr had, in the midthirties, formulated the task of joining traditional Christian convictions to a radical political ethic. That agenda was framed by his Christian realism. The tension between the ideal and the actual established the criteria for retrieving traditional Christian doctrines. As he put it in 1935: "The ethical fruitfulness of various types of religion is determined by the quality of their tension between the historical [actual] and the transcendent [ideal]." This quality was measured by two considerations: (1) the degree to which religious ideas truly transcend every value and achievement in history and (2) the degree to which they remain in "organic contact" (i.e., relevance and credibility) with history so that it is not robbed of all meaning and significance.[1] As in the twenties, the ethical fruitfulness of religious ideas was still the overriding criterion for their adoption. In order to bear fruit within the frame of Christian realism, Christian doctrines must maintain a tension between the ideal and the actual. This tension must first illumine the ethical problems of history without sanctifying any actual condition in history, and second, be credible in light of modern science and experience. For Niebuhr, the concept of myth functioned to resolve both these problems.

Retrieving Christian Doctrine

We will first consider how the concept of myth enabled Niebuhr to retrieve traditional Christian doctrines within his realist framework.

---

1. Niebuhr, *An Interpretation*, 18.

Already in *Does Civilization Need Religion?* Niebuhr was rejecting various liberal theologies and secular philosophies that abandoned traditional Christian doctrines in order to be intellectually acceptable in the modern world. These systems of thought fail on the first consideration above; in seeking to be rational and scientific, they sanctify the actual as though it were the ideal. They suppose that "transcendent ideals of Christian morality have become immanent possibilities in the historic process."[2] Yet orthodox Christianity, adopted without modification, fails to satisfy the second consideration; its "religious truths" are embedded in outmoded science and are associated with canonical moral codes that are merely primitive moral standards.[3] It fails to make "organic contact" with modern science and moral perspectives. Hence, it fails to illumine the modern ethical problem.

This defect of orthodox Christian doctrines can be overcome if we understand them as myths. They are myths in two senses. They are both "prescientific" and "suprascientific." As prescientific, they make claims about causal relations that defy modern science, and they should be rejected as primitive. They should not simply be appropriated; they must be restated in ways that do not reject the findings of science. As suprascientific, these myths contain permanent truths that can be defended against the criticisms of the scientific age.[4] In fact, this suprascientific quality of myth plus its supra- or ultrarational character is its genius. These are the qualities of myth that allow it to challenge the actual moral conditions of modern culture. How is this so? Let us consider first its suprascientific character and then its suprarationality.

Niebuhr understood science as capable only of describing cause-effect relations after the fact.[5] Scientific reasoning is incapable of knowledge beyond the cause-effect sequences on the surface of history.[6] Applied to interpretations of human nature and history, it perceives human interrelations and relations to the world as mechanical, valueless, and meaningless.[7] Purely naturalistic interpretations of human nature tell little truths in the interest of a great lie. The lie is that "spatio-temporal realities are self-contained and self-explanatory and that a scientific description of

---

2. Ibid., 19.
3. Ibid., 14, 18.
4. Reinhold Niebuhr, "The Truth in Myths," in *Faith and Politics*, 16. First published in 1937. This analysis of Niebuhr's idea of myth cites materials from the late thirties and forties, as well as writings from the fifties. The earlier writings, especially "The Truth in Myths," clearly demonstrate that Niebuhr's concept of myth was operative in his retrieval of Christian doctrines in *The Nature and Destiny of Man*.
5. Ibid., 18.
6. Niebuhr, *An Interpretation*, 20–21.
7. Niebuhr, "The Truth in Myths," 17, 20.

sequences is an adequate analysis of causes."[8] Science comprehends neither the depth of human sin and evil in history nor the transcendent possibilities of humans, for example, neither the height of love nor the depth of self-love. The suprascientific genius of myth is "to suggest the dimension of depth in reality and to point to a realm of essence which transcends the surface of history."[9] As long as we understand these myths as paradoxical rather than literal truths, they are not incompatible with the little truths of science. They point to a transcendent truth for which the little truths of science have no implications.

There are rational understandings of humans that are not purely scientific or naturalistic. Whenever ideals and meaning are introduced into interpretations of human nature, human history, human origins, and human destiny, something transcendent and mythical is also covertly introduced into purportedly scientific accounts of life and history.[10] For that reason, Niebuhr understood the liberal idea of evolutionary progress and the Marxist idea of the revolutionary achievement of human destiny as mythologies.[11] These, and still more idealistic philosophies, contain some measure of the larger truth that pure naturalism misses, but all rational mythologies (by which Niebuhr meant those mythologies that try to establish coherent interpretations of human nature and history) fail "to do justice to the tragic realities of evil [the depths of human life] and to its paradoxical relation with the good [the heights of human life]."[12]

Rationalized myth destroys the paradox of true myth in one of two ways. It either "loses its virtue because it ceases to point to the realm of transcendence beyond history, or, pointing to it, fails to express the organic and paradoxical relationship between the conditioned and the unconditioned."[13] (Rational myths necessarily fail on either the first or the second criterion for the ethical fruitfulness of religion cited above.) The first error is committed by monistic (naturalist or idealist) philosophies that leave out or reduce the transcendent ideal in their attempt to comprehend the harmony of human temporal existence.[14] Niebuhr no doubt would have included both Rauschenbusch and Ryan in this category of error: Rauschenbusch due to his scientific account of redemption and Ryan due to the continuity he asserted between the proximate end

---

8. Ibid., 26.
9. Niebuhr, *An Interpretation*, 21.
10. Niebuhr, "The Truth in Myths," 20.
11. Niebuhr, *Reflections on the End of an Era*, 121–136.
12. Niebuhr, "The Truth in Myths," 23, 21.
13. Ibid., 26.
14. Ibid., 28–29.

and ultimate end of human nature. The second error is committed by dualistic philosophies, such as mysticism, when they locate meaning in a transcendent realm that negates the reality and destroys the meaning of mundane existence.[15] Both errors fail to maintain the creative tension between the ideal and the actual. An example of the first error, particularly pertinent to this study, is when love is identified with or reduced to justice between conflicting groups. The second error occurs where love becomes a transcendent communion with God that is irrelevant to a just arbitration of conflicts in history. The perfect harmony of the ideal of love cannot be made to cohere with highest expressions of justice, but, paradoxically, love is the transcendent goal of justice and is therefore relevant to justice.

Niebuhr called true myth supra- or ultrarational as well as suprascientific. True myth relates the transcendent ideal and the actual of history in terms "embodying paradox and contradiction and straining the limits of rationality"[16] or in terms that "elude the canons of logic."[17] Only this paradoxical quality enables myth to maintain an ethically fruitful tension between the ideal and the actual. It can

> discover symbols of the transcendent in the actual without either separating the one from, or identifying it with, the other. . . . [I]t points to the timeless in time, to the ideal in the actual, but does not lift the temporal to the category of the eternal (as pantheism does), nor deny the significant glimpses of the eternal and the ideal in the temporal (as dualism does).[18]

In sum, myth was the key to Niebuhr's retrieval of Christian doctrines because it expresses truth paradoxically. It uses symbols from the temporal world that point to a transcendent dimension of reality.[19] That transcendent ideal is the goal of and relevant to temporal existence but never fully true nor achievable within it. The ideal of love, for example, is intellectually incoherent and morally impossible within the inevitable conflicts of history, but it contains the ultimate truth about how humans ought to live together within history. The love symbolized in the cross is paradoxically an impossible possibility within history. The claim that this

---

15. Ibid., 28.
16. Reinhold Niebuhr, "Coherence, Incoherence, and Christian Faith," in *Christian Realism and Political Problems* (New York: Charles Scribner's Sons, 1953), 185.
17. Niebuhr, "The Truth in Myths," 18.
18. Niebuhr, *An Interpretation*, 80.
19. Niebuhr later dropped the word "myth" in favor of "symbol" because of the skeptical connotation of "myth" (see Reinhold Niebuhr, *"The Self" and the Dramas of History* [New York: Charles Scribner's Sons, 1955], 97), but his emphasis upon paradox was crucial to both.

love is the standard for human relations cannot be made without deceiving; yet attempts to understand love so that it does not deceive anyone about what is possible in history are "immeasurably less profound."[20] The love symbolized by the cross is, therefore, a paradoxical truth for our historical existence. In the language of Paul, which Niebuhr used in his lead essay in *Beyond Tragedy,* it is deceptive, yet truer than an understanding of love or justice fully attainable within history, or than insisting that this ideal of love is simply impossible in history. It is truer than either scientific descriptions or rational mythic accounts of human possibilities.

For Niebuhr, Hebrew prophecy exemplified the paradoxical relation between the transcendent and the historical characteristic of this permanent truth of myth. This quality of mythic paradox is endemic to Christianity, which arose out of the mythical heritage of the Hebrew prophetic movement.[21] Jesus' ethic of love is, for example, "the perfect fruit of prophetic religion."[22] Although Christian doctrines have been interpreted in ways that lead to a dualism that isolates the ideal from the actual or a monism that too readily sanctifies the actual, they are appropriately interpreted as paradoxical myths. This hermeneutical basis for understanding Christian doctrines dealing with creation, sin and evil, and redemption enabled Niebuhr to retrieve these doctrines as backing for his Christian realist theory of justice. It allowed him to reject the primitive prescientific elements in these myths, which prohibit or hinder their "organic contact" with the modern mind, yet to express their permanent, paradoxical truth in ways that challenged the inadequacies of scientific and philosophical interpretations of human nature and history.

Armed with this mythical interpretation of Christian doctrines, Niebuhr was no longer left with endorsing intellectual and social movements based on illusions that are useful in approximating justice. He could now endorse the myths of the Christian tradition, kept vital in the church, as the practical basis for his political ethic. Niebuhr, of course, never abandoned the Christian tradition or the church, but for a time the focus of his attention was on the proletarian movement, having lost confidence in the church as a force for greater justice. In the midthirties, according to Richard Fox, Niebuhr began to withdraw from active participation in the Socialist Party and increased his interest in his vocation as a seminary teacher, theologian, and religious spokesman.[23] Perhaps the shift from

---

20. Reinhold Niebuhr, *Beyond Tragedy: Essays on the Christian Interpretation of History* (New York: Charles Scribner's Sons, 1937), 20–21.
21. Niebuhr, *An Interpretation,* 31.
22. Ibid., 43.
23. Fox, *Reinhold Niebuhr,* 157–161, 170.

thinking in terms of useful illusions to thinking in terms of true myths helps to explain this change in where Niebuhr focused his energy. Unlike Rauschenbusch, Niebuhr never viewed the church as an agent for progress toward justice, but the importance of myth for his realist strategy for justice gave the church a vital role in maintaining cultural awareness of the tension between the ideal and the actual.

The Credibility of Christian Doctrine

In order to bear fruit in the struggle against injustice, Christian doctrines must do more than maintain a creative tension between the transcendent and the historical. They must be credible. Credibility involves more than avoiding outright contradictions with science. It also requires that the permanent paradoxical truth of myth be in some way verified. Niebuhr chided Barthianism for a dogmatism, which although avoiding primitive, prescientific myth makes "no effort to validate Christianity in experience against competition with other religions."[24] (By "other religions" Niebuhr intended what he called rational mythologies, e.g., Marxism, bourgeois liberalism, and Buddhism.)

Niebuhr no longer hoped, as he had in the twenties, to demonstrate the credibility of Christian doctrine by claiming that its transcendent values would be proven true as the ideal subdues the actual. If, however, the paradoxical structure of myth requires a dialectical relation between the transcendent and history, it can and must be partially verified in history. Myths are, asserted Niebuhr, "subject to [partial?] verification by experience."[25] By experience he meant interpretations of personal, political, and economic events, interpretations that Christians and non-Christians share. His writings were peppered with such interpretations, which Niebuhr intended to validate (as well as illustrate and explicate) his understandings of Christian doctrines.

Niebuhr appealed to experience in two ways: one positive, the other negative.[26] Positively, experience corresponds in part to the Christian views of love and sin. First, there are glimpses or suggestions of the transcendent in experience; every moral experience suggests the ultimate possibilities of love.[27] These glimpses are built into the character of myth. Because the paradox of myth does not separate the ideal from the actual, the ideal is always suggested (but only suggested) by the actual.

24. Niebuhr, "The Truth in Myths," 29.
25. Ibid., 30.
26. Reinhold Niebuhr, *Faith and History: A Comparison of Christian and Modern Views of History* (New York: Charles Scribner's Sons, 1949), 165.
27. Niebuhr, "The Truth in Myths," 30, 31.

The other side of the paradox is that experience also manifests the depths of sin, which corrupt our thinking as well as our acting.

Any system of thought that evades this paradox is itself corrupt and inadequate to explain the constant tension between the ideal and the actual in experience. This inadequacy constitutes the basis for Niebuhr's negative appeal to experience. All scientific and rational schemes, because they try to demonstrate the rational coherence of nature and history, fall short of their own standards. The chaos, tragedy, and novelty in our experience of history defy rational schemes to demonstrate the coherence of experience. "[T]he totality of reality is more complex than any scheme of rational meaning which may be invented to comprehend it."[28] Highly sophisticated reason can recognize these limits of rational coherence in understanding the contradictory aspects of reality.[29] Christian myths are, consequently, partially verified by the proof that the alternatives lead to observable miscalculations in interpreting human nature and history.[30] Only the paradoxes of freedom and necessity, love and justice, and so forth, are capable of providing a coherent meaning for total reality.

Niebuhr constantly employed these appeals to demonstrate the credibility of his Christian interpretations of the nature, history, and the origin and destiny of humans. He never worked out a systematic religious epistemology. He sometimes said myths are "born out of profound experience."[31] Yet he insisted that experience does not "yield" the wisdom of the myth of grace.[32] A special revelation[33] or particular encounter with God[34] is a necessary source for true myth. He unqualifiedly claimed that myth can be verified in experience,[35] but the true myth, by his own description, can be only suggested in experience. The truth of faith must remain partially shrouded in mystery that cannot simply be resolved into rational intelligibility.[36] The full validation of love, for example, must await the final consummation of history.[37]

The present point is that his concept of myth enabled Niebuhr to argue for the credibility of his interpretations of Christian doctrines in constant dialogue with various philosophical and social scientific theories without

---

28. Niebuhr, "Coherence, Incoherence, and Christian Faith," 196.
29. Ibid., 201.
30. Niebuhr, *"The Self" and the Dramas of History*, 98.
31. Niebuhr, "The Truth in Myths," 30.
32. Niebuhr, *The Nature and Destiny*, vol. 2, 121.
33. Niebuhr, "The Truth in Myths," 15; idem, *Beyond Tragedy*, 20.
34. Niebuhr, "Coherence, Incoherence, and Christian Faith," 199–200.
35. Niebuhr, "The Truth in Myths," 30; idem, *Beyond Tragedy*, 20.
36. Niebuhr, *Faith and History*, 167.
37. Niebuhr, *The Nature and Destiny*, vol. 2, 96.

being bound by the canons of rationality established by any of these disciplines.[38] He could, therefore, retrieve traditional Christian doctrines to back his theory of justice without losing "organic contact" with the modern mind. Niebuhr's influence upon non-Christian proponents of these cultural disciplines is one measure of his success in using this concept of myth.

We will now examine Niebuhr's use of this concept of myth in retrieving Christian doctrines that backed his Christian realist theory of justice.

HUMAN NATURE AND AGENCY

As the title of *The Nature and Destiny of Man* implies, the interpretation of human nature and agency (individual and collective) received more of Niebuhr's attention than the other three base points Gustafson delineates. Niebuhr's reconstrual, in the early thirties, of how persons and collectivities should make judgments about matters of justice had followed primarily from his reinterpretation of the limitations and possibilities of human nature and agency. He had not come to Christian realism through a reinterpretation of practical reasoning. Indeed, Niebuhr never attended systematically to his method of practical reasoning.[39] Although his way of reasoning about matters of justice had changed dramatically in the early thirties and was further modified in the forties, this base point did not receive his systematic attention.

The Nature of Destiny of Man built upon Niebuhr's earlier reinterpretation of human nature and agency and deepened it in light of traditional Christian doctrines. And this base point remained paramount for Niebuhr's thinking about justice. What Niebuhr had to say about God was stated, almost incidentally, in relation to his theological anthropology. For Niebuhr, knowledge of God's will for social policy was not possible without first understanding human nature and agency. The interpretation of the historical circumstances, in which just social policies must be formulated and executed, did receive Niebuhr's systematic attention. But this interpretation was dependent upon the insights of his theological anthropology. Hence, we begin there.

For Niebuhr, human agents are a compound of the transcendent possibility of the ideal of love, the actuality of prideful self-love, and dependence upon divine mercy and forgiveness in order to approximate their potential for love. We will consider each of these elements as

---

38. See Niebuhr, *Faith and History,* 166–167.
39. Gustafson, "Theology in the Service of Ethics," 30.

Niebuhr developed them in light of the myths of creation, the fall, and justification and redemption. First, we must consider human nature, which gives rise to these elements of human agency.

Humans as Spirit and Nature

Niebuhr's earlier view of humans as a compound of natural impulse and self-consciousness arising from reason gave way to an interpretation of humans as a paradoxical unity of spirit and nature. In *Moral Man and Immoral Society,* Niebuhr had asserted the human possibility for love that transcends reason and natural impulse without offering an account of human nature that could explain this transcendence. In *The Nature and Destiny of Man,* he grounded this freedom for transcendent possibilities in the spirit. The spirit, in the "essential structure" of human nature, provides a basis for the freedom Niebuhr claimed for moral agents to practice sacrificial love. This spirit transcends human creatureliness but is in ultimate unity with the finite impulses and finite rationality of humans. Niebuhr saw this unity of spirit and nature as distinctively expressed in the Christian doctrine of creation, in which the human is understood as in the "image of God and as creature."[40]

The paradoxical assertion that humans are both creatures and in the image of God joins three aspects of human existence: (1) the height of self-transcendence in humans' spiritual stature; (2) humans' weakness, dependence, and finiteness in their involvement in the natural world; and (3) human evil as a consequence of their inevitable, though not necessary, unwillingness to accept their finiteness.[41]

Humans in the Image of God

Although the Christian tradition has sometimes identified the image of God with human rational capacities, the most profound theologians, beginning with Augustine, have associated the image of God with a human capacity to transcend reason, world, and the self. This radical self-transcendence was important for Niebuhr because the "perfect love of Christ, which ends on the Cross" and gives meaning to life, transcends reason, history,[42] and all interests of the self.[43] It is this love that humans in the image of God are free to imitate.

In the abstract, this freedom Niebuhr claimed for humans is stupefying.

---

40. Niebuhr, *The Nature and Destiny,* vol. 1, 150.
41. Ibid.
42. Ibid., 163–166.
43. Ibid., 287.

"The human spirit cannot be held within the bounds of either *natural necessity* or rational prudence."[44] Humans are "free enough to violate both the *necessities of nature* and the logical systems of reason."[45] "Christianity measures the stature of man in terms of a freedom which transcends the *necessities of nature.*"[46] Taken in isolation, these and other similar assertions are incredible, but Niebuhr sometimes used the word "necessity" to include more than a strict meaning of the word allows.[47] Due to his vague use of "necessity," it is difficult to discern what Niebuhr meant by these references to human freedom from natural necessities.

If we interpret these claims to freedom from natural necessity in the context of Niebuhr's claims for the freedom to love, they refer generally to "necessary" interests of "fallen" human nature (e.g., interests in self-preservation[48] or interests that dictate inequalities).[49] On Niebuhr's view of human nature, it could be said that these interests appear to us only as necessities of our created nature. He was, however, reluctant to make a sharp distinction between our sinful and our finite nature. "[I]t is not possible to ascribe some human actions to mere finiteness and others to sin."[50] "[S]acrificial love is the harmony of the soul with God beyond the limitations of *sinful and finite* history."[51] Because Niebuhr affirmed the goodness of our created nature, this sentence cannot mean that we overcome our creatureliness. It presumably reflects Niebuhr's view that sin and finitude are so intermixed in the dynamics of history that limits upon human possibilities (e.g., limits on equality among the sexes)[52] that we associate with creaturely finitude turn out to be limits humans can transcend.

We can conclude that Niebuhr's point was that the limits that philosophers and social scientists believe natural and rational interests place upon the highest demands of morality are surpassed in the Christian understanding of self-transcendence. He observed that modern estimates of human nature do not measure humans sufficiently high to do

---

44. Ibid., 122, my emphasis.
45. Ibid., 124, my emphasis.
46. Ibid., 298, my emphasis.
47. See John Howard Yoder's comments, in a pamphlet entitled "Reinhold Niebuhr and Christian Pacifism," about Niebuhr's view that violence is a necessity in a sinful world. See Heerewegen pamphlet no. 1 (Heerewegen-Zeist, Netherlands, 1954; repr., Scottdale, Pa.: Herald Press, 1968), 18.
48. Niebuhr, *The Nature and Destiny,* vol. 2, 76.
49. Niebuhr, *The Nature and Destiny,* vol. 1, 297.
50. Reinhold Niebuhr, "Christian Faith and the Common Life," in *Christian Faith and the Common Life,* by Nils Ehrenstrom, M. G. Dibelius, et al. (Chicago: Willett, Clark & Co., 1938), 73.
51. Niebuhr, *The Nature and Destiny,* vol. 2, 78, my emphasis.
52. Niebuhr, *The Nature and Destiny,* vol. 2, 282.

full justice to their capacity for the good.[53] His understanding of human freedom was a correlate of the freedom from natural and rational boundaries that the Christian myth requires to affirm the ideal of love embodied in the cross of Christ.

As a correlate of the possibility of love, our freedom does not transcend natural necessities, strictly understood, but it transcends what both idealist and naturalistic philosophies claim to be natural necessities. It transcends all natural contingencies (such as of nation, race, time, and place) that give rise to conflicting interests or justify less than complete liberty and equality.[54] It also transcends interests the self may have in a particular rule of justice. Love is never satisfied arbitrating the interests of the other with those of the self.[55] Freedom for love is not merely a freedom from selfish interests. It is a freedom to rise above any ego interest that conflicts with another. The cross symbolizes a love that transcends "the sinful rivalries [rivalries are by definition sinful] of ego with ego."[56] The freedom Niebuhr claimed for humans is radical; it had to be to provide the basis for the ideal of disinterested love for which he had argued since the early thirties.

Niebuhr's view of love as disinterested and self-sacrificial was grounded in an understanding of human freedom from natural interests that neither Rauschenbusch nor Ryan asserted. The healthy "selfish" interests that Rauschenbusch thought should be balanced with fully developed instincts for solidarity were to Niebuhr "necessities" of sinful human nature but unnecessary capitulations of the human spirit. Rauschenbusch's understanding of human freedom was, from Niebuhr's perspective, limited due to Rauschenbusch's acceptance of the evolutionary social science of his day. It is no wonder that Niebuhr believed Rauschenbusch failed to comprehend the height of Christian love.[57]

Humans as Creatures

Freedom was not the whole story for Niebuhr. According to the creation myth, humans are not only in the image of God; they are also creatures: weak, dependent, finite. Humans are free to transcend nature (as understood by science), reason, and self, but they are bound by the weakness, dependence, and finitude of their creatureliness. Their freedom is limited. Humans are not free to be God, which means they are

---

53. Ibid., 124.
54. Ibid., 296–297.
55. Ibid., 295.
56. Niebuhr, *The Nature and Destiny*, vol. 2, 72–73.
57. Niebuhr, "Walter Rauschenbusch in Historical Perspective," 38.

not free to comprehend the whole by their own wisdom or to realize self- or collective-fulfillment by their own power. Consequently, no human conception of justice can bring the chaos of existence into a meaningful total harmony.[58] Indeed, the attempt, by idealist philosophies, to formulate universal principles is a sin.[59] It is idolatry because it makes reason, which is finite, God.[60]

The apparent paradox of the myth of creation is that humans are free for an ideal of love that gives meaning to history but not free to realize this ideal through their creaturely resources. In Niebuhr's words, a human "is conceived of as a creature of infinite possibilities which cannot be fulfilled within [the] terms of this temporal existence."[61] There would be a rational way out of this paradox if the ideal of love were possible independent of creaturely existence in the actual conditions of history. The meaning and fulfillment of human life could then be conceived in terms that ignore the problem of justice in mundane existence. This assertion of a transhistorical fulfillment is, Niebuhr argued, an error committed by dualistic philosophies, especially mysticism. The myth of creation rejects it because this myth asserts the goodness of the created world.[62] Consequently, "salvation never means the complete destruction of [humans'] creatureliness and absorption into the divine."[63] Christian love fulfills justice even as it rejects all formulations of it.

At the risk of denying the mystery, which Niebuhr noted as an essential concomitant of myth,[64] I suggest that there is also an ultra-

---

58. Niebuhr, *The Nature and Destiny*, vol. 1, 168.
59. Ibid., 170.
60. Ibid., 165.
61. Ibid., 170.
62. Ibid., 169.
63. Ibid., 170.
64. Niebuhr persistently insisted that the meaning of myth contains a penumbra of mystery that cannot be fully illumined; e.g., Reinhold Niebuhr, "Mystery and Meaning," in *The Essential Reinhold Niebuhr*, 237–249 (first published in 1946). In the context of considering attempts to assert an ultimate coherence between the ideal in which humans are meaningfully fulfilled and human nature (created, not sinful), Niebuhr wrote: "[H]uman life is meaningful even though its existence in a world of nature, which is not completely sympathetic to the human enterprise, is not fully explained." This meaning for human life can be asserted, but it remains a mystery. He went on to say that humans and nature are reconciled by a meaning (derived from the social ideal) that transcends both humans and nature. See Reinhold Niebuhr, "Optimism, Pessimism, and Religious Faith," in *The Essential Reinhold Niebuhr*, 13 (first published in 1940). Perhaps we should take such statements to indicate that the paradox between human self-transcendence and human creaturely finitude cannot be resolved, but if Niebuhr pushed this incoherence to include what he called the ultrarational level, he would have fallen into the dualism between human fulfillment and the good of creation, which he sought to avoid. I take him to have meant that the ideal transcends the limitations that we, in our corrupted reason and sciences, attribute to nature and not that human fulfillment transcends our created nature.

rational way out of this paradox, one that Niebuhr could have accepted. What if we understand the human capacity to transcend nature, reason, and self as freedom to deny interests that only appear to us, "fallen" as we are, to be necessities of our creatureliness? We are, then, free to transcend these interests without rising above our creaturely limitations. In fact, the ideal of love that gives meaning to our creaturely existence by standing above all assertions of interest[65] can be realized only within that existence. It can be realized only by trusting in the goodness of the weakness, dependence, and finitude of our creaturely existence, for we fulfill the possibility of love by faith in God's will for us, not by efforts or hopes to rise above our creatureliness. This faith transcends, along with other interests, our interest in being more than finite creatures. It even transcends a human interest in self-perfection. Niebuhr's favorite text for expressing this possibility was Jesus' saying: "He that loseth his life for my sake shall find it." In this faith, which enables a love that surpasses what rationally appears to be our creaturely interests, we realize rather than negate our creaturely selves.[66] Such love presupposes an ultrarational faith in God's providence that dissolves anxiety about satisfying even reasonable finite interests,[67] but it nonetheless fulfills the creaturely self. From any rational perspective that asserts interests of the self, this fulfillment in love remains an incoherent paradox; but from the perspective of the ultrarational myth of creation, love is the law of nature, and this view of the self is coherent.[68]

This love is a possibility that entails perfect justice as it fulfills and rejects all conceptions of justice based upon natural or rational interests of the self. The ideal of love, entailing the perfection of justice and meaning for temporal life, can be achieved within the actual creaturely existence of humans. Niebuhr could, therefore, portray the social ideal, to which conceptions of justice point, as an ideal that is possible within human creaturely existence. He did so in the myth of original perfection before the "fall," which for Niebuhr meant before history.

This social ideal is a condition in which there is "perfect accord of life with life and will with will."[69] There is perfect harmony; that is, there are no conflicting interests to be arbitrated by rules of equity. There is also "complete liberty and equality,"[70] which Niebuhr understood as a situa-

---

65. Niebuhr, *The Nature and Destiny,* vol. 2, 89–90.

66. Niebuhr, *The Nature and Destiny,* vol. 1, 251.

67. Ibid., 271–272, 289.

68. For one claim that the myth of creation is ultimately coherent, see Niebuhr, *An Interpretation,* 32. Although this passage refers to the myth as paradoxical, the coherence he asserted presumably resolves the paradox.

69. Niebuhr, *The Nature and Destiny,* vol. 1, 293.

70. Ibid., 297.

tion where "every one 'will give according to his ability and take according to his need.' "[71] As in his earlier use of it,[72] Niebuhr understood this formula as a description of what will be freely given and received where all persons are considered equal, not as a rule to be enforced. In this perfect harmony of selves, no one will assert an interest in having his or her needs met or in having others give according to their abilities. It is an uncoerced social condition.[73] This portrayal of social relations in original perfection is the social ideal of anarchy and communism that Niebuhr delineated in 1932.[74] It is here portrayed on the basis of Niebuhr's understanding of the creation of humans as a unity of spirit and finite nature.

This social ideal must be a possibility within human creaturely existence; otherwise, Niebuhr could not claim even an ultimate coherence between the freedom for the ideal of love and the goodness of human creation in finitude. The ideal requires freedom from all natural and rational interests. Such interests necessarily conflict. But it also presumes that persons are fulfilled only in and through their finitude, weakness, and dependence upon each other and God. Humans are not free to transcend their creatureliness. The social ideal contains no place for either individual or collective assertions of interest in human fulfillment.

Niebuhr's social ideal, I believe, established coherence between his understanding of humans as self-transcendent in the image of God and his view of humans as weak, dependent, and finite creatures. His understanding of human creatureliness, however, differed quite sharply from the views of Rauschenbusch and Ryan, for whom created nature entailed rational interests in self-preservation and in the means for developing the personality. From Niebuhr's perspective, such interests not only fall short of the transcendent ideal of love; they are attempts to seek fulfillment by denying our created weakness, dependence, and finitude. Because all conceptions of justice assert some interests against others, all conceptions of justice that purport to unite the ideal of love with the limits of human creatureliness fail. Only faith and love, which assert no interests in self-development or in enforcing a pattern of justice, can unite the spirit and nature of humans. Love, thus, fulfills what conceptions of justice can only point to.

If Niebuhr's social ideal could be achieved in history, the paradox between the ideal and the actual in the myth of creation could be resolved. Such a resolution fails, however, to account for the third aspect of human existence that Niebuhr inferred from the myth of creation.

---

71. Ibid., 295.
72. See *supra*, chapter four, 212–213.
73. Niebuhr, *The Nature and Destiny*, vol. 2, 87.
74. See *supra*, chapter four, 203.

Humans as Willing but Inevitable Sinners

As constituted in the juncture between spirit (freedom) and nature (creaturely necessity), humans freely but inevitably succumb to the temptation to place their interests at the center of existence. The character of this freedom and its inevitable use for evil are indispensable for a full understanding of the paradox of the myth of creation and its implications for Niebuhr's theory of justice.

The freedom of humans to transcend nature, reason, and self in sacrificial love is also freedom to transmute their natural and rational interests into a powerful force for evil. Knowing we have the possibility of rising above our creaturely existence in a perfect, eternal fulfillment of the self, we are anxious about our weakness, dependence, and finitude. This anxiety is both a creative impulse toward perfection in love and a temptation to use our freedom for perfection to transmute "finiteness into infinity," "weakness into strength," and "dependence into independence."[75] This is not a temptation to gratify animal desires but a temptation to exercise our freedom over those desires in a sinful assertion of the universality of our particular and finite values. Rational estimates of human nature, which do not comprehend our freedom for love, cannot fully appreciate this capacity for evil either.[76] Paradoxically, any attempt, including rational ones, to assert the universality of a necessarily particular system of values and justice is a prideful denial of our finitude. It "subordinates other life to [our] will and thus does injustice to other life."[77] Prideful humans do not see their finitude as good but as an undesirable limit on their possibilities. We are not free to overcome this finitude, but we are free to put it unjustly at the center of our world.

This freedom in its juncture with finitude is the basis for Niebuhr's understanding of the human will-to-power with its almost unlimited potential for injustice. Humans, free from the limited animal desires, are also free to assert their interests in a particular scheme of justice as though it were universal. This will-to-power is present in every human effort to establish a scheme of justice.

This prideful assertion of our finite interests was the only account of sin for which Niebuhr provided in his interpretation of the myth of creation, but in his chapters on "Man as Sinner," he offered a second account of how sin issues from the juncture between spirit and freedom. In their anxiety about how to live out perfect love under the condition of

---

75. Niebuhr, *The Nature and Destiny*, vol. 1, 251.
76. Ibid., 124.
77. Ibid., 179.

finitude, humans are tempted to escape from their freedom to transcend self-interests by indulging themselves in devotion to limited values in creation. This attempt to escape freedom Niebuhr called "sensuality."[78] This view of sin as sensuality did not fit easily with Niebuhr's earlier interpretation of the myth of creation in which the third aspect of human existence is an inevitable unwillingness to accept human finitude. Nevertheless, Niebuhr was not satisfied with traditional Christian explanations of sensuality as always derivative from self-love or pride. The Christian tradition correctly rejected the view that sensuality is a simple failure to control the animal desires. Sensuality, like pride, is a temptation that emerges from anxiety about how to exercise one's freedom for love. Unlike pride, however, sensuality sometimes results from a surrender of freedom in an effort to avoid an uneasy conscience rather than from an attempt to center all of existence in the self.[79]

On this second account of sin, the anxiety inherent in human existence does not always lead to a willful refusal to acknowledge one's finitude. It may also lead to an unwillingness to accept the responsibilities of human freedom. Understood this way, namely, as an attempt to avoid the anxiety of human life by ignoring the responsibilities concomitant with human freedom, sensuality is also sloth born of despair. In matters of justice, this form of sin would manifest itself as neglect for the possibilities of relative justice rather than as a centering of justice in one's self-interest.[80]

Unfortunately, Niebuhr never fully explored this second account of sin or its implications for justice. His brief treatment of sin as sensuality stands in relative isolation from the remainder of his theology and from his thinking about justice. Sin as a prideful assertion of the will-to-power had a much more profound influence on Niebuhr's understanding of injustice and his realist response in order to approximate justice. Had he integrated sin as an escape from freedom into his theory and conception of justice, Niebuhr might have had more to say about the dangers of passivity in the face of injustice. Although he criticized Protestant orthodoxy and neo-orthodoxy for "defeatism" in the early thirties[81] and again in the second volume of *The Nature and Destiny of Man,*[82] Niebuhr was far more concerned about injustice resulting from inordinate asser-

---

78. Ibid., 185–186.

79. Ibid., 233–234.

80. Joseph Allen observed that I had omitted this second interpretation of sin in an earlier draft and pointed out to me the close relationship between sloth and what Niebuhr called "sensuality." I am responsible for this particular interpretation of Niebuhr's understanding of sensuality and its implications for justice.

81. See *supra,* chapter four, 208.

82. See *infra,* chapter six, 293–294.

tions of power than about injustice as a consequence of refusing to exercise our freedom to achieve relative justice.

Although Niebuhr did not integrate this second account of sin into his interpretation of the myth of creation, he could have done so. In both accounts, sin arises out of the temptations that follow from human anxiety inherent to existence in the juncture between freedom and creaturely necessity. This anxiety does not entail either pride or sensuality. Sin is not a necessary outgrowth of our created nature. Anxiety about our freedom can theoretically create a drive toward perfection in love, but these creative aspects of anxiety are inextricably admixed with its destructive possibilities. Consequently, prideful assertions of our finite interests or attempts to escape from freedom in sensuality are inevitable.[83]

The crucial point is that according to Niebuhr's interpretation of the myth of creation, injustice is inevitable in history. We are free for perfection and therefore are responsible for our willful pride and/or sensuality, but sin and injustice are an inevitable consequence of human freedom exercised in its juncture with human finitude. Niebuhr needed no doctrine of a fall in history; the Christian doctrine of original sin is nestled in the myth of creation itself.[84] Therefore, Niebuhr asserted, in continuity with the Christian doctrine of original sin: "Sin is natural for man in the sense that it is universal but not in the sense that it is necessary."[85] Original perfection is prior to human acts;[86] it never existed in history. "Where there is history . . . there is freedom; and where there is freedom there is sin."[87]

Implications for Justice

When we add this third aspect of Niebuhr's view of humans as creatures in the image of God, we can draw three inferences that have important implications for his theory of justice. First, humans are free within the limits of their creaturely existence for sacrificial love that transcends the interests of natural impulses, reason, and self. This love would entail a

---

83. Ibid., 185–186.

84. The myth of the "fall" (more properly understood as the universality of sin) is, like all Christian myths, confirmed in the experience of history (ibid., 244), but Niebuhr did not claim a time when humanity fell because of the sins of actual persons. Nor did he need evidence to prove that actual persons or groups sin. He knew they sin on the basis of his understanding of humanity's created nature. He then applied this understanding to actual persons and groups in history to interpret their capacities as moral agents.

85. Ibid., 242.

86. Ibid., 278.

87. Niebuhr, *The Nature and Destiny*, vol. 2, 80.

perfection of justice in temporal social relations through which all selves would be fulfilled. In this love, the paradox of humans as spirit and nature would be overcome in a coherent unity of the image of God and creaturely finitude. Second, in history the anxious self freely but inevitably asserts his or her interests as though satisfying these interests, and not God or love, were the means to universal justice and self-fulfillment.[88] This assertion of interests does not arise from creaturely desires but from within the freedom to transcend these desires. Consequently, human freedom for justice and self-realization is also a freedom that inevitably transmutes our efforts to harmonize various finite interests into terrible injustices. Thus, the third point is that the ultrarational resolution of the apparent paradox between the *ideal* possibilities of love in the human spirit and finite necessities of human creaturely nature is not resolvable in the *actual* conditions of history. We are left with a view of human nature in which the juncture between spirit and nature is, within history, a paradoxical juncture between the *ideal* possibility of love and the *actual* "necessity" or inevitability of asserting the interests of the self. The capacity for self-transcendence is always exercised in an admixture of love and self-love. This is the condition in which we must make judgments about what is just.

This understanding of human nature provided a theological foundation for the tension between ideal and actual possibilities of human agency that Niebuhr had asserted in the early thirties. It did not, in my judgment, radically change his previous views, but it helped him to clarify and expand them. We will now turn to this more comprehensive understanding of human agents.

Humans as Agents: An Admixture of Ideal and Actual Possibilities

Although Niebuhr could conceive of a transcendent self in which the freedom for love and the limitations of creaturely existence are unified, this self is distinguishable from the "self-as-agent of action."[89] As moral agents, humans are in history. They inevitably act in the tension between the transcendent ideal of love, of which they are more or less vaguely cognizant as a human possibility, and the actual realities of self-assertion. The key for Niebuhr's interpretation of moral agency is the freedom he posits for humans on the basis of the myth of creation.

---

88. As I observed above, Niebuhr did not integrate his account of sin as sensuality (or sloth) into his thinking about justice. Consequently, this interpretation of Niebuhr's understanding of human agency will proceed as he did, that is, on the view that self-love or pride is the reality for which a theory of justice must account.

89. Niebuhr, *The Nature and Destiny,* vol. 1, 284, 292.

Humans, unique among creatures, are agents (1) free to transcend the natural and rational interests of finite selves and (2) free to act as though their interests were universal and absolute (i.e., free to posit their interests at the center of existence). Conceptions of the self-as-agent that fail to comprehend this freedom misjudge the height of humans' transcendent possibilities and the depth of their capacity for evil. As Niebuhr would put it later: "[T]here are indeterminate desires within the self, both for self-aggrandizement and for self-giving."[90]

Free for Self-giving

As individual agents, humans are free for sacrificial love that transcends all interests of the self, both those arising from natural impulses and those derived from reason.[91] Unlike animals, humans are free from all natural interests. No social scientific scheme of natural causality can explain the actions of human agents.[92] They are free to transcend the natural will-to-live. "There is always the possibility of sacrificing our life and interest."[93] Nor does a view of the self-as-rational comprehend human agency. Philosophical idealists are correct in claiming that human agents are capable of transcending natural impulses.[94] They do not see that human reason is bound by the contingencies of nature nor that the agent is free from the dictates of reason.[95] As an assertive activity linked to our finitude, reason is contingent upon the interests of our particular situation. If reason were the cause of human actions, humans could not transcend this particularity characteristic of reason. Fortunately, human agents are not bound by their interest in rationally conceived values or principles. They are, for example, free from a rational interest in reciprocity from others because they are free to surrender the rational self in love for the other.[96] They are also free from interest in all rational schemes of justice. All such schemes seek to justify assertions against the interests of some in the name of a rational harmony of conflicting interests. Agents free for love cannot be bound by any rational system of justice.

In sum, the agent free for sacrificial love is free from all assertions of the self.[97] This freedom should not be reduced to mere freedom from

90. Niebuhr, *"The Self" and the Dramas of History,* 139–140.
91. Niebuhr, *The Nature and Destiny,* vol. 1, 96.
92. Ibid., 95.
93. Niebuhr, *The Nature and Destiny,* vol. 2, 74–75.
94. Niebuhr, *The Nature and Destiny,* vol. 1, 120.
95. Niebuhr, *The Nature and Destiny,* vol. 2, 112.
96. Ibid., 82.
97. Ibid., 90.

selfish interests. It includes interests in any group's welfare or values or any scheme of justice. It is freedom for "pure non-resistance."[98] From this transcendent perspective, the moral agent is free to criticize all schemes of justice, including his or her own. In fact, he or she is morally bound to do so because all systems of justice approve of some forms of coercion and conflict.[99] This freedom from all interests is incompatible with claims that agents are free to create universal harmony by enforcing a system of morality or justice. As dependent and finite creatures, agents are not free, either individually or collectively, to master their own existence by enforcing rational moral schemes. Modern culture has generally understated the agent's freedom from natural and rational interests and overestimated his or her freedom to create harmonies of interests.[100] Such miscalculations result in the confident imposition of schemes of justice that are based on natural and/or rational interests of the self humans are free to transcend.

Free for Self-aggrandizement

Despite their inability to master history, agents free to transcend their natural and rational interests are also free to assert and enforce those interests as if they were the center of history. Unbounded by limited animal interests in survival, human agents are free to pursue their eternal security by seeking power over threats from nature or competing human interests. Unlike animals whose interests are satiated by the necessities for immediate physical survival, humans are free to envision and pursue their interest in an eternal preservation of their finite values and ways of life. Humans are in fact dependent upon God for their survival, but they have the capacity to pursue inordinate ambitions, which animals, with their competing impulses of survival, do not know.[101] There are, says Niebuhr, no limits to this human ambition for power.[102]

Their transcendence over the dictates of reason also raises human agents above rational limits on this will-to-power. Although all creaturely knowledge is limited by particular perspectives, human agents are free to pretend that their knowledge is final and ultimate.[103] In moral and

---

98. Niebuhr, "Why the Christian Church Is Not Pacifist," 107. Compare Niebuhr's earlier statement that even Gandhi's nonviolent resistance falls short of the ethic of Jesus. See *supra,* chapter four, 202.

99. Ibid., 113–116.

100. Niebuhr, *The Nature and Destiny,* vol. 1, 101.

101. Ibid., 192.

102. Ibid., 194.

103. Ibid., 194, 197.

religious matters, this is a freedom to claim final righteousness and even divine sanction for rational interests, which are necessarily condi-tional.[104] From Niebuhr's perspective, reason is properly a tool for discriminating among finite possibilities, but humans in their capacity for self-transcendence are free to deify reason as the source of their uncondi-tional virtue.[105] In doing so, they exploit reason for their own interest in securing the eternal righteousness of their ways of life. Thus, humans are free to use reason as an "instrument" by which the self "seeks to give the sanctity of a false universality to its particular needs and partial in-sights."[106]

This freedom would not be destructive if humans were actually free from their own creaturely finitude, but all human interests are contin-gent. The absence of natural or rational limits on the assertion of those interests leads to highly destructive conflicts among finite interests. In some cases, it permits the total subjection of one group's interest to another's. For Niebuhr, a conception of justice that fails to account for this inordinate ambition of humans to dominate others will not provide for the checks on concentrations of power that can prevent the terrible injustices of which humans are capable. In a later essay, he asserted that classical liberalism and Marxism generated monstrous contrasting evils from the identical mistake of underestimating the destructive potential of unfettered human interests. Classical liberalism failed to see that individual interests are not limited by material needs and cannot be harmonized by uncontrolled competition. It left individuals free to create horrendous economic inequalities. Marxism failed to see that the concentration of political power required to equalize private economic powers could not be limited to an interest in economic equality. It allowed a tyrannical oligarchy to subject human liberties to its lust for power.[107]

The Inevitable Admixture of Self-giving and Self-aggrandizement

A conception of justice must account for this interpretation of both the heights and depths of agential freedom. Humans are free for sacrificial love that transcends all interests and free to defy their creatureliness in assertions of power that place their interests in ultimate security at the center of human existence. But it must go one step further. It must account for the fact that this is not freedom to choose *either* sacrificial

---

104. Ibid., 199–200.
105. Niebuhr, *"The Self" and the Dramas of History*, 118.
106. Niebuhr, *The Nature and Destiny*, vol. 1, 284–285.
107. Niebuhr, "Why the Christian Church Is Not Pacifist," 150–153.

love *or* injustice rooted in the prideful deification of self. The purely transcendent self, in original perfection, is free for either love or self-love, but the self-as-agent lives in history. The self-as-agent exists in the tension between this ideal as an impossible possibility and the actual reality that her or his actions are corrupted by pride. Only this second step, which interprets moral agency in light of the myth of the "fall," can account for the paradox of the self-as-agent.

Freedom for either the height of love or the destructiveness of self-love is theoretically possible within Niebuhr's understanding of humans as spirit and nature. A purely transcendent self could choose one or the other without contradiction. But when he adds that the self in history inevitably sins, Niebuhr interprets the freedom of the agent as a paradoxical admixture of the responsibility for love and the necessity of profoundly destructive self-love and injustice. The agent is an unresolvable admixture of the ideal and the actual. The agent can neither deny her or his responsibility nor fulfill it. This paradox of agency is inevitable for several reasons.

First, every individual action contains an element of self-assertion that corrupts the ideal of love. This was a change from *Moral Man and Immoral Society,* in which a few individuals may achieve the ideal of love, although collective agents cannot. This change was based on two Christian myths. We have considered the doctrine of original sin. Niebuhr also shifted the source for the norm of love from the Jesus of history to the doctrine of the crucifixion, which is both in and beyond history.[108] Gustafson notes that this latter change in doctrine occurs between *An Interpretation of Christian Ethics* and *The Nature and Destiny of Man.*[109] It clearly places the norm of love beyond history, even for individuals.[110] This change is one way in which Niebuhr's retrieval of traditional doctrines clarified his theory of justice. He became clearer that injustice is ultimately rooted in the willful sin of every individual and not in interests dictated by the structures of economic relations, and he softened his earlier dualism between individual and collective morality. Now both individuals and groups are always sinful, though collective egoism remains more intractable to correction.

Second, even when the individual sacrifices his self-interests for the cause of a larger group, he gives himself over to a collective self-

---

108. Niebuhr, *The Nature and Destiny,* vol. 1, 164.

109. James M. Gustafson, "Christian Ethics in America," in *Christian Ethics and the Community* (Philadelphia: Pilgrim Press, 1971), 33.

110. Notice how this shift in the source of the norm of love confirms my observation that Niebuhr's earlier conception of love was contradictory within history (see *supra,* chapter four, 203).

assertion. Collective assertions are all the more unjust because of the power of groups and the plausibility of their claims to embody unconditional value.[111] Niebuhr considered the agent's participation in collective self-assertions his last and most destructive "effort to deny the determinate and contingent character of his existence." These collective assertions are prideful and unjust even when the group "incarnates values [e.g., democracy or communistic equality] which transcend its immediate interests."[112] Niebuhr clearly rejected Rauschenbusch's view that collective agents could have a redemptive effect on individuals.

Third, even as the agent participates in these sinful assertions of interests, she has a residual knowledge of and capacity for the ideal of love. This residual freedom is manifest in the agent's unsuccessful efforts at self-deception through veiling her assertions of interests with claims for their unconditional value.[113] If the agent did not feel compelled to deceive herself or were successful in doing so, she would not feel the tension between her actual conduct and the ideal of love. Niebuhr saw a refutation of the doctrine of total depravity in these efforts at self-deception.[114] For agents who are the most honest, the tension is even more taut. Their freedom "is such that no rule of justice . . . can leave the self with the feeling that it has done all that it could."[115]

Finally, even if the individual agent could achieve the ideal of love, he could not apply it to secure justice for others. He cannot achieve justice for them without taking actions that assert their interests against others.[116] Here again is the necessary self-contradiction of sacrificial love within the realm of history.

Grace: The Tension Relaxed

Human agents are caught in the paradox of knowing that they inevitably use their freedom to love for assertions of interests (whether selfish, collective, or in justice for others) that disrupt the harmony of life. This tension between the ideal and the actual is so taut that the agents most perceptive about their own responsibilities and capacities would be cynical about the possibility of even relative justice, were it not for God's grace. Grace is another paradoxical myth based upon the biblical doctrines of justification and redemption. The paradox is that by relying

---

111. Niebuhr, *The Nature and Destiny*, vol. 1, 208–214.
112. Ibid., 213.
113. Ibid., 203–207.
114. Ibid., 203.
115. Ibid., 295.
116. Niebuhr, *The Nature and Destiny*, vol. 2, 88.

upon God's love rather than her own moral capacities, the agent abandons her anxious self-interest in perfection. She is thereby enabled to approximate more nearly the perfect love that transcends all interests.

There are two effects in agents arising from two aspects of God's power in grace: "the power of God within the life of man, making for newness of life, and the power of God's love over man, annulling his sin by His mercy."[117] The effects are interrelated. The agent who has faith (trust) in God's merciful love in Christ for his completion is a new self, capable of transcending his own interests because he no longer has to center existence around his interests.[118] This agent is less disposed to fanatical commitments to schemes of justice that promise universal fulfillment. He is more capable of perceiving his own and his group's self-interest in even the highest formulations of justice. By relaxing the tension between an agent's responsibility for the ideal and his actual inability to fulfill it, grace enhances his capacity for love and justice.

Yet if this power of grace is thought to perfect the self, "it becomes the vehicle of sin from which it ostensibly emancipates."[119] It becomes a source of pride in one's own achievements that again places an agent's interests at the center of existence. Consequently, even in the experience of grace, the agent "regards all truth and goodness as merely a cloak of self-interest."[120] The agent relies on the second power of grace, forgiveness. This experience of forgiveness nourishes a continuing humility about one's moral achievements. It also frees the agent to act for relative justice, thus taking responsibility to secure justice for others without undue anxiety about the personal sins such acts inevitably involve. In a 1940 essay arguing against the perfectionism of pacifists, Niebuhr wrote: "The Christian is freed by . . . grace [from the paralyzing effects of guilt] to act in history, to give his devotion to the highest values he knows, . . . and he is persuaded by that grace to remember the ambiguity of even his best actions."[121]

By relaxing the tension between the ideal and the actual, grace enables the self to be a more effective agent for approximating justice. It does not resolve the tension. The agent under grace is a new self, but she is not free from prideful assertion of her interests. Further, grace does not directly alter the collective consciousness. The individual, who remains dependent upon communities for her fulfillment, remains inextricably involved in the injustices of collective egoism. Faith in future

---

117. Ibid., 104–105.
118. Ibid., 110.
119. Ibid., 147.
120. Ibid., 122.
121. Niebuhr, "Why the Christian Church Is Not Pacifist," 118.

forgiveness frees the agent to act for relative justice, but it does not free those actions from the moral ambiguity intrinsic in all assertions of interests. In short, grace releases the agent from a paralyzing conscience enabling her to act for justice in a sinful world, but it does not give her an "easy conscience"[122] regarding those actions. She remains in an uneasy, but not paralyzing, tension between the ideal of love and the actual possibilities for justice.

Implications for Justice

The interpretation of agency Niebuhr elaborated on the basis of the Christian doctrines of creation, original sin, and justification and redemption is a compound of four elements: (1) freedom from all interests of the self (for sacrificial love), (2) freedom to make its interests the center of existence (for tyrannical injustice), (3) an inevitable admixture of this height of love and destructive injustice, and (4) the continuing possibilities for renewal and forgiveness. In this freedom, humans remain bound by their weakness, dependence, and finitude. In grace, they remain in sin, that is, in need of forgiveness. Thus, agents (individual and collective) are free for indeterminate renewal and indeterminate injustices yet organically related to their finitude and to their individual and collective injustices. Their freedom for justice and injustice is indeterminate, but it is not freedom to construct a perfectly just society.

As free, they have "infinite possibilities of organizing life from beyond the center of the self; and equally infinite possibilities of drawing the self back into the center of the organization."[123] This is not, however, a freedom to master one's own destiny. As finite, the agent (individual and collective) is dependent for its fulfillment upon larger communities and upon God, not upon its pursuit of its own interests in perfection. Further, the communities to which it is organically related necessarily blend order and injustice in a way that prohibits their reconstruction as though they were artifacts.[124] Individuals or collectivities that ignore this

---

122. Niebuhr, *The Nature and Destiny*, vol. 2, 141.
123. Ibid., 123.
124. This organic aspect of agency is operative in *The Nature and Destiny of Man* in Niebuhr's understanding of grace as a continuing dependence on the power of God's mercy. Because the agent is in persistent need of forgiveness, it should not "desire to stand beyond the contradictions of history, or to eliminate the final corruptions of history," ibid., 207. The agent is inextricably bound to the finitude and injustices of history. This theme was developed more explicitly in Niebuhr's later writings (e.g., Niebuhr, *"The Self" and the Dramas of History*, 159–182). Niebuhr noted his increasing appreciation for "organic factors in social life" in his reply to his critics in Charles Kegley's edited volume on his thought. See Reinhold Niebuhr, "Reply to Interpretation and Criticism," in *Reinhold Niebuhr: His Religious, Social, and Political Thought*, 510. First published in 1956.

organic aspect of agency will produce injustice in the name of constructing absolutely just societies.

The tension between the ideal and the actual that characterized
Niebuhr's Christian realist theory of justice in the early thirties remained
intact in *The Nature and Destiny of Man*. It was elaborated in light of his
mythic interpretation of traditional Christian doctrines and grounded in
the radical freedom of created human nature. Niebuhr became clearer
that the ultimate roots of injustice are in the universal perversion of this
freedom by individuals and not in economic institutions. He, therefore,
criticized Marxism more forcefully for linking sin exclusively to economic relations and interests.[125] Nevertheless, it was still the tension
between the ideal of disinterested love (now sacrificial) and the actuality
of the individual and collective will-to-power, which characterize all
moral agents, that a realistic conception of justice must account for.

This understanding of agency differed from Rauschenbusch and Ryan
both in its potential for love and injustices and in the effects of grace for
determining justice. Like Rauschenbusch and unlike Ryan, Niebuhr
believed that grace influenced the capacity of agents to discern justice.
He differed from Rauschenbusch (and to some extent with his earlier
realism) in that grace never redeems agents sufficiently to identify
progress toward justice with a particular social movement or with an
ideal conception of justice. Grace should make us "uneasy" about all
social movements and conceptions of justice, including our own.
Niebuhr clearly did not share Ryan's confidence in the capacity of
rational agents to know the laws of a divine natural order. On Niebuhr's
view of human agents, no conception of justice is even theoretically
compatible with Christian love. Rauschenbusch and Ryan failed to
realize that if justice is to approximate the social ideal of love, it must
account for the necessity that all principles of justice are assertions of
sinful interests. Justice must seek a balance of sinful interests, not an
adjudication between right and wrong interests.

INTERPRETATION OF CIRCUMSTANCES

On this account of agency, Niebuhr interpreted the circumstances in
which justice must be done in terms of a divine-human encounter in the
"dramas of history" rather than in terms of natural human interests or
natural orderings of human life. In her or his freedom, the agent is more
like a participant in the "dramas of history" than a participant in patterns

---

125. Niebuhr, *The Nature and Destiny*, vol. 1, 35.

and structures, whether of nature or of history.[126] Neither the height nor the depth of individual life of collective enterprises can be understood within the necessities and limitations of the natural process.[127] Consequently, Niebuhr focused more on the historical circumstances and destiny of humans than on their circumstances in nature. Furthermore, he asserted that history should be distinguished radically "from the slow mutations of forms known in nature."[128] History contains elements of novelty and chaos that are absent from natural evolution.

History resists all attempts at explanation within scientific models of cause and effect. Social scientific analyses of the circumstances of justice are generally detrimental. "[N]o respectable novel has ever pictured human life as vapidly as some of our more theoretic social and historical sciences."[129] In *The Irony of American History*, Niebuhr noted that when political science is severed from its roots in the humanities and becomes "enriched" by the social sciences, it "obscures the grand and tragic outlines of contemporary history, and offers vapid solutions for profound problems."[130] In the second volume of *The Nature and Destiny of Man* and in many of the books and articles that followed, Niebuhr sought to interpret these "grand and tragic outlines of contemporary history" in which just solutions to profound problems must be worked out.

His outline was set within the poles of the renewing and forgiving aspects of grace, which Niebuhr used to synthesize the Reformation and Renaissance/modern views of human destiny. The Renaissance/modern view correctly sees that "life in history . . . [is] . . . filled with indeterminate possibilities." Humans always "face new possibilities of the good and the obligation to realize them." On the other hand, "every desire to stand beyond the contradictions of history, or to eliminate the final corruptions of history must be disavowed." The Reformation view corrects optimistic illusions about history by comprehending the continuing need for God's mercy and forgiveness.[131] These two aspects of grace embody the features of agency that, for Niebuhr, illumine the indeterminate but limited possibilities for justice within history.[132]

First, the power of renewal indicates the ever-present possibilities of new and better schemes of justice. History is a "realm of endless

---

126. Niebuhr, *Faith and History*, 27, 56.
127. Ibid., 66.
128. Ibid., 55, see also Niebuhr, "Coherence, Incoherence, and Christian Faith," 199.
129. Niebuhr, *Faith and History*, 92.
130. Reinhold Niebuhr, *The Irony of American History* (New York: Charles Scribner's Sons, 1952), 60.
131. Niebuhr, *The Nature and Destiny*, vol. 2, 207.
132. Ibid., 210–211.

possibilities of renewal and rebirth."[133] Niebuhr was pessimistic about the prospects for steady progress toward perfect justice but not about improving on existing schemes of justice.

The renewing power of grace also reminds us that humans are not the instigators and managers of these new possibilities. Renewal in history depends upon God's judgment and mercy.[134] Humans are participants in, not the authors of, the dramas of history. Grace renews by bringing agents to surrender their prideful attempts to master their existence. It reconciles humans to (rather than liberating them from) their finitude, weakness, and dependency. Even if grace were to free a historical movement from sin, this freedom would remind it of "the fixed limits of man's creaturely finiteness."[135] This agent would be especially aware that it cannot remold history after its particular, finite interests in justice. This connecting of history to human creatureliness qualified the distinction Niebuhr made between history and nature. Due to human creatureliness, the human capacity to control history, even under the renewing power of grace, is severely limited. This is one reason Niebuhr used the organic metaphor to describe the circumstances in which justice must be done.

The other reason is the persistence of sin vivified by the second aspect of grace, divine forgiveness. The mercy of God, in a dialectical relation to God's judgment, "points to the incompleteness of all historic good, [and] the corruption of evil in all historic achievements."[136] The achievements in history inevitably remain short of the social ideal of justice. Unless we recognize that the possibilities of justice are enmeshed in the actualities of sin, our optimism will prevent us from even approximating the social ideal of love. This is so for two reasons. First, we will not realize that sacrificial love is ineffective in dealing with the powerful interests of unjust groups. Niebuhr had pressed this point in the early thirties. Second, we will not be fully cognizant of wrongful assertions of power in our group's efforts to achieve justice. No agent or historical movement powerful enough to change history is free of pride and self-assertion that creates new injustices. "[E]ach new power and potency of life creates its own new problem."[137] An agent or movement that is not cognizant of this limitation will unjustly impose its scheme of "justice" on others. This theme was also present in Niebuhr's earlier writings, but he emphasized and deepened it in the forties and fifties so that it altered his working standards of justice.

---

133. Niebuhr, *Faith and History,* 28.
134. Ibid., 27–28.
135. Ibid., 74ff.
136. Niebuhr, *The Nature and Destiny,* vol. 2, 212.
137. Ibid., 182.

Because these limitations resulting from finitude and from sin are inextricably intermeshed in history, Niebuhr often referred to natural necessities and limitations in ways that do not distinguish sin and finitude. His references to the organic character of history account for both. A theory of justice should be based on historical circumstances that reflect both the inability of finite creatures to master their existence and the reality that no historical period or movement can rise above sin.

In order to understand how this grand and tragic outline of history informed Niebuhr's working standards of justice, we will examine in more detail his criticisms of other interpretations of history. According to Niebuhr, these interpretations failed to comprehend either the limitations history places on justice or the indeterminate possibilities for justice that exist within those limitations. We will then be able to see how the social ideal entailed by love indicates the direction in which the structures of justice should move, even though it is not a goal in history. Finally, these circumstances would produce cynicism about the prospects for meaningful justice, were it not for the hope engendered by faith in God's fulfillment at the end of history.

Limitations

Niebuhr thought that the Renaissance understanding of history as a cradle for the possibility of human self-fulfillment had eclipsed the classical Christian view of history.[138] He maintained that, despite its diversity, modern culture is united by the "article of faith" "that historical development is a redemptive process" and that the "ambiguities of man's historic existence would be overcome in history itself."[139] Niebuhr agreed with the modern view that history develops through either evolution or catastrophe and revolution. There is no static natural order. Further, there is growth in this change insofar as growth means humans have developed the technical capacity to focus power against nature and each other. He objected to the modern notion that this growth is progress[140] and that this growth can perfect justice. Niebuhr's comments on this modern optimism about progress focused primarily upon multiple versions of the liberal bourgeois and Marxist views of history.

The earliest form of bourgeois liberalism contended that by unfettering individual interests from the restrictions of feudalism, modern civilization had created the conditions for perfecting justice. These individual

---

138. Ibid., 182–183.
139. Niebuhr, *Faith and History*, 1–2.
140. Niebuhr, *The Nature and Destiny*, vol. 2, 205–206.

liberties were expected to lead to equality and to a natural harmony of
self-interests. The bourgeois classes assumed that "all injustice had
disappeared or would disappear when feudalism had been completely
vanquished."[141] When it became obvious that these liberties produced
inequalities and class conflict, various explanations and remedies—for
example, Social Darwinism,[142] rational principles of justice to curb
natural selfish interests,[143] liberal Christian love as a force in history,[144]
Deweyian ideas of cultural lag to be remedied by the application of social
science and universal education[145]—were proposed to justify the view
that history can be managed so as to evolve toward fulfillment. The
common thread in these diverse views is that liberal culture is evolving
toward fulfillment.[146] History is considered sufficiently malleable that it
can be managed, or at least cajoled, toward perfect justice. Like Renaissance thought, these modern liberal views are founded on the belief that
history can be fulfilled without continuing grace and without a final
judgment.[147] "Everything in the Christian faith which points to ultimate
and transcendent possibilities is changed into simple historical achievements."[148] Liberal culture correctly discerned dynamism and growth
within history, but it could not comprehend the tension between the
ideal and the actual.

Niebuhr took three lessons from his Christian interpretation of the
history of liberal culture. First, the theories of progress based on unfettered individual liberty were grossly mistaken in their claims that liberty
would produce equality and natural harmony. Oblivious to the destructive
possibilities in human freedom, this liberal theory was blinded to the
injustice of the concentrations of power that developed in the economic
realm. It did not see how unfettered liberty had disrupted harmony and
produced unjust inequalities.[149] The Christian myths of sin and grace allow
us to see that history does not present circumstances in which absolute
liberty is compatible either with community[150] or with equality.[151] Be-

---

141. Ibid., 181.
142. Niebuhr, *Faith and History*, 4–5, 81.
143. Ibid., 5.
144. Niebuhr, *The Nature and Destiny*, vol. 2, 45, 49.
145. Niebuhr, *The Nature and Destiny*, vol. 1, 113–114; idem, *The Nature and Destiny*,
vol. 2, 237; idem, *Faith and History*, 67–68, 83.
146. Niebuhr, *The Nature and Destiny*, vol. 2, 240.
147. Ibid., 166.
148. Niebuhr, *The Irony of American History*, 12.
149. Ibid., 92–94; idem, "The Christian Faith and the Economic Life of Liberal
Society," in *Faith and Politics*, 140–141. First published in 1953.
150. Reinhold Niebuhr, "Liberty and Equality," in *Faith and Politics*, 186. First
published in 1957.
151. Ibid., 192.

cause the Christian social ideal combines liberty, equality, and social harmony, there is no hope for the fulfillment of history, or even for approximating the social ideal, in these theories of justice founded upon absolute liberty.

Second, Niebuhr came to see resources for justice in the liberties nourished by liberal theory, which neither he nor the theory had anticipated. As these new liberties spawned inequalities and class conflict, the recipients of economic power who continued to espouse laissez-faire theory were only disguising their own self-interest and degrading the liberal dogma.[152] It was inevitable that Marxism would arise to challenge these injustices, but the liberties and democratic institutions, which this liberal theory helped to create, demonstrated greater capacity for meeting the Marxist challenge than the liberal theories about them. Instead of the fascism, which Niebuhr had anticipated in the thirties, American history, according to Niebuhr in the early fifties, produced a balance of power and consequent justice that robbed the Marxist challenge of its sting.[153] This rough justice resulted from the wisdom of the common sense of democracy that produced an ironic triumph over both Marxist and bourgeois ideologies.[154] The triumph was ironic (in another context he called it the "grace of common sense")[155] because democracy allows for "values and virtues to enter into history in unpredictable ways" that neither liberal nor Marxist theories could have conceived or controlled.[156] The triumph of tolerable justice in the West occurred as an unanticipated by-product of liberal social theories, not as a product of their conscious application. Another way to put this point, in keeping with Niebuhr's doctrine of grace, is that the liberties of democratic cultures allowed for renewals of the structures of justice that the pretensions of liberal theories of justice, clinging to their past "self," did not encourage.

One limitation modern theories of justice failed to recognize is our inability to predict the creative as well as the destructive consequences of human liberties. This realization led Niebuhr to appreciate the value of political and economic freedoms more than he had in the thirties. He had come to this conclusion when, in *The Nature and Destiny of Man*, he insisted that modern views of history are wrong to hope for the ever-increasing dominance of " 'order' over all historical vitalities." History cannot move toward "cosmos without developing the possibilities of

---

152. Niebuhr, *The Irony of American History*, 93–94.
153. Ibid., 91.
154. Ibid., 106–107.
155. Ibid., 75.
156. Ibid., 79.

chaos by the very potencies which have enhanced cosmos."[157] In the fifties, he stated the point in bold contradiction to his earlier views. The libertarians, he wrote in 1957, despite their illusions about liberty leading to equality, were more right in the long run than the equalitarians. The libertarians were closer to being right because their illusions were harmless "so long as a free society made it possible to create balances of power . . . which would make for justice."[158] This is not to say that their theories of justice were right or even adequate. No conception of justice based on the illusion that history can rise above the ambiguities and corruptions of history is adequate.

We should not conclude that Niebuhr, in the fifties, had become a defender of liberal culture. The third lesson Niebuhr took from his analysis of liberal theories of history was that liberalism had not generated an interpretation of history that could account for the circumstances of justice as well as the Christian paradox of grace does. Even liberal theories that called for a balance between liberty and equality still presumed humans could master the moral problems of history. The focus of Niebuhr's polemical sting shifted away from the moribund religious liberalism of the social gospel to those who wanted to apply social science to manage the evolution of history. Their pretension to manage history ignored two limitations established by the myth of grace. First, it rejected the limits of humans' creatureliness, which prohibits any group from attaining a universal perspective from which to manage. Second, it ignored the limits on management posed by humans' unique endowment with freedom, which issues in both creative and destructive actions that cannot be controlled.[159]

This pretension undermines efforts to approximate the social ideal. It encourages pride and complacency about the culture's achievements and its immediate prospects for justice. A prideful and complacent culture is unable to convict its present conception of justice by the judgment of sacrificial love. Consequently, the renewal that the power of grace affords is forfeited. These liberal claims that Western cultures are progressing toward perfect justice blind their adherents to what the paradox of grace enables one to comprehend: "the fulfillments of meaning in history will be the more untainted in fact, if purity is not prematurely claimed for them."[160] For Niebuhr, the ambiguities of history are such that justice is more likely to be approximated by those who recognize the impossibility of perfect conceptions or structures of justice, that

---

157. Niebuhr, *The Nature and Destiny*, vol. 2, 169.
158. Niebuhr, "Liberty and Equality," 192.
159. Niebuhr, *Faith and History*, 83; idem, *The Irony of American History*, 83–84.
160. Niebuhr, *The Nature and Destiny*, vol. 1, 213.

is, by those who understand the permanent tension between the ideal and the actual.

Niebuhr also accused Marxism of repeating this last misunderstanding of the historical circumstances for justice. He came to understand Marxism as "a variant of the liberal dogma."[161] It affirmed the same mistaken hope that humans will become "unequivocally the master of [their] own destiny"[162] and "establish perfect justice."[163] As a variant of bourgeois liberalism, Marxism displayed differences from liberalism. First, though both trace injustice to social factors, which if eradicated will eliminate injustice, for Marxism the social problem is private property rather than feudal and monarchical restraints on liberties or social ignorance.[164] Socialistic equality (rather than liberty and/or education) is made the foundation for perfect justice.[165] Second, Marxism challenges the liberal illusions about the evolution of history toward perfection with the illusion that perfection is obtainable only by a revolutionary assertion of power by the proletariat.[166] These differences, however, are disputes within the common view that humans can redeem history. Liberalism and Marxism share this error of the modern culture that history can progress to perfection.

This assessment of Marxism was not in itself new. Niebuhr challenged Marxist utopianism in the thirties. There was, however, a change in Niebuhr's assessment of the Marxist view of history. Even as late as the forties (when he had abandoned his earlier claim that Christianity should endorse the proletarian mission), Niebuhr continued to maintain that the Marxist view of history is truer than the liberal view. Niebuhr preferred the Marxist view because it does not claim simple harmony but the possibility of harmony emerging out of chaos.[167] But by the fifties, Niebuhr wrote that "communism changes only partly dangerous sentimentalities and inconsistencies in the bourgeois ethos into consistent and totally harmful ones."[168] The author of *Moral Man and Immoral Society*, who found the Marxist illusion a useful instrument for approximating justice, now wrote of "a foe who has transmuted our [liberal] harmless illusions into noxious ones."[169]

Niebuhr claimed that the communists' illusion about mastering history

161. Niebuhr, *The Irony of American History*, 19.
162. Ibid., 66–67; idem, *Faith and History*, 84.
163. Niebuhr, *The Nature and Destiny*, vol. 2, 181.
164. Niebuhr, *The Irony of American History*, 19.
165. Niebuhr, *Faith and History*, 187.
166. Niebuhr, *The Irony of American History*, 13–14.
167. Niebuhr, "Optimism, Pessimism, and Religious Faith," 10–11.
168. Niebuhr, *The Irony of American History*, 15.
169. Ibid., 153.

is more dangerous because they specify who should use a detailed scheme of political power for what precise goals in history.[170] They fail to see the possibilities for injustice in unchecked political power or in the power of economic managers.[171] There was nothing new in this observation. Niebuhr had, in the thirties, warned of the dangers of using political power to eradicate economic inequalities. At that time, however, he did not see the threat of communist tyranny as greater than capitalist inequality. He had, in the intervening period, become clearer about the error of rooting injustice in historical phenomena rather than in original sin, but that clarity hardly explains why he now saw Marxism as more dangerous than liberalism. The major factor in Niebuhr's reassessment of Marxism was, I think, the application of his developing myth of grace to unfolding events.

The important events were Stalin's purges and pact with the Nazis, the postwar Soviet threat to Western nations, and achievement of tolerable equality in democratic-capitalist societies. Interpreting these events in the light of grace, Niebuhr came to view the conscious application of power for the purpose of creating equality as less open to renewal than the inequalities produced by economic anarchy in democratic societies. The power of renewal in grace is not just a turning away from one mode for obtaining perfection to another. It is a recognition of our limited capacities and a faith in the providence of God. There is no such recognition or faith in the pretensions of the liberal creed. Yet liberalism's vagueness about the use of power and its institutions that allow for the vitalities of the human spirit leave room for the irony of a "grace of common sense," which liberalism's theories belie. Marxism, with its clarity about the use of power, impedes this capacity for ironical renewal. This understanding of the irony in history was absent from Niebuhr's earlier qualified endorsement of Marxism.

Recall that Niebuhr understood his earlier choice for Marxism as a tragic choice between "hypocrisy and vengeance."[172] A tragic situation, he wrote in *The Irony of American History,* is "constituted of conscious choices of evil for the sake of good."[173] As Ronald Stone notes, the experience of the thirties and forties gradually moved Niebuhr from a "tragic" to an "ironic" interpretation of history.[174] An ironic interpretation does not eliminate tragedy from history, but it offers a different view of human participation in history. An ironic situation is distinguished

---

170. Ibid., 67.
171. Ibid., 95.
172. See *supra,* chapter four, 225.
173. Ibid., vii.
174. Stone, *Reinhold Niebuhr,* 72–73.

from a tragic one, according to Niebuhr, "by the fact that . . . responsibility is related to an unconscious weakness rather than to a conscious resolution."[175] Niebuhr now considered the ironic view normative for Christian faith.[176] In his earlier, primarily tragic, view of history, he clearly did not believe humans could redeem history, but he did believe Christians would have to make tragic choices in order to approximate the social ideal in history. "The irony of American history" is that it produced a tolerable justice notwithstanding its refusal to take Niebuhr's tragic choice for Marxism. The calamity of Russian history is that its tragic choice for equality over democracy and its attendant freedoms left no room for ironic renewal.

The lesson for Niebuhr was that humans are even less able to control history than the idea of tragic choices for approximating justice implies. This lack of control need not bring us to despair, because the ironies of history may produce a more tolerable justice than our tragic choices. It does mean that the power of grace, which allows us to trust the providence of God, requires that our conceptions of justice offer greater latitude to freedom and human vitalities than Niebuhr had allowed in the thirties. This higher evaluation of freedom is necessary even though we know it is incompatible with the ideal of equality. One of the limitations that history places on justice is that we cannot approximate it by aiming to achieve any one of the ideals it incorporates.

The circumstances of history limit the possibilities for justice because the proponents of justice can never stand above the continuing tension between the ideal and the actual. Attempts to achieve perfect justice, whether through the liberal ideal of liberty or the Marxist ideal of equality, fail even to approximate justice. Even more modest attempts to approximate justice by tragic choices for a particular social movement, such as Niebuhr's in the early thirties, are too sanguine about controlling history. Our efforts to achieve justice will prove most successful if we are sufficiently humble about our own righteousness and capacities to manage history that we permit human vitalities that do not conform precisely to our conception of a just order.

Possibilities

For Niebuhr, there is no full redemption in history, but there are indeterminate possibilities for approximating the social ideal. Most of his polemics were directed against the failure of modern culture to recognize

---

175. Niebuhr, *The Irony of American History*, viii.
176. Ibid., 155.

the limits history places upon justice, but Niebuhr also castigated the "pessimism" and "defeatism" that he thought the Reformation bequeathed to dialectical theology. This theology, Niebuhr contended, was inclined "to exclude the possibility of redemption and a new life in man's social existence."[177] It is keenly aware of the inadequacies of all historical achievements. Its hope is almost exclusively for a transcendent kingdom. The result is an "absolute distinction" between the transcendent (ideal) and historical (actual) that "destroys the tension between the final demands of God upon the conscience, and all the relative possibilities of realizing the good in history."[178] What is hoped for is disassociated from the task of securing justice. Love becomes irrelevant to justice. By contrast, a theology that interprets history as a field of creative tension between the "demands of perfect love" on the one hand and "every political system" and "every social situation" on the other can see the indeterminate possibilities for higher justice.[179] Social institutions open to renewal can more closely approximate the social ideal, even though perfect justice is an impossibility. The "defeatist" destruction of this tension has two untoward effects on approaches to the problem of justice.

First, it leads to indifference to "relative moral discriminations."[180] All human actions are interpreted as equally sinful. Hence, judgments about the relative moral achievements of history are imperiled.[181] Further, grace is understood as love that frees us from the imperfect obligations of the law rather than as increasing a still imperfect sense of obligation. Consequently, discriminations among obligations, which justice requires, are eliminated.[182]

Niebuhr argued against this pessimistic and one-dimensional interpretation of history. He agreed that all persons are equally sinful before God but insisted that we can distinguish among better and worse "historical consequences of sin." On that distinction, we can determine that some persons and institutions are more guilty of injustice than others.[183] For Niebuhr, discriminate judgments about justice should be based on

---

177. Niebuhr, *Faith and History,* 199.
178. Niebuhr, *The Nature and Destiny,* vol. 2, 195.
179. Ibid., 192.
180. Ibid., 190.
181. Niebuhr, *The Nature and Destiny,* vol. 1, 220.
182. Niebuhr, *The Nature and Destiny,* vol. 2, 189–190.
183. Niebuhr, *The Nature and Destiny,* vol. 1, 222. Niebuhr later confessed the error of this distinction between the " 'equality of sin and inequality of guilt,' " but he continued to maintain that we must find a way to describe our "situation" that "will allow for discriminate judgments between good and evil" while "preserving the Biblical affirmation that all men fall short before God's judgment." See Niebuhr, "Reply to Interpretation and Criticism," 513.

the "fact that those who hold great economic and political power are more guilty of . . . injustice against the weak than those who lack power and prestige."[184] Schemes of justice that restrict inequalities of power are relatively better than those that endorse them. Niebuhr also understood the power of renewal in grace as "increasing [a] sense of social obligation" so that grace is related to indeterminate "proximate possibilities of liberty and justice, which must be achieved in history."[185] The love in grace will ultimately fulfill history by forgiveness, which no system of justice can do, but it is also a source for enhancing the relative discriminations of justice. As Niebuhr wrote in another context, love is a "principle of discriminate criticism" that requires a scheme of justice that is the "closest approximation to love."[186] For Niebuhr, history is neither so thoroughly determined by sin nor so intractable to renewal by grace that the relative distinctions of justice are irrelevant to its final fulfillment in God's love. Imperfect schemes of justice that balance liberty and equality in a relatively stable equilibrium of power can approximate love.

Second, a "defeatist" interpretation of history can lead to complacency or an easy conscience about the extant systems of "justice." This problem, which also exists for modern views of history, arises in the Reformation heritage for the opposite reason. The Renaissance heritage encourages complacency because it claims the ideal has been or soon will be achieved in history. Protestant, especially Lutheran, views of history, on the other hand, heighten the religious tension between the ideal and the actual to the point that "it breaks the moral tension from which all decent action flows." The conscience is uneasy about the sin in all human enterprise, but all alternative courses of action are seen as equally tainted. Confidence is placed solely in the hope that divine forgiveness will sanctify what is really unholy. Consequently, the uneasy conscience is eased "prematurely," and saints are tempted to sin so that grace may abound while the sinners are left with the task of making human relations slightly more just.[187] This "defeatist" theology is not pretentious about mastering history, but history is understood as so sinful and impenetrable by grace that there is "complacent acceptance of whatever imperfect justice a given social order [has] established."[188]

Niebuhr believed his twofold understanding of grace (i.e., combining renewal and forgiveness) called for understanding history as subject to

---

184. Niebuhr, *The Nature and Destiny*, vol. 1, 225.
185. Niebuhr, *The Nature and Destiny*, vol. 2, 190, 193.
186. Niebuhr, "Why the Christian Church Is Not Pacifist," 116.
187. Niebuhr, *The Nature and Destiny*, vol. 2, 196–197.
188. Niebuhr, *An Interpretation*, 129.

indeterminate possibilities for greater justice but not to the perfection of justice. The tension between love and justice is a constant part of historical existence. Love, said Niebuhr, is "a principle of indiscriminate criticism" because it is (1) the "law of life" pertinent to history, yet (2) an impossibility for all "forms of community in which elements of coercion and conflict destroy the highest type of fellowship."[189] A conception of justice, based on this interpretation of history, must incorporate the ideal of love as a basis for constant criticism that prohibits complacency about the final validity of any principles of justice.

In sum, the historical possibilities for justice warrant both judgments about which economic and political structures are relatively more just and a constant uneasiness about why the relatively better is not a closer approximation of the social ideal. The limitations history places on the possibility for perfect justice should never chasten enthusiasm for greater justice.

Direction and Fulfillment

For Niebuhr, the circumstances of history are such that the "achievements of justice . . . may rise in indeterminate degrees to . . . a more perfect love . . . ; but each new level of fulfillment [achievement would be more accurate] also contains elements which stand in contradiction to perfect love."[190] The social ideal entailed by love provides the direction toward which justice should move, but it is not the goal (in history) of justice. History is not one damn injustice after another. Justice should be extended in the direction of universal love,[191] even though love should not be viewed as a possible goal of justice. "History moves towards the realization of the Kingdom [perfect love] but yet the judgment of God is upon every new realization."[192] All achievements in history stand under God's final judgment at the end of history. There is no progressive fulfillment of humankind within history.[193] The highest realizations of justice are possible only when it is understood that they contradict, as well as approximate, the ideal of love.[194]

Niebuhr's view of the relation between love and justice had not changed since the early thirties. He continued to view his conception of justice as a strategy for approximating the ideal of love within the

---

189. Niebuhr, "Why the Christian Church Is Not Pacifist," 113–114.
190. Niebuhr, The Nature and Destiny, vol. 2, 246.
191. Niebuhr, "Christian Faith and the Common Life," 81.
192. Niebuhr, The Nature and Destiny, vol. 2, 286.
193. Ibid., 293.
194. Ibid., 246–247.

actualities of conflicting interests where the ideal of love can never be fully achieved. Historical circumstances require that we use strategies of justice that balance individual and collective interests rather than making love the norm (or goal) in history. Yet these strategies will work only if they take their inspiration (and direction) from the ideal of love.[195] This strategy, which takes its direction from love, requires relative principles of justice. Love that discriminates among better and worse schemes of justice encourages relative principles of justice. It prohibits claims for absolute principles of justice because love is also indiscriminately critical of every conception of justice. Herein was the basis for Niebuhr's developed views toward what he almost interchangeably called natural law or rational principles of justice.

What Niebuhr, following Ernst Troeltsch, called relative natural laws or regulative or guiding principles of justice are "the servants and instruments" of love in that they extend the sense of obligation toward others. They are required to apply love to the enduring obligations that communities must specify for complex situations.[196] The most general principles, namely, liberty and equality, are "in a medial position between love and justice."[197] ("Justice" in this context means more specific principles and actual structures of justice.) Niebuhr clearly believed that these principles are necessary for justice to approximate love. On the other hand, they are never absolute. Absolute principles always fail to account for the freedom history allows for indeterminate higher possibilities of love.[198]

All principles of justice legitimate some assertions of interests against others, while the social ideal of love eliminates all conflicts of interest. "[E]very effort to enforce [love] negates it."[199] Principles of justice, which by their nature sanction enforcing a distributive pattern in conflict situations, necessarily fall short of love. "The heedlessness of perfect love can not be present in the rational calculations of justice."[200] As long as love provides direction for justice, no principles of justice can determine the ideally right distribution of benefits and burdens. Love determines the ideal, which can never be achieved but can be approximated by principles of justice that do not claim to be absolute reflections of love. The principles of justice or the natural law are constitutionally

195. Ibid., 95–96.
196. Ibid., 248.
197. Niebuhr, *Faith and History*, 189.
198. Niebuhr, *The Nature and Destiny*, vol. 1, 280–286; idem, "Reply to Interpretation and Criticism," 511.
199. Niebuhr, "Christian Faith and the Common Life," 20.
200. Niebuhr, *Faith and History*, 190.

relative. They are instruments in a strategy for achieving whatever tentative harmony of interests most nearly approximates the ideal of love.

Given this constitutional tension between love, which transcends all interests, and standards of justice, which necessarily adjudicate among interests, love must never be considered a goal *in* history. As a goal in history, love would become identified with a particular social movement or conception of justice. It would no longer provide direction for the indeterminate possibilities of justice. Love always stands above history in judgment upon every approximation of it within history. But love is also the goal *of* history. At the end of history, love fulfills the approximations of it in history. If it merely stands above history, the consequences of justice for the direction of history would not be a serious matter for Christians. Only the purity of an action in relation to love would be important. Only by viewing love as the goal of history that fulfills justice can we assert that love provides meaningful direction for justice.[201] Thus, Niebuhr's eschatology was a faith and hope that the suffering love of Christ is ultimately triumphant at the end of history.[202]

Two salient features of this eschatological faith were significant for Niebuhr's theory of justice. First, the fulfillment transfigures but does not annul the temporal process.[203] Consequently, the historical struggle for justice, even though it has no hope for achieving perfection, finds meaning in hope for the resurrection at the eschaton. Christians should not hope for an escape from the historical struggles for justice, thereby rendering these struggles meaningless. They should hope for a final redemption that gives meaning to the struggle by transfiguring and completing justice. Second, this eschatological hope is based on faith in the sovereignty of divine suffering love, not on a human or historical resolution to the problems of injustice. Only faith "in the God who is revealed in Christ" is an answer to the problems of the meaning and fulfillment of history.[204] Only this faith in "security beyond all the securities and insecurities of history . . . [can] dissuade men from the idolatrous pursuit of false securities and redemptions in life and history."[205] Only this faith can bring us to abandon the modern pride that a particular historical movement to which we are loyal is progressing toward perfect justice. Only this faith gives us the security to submit our

---

201. Reinhold Niebuhr, "Is Religion Counter Revolutionary?" *Radical Religion* 1, no. 1 (Autumn 1935): 17; idem, *The Nature and Destiny,* vol. 2, 299–301.

202. Ibid., 290.

203. Ibid., 295; idem, *Faith and History,* 237.

204. Niebuhr, *The Nature and Destiny,* vol. 2, 295.

205. Ibid., 320–321.

best conceptions of justice to the indiscriminate criticism of the ideal of love.

This understanding of the circumstances in which justice must be done differed dramatically from both Rauschenbusch and Ryan. The differences had significant influence on their respective conceptions of justice.

Ryan's analysis of economic conditions for the purpose of securing natural rights through just economic institutions did not locate the circumstances of justice in the "dramas of history." Ryan's focus on economic patterns and structures provided no basis for seeing either indeterminate possibilities for Niebuhr's social ideal or the sinful forces in history Niebuhr believed were impeding the realization of that ideal. Niebuhr located the problem of justice in the context of a grand historical struggle between divine love and human sin that Ryan simply did not consider.

Rauschenbusch's analysis of the forces of redemption in history placed him closer to Niebuhr's concern that justice be understood in the context of a struggle between divine love and forces of evil. Both Niebuhr and Rauschenbusch attempted to discern how divine grace shaped the circumstances for justice. These common elements in their analyses of the circumstances of justice explain why both Niebuhr and Rauschenbusch, unlike Ryan, developed strategies to secure justice through a historical struggle. Still, Rauschenbusch's sociological analysis of history left no room for the indeterminate possibilities of Niebuhr's ideal of love. Nor did Rauschenbusch perceive the will-to-power that Niebuhr saw in every collective movement. (Recall that Rauschenbusch believed that collectivities could foster good character as well as reinforce selfish interests.) The unresolvable tension between the ideal and the actual in history that characterized Niebuhr's understanding of the circumstances of justice was no more part of Rauschenbusch's analysis than it was of Ryan's.

Both Rauschenbusch and Ryan considered justice an appropriate, though not necessarily attainable, goal in history. Thus, both developed conceptions of justice they viewed, at least tentatively, as more or less adequate reflections of God's order (Ryan) or ordering (Rauschenbusch) of nature and history. For them, the divine order accommodates principles of justice that discriminate among conflicting interests. For Niebuhr, such claims for the possibility of an ideal conception of justice reach beyond the limitations endemic to standards for justice. These claims also necessarily fall short of the possibilities for justice created by the divine-human encounter in history.

For Niebuhr, God's will could not be perceived in patterns and structures (not even in evolving ones such as Rauschenbusch discerned) of nature or history. For Niebuhr, the possibility of the fulfillment of justice in divine love could only be encountered, not embedded, in history. It necessarily conflicts with every conceivable ordering of history.

Niebuhr's interpretation of history as a continuing tension between the ideal and the actual and between love and justice relied ultimately upon his doctrine of God. Only by faith in a particular conception of God as love could he view the human condition so that love provides direction for indeterminate possibilities for justice that are fully realizable only beyond history. We now turn to that conception of God.

GOD

Niebuhr never gave systematic attention to a concept of God. He, nevertheless, used the term *God* frequently.[206] These references to God are not surprising because faith in a partially specified concept of God offered backing for his interpretations of human nature and history. We must ferret out that concept from scattered passages in order to comprehend fully the theory for his conception of justice, especially as it relates to love.

God Is Love

The central concept for Niebuhr's understanding of God was disinterested love. H. Richard Niebuhr, in the context of a stinging criticism of liberal Christianity for its "disposition to identify God with love," observed that his brother made the same error. H. Richard cited several passages from *An Interpretation of Christian Ethics* and criticized them for implying that Jesus interprets God as though God were love only.[207] My present purpose is not to assess H. Richard's criticism but to develop Reinhold's understanding of God in light of H. Richard's interpretation.

In *An Interpretation of Christian Ethics,* Niebuhr wrote: "[T]he will of God is defined in terms of all-inclusive love."[208] We need not infer that Niebuhr defined God exclusively in terms of love. He, especially during the forties, developed concepts of God's justice, judgment, wrath, power, sovereignty, providence, majesty, and so forth. However, as this 1935 passage implies and Niebuhr's later development of other attributes of God confirms, love was, for Niebuhr, the primary attribute of God. All other attributes are ultimately extensions of God's love. It is not just that these attributes cohere with love (in fact, within history they

---

206. See Stone, *Reinhold Niebuhr,* 225–226.
207. H. Richard Niebuhr, *Christ and Culture* (New York: Harper & Row, 1951), 15–17.
208. Niebuhr, *An Interpretation,* 54.

are permanently in paradoxical tension with love); it is rather that they have their source solely within love. They do not qualify a description of God as love. Furthermore, God's love is "the perfect disinterestedness" revealed by the cross.[209] Niebuhr understood God primarily in terms of sacrificial love that eschews all assertions of interests in indiscriminate care for others.

How can God so conceived act in history with sufficient judgment and power to secure the ultimate triumph of justice? How can the God of love also be the God of justice? This question was the burden of Niebuhr's attempt to understand God and God's relations to the world. His answer came on two levels.

God as Transcendent: Love and Justice Unified

First, there is the transcendent level. Only at this level can God's justice, power, judgment, and so forth, be fully united with God's love, mercy, forgiveness, and so forth. In a sermonic essay on the goodness (love) and power of God, Niebuhr wrote: "Perfect power and goodness can be united only in God, where the contest of life with life is transcended and where the possession of power does not lead to its use in the struggle for existence."[210] Niebuhr made a similar claim in his most systematic theological writing: "The final majesty of God is contained not so much in His power within the structures as in the power of His freedom over the structures." God's majesty and God's agape are one but only in God's transcendent freedom.[211] If love is nonassertive, it cannot be powerful and majestic within the conflicts of history. Consequently, Niebuhr emphasized that the "radical otherness of God" is required in order to provide a unified meaning for history. God is too transcendent of human desires, capacities, and powers to simply be comprehended or associated with natural human purposes.[212]

This emphasis upon transcendence allowed Niebuhr to unite divine justice with his conception of totally disinterested love. At the level of divine transcendence, "the highest justice of God *is* the holiness of His love."[213] This transcendent unity of love and justice (unity through love

---

209. Niebuhr, *The Nature and Destiny*, vol. 2, 72.
210. Reinhold Niebuhr, "The Power and Weakness of God," in *The Essential Reinhold Niebuhr*, 26. First published in 1946.
211. Niebuhr, *The Nature and Destiny*, vol. 2, 71.
212. Niebuhr, *Faith and History*, 103.
213. Niebuhr, *The Nature and Destiny*, vol. 2, 56, my emphasis. Most of Niebuhr's references to divine justice pertained to retributive justice, but because they concerned the problem of discriminations about what is due persons, they apply to distributive justice as well.

fulfilling justice) stands in judgment upon every human conception of justice. The latter necessarily employ power and assert some interests against others. They necessarily disrupt the harmony of sacrificial love. Thus, the highest principles of justice (absolute liberty and equality), which approach the social ideal entailed by divine love, are themselves too transcendent to be constitutive of actual justice. They are transcendent principles. Love and justice are never fully united within history, not even by the acts of God in history (most especially not by the cross, which stands above the problem of relative justice in history).

In accord with H. Richard's interpretation of his brother's understanding of God, love was as central for Reinhold Niebuhr's understanding of God as it was for liberal theology. It was not the primacy of love in understanding God that distinguished Niebuhr from liberal theology. Niebuhr's problem with liberal theology was that it reduced the ideal of love to prudential mutuality. It identified love with the historical person of Jesus, "the good man of Galilee." Hence, it missed the transcendence of divine love and divine justice.[214] Recall Rauschenbusch's emphasis upon the immanence of God's love.[215]

Niebuhr perceived the unity of love and justice, and so forth, most clearly in God as creator, that is, source of the world, and God as final judge and final redeemer, that is, goal of the world's perfection. These myths about God as the transcendent source and transcendent goal of the world provide meaning that justifies Christian optimism about the ultimate course of history.[216] In God as creator and final judge and final redeemer, divine love unites with divine majesty and justice. Viewed within history, this unity is an ultrarational myth known only in faith. It remains shrouded in mystery. Niebuhr took great pains to assert the radical otherness of God as creator and end from any natural or temporal process or achievement.

In the original perfection of creation, humans are, as I have noted, free to transcend all "natural" desires and interests in perfect love while remaining fully dependent upon God's power for fulfillment. God's power and love are united but not in a way that pertains to a natural or historical ordering of life. Niebuhr unrelentingly criticized doctrines of creation that understate God's transcendence of nature and history. He objected again and again to rational proofs for God as the first cause. The resulting view of God as creator, he observed, understands creation as a self-explanatory chain of causation. It underestimates arbitrariness

---

214. Niebuhr, *An Interpretation*, 23.

215. See *supra*, chapter two, 81–82.

216. Niebuhr, "Optimism, Pessimism, and Religious Faith," 4–5; idem, *An Interpretation*, 16–17; idem, *Faith and History*, 103–104.

and novelty in the created world. This view identifies God too closely with the totality of things.[217] It too severely restricts the transcendence and freedom of God and the openness of history.

This emphasis upon God's transcendence over creation is manifest in Niebuhr's conspicuous silence about God as governor, orderer, or as ordering. He was particularly critical of naturalistic theologies, which he thought identified God with process. In response to criticisms by Henry Nelson Weiman, Niebuhr charged that Weiman "believes in a 'process' which he call [sic] 'God.' " Niebuhr argued that the "divine person possess[es] a freedom over and above the processes and structures."[218] He was also critical of those who attributed final or divine meaning to a coherent scheme or sequence of history.[219] God is neither nature nor time.[220] As creator and source of meaning, God transcends all natural and historical orderings that might be the basis for a system of justice. Justice based on divine ordering identifies God's purposes with assertions of power and interests that fall short of the nonresistant and disinterested love God discloses in Christ.

As the goal of the world, God is characterized by the same transcendent unity of divine love with divine power and justice. The eschaton is, as I have noted, the uniting of divine love and divine sovereignty in the triumphant return of Christ.[221] Here again, this unity in God cannot be directly related to temporal existence. The final consummation "lies beyond the conditions of the temporal process," even though it does not annul justice in history.[222] As the goal of history, God is not known by an argument from design that could disclose a natural or historical ordering toward God as final cause. Rather, the divine judgment and mercy place a wide gap between all conceivable orderings of history and God's love as the triumphant goal of history. Niebuhr could write of Christian love as the "final and authoritative definition of the 'order of God,' " but that "order" is no basis for "specific laws and rules of justice."[223] Faith asserts the perfection of justice in the love of God as the goal of history, but that unity is a mystery transcending any temporal ordering that might be the basis for a conception of justice.

By emphasizing the transcendence of the source and goal of the world,

---

217. See, for example, Niebuhr, *An Interpretation*, 32–33; idem, *Beyond Tragedy*, 7–9; idem, "The Truth in Myths," 18–19; Niebuhr, *The Nature and Destiny*, vol. 1, 133–134.

218. Niebuhr, "Reply to Interpretation and Criticism," 523–524.

219. Niebuhr, *Faith and History*, 105.

220. Ibid., 43–45.

221. Niebuhr, *The Nature and Destiny*, vol. 2, 290.

222. Ibid., 291.

223. Reinhold Niebuhr, "God's Design and the Present Disorder of Civilization," in *Faith and Politics*, 105–106. First published in 1948.

Niebuhr could envision a unity of disinterested love and justice that is impossible where justice must deal with natural interests and conflicts. The unity of divine love and justice presumes transcending all conflicting interests. To lose sight of the transcendence of God reduces love to mutuality of interests and perfect justice to tentative harmonies among conflicting interests. This reduction of the divine purposes to historical possibilities is the common idolatry of liberal Christianity and secular philosophies. It is idolatry because it identifies God with schemes of justice, which always contradict disinterested love. It dissolves the tension between the ideal of love and the actual achievements of justice.

God Acting in History: Love and Justice in Paradox

Divine transcendence solves the problem of uniting love and justice, but it begs the question of what this transcendent ideal has to do with the struggle for justice within history. A God who only transcends history dissolves the creative tension between the divine ideal and actual human existence as surely as do idolatries that reduce divine love to the actual conditions of history. If the transcendent God is not related to and involved in history, divine love becomes irrelevant to justice in history.

This brings us to the second level of Niebuhr's attempt to relate God's disinterested love to justice, that is, the level of God's involvement in history. Niebuhr consistently opposed any strict dualism between a transcendent God and history; he insisted that God is involved in history in both divine love and divine majesty.[224] This assertion that God is involved in history allowed him to account for the relevance of God's will to justice. At this level, his problem was to maintain unity between God's love and God's majesty and justice.

Niebuhr began by noting that the relation between God's love and God's justice[225] and God's love and God's majesty[226] are only paradoxically manifested in history. God enters history as love that finally subsumes divine power and judgment, but the unity remains "hidden." God defies and destroys unjust interests as well as overcoming them with love and forgiveness. Thus, the tension between the ideal of love and actual justice is reflected in the paradoxical actions of God in history. Agents seeking to comply with God's purposes act within the tension of using power to secure a tentative level of justice that continues to stand under the judgment of divine love.

224. Niebuhr, *The Nature and Destiny*, vol. 2, 46, 90–95.
225. Niebuhr, *Faith and History*, 126.
226. Niebuhr, *The Nature and Destiny*, vol. 2, 71.

God engages history primarily through the judging and redeeming grace most fully disclosed in the disinterested love symbolized by the cross. Divine love is primary, and it can enter history only as "powerless." Niebuhr distinguished the divine power that underlies creation at the "trans-historical" level from the divine love as "powerless" in Christ at the "historical" level. This powerless love is a "self-imposed weakness" of God.[227] Thus, this weakness reveals the (moral) character of God.[228] Langdon Gilkey writes: "The divine will (precisely because it is righteous) cannot in Niebuhr's view reveal itself as sheer power, even righteous power. . . . For all power in history, even that which seems most righteous, is . . . in actuality corrupt."[229] God chooses to enter history as love and not as an omnipotent sovereign who rules history. God's love will be sovereign, but that sovereignty is not fully established in history.[230]

This weak love must always be suffering love. It is not triumphant in history.[231] Those who represent it will be tragic victims of all systems of justice. This love, Niebuhr indicated, will fall victim not only to excessive self-assertion by others but even to "the most perfectly balanced system of justice." This justice "is [still] a balance of competing interests, and must therefore worst anyone who does not participate in the balance."[232] Niebuhr disassociated divine love not only from unjust exercises of power but also from the power to support perfectly balanced systems of justice. Where then is the divine wherewithal to effect justice in history? Niebuhr had two answers to this question. Both reflect the paradox of God's acts in history.

First, Niebuhr believed that it is only because there is power, albeit paradoxical power, in the suffering love of Christ that the renewal of history is possible. Without God's love, mercy, and forgiveness, the power of judgment cannot effect the repentance and renewal.[233] Herein lies the power of grace to create the indeterminate possibilities for justice. Further, the ultimate perfection of history is possible only by the grace of God's forgiving love. Thus, Niebuhr could write: "Faith rises above all philosophies and theologies in sensing that the weakness of God is His final power. It is the weakness of love which touches the heart

227. Niebuhr, "The Power and Weakness of God," 26–28.
228. Ibid., 28, 32; idem, *The Nature and Destiny*, vol. 2, 55, 96.
229. Langdon Gilkey, "Reinhold Niebuhr's Theology of History," in *The Legacy of Reinhold Niebuhr*, ed. Nathan A. Scott, Jr. (Chicago: University of Chicago Press, 1974), 53.
230. Niebuhr, *The Nature and Destiny*, vol. 2, 49.
231. Ibid., 49, 51.
232. Ibid., 72.
233. See, for example, Niebuhr, "The Power and Weakness of God," 29.

of the offender." "[T]he final majesty of God is the majesty of his mercy."[234] God has "resources of mercy great enough to redeem as well as to judge all men."[235] The mercy of God "strangely fulfills and yet contradicts the divine judgment."[236] "The justice and forgiveness of God are one."[237] Using the myth of atonement, Niebuhr asserted that the ultimate reconciliation of God's justice and love occurs as God takes the consequences of just judgment into divine suffering love.[238] These statements reflect Niebuhr's beliefs that the love of God *in history* contains power for renewal and that divine judgment is ultimately a matter of being touched by the mercy of divine love.

If this were the only dimension of God's involvement in history, Niebuhr would have been committed to an ethic of nonresistant love as the only means to justice, an ethic he persistently criticized for lacking realism. Indeed, the relevance of love for securing relative justice indicates that Niebuhr believed that this divine love has some power in history. But God's power in history is not contained in divine love alone. The power of God's love to effect justice remains partly hidden in history. It is hidden not only because God's love has not yet triumphed but also because the love in God's acts is sometimes hidden in a paradoxical relation to God's judgment. In history, the power of God's grace to renew is not only in God's love. It is also in God's powerful and wrathful judgment. God is sovereign not only through divine love that touches the rebellion of the heart but also "partly by the power which places an ultimate limit upon human defiance."[239]

This power is not a nonassertive judgment of love on all self-assertions. It is the power of judgment that brings "doom" upon Germany and Japan.[240] In his more anticapitalist period, Niebuhr considered the self-destruction of capitalism an example of this divine judgment.[241] It contains "a hard and terrible facet . . . which stands in contradiction to love."[242] This power is in the prophets' judgment of doom upon Israel and the divine judgment that destroys nations, cultures, and empires.[243] The catastrophes of history in which nations,

---

234. Ibid., 29–30.
235. Niebuhr, *The Nature and Destiny*, vol. 2, 30.
236. Ibid., 212.
237. Ibid., 56.
238. Ibid., 55, 292.
239. Niebuhr, *Faith and History*, 125.
240. Niebuhr, "The Power and Weakness of God," 29.
241. Reinhold Niebuhr, "Culture Religions," *Radical Religion* 3, no. 3 (Summer 1938): 10.
242. Niebuhr, "The Power and Weakness of God," 29.
243. Niebuhr, *Faith and History*, 126–130.

cultures, and civilizations are destroyed are signs of God's punishment of human pride.[244]

These destructive events are not merely a divine ordering to restrain evil. They limit injustice, but they also present occasions for renewal that create the possibilities for higher justice. In both respects, they partially disclose God's will for moral agents.

Niebuhr was careful not to identify God's wrath with a particular historical judgment on injustice. The divine judgment is exercised "above and beyond the rough and [morally] inexact historical judgments."[245] Consequently, agents who carry out this judgment are never purely doing God's will. These agents are not always good. They are never solely good. Christians exercising this power against injustice ought not consider themselves purely righteous agents of divine power who will be vindicated through God's providence over history. God's ultimate providence is not located in particular events of history that favor the power of the just but in the grace that transcends good and evil in impartial love for all of God's children.[246] Christians, therefore, should always exercise power with an uneasy conscience. They, nevertheless, sometimes come closer to serving God's will (as paradoxically understood in history) by powerful judgments against injustice than by nonresistant love. In such uses of power they may be, as the Allies were, positive "instruments of the divine justice." Mercy is not always in the service of God's will. Wrathful judgments upon injustice are morally necessary. They can provide a negative basis, which is often necessary, for repentance and renewal. They also restrain injustice.[247]

In sum, the divine grace that provides for the indeterminate possibilities of justice in history is characterized by this tension between God's disinterested love and the power of God's wrathful judgment. This tension is ultimately overcome in God's merciful and forgiving love. "[J]udgment is not the final word of God to man."[248] But the final word transcends history. God as judge and redeemer enters history and completes history as love, but, in order to prevent human injustice from defeating divine love in history, God is also a wrathful judge in paradoxical tension with divine love.

---

244. Niebuhr, *The Nature and Destiny*, vol. 1, 138–141. In this section, Niebuhr related God as creator to God as judge engaged in history, observing that the essential structure of creation punishes sin and limits human freedom as humans rebel against it. The transcendent Creator is, here, also involved in history, but along with the involvement comes a tension between God's love and God's wrathful judgment. See also Niebuhr, *The Nature and Destiny*, vol. 2, 56.
245. Niebuhr, *Faith and History*, 126.
246. Niebuhr, "The Providence of God," in *The Essential Reinhold Niebuhr*, 33–40.
247. Niebuhr, "The Power and Weakness of God," 29–30.
248. Niebuhr, *The Nature and Destiny*, vol. 2, 142.

Neither Ryan nor Rauschenbusch understood God as disinterested love in which resides power that ultimately absorbs into love the divine justice that is only paradoxically related to love in history. Consequently, they did not understand God in terms of these paradoxes of transcendence and involvement or powerless love and wrathful judgment. Ryan separated God as the ultimate end from the proximate end for humans in the divine order of creation, but God orders nature in a way that is conducive for humans' ultimate end in God. God has ordered human life so that justice provides the means to the proximate end of rational nature, which is conducive to God as the ultimate end. Rauschenbusch's more Protestant uniting of God as orderer and as redeemer in history related divine love to justice, as Niebuhr did, but for Rauschenbusch divine love was obviously not radically transcendent. Nor was it in paradoxical conflict with God's just judgment in history. To be sure, the work of redemption requires acts of sacrificial love and the suffering of the innocent that are not in immediate and strict compliance with justice, but Rauschenbusch considered divine redemption and divine judgment reconcilable in history.

Because neither Rauschenbusch nor Ryan perceived the tensions between divine love and divine power and justice that characterized Niebuhr's conception of God, they are among those whom Niebuhr considered idolaters. They both believed justice, which discriminates among conflicting interests and enforces its discriminations, is compatible with God as the orderer of history and nature. No such ideal justice was conceivable on Niebuhr's understanding of God as disinterested love in paradoxical tension with every act of divine wrathful judgment in history.

Implications for Justice

Niebuhr's conception of justice was informed both by the tension in God's acts in history and by the perfecting of justice in God's love as the transcendent source and goal of history. Justice requires assertions of power to approximate the ideal of love, which would otherwise face certain tragic defeat in the realities of history. But justice must also be tempered by the resources of sacrificial love in order to halt the degeneration of mutuality and justice based upon a balance of power alone. Justice requires both the power of wrathful judgment and the power of "powerless" love to attain its proximate possibilities in history. Yet it can never overcome the tension between them. It remains incomplete because its assertions of power, though necessary in history, are always under the higher judgment of the transcendent unity of God's majestic and perfectly just love.

Faith in God acting in history for the indeterminate possibilities for justice to approximate love informs and sustains the struggle for proximate justice. Faith in God as the transcendent source and goal of history who ultimately joins power and justice to love prevents absolute devotion to any system of justice, yet makes the struggle for imperfect justice ultimately meaningful.

THE IDEAL AND ACTUAL REVISITED

Niebuhr began his theological investigations convinced that religion, in order to be ethically fruitful, must maintain a creative tension between the historical and the transcendent. He utilized his concept of myth as the best method for interpreting Christian doctrines because he thought the paradoxical character of myth sustained this tension, and for Niebuhr it did. The tension between the ideal of love and the actual capacities of individual and collective agents remained his overarching theological and ethical frame of reference.

The Ideal

Niebuhr's understanding of human nature as created in the image of God portrayed humans as free for love and for a social ideal transcending all interests and conflicts. God created humans free from all interests and desires so that they could live in perfect harmony with each other and with God. By relying upon God's love as power sufficient for individual and social fulfillment, humans in original perfection do not even assert their interests in this individual and communal perfection.

No conception of justice complies with this ideal of original perfection. Justice adjudicates among conflicting interests and establishes itself by coercion. It necessarily falls short of the harmony in absolute anarchy and absolute communism for which humans were created. It necessarily contradicts God's love, which Christians trust will fulfill history. Because justice is perfected in this social ideal, standing at the source and end of history, all principles and schemes of justice are constitutionally incapable of achieving the aim of justice. "[T]he very freedom of man over nature . . . places him . . . in a state of tension with every form of justice which can be devised in history."[249]

The social ideal that instructed Niebuhr's conception of justice in the

---

249. Reinhold Niebuhr, "Christianity as a Basis of Democracy," *The Listener* 37 (January 1, 1947): 69.

early thirties did not change. It was now backed by a more fully articulated theology. His doctrine of creation conceived of humans as a unity of spirit and nature, free to transcend their natural interests without denying their finitude. His doctrine of eschatology conceived of God as divine love whose power of grace will fulfill the social ideal at the end of history.

The Actual

Niebuhr's doctrine of original sin portrayed humans in history as inevitably bound to use their freedom in prideful assertions of finite individual and collective interests. As earlier, Niebuhr understood these assertions of interests as rooted in the individual will-to-power. They are unbounded by the limits that characterize animal desires, and they cannot be eliminated by changes in economic or political institutions. These conflicting interests cannot be subdued by love nor harmonized by rational principles of justice. A realistic effort to achieve justice must accept them as "necessary," albeit sinful, and develop a strategy to restrain them in a balance of power. Even the highest conceivable justice in history is not ideal. It is the best possible harmony "within the conditions of human egoism."[250]

Niebuhr's doctrine of original sin stated more clearly than he had in *Moral Man and Immoral Society* that the will-to-power arises in human freedom and is universal. To the extent that he had thought a few individuals could achieve the ideal of love or that the worst aspects of the will-to-power could be corrected by eliminating concentrations of economic power, his retrieval of the Christian doctrine of sin made his understanding of the actual human condition even more intractable to correction. The limits his doctrine of grace placed upon the possibility for renewal reinforced this view.

There was also a slight change in Niebuhr's understanding of the collective manifestations of sin. Although he had never understood injustice as solely a phenomenon of economic institutions, Niebuhr increasingly emphasized the political and spiritual manifestations of the collective will-to-power as much or more than its economic manifestations.[251] This new emphasis resulted more from the failure of the Russian experiment with Marxism than from Niebuhr's retrieval of the Christian doctrine of sin. For the most part, Niebuhr's developed theology of sin

---

250. Niebuhr, *The Nature and Destiny*, vol. 2, 252.
251. E.g., Reinhold Niebuhr, "Some Remarks About the Economic Interpretation of History," *Christianity and Society* 11, no. 4 (Fall 1946): 8–10; idem, *The Nature and Destiny*, vol. 2, 260–265.

simply reinforced and deepened his earlier understanding of the actual human condition.

The Tension

Niebuhr's theological investigations also backed his earlier understanding of the creative tension between the ideal of love and actual human condition. Here, the doctrine of grace is most relevant. First, as we stand under the continual divine judgment in need of forgiveness, we are constantly reminded of the limits of our individual and collective capacity for justice. Grace provides no hope for individual or collective perfection in history. Niebuhr never shared Rauschenbusch's confidence that God's grace enables pursuit of perfect justice. Grace even frees us from seeking perfect justice. It encourages us to aim for more modest possibilities that assert power against power in order to achieve tentative harmonies that balance liberty and equality. Even God's involvement in history for the sake of justice paradoxically includes power exercised as wrath, not just the "power" of disinterested love.

On the other hand, the power of grace to renew offers indeterminate opportunities for justice that more closely approximate the social ideal of love. It undercuts a too consistent realism or defeatism that ignores the lure of the ideal to higher forms of actual justice than have yet been achieved. One who trusts in the providence of God's grace knows that even the highest justice stands in tension with the social ideal, but one also knows that God's love makes better schemes of justice possible.

This doctrine of grace sustained Niebuhr's earlier realist understanding of the tension between the ideal and history, but it also contributed to the most significant change in his understanding of the tension. In the thirties, Niebuhr thought that the ideal could be most closely approximated by a tragic choice to sacrifice liberty and peace in an effort (perhaps revolutionary) to move history toward the goal of equality. By the time he wrote *The Irony of American History*, Niebuhr concluded that the pragmatic efforts of the New Deal had ironically produced a more tolerable justice than Marxism or dogmatic democratic socialism. Moreover, the achievement of the New Deal had occurred without a Promethean effort to direct the course of history and without a radical sacrifice of liberty. Niebuhr's strategy for approximating the ideal of love changed. He had become increasingly sensitive to limits upon the human capacity to direct history, even toward goals that fall tragically short of the social ideal. He now thought that the closest approximation of the social ideal occurs where liberties and order (peace) are balanced with equality.

This change arose from two interrelated sources: Niebuhr's retrieval of the doctrine of grace and his response to historical events. We have seen how Niebuhr drew upon the twofold aspect of grace to emphasize limits to our capacity to manage history and to notice that justice is renewed unpredictably, through the "grace of common sense," where liberties are not unduly restricted. This new emphasis on liberty did not, however, result solely from Niebuhr's retrieval of the myth of grace. Events in the Soviet Union and the United States influenced his interpretation of the circumstances of justice directly, and indirectly by informing his understanding of grace. In 1938, Niebuhr noted that changes in his theological ideas through the thirties came "not so much through study as through the pressure of world events."[252] This observation pertains to the forties as well. His method for recovering Christian myths was to test them in light of experience. His editorials in *Radical Religion* and *Christianity and Society* during this period reveal Niebuhr's increasing alarm over the moral failures of communism and, to a lesser extent, dogmatic democratic socialism.[253] Simultaneously, Niebuhr was increasingly astonished that American democratic liberalism contained resources to produce a tolerable equality of distribution. In 1953, commenting on the relegation of Norman Thomas's socialism to the periphery of the struggle for justice, Niebuhr wrote that the changes that have occurred in the political climate are "due both to the corruption of the alternative to capitalism and to the revelation of resources of justice in a free society which were not suspected two decades ago."[254]

What had happened to Niebuhr's earlier realism? He had not abandoned the creative tension between the ideal and the actual or his understanding of justice as a strategy for approximating love. He had (on the basis of his retrieval of traditional Christian doctrines informed and supplemented by the experience of historical events) modified his realist strategy of justice. He had rejected the view that the ideal could be best approximated by singular pursuit of the goal of equality. His modified strategy relied more heavily on freedom and order. These changes in his theory and conception of justice were, of course, accompanied by revisions in his judgments about ownership of property, democracy, and the proletarian movement.

---

252. Reinhold Niebuhr, "Ten Years That Shook My World," *The Christian Century* 56, no. 17 (April 26, 1939): 546.

253. See Reinhold Niebuhr, "Christian Faith and Social Action," in *Faith and Politics,* 121–122, for a summary of Niebuhr's revised views of Marxism and democratic socialism. Niebuhr noted that these revisions arose from both deepening theological convictions and the experience of history.

254. Reinhold Niebuhr, "Norman Thomas," *Christianity and Society* 18, no. 2 (Spring 1953): 5.

In the midthirties, Niebuhr had set out to provide theological backing for the mission of the proletariat without endorsing Marxist religious illusions. His theological investigations and world events led him to reject that mission. Nevertheless, his modified working standards of justice and policies were still, as they were in the thirties, backed by a Christian realist strategy for approximating love where actual conditions make this ideal inapplicable (but not irrelevant) to problems of justice. The working standards of justice, though changed, were still instruments in this strategy rather than guides for determining an ideal distribution of benefits and burdens.

The next chapter examines that revised conception of justice and its application to what Niebuhr, during this period, considered the major problems of distributive justice.

7

A MODIFIED STRATEGY FOR APPROXIMATING LOVE

Niebuhr's general principle of justice remained a consequentialist strategy for approximating the ideal under conditions in which the direct application of love would have terrible consequences for its own approximation. Because the gospel ethic of love offers no "strategy for dealing with relative requirements of a sinful world," it must be supplemented with a "strategy for dealing with the immediate requirements."[1] Niebuhr's revised working standards of justice outline this supplemental strategy. They are neither "in-principled" love nor valid independent of love. They are instruments of love valid only insofar as their application produces "an approximation of the law of love."[2] This view of the relation between the ideal of love and the principles of justice recurred throughout Niebuhr's later writings. In 1952, Niebuhr wrote: "The law seeks for a tolerable harmony of life with life, sin presupposed. It is, therefore, an approximation of the law of love . . . and an instrument of love."[3] In 1963, he reaffirmed: "The real problem of a social ethic is how to make justice, with its calculations of rights, the instrument of love."[4]

---

1. Niebuhr, "Christian Faith and the Common Life," 82–83.
2. Ibid., 71.
3. Reinhold Niebuhr, "Love and Law in Protestantism and Catholicism," in *Christian Realism and Political Problems* (New York: Charles Scribner's Sons, 1953), 171.
4. Reinhold Niebuhr, "The Development of a Social Ethic in the Ecumenical Movement," in *Faith and Politics,* 166. First published in 1963.

As in the early thirties, principles of justice, as well as the intellectual and social movements that embody them, are resources to be *used* in a strategy to approximate love. The major difference is that Niebuhr no longer had confidence that illusions or missions (whether religious, proletarian, bourgeois, etc.), if they are endorsed too wholeheartedly, have positive consequences for approximating love. These general programs for justice tend to be used as weapons to further the interests of particular groups, which the programs hide.[5] The interests and power that these various movements embody should be "used, beguiled, harnessed and deflected for the ultimate end," that is, establishing the highest possible justice.[6] This modification of Niebuhr's strategy, which occurred under the influence of his interpretation of history on the basis of his doctrine of grace, backed changes in working standards of justice.

The Working Standards of Justice
Regulative Principles of Justice

The most obvious change was a gradual abandonment of equality or equal justice as a goal, which, if pursued, would have the best consequences for approximating love. In place of the goal of equality, Niebuhr posited a balance between equality, freedom, and order as "regulative principles."

Already in 1935, Niebuhr included freedom with equality as one of two absolute "natural laws" (transcendent principles) of justice. He also noted that limits on equality are required by "the necessities of social cohesion and organic social life." He warned that the principle of equality should not be made so transcendent that it is robbed of its regulative function, yet equality is not a goal, certainly not the sole goal, for approximating love in history. This discussion, however, still gave preeminence to equality. There was no clear indication of what regulative function freedom has in determining which policies are just.[7] In 1938, Niebuhr still referred to equality as the only regulative principle of justice.[8]

As we will see momentarily, Niebuhr's discussion of the balance of power in the second volume of *The Nature and Destiny of Man* demonstrated that liberty and order were already functioning as regulative principles alongside equality, even though equality was still given supe-

---

5. Niebuhr, "Christian Faith and Social Action," 125.
6. Ibid., 136.
7. Niebuhr, *An Interpretation*, 132–136.
8. Niebuhr, "Christian Faith and the Common Life," 85.

rior status in his explicit discussion of the principles of justice.[9] By the fifties, Niebuhr explicitly offered an equivalent (or slightly superior) status to liberty as a regulative principle of justice. In a 1957 essay on liberty and equality, they are viewed as twin regulative principles that stand in tension with the social hierarchy and unity needed to maintain community[10] and with each other.[11] The importance of order for the sake of preserving community, which this essay stressed, was explicitly given equal status in a 1959 essay in which Niebuhr referred to "the principles of order (peace), liberty, and equality as transcendent or regulative principles of justice."[12]

These revisions were important. We will see that they cohere with considerable changes in the policies Niebuhr advocated. But why did Niebuhr demote equality, and how did these revisions alter his conception of justice? They do not indicate modifications in his distributive ideal (i.e., to each according to needs and from each according to abilities) or in his insistence that this ideal must be adjusted to the realities of the actual. To the extent that they transcend what is realizable in history, these three principles approximate the three elements of the social ideal, as Niebuhr conceived it in 1932: anarchy (freedom), communism (equality), and perfect harmony (peaceful order). To the extent that they are regulative for just policy, they are, as the goal of equality was earlier, strategic guides for approximating this social ideal in light of the actual human condition.

Why did his strategic guides change? They changed because Niebuhr's developed theology and interpretations of new events in history indicated an enlarged role for freedom and order as realistic means for approximating the same social ideal. Theologically, his understanding of God's providence as grace left him less confident of the human capacity to improve justice by a tragic choice for equality. Historically, the unanticipated resources of democratic societies to produce greater

---

9. See also Niebuhr's observations on "The Limits of Liberty" in a 1942 issue of *The Nation*. This essay implies that liberty and order function as regulative principles for democracies. Reinhold Niebuhr, "The Limits of Liberty," *The Nation* 154, no. 4 (January 24, 1942): 86–88.

10. Niebuhr, "Liberty and Equality," 186.

11. Ibid., 192.

12. Niebuhr, "The Problem of a Protestant Social Ethic," 10. Throughout the fifties, Niebuhr offered relatively equal status to freedom, equality, and order, but his thinking was inconsistent and perhaps continued to develop in regard to whether freedom and order are actually principles of justice. In the early fifties, he tended to list "order, freedom and justice" (i.e., equality) as considerations to be balanced in social policy. See Niebuhr, "Christian Faith and Social Action," 131. By the late fifties, he seemed to consider freedom and order as regulative principles of justice along with equality. See Niebuhr, "The Development of a Social Ethic," 177.

equality gave him more confidence in what he came to call the "common sense,"[13] the "common grace,"[14] or even the "grace of common sense."[15] This "common grace" is operative when human vitalities are free for creative efforts to enhance justice within an ordered community. In addition, the Marxist strategy of making equality the sole goal of justice had produced the political tyranny that Niebuhr earlier had only feared. Niebuhr's claim that the highest justice can be achieved via a Christian realist strategy remained, but theological and historical considerations persuaded him to abandon a strategy based on equality as the goal in history. He now saw love as most likely to be approximated where freedom and order are combined with equality and where all three are viewed as transcendent and regulative principles rather than as goals.

As transcendent, these principles are unrealizable. They lose their transcendent purity when they are elaborated in formulations sufficiently precise to discriminate among just and unjust claims. If, for example, absolute equality is made definitive for social policy, it becomes tainted. As a principle of discrimination, equality fails to account for actual circumstances of justice that require inequalities based on need, social function, or reward required for inducement. In the social ideal of the kingdom of God, there would be no need for these qualifications on equality. The first two qualifications would be satisfied freely by love without the sanctions of principles, and requirement for inducement would be dissolved by love. But within the realities of history, these qualifications must be incorporated into the regulative principle of equality. On the other hand, principles that incorporate these qualifications on absolute equality are also tainted by the interests of the privileged classes. Thus, no principle of equality (or of freedom) should be definitive for justice. All applicable principles are tainted by self or group interests.[16] This taintedness is the reason that Niebuhr had no interest in precise formulations of the principles of justice. Equality and freedom are absolute and definitive only insofar as they transcend the realities of human conflict.

Yet these regulative principles of justice, which are always corruptions of love, are also means for the indeterminate approximation of love.[17] Traditional principles and natural laws should not simply be abandoned. They should be used as regulative for a strategy to approximate the

---

13. E.g., Niebuhr, "Liberty and Equality," 197.
14. E.g., Niebuhr, "The Development of a Social Ethic," 168.
15. E.g., Niebuhr, *The Irony of American History*, 75.
16. Niebuhr, *The Nature and Destiny of Man*, vol. 2, 255; idem, *The Children of Light and the Children of Darkness* (New York: Charles Scribner's Sons, 1944), 74.
17. Niebuhr, *The Nature and Destiny*, vol. 2, 256; see also idem, "The Development of a Social Ethic," 178.

social ideal rather than as definitive (either of goals to be achieved or rights to be respected) of a just distribution. "A Christian contribution to standards of justice . . . must . . . not be found primarily in a precise formulation of the standard."[18] Niebuhr's theory of justice provided no basis for the formulation of principles or canons, as Rauschenbusch and Ryan did, to determine what is ideally just. His regulative principles were strategic guides for approximating a social ideal that transcends and fulfills all formulations of justice.

How did these regulative principles alter Niebuhr's previous working standards for justice? His earlier positing of equality as the goal, even though it was part of a strategy rather than definitive of ideal justice, clearly backed his endorsement of socialism and of the proletarian mission. His later strategy of balancing the regulative principles of equality, freedom, and order backed a "pragmatic" (nonrevolutionary)[19] and ad hoc[20] approach to policy questions. These regulative principles throw "some light on our present dilemmas," but they do "not solve them. No principles solve them."[21] Whereas Niebuhr, in the thirties, asked what consequences supporting an intellectual or political movement or general program of socialism had for furthering equality, Niebuhr, in the fifties, asked about the consequences of specific policies; for example, socializing steel may have different consequences than socializing coal.[22] If the effects of a policy maintain an appropriate balance between freedom, equality, and order, it is likely to approximate the ideal of love, which the regulative principles of justice are intended to serve. There is no basis here for endorsing a political mission or a general program, either of socialism or of capitalism.

Niebuhr's regulative principles of justice made his policy concerns less sweeping and more conservative. He was not only more conservative than he had been in the thirties. He was also more conservative than Rauschenbusch, who was willing to back the social and labor movement and a sweeping program for change, and Ryan, who proposed a comprehensive program for legislative action.

Balance of Power

Regulative principles of justice alone are obviously insufficient to determine what policies and structures are most just. The structures of justice

---

18. Niebuhr, "The Christian Faith and the Economic Life," 145.
19. E.g., Niebuhr, "The Problem of a Protestant Social Ethic," 9.
20. E.g., Niebuhr, "The Christian Faith and the Economic Life," 157.
21. Niebuhr, "The Problem of a Protestant Social Ethic," 10.
22. Niebuhr, "Christian Faith and Social Action," 128.

are at least as much a factor of equilibria of existing and developing forces and vitalities of a community as they are of rational principles or laws. Neither moral nor civil laws muster sufficient power to impose a pattern of justice on these structures.[23] Moreover, laws are themselves often instruments of powerful unjust interests. As he did in the thirties, Niebuhr continued to insist that the most successful way to deal with the realities of conflicting human wills is through an equilibrium of powers.[24] He even allowed that the "principle of the equilibrium of power" is itself a "principle of justice."[25] There were, however, changes in the way he conceived the problem of equilibrium and in his understanding of it as a working standard for justice. These changes cohere with his increasing emphasis upon freedom and order as regulative principles.

Niebuhr's most sustained treatment of the balance of power occurred in the second volume of *The Nature and Destiny of Man*.[26] In that discussion, he saw the problem of establishing relatively just structures of justice as one of joining "the coercive and organizing power of government" with "the balance of vitalities and forces" in a given situation. The balance of vitalities and forces is a natural and historical given. The use of government is a conscious use of power to reshape the given balance of forces into one somewhat more just. Total reliance on the organizing power may degenerate into tyranny. Passivity toward the balance of vitalities and forces may permit anarchy.[27]

This conception of the problem of balancing powers differed from Niebuhr's earlier view. Earlier, the problem had been primarily one of equalizing economic power by political force from outside and/or through the existing government. To the extent that he attended to what he now called the vitalities of a social situation, they were viewed as an economic imbalance of powers due to private property. Niebuhr's revised description of the given, as a balance of vitalities and forces (embodying the contingencies of both nature and sin), was a much more complex portrayal of the powers that government must organize.

First, the powers that constitute this initial equilibrium are spiritual and political as well as physical and economic. Niebuhr explicitly disassociated himself from the "modern belief that economic power is the most basic form."[28] Second, these various powers, independent of a conscious effort to organize them through government, form their own

23. Niebuhr, *The Nature and Destiny*, vol. 2, 257.
24. Ibid., 265.
25. Ibid., 266.
26. See ibid., 256–269.
27. Ibid., 257–258.
28. Ibid., 261.

tentative, albeit inadequate and unstable, balance of power. Further, this tentative balance of vitalities is creative of higher forms of justice than conscious political judgments can anticipate.[29] Because unrestrained vitalities can also be destructive, the organizing power of government is required to manage and manipulate the balance, but its role is greatly reduced from what it was before.[30] His earlier worries about concentrations of political power were now emphasized, and he was prepared to celebrate the diffusion of political power in democracies as a move toward a more just equilibrium of power.[31]

This reconception of the problem of balancing powers coheres with Niebuhr's theological backing for combining the metaphor of organism and the theme of self-transcendence in an interpretation of history as a drama in which the possibilities for justice are limited yet indeterminate. In these circumstances, conscious attempts to organize history through political activity are disastrous for two reasons.

First, such attempts fail to recognize that the vitalities and forces of history are not a chaos to be shaped into a just product but a semiordered balance of power subject to "refinement."[32] Here the organic metaphor influenced Niebuhr's emphasis upon the limits of consciously constructing just structures. We now find Niebuhr referring to the task of political activity as one of "mitigating" conflict,[33] of using, beguiling, harnessing, and deflecting rather than controlling interests.[34] The Marxists' excessive confidence in political activity is wrong because it fails to see (1) that the given balance of power can be adjusted by pragmatic and ad hoc policies without revolutionary disorder and (2) that successful political revolution will lead to a tyrannical order due to a disproportionate concentration of political power. By presuming that history is a moral chaos to be consciously ordered by political activity, Marxism leads to a static and tyrannical order.

When conscious construction of the structures of justice leads to tyranny, it stifles the capacity for transcendence essential for achieving the indeterminate possibilities of justice. Herein was Niebuhr's second reason for limiting the application of political force to the problem of shaping a just balance of power. Concentrated political force suppresses freedom issuing from the given vitalities and forces. This freedom

---

29. Niebuhr, *The Children of Light*, 63–64.
30. Niebuhr, *The Nature and Destiny*, vol. 2, 265–266.
31. Ibid., 262.
32. Ibid., 258.
33. Ibid., 265.
34. Niebuhr, "The Christian Faith and Social Action," 136; idem, "The Christian Faith and the Economic Life," 153.

permits a dynamic balance of power that adjusts to new realities and produces higher forms of justice than those consciously created. Here the themes of irony and common grace in history influenced Niebuhr's understanding of the criterion of a relatively just balance of power. Too much reliance on the organizing center of government can "destroy the freedom of component elements in the community in the name of 'order.' "[35] He could have added: even when the ordering is for the sake of equality. In his later writings, Niebuhr's discussions of "harnessing" interests allowed "a certain free play [of self-interests] for . . . the reason that there is no one in society good or wise enough finally to determine how the individual's capacities had best be used for the common good."[36]

This change in Niebuhr's understanding of the balance of power can be overemphasized. He had never held that power was solely a product of economic structures or that achieving equality by political activity was without dangers. Moreover, economic powers and inequalities are not dropped from the equation. It is, wrote Niebuhr, "axiomatic that great disproportions of power lead to injustice" and "the concentration of economic power in modern technical society has made for injustice."[37] In 1953, he was still observing that where disproportionate economic power exists, economic freedom must be curtailed by conscious political activity.[38] "There must be an organizing center within a given field of social vitalities."[39]

In sum, Niebuhr's view was that a balance of power is best established where the organizing center of government refines (he sometimes used stronger language) a given equilibrium of vitalities and forces. This view incorporated freedom and order alongside equality as regulative principles for the type of balance that will be most just.[40] As in his earlier thought, Christian realism requires that balancing powerful interests be used as a tool and criterion for justice. Neither love nor rational principles and laws alone can subdue the will-to-power that creates intolerable injustice. It must also be restrained by a countervailing will-to-power.

---

35. Niebuhr, *The Nature and Destiny,* vol. 2, 267.
36. Niebuhr, "The Christian Faith and the Economic Life," 151.
37. Niebuhr, *The Nature and Destiny,* vol. 2, 262.
38. Niebuhr, "Christian Faith and the Economic Life," 143.
39. Niebuhr, *The Nature and Destiny,* vol. 2, 266.
40. It is instructive, in this context, to contrast Niebuhr's understanding of freedom with Rauschenbusch's and Ryan's. For the latter, persons have a just interest in freedom insofar as it is necessary to develop the personality. For Niebuhr, individual and group interests are permitted freedom, even though their interests are not just, whenever that freedom is seen as a useful tool in maintaining a balance of power that approximates the ideal of justice.

As previously, those who think solely in terms of balancing powers are too consistent realists. This criterion for justice should stand under the constant criticism of the regulative principles of justice, but even that combination is insufficient. Any structure of justice will degenerate into gross injustice if it is not constantly judged and tempered by the ideal of love.[41]

The Relevance of Love

The regulative principles and the balance of power are necessary to approximate the ideal of love, even though they contradict it. Nevertheless, love is more than an impossible goal to be approximated by compromising means. It is also a resource to be applied in the formulation of just policies when the consequences of applying love advance its approximation as a social ideal. The crucial point here is that love as a working standard in Niebuhr's conception of justice is not the universal law of love. It is a resource where it has positive consequences for the strategy of justice. Love was also such a resource in Niebuhr's earlier conception of justice. In the forties and fifties, he specified its usefulness with greater clarity.

First, love is a resource for the discriminations justice requires. Love as an uncalculating concern for the dignity of every person is paradoxical (i.e., self-contradictory) within the conflicts of history. As uncalculating, it asserts no interests. As concern for the dignity of each person, love motivates a "passion for justice."[42] It seeks a way to determine who is being treated unjustly and to enforce its "interest" in their dignity. The way is to compromise its own indiscriminate care and endorse discriminations among interests. This discrimination requires principles of justice. Consequently, Niebuhr asserted, "as soon as the third person is introduced into the relation even the most perfect love requires a rational estimate of conflicting needs and interests."[43]

Love, however, does not license a rational formulation of principles independent of the social ideal it entails. In the forties, Niebuhr no longer argued that his principles of justice (unlike the goal of equality in the thirties) could be rationally derived. They are "not so much fixed standards of reason as they are rational efforts to apply the moral obligation, implied in the love commandment, to the complexities of life and the fact of sin."[44] Equality, freedom, and order are transcendent

41. Niebuhr, "Justice and Love," in *Love and Justice*, 28.
42. Niebuhr, "The Problem of a Protestant Social Ethic," 11.
43. Niebuhr, *The Nature and Destiny*, vol. 2, 248.
44. Niebuhr, *Faith and History*, 188–189.

principles of justice because they are the nearest discriminating approximation to the communism, anarchy, and harmony of the social ideal of love. They are regulative rather than definitive because they are partially corrupt instruments. Treated as definitive, principles of justice are closed to the higher possibilities of love. As regulative, they are open to the indeterminate possibilities of justice inspired by love. In this sense, Niebuhr could say that love is the guiding principle of our social relations.[45]

In sum, love, though it is not as an absolute standard applicable to social problems, is a resource for the discriminations of justice. It motivates and funds the regulative principles of justice. As such, love is a practical resource for approximating the social ideal it entails.

Second, love is a resource for justice in its indiscriminate criticism of all systems of justice. Even as it encourages provisionally discrimination among conflicting interests and use of a balance of power in order to approximate the social ideal, love reminds us of the corruption in all discriminations and all uses of power. Love "remains a principle of [indiscriminate] criticism over all forms of community in which elements of coercion and conflict destroy the highest type of fellowship."[46] By nourishing our dis-ease about the calculations and coercion of the highest principles and structures of justice, love engenders attitudes of contrition and humility. These attitudes mollify the pride in our particular views of justice. This pride would, otherwise, prevent the partial realization of love that makes a tolerable harmony of life with life possible.[47]

The ideal of love does not offer a realistic alternative to the present schemes of justice,[48] but it engenders attitudes that produce consequences necessary for a tolerable justice. The highest relative justice is possible only when we are not too sure of our principles and schemes of justice, that is, when the "heedlessness of love . . . enters into the calculations of justice by becoming the spirit of contrition."[49] This judgment of love is the grace that makes renewal toward the indeterminate possibilities of higher justice possible. Though it provides no principles, it reminds us that our principles of justice are regulative rather than definitive. It chastens those who would otherwise enforce their vision of justice upon the powerless.

In sum, the attitudes generated by love's indiscriminate judgment

---

45. Niebuhr, "Christian Faith and Social Action," 132.
46. Niebuhr, "Why the Christian Church Is Not Pacifist," 114.
47. Ibid., 113.
48. Ibid., 115; idem, *Faith and History,* 184.
49. Niebuhr, "Christian Faith and Social Action," 134.

enter into deliberations about justice to prevent a relatively just balance of power from degenerating into an imposition of power by those in control of the organizing center. This function of love, however, must not be allowed to generate such an extreme tension between the ideal and the actualities of justice that persons reject the discriminating function of love. Faith that we are forgiven, as well as judged, by God's grace eases this tension. This faith prevents us from being paralyzed in inaction by an overly scrupulous conscience. It frees us to accept the sin that inevitably accompanies enforcement of the discriminations required for a relatively just balance of power.

Love also serves justice in a third way. In addition to nourishing attitudes that color deliberations about justice, heedless love is a disposition or readiness to forgive and to sacrifice our "just" interests. This disposition should occasionally venture forth into action. Ordinarily, justice is undergirded by mutual love in which concessions to the other are made only when reciprocity is expected. This mutual love is the highest form of love justified by predictable consequences.[50] There are occasions, however, when acts of sacrificial love, heedless of consequences, will have the "unintended" consequence of eliciting reciprocity and preserving mutuality. In this way, acts based upon faith in God's love and grace, without consequentialist justification, have the effect of making "new ventures in brotherhood possible."[51] This effect of sacrificial love is possible because it stands, paradoxically, both inside and beyond history.[52] As a myth, Christ's love is partially validated by its consequences in history, even though it is a transcendent reality fully confirmed only in faith.[53]

These occasional acts of sacrificial love, Niebuhr believed, are necessary to preserve mutuality and justice. Acts of love, heedless of consequences, must be a part of any strategy that hopes to maintain mutuality or justice. Thus, Niebuhr claimed that grace, which enables love, is necessary to prevent justice from degenerating into sheer conflict among self-interests.[54] "[W]ithout love the frictions and tensions of a balance of power would become intolerable."[55] His argument is paradoxical: a fully adequate conception of justice requires acts of love that disregard consequences, because the consequences of such uncalculating acts are necessary to preserve and extend justice. These acts are, however, only

---

50. Niebuhr, *The Nature and Destiny*, vol. 2, 247.
51. Ibid., 83, 247.
52. Ibid., 247.
53. Ibid., 96.
54. Ibid., 96; idem, *Faith and History*, 185.
55. Niebuhr, "Why the Christian Church Is Not Pacifist," 116.

occasionally justified. Their consequences are normally disastrous for a reasonably just balance of power. Niebuhr was left with a consequentialist justification for occasional sacrificial actions performed only by agents who could ignore consequences.

In sum, Niebuhr considered the attitudes engendered by indiscriminate sacrificial love and the disposition to act sacrificially on occasion crucial elements in his strategy of justice. But love also endorses and funds discriminating principles of justice. Niebuhr was unable to specify when and how the attitudes and disposition of heedless love, antithetical to the calculations of justice, should enter into discriminating judgments and actions of justice. These indefinite elements in Niebuhr's conception of justice are apparently what prompted Dennis McCann to suggest that Niebuhr's proposal is not much more than a dispositional ethic, without adequate criteria for distinguishing between just and unjust uses of power.[56] Although McCann's criticism is, in my judgment, partially correct, two qualifications are in order.

First, Niebuhr's Christian realist tension between the ideal and the actual requires that the possibilities of justice remain indeterminate. From this perspective, definitive criteria for justice cannot attain the highest approximation of the social ideal. Uneasiness about pressing one's particular scheme of justice and a readiness to act sacrificially, without specification of when to do so, reflect that indeterminacy. In order to criticize Niebuhr's conception of justice for failing to offer more definitive criteria, one must challenge his understanding of the tension between the ideal and the actual and the theology that backs it. Christian realism does not permit criteria for when sacrificial love advances or hinders justice.

Second, love is itself paradoxical. Although it is heedless, love also encourages and provides direction for consequentialist calculations to approximate the social ideal. The regulative principles of justice and the balance of power are more than dispositions; they are guides for consequentialist deliberations.[57]

Niebuhr's mature conception of justice remained a Christian realist strategy for approximating love, but he modified the strategy. Instead of equality as the goal in history, Niebuhr employed freedom, order, and equality as regulative principles of strategy. He reconceived the balance

---

56. McCann, *Christian Realism and Liberation Theology*, 80, 93, 103.
57. See James Gustafson's comment that McCann is incorrect insofar as he reduces Niebuhr's ethic to a dispositional one. Gustafson, "Theology in the Service of Ethics," 45. McCann also qualifies his own claim by explaining how Niebuhr attempts to move beyond a strictly dispositional ethic by using middle axioms. See McCann, *Christian Realism and Liberation Theology*, 93.

of power, enlarging the importance of preserving existing vitalities and forces in keeping with his increased emphasis upon freedom and the given order. He clarified the role of love as a resource for this strategy, but love remained paradoxical and self-contradictory in history. On the one hand, love encourages and provides direction for the discriminations that justice must make. On the other hand, it reminds us that all discriminations are corrupt, and it must, on occasion, venture forth in indiscriminate acts of care that sacrifice just claims. These standards guided Niebuhr's judgments about democracy and property during the forties and fifties. They also convinced him to address more specific issues; for example, taxation and inflation and how far to go in providing free public health care.

JUSTICE APPLIED

It is well known that Niebuhr, during the late thirties and forties, moved away from his commitment to the Marxist mission, dropped his total opposition to private ownership of industrial property, and came to defend democracy. My purposes in this section are (1) to describe Niebuhr's revised positions on democracy and ownership of property and (2) to show how these revisions cohere with his modified conception of justice.

It is wrong to portray this change as a conversion from Marxist socialism to democratic capitalism. Niebuhr did not become a democratic capitalist. He gradually withdrew his qualified endorsement of the Marxist mission as unfolding events and his theological interpretation of history convinced him that justice was more a matter of ad hoc judgments and piecemeal change than a tragic choice to back one movement or another. All social movements, the liberalism of the commercial classes as well as Marxism, tend to claim godlike qualities for themselves.[58] The question was no longer what extant sociopolitical movement to endorse in order to produce the best consequences for achieving justice. Niebuhr came to be identified with a Christian community whose business is to mediate the judgment and mercy of God's grace upon all nations and cultures.[59]

This Christian distance from social movements is compatible with advocating specific forms of democratic government and ownership of property. It is not compatible with endorsing democratic capitalism. Niebuhr denounced anyone who identified Christian faith, or even

---

58. Niebuhr, *Faith and History*, 228.
59. See ibid., 227–230; idem, "God's Design and the Present Disorder," 114–118.

justice, with democracy or capitalism. Niebuhr, in a 1947 essay, chided Americans for the "sin" of identifying democracy, especially our particular brand of democracy, with the ultimate values of life. He noted that democratic societies are not the only societies in which justice prevails.[60] In 1948, he ridiculed American critics of the report on social justice from the Amsterdam meeting of the World Council of Churches for their "complacency" about the injustices that flow from laissez-faire capitalism.[61] Niebuhr came closer to embracing democracy than capitalism, but we will see that certain forms of democracy as well as pure capitalism violated his revised working standards of justice. For Niebuhr, the choices were not for or against democracy or between socialism and capitalism. They were ad hoc choices about how government could be constituted to limit the excesses of individual liberties without stifling the creative vitalities in a society. They were choices about how private property interests could be balanced by government without concentrating economic power in the hands of the state.[62]

Democracy

Because Niebuhr altered his view of democracy by degrees, we cannot establish a time when he became a defender of democratic government. By 1936, Niebuhr was already arguing, in *Radical Religion,* that the threat of fascism required a defense of democratic institutions, even at the expense of delaying socialism.[63] This defense of democracy was, however, in response to the threat of international fascism. It was not a change in judgment about the justice of democratic institutions. In the same issue of *Radical Religion,* Niebuhr wrote an editorial responding to the Supreme Court decision declaring the Agricultural Adjustment Act unconstitutional. He lamented the rigidity of the U.S. constitutional system and asserted that the Court was an instrument of "a nationally integrated capitalist system [that] has developed among us which only a nationally centralized political system can control."[64] In 1938, Niebuhr

---

60. Reinhold Niebuhr, "Democracy as a Religion," *Christianity and Crisis* 7, no. 4 (August 4, 1947): 1.

61. Reinhold Niebuhr, "The Cult of Freedom in America," *Christianity and Crisis* 8, no. 1 (February 7, 1948): 4–7; see also idem, "God's Design and the Present Disorder," 112–113.

62. Although this analysis focuses on the mistake of those who identify the later Niebuhr closely with democratic capitalism (see Michael Novak, *The Spirit of Democratic Capitalism* [New York: Simon & Schuster, 1982], 313–329), it also contrasts Niebuhr with Rauschenbusch. For Niebuhr, the role of the church, to keep its critical distance from all social movements and programs, was incompatible with "christianizing" society.

63. Reinhold Niebuhr, "The United Front," *Radical Religion* 1, no. 2 (Winter 1936): 4.

64. Reinhold Niebuhr, "The Supreme Court Decision," *Radical Religion* 1, no. 2 (Winter 1936): 9.

could still write: "There are moments in history in which we might have to deny democracy for the sake of a higher justice [socialism] which current democracy could not establish."[65]

This tentativeness about democratic politics reflects Niebuhr's persistent connecting of political and economic justice, a connection he continued to make in the forties and fifties. This linkage was grounded in his view that powerful interests are inordinate and expand to dominate all areas of social life. Niebuhr had always valued the freedoms associated with democracy, but he was convinced that these freedoms were manipulated by capitalist economic power in order to preserve unjust inequalities. Only a centralized organizing center could rectify this imbalance. As long as Niebuhr saw the private ownership of productive property as the major cause for an unjust imbalance of power, he remained dubious about the future of democracy. Niebuhr's affirmation of a particular kind of democracy coincided with his move away from socialism. Underlying both these revisions of social policy was Niebuhr's reconception of the balance of power, articulated in *The Nature and Destiny of Man* and applied both to democratic politics and to property in *The Children of Light and the Children of Darkness*.

The Children of Light and the Children of Darkness developed fully, for the first time, Niebuhr's defense of democracy and his increasing retreat from the claim that public ownership of productive property is a prerequisite for justice. Although Niebuhr's criticism of U.S. democracy and its economic system continued to soften after 1944, the arguments in *Children* continued to provide the basis for his policy judgments.[66] Democracy is our present focus.

The key to Niebuhr's modified judgment about democracy was his assertion that the "undemocratic constitutionalists saw the destructive but not the creative possibilities of individual vitality and ambition, and appreciated the necessity, but not the peril, of strong government."[67] This statement was directed at cynics who see little human capacity for justice; it also applies to Marxists and to Niebuhr's former views. In the thirties, Niebuhr perceived the vitalities in capitalist economies as anarchical economic interests. They could be controlled only by a strong government, one unobtainable by democratic processes. On the basis of his reconception of the balance of power, the problem was to refine and mold an equilibrium of power already partially established. The problem

---

65. Niebuhr, "Socialist Decision and Christian Conscience," 1.
66. See Merkley, *Reinhold Niebuhr*, 180. Perhaps some of these arguments were developed earlier. See Fox, *Reinhold Niebuhr*, 219, for Niebuhr's defense of democracy in *Christianity and Crisis* and the *New Leader* in 1941.
67. Niebuhr, *The Children of Light*, 47.

was no longer to create a balance of power out of existing anarchy. The function of government, as the central organizing center, is to restrain the destructive tendencies of capitalist vitalities without repressing individual and collective creativity.

The critics of democracy are preoccupied with "the perils of individual inordinateness" and insufficiently aware of the perils of reining in all these vitalities. They fail to understand the complexity of actual human vitalities that express themselves in many directions capable of unpredictable creative and destructive consequences.[68] "[T]he social substance of life is richer and more various, and has greater depth and tensions than are envisaged in the Marxist dream of harmony."[69] These were the words of a Niebuhr who had come to emphasize that the inordinate will-to-power manifests itself in political as much as in economic power. They are words written after Niebuhr discovered that the given social situation (including its economic dimension) is a semiordered and creative balance of vitalities to be refined, but not reconstructed, by a government.

On the basis of his new emphasis on political power, Marxists are, even more than previously, viewed as sentimental idealists. Only a naive "child of light" could believe that the dictatorship of the proletariat can produce a perfect harmony between the individual and the community.[70] Because they associate the self-interested use of power solely with private ownership, Marxists do not realize that political, managerial, and technical power must also be restrained after private ownership has been eliminated. Because the Marxist elite class controls both political and economic power,[71] its power is likely to be even less restrained than that of the capitalists. Niebuhr did not ignore these themes in the thirties. Nonetheless, increased appreciation for the many directions in which the destructive forces of human vitalities express themselves persuaded him that a government sufficiently centralized to control all private economic vitalities permits even more unrestrained destructive vitalities in a different direction.

This enhanced appreciation for the depth and multifaceted expressions of sin was one of the two parts in Niebuhr's often-cited justification for democracy. "[M]an's inclination to injustice makes democracy necessary."[72] Democracy is necessary because it can provide checks and balances on the power of government that more centralized forms of

---

68. Ibid.
69. Ibid., 59.
70. Ibid., 58.
71. Ibid., 113.
72. Ibid., xiii.

government cannot. "[O]ne perennial justification for democracy is that it arms the individual with political and constitutional power to resist the inordinate ambition of rulers, and to check the tendency of the community to achieve order at the price of liberty."[73]

Niebuhr's discovery that vitalities in the given situation are already in partial equilibrium provided the second leg of his justification for democracy. If the given vitalities are not simply anarchical and destructive but in partial equilibrium and also creative, conscious political control is neither as large a task nor as desirable as the Marxists assert. Niebuhr observed that we should "preserve whatever self-regulating forces exist in the economic process" so that "the task of control" does not become "too stupendous" and "achieve proportions which endanger our liberty."[74] This view of the ungoverned vitalities and forces neither requires nor permits the invasive political control Niebuhr earlier called for in order to remedy the inequalities of unfettered capitalism. This view backs the second part of his famous justification for democracy. "Man's capacity for justice makes democracy possible."[75] Democracy permits the creative capacities of individual and collective vitalities to produce higher structures of justice than a governing elite can imagine. "The indeterminate creativity of history validates . . . a democratic society, which refuses to place premature checks upon human vitalities."[76]

Niebuhr's justification for democracy was definitely not based on an individual's right to liberty. Liberty is a value to be considered for its own sake, but this justification of a larger place for liberties depends more on their effectiveness as means to approximate the social ideal, which also includes equality and harmony. Individual and group liberties are just insofar as they contribute to a balance of power that is open to the indeterminate possibilities for a higher approximation of the social ideal. Democracy and the freedom it affords are validated more on the grounds that they are instrumental for a relatively just community than because they are due individuals.[77]

Because unrestrained human vitalities can also be destructive, far more so than liberal optimists' justifications for democracy assumed, Niebuhr emphatically rejected both liberal democratic theory[78] and its identification of liberty with democracy.[79] The kind of democracy he

---

73. Ibid., 46–47; see also idem, *The Nature and Destiny*, vol. 2, 268.
74. Niebuhr, *The Children of Light*, 76.
75. Ibid., xiii.
76. Ibid., 49.
77. Ibid., 4–5.
78. Ibid., 40.
79. Ibid., 3.

defended was not the inherited democracy of bourgeois culture; it, he insisted, faces doom.[80]

If Marxists were naive about the destructive capacities of unrestrained government, the liberal children of light failed to understand the depth of human freedom for sin manifest in economic affairs.[81] Niebuhr's newfound appreciation for the complexity of ungoverned vitalities did not exclude the continuing dangers of unfettered economic powers. These private powers "must be managed, supervised, and suppressed by the community, precisely because they do not move within the limits of 'nature.' "[82] Democracy is justified only because it demonstrates some capacity "to redress economic inequalities through the use of political power."[83]

The test for any type of democracy, and its concomitant freedoms, is whether it performs the function of the organizing center. This function is to harness, deflect, beguile, and so forth, the destructive vitalities (especially economic interests) into a relatively just balance of power. In 1950, Niebuhr was still calling for "correcting our unique conceptions of democracy" that equate democracy and liberty and fail to "relate freedom to justice, to community, and to equality as the regulative principle of justice."[84] He was still insisting that "in America our business is to challenge bourgeois rather than the proletarian illusions."[85]

Niebuhr's evaluation of democracy did change between the midforties and the fifties. In the forties, he still wondered "whether democratic society has the resources to compose [the struggle between classes] by the achievement of higher forms of justice."[86] In the fifties, he was convinced that democracy had provided a tolerable justice by the "intervention of the state . . . in the pragmatic terms of the New Deal [that] provided the necessary balances which the economic realm lacked."[87] There was no change in the "duty of democratic society to achieve economic justice,"[88] but Niebuhr came to believe that American democracy had passed this test. Its performance had proven morally

---

80. Ibid., 2.
81. Ibid., 61–66.
82. Ibid., 64–65.
83. Ibid., 104.
84. Reinhold Niebuhr, "The Idolatry of America," in *Love and Justice*, 95. First published in 1950.
85. Reinhold Niebuhr, "Social Christianity," *Christianity and Society* 16, no. 1 (Winter 1951): 5.
86. Reinhold Niebuhr, "Marxism in Eclipse," *The Spectator* 170, no. 5997 (June 4, 1943): 519.
87. Niebuhr, "Norman Thomas," 5; see also idem, *The Irony of American History*, 100–101.
88. Niebuhr, "Social Christianity," 4.

superior to the liberal theories that defended it on the grounds that democracy maximizes freedom.[89] This was one of the ironies of American history that persuaded Niebuhr that there is a grace of common sense, even where a culture does not adhere to the Christian doctrine of grace.

Niebuhr's justifications for this particular form of democracy were largely couched in terms of his reconception of the balance of power, but his understanding of what constitutes a relative just balance of power was also instructed by his regulative principles of justice. Clearly, Niebuhr did not defend democracy as the best means for achieving the goal of equality. The checks and balances democracy places on the organizing center preserve freedoms only at some loss in equality. The kind of democracy Niebuhr desired is justified because it balances "a struggle for liberty and a struggle for equal justice" under conditions in which neither "can be completely achieved."[90] "[S]ome inequality is inevitable in a sinful world."[91]

Niebuhr also believed democracy can balance freedom with order. Because the vitalities to be balanced are semiordered, a democratic organizing center can unite liberty, which prevents the community from becoming a "forcibly unified mass," with equality, which orders economic freedoms that would otherwise "destroy the community of persons."[92] What had been, in the thirties, a tragic choice between the chaos of capitalism and the potential tyranny of a Marxist state became a less tragic pragmatic trade-off between the regulative principles of order and freedom.[93] Put differently, the pragmatic objective is a compromise between the "contrasting perils of anarchy and injustice" to be "continually solved within the framework of the democratic process."[94]

In sum, Niebuhr defended a democracy that seeks a balance of freedom, equality, and order by refining, deflecting, beguiling, and so forth, the vitalities and forces of society into a relative just balance of power. Niebuhr's application of these principles reflects his commitment to the discriminating function of love "to realise the obligation of [the love] commandment within the terms of given civilisations."[95]

Love as the basis for indiscriminate criticism and sacrificial acts also had a role in Niebuhr's conception of a defensible democracy. First,

89. Niebuhr, "Liberty and Equality," 198.
90. Niebuhr, "Christianity as a Basis of Democracy," 65.
91. Ibid., 68.
92. Ibid., 65.
93. Niebuhr, *The Children of Light,* 78.
94. Ibid., 115.
95. Niebuhr, "Christianity as a Basis of Democracy," 69.

"concern for the other rather than the self" (sacrificial love) contributes to "consideration of the needs of others" (mutual love) without which any democratic process would be wrecked.[96] Second, and more important for democracy, religious humility is a prerequisite for democratic tolerance and mutuality between classes, ethnic groups, and so forth.[97] This attitude of humility maintains a "state of tension with every form of justice which can be devised in history."[98] It prevents identification of the ideal of love with any form of government, including democracy, or any definitive principles of justice devised to support it. In this way, the indiscriminate criticism of Christian love provides necessary support for democracy. "This spirit [of contrition and humility] lies at the foundation of what we define as democracy."[99] In turn, the democratic freedom to criticize all areas of authority (including the authority of a natural right to liberty) is justified because it leaves room for criticism from the perspective of love.[100]

Clearly, Niebuhr's defense of democracy reflected a continuing application of Christian realist tension between the ideal and the actual that he developed in the early thirties. In the foreword to *The Children of Light and the Children of Darkness,* Niebuhr noted that his arguments "are informed by the belief that a Christian view of human nature is more adequate [than other available views] for the development of a democratic society."[101] It is more adequate precisely because it alone approaches issues of justice from the perspective of a permanent tension between the ideal as love and the actual as a mixture of love and self-love.

It is sometimes observed that Niebuhr was not fully a realist until this period in which he offered a pragmatic defense of democracy.[102] I disagree. In fact, insofar as realism refers to pessimism about the actual human condition and a consequent need for a tragic choice to use political power to forge justice, Niebuhr's defense of democracy reflected a softening of his earlier realism. His reconception of the balance of power gave a larger role to the creative capacities of relatively free human vitalities. His justification for democracy depended heavily upon

---

96. Niebuhr, *The Children of Light,* 151.

97. Ibid., 150–152.

98. Niebuhr, "Christianity as a Basis of Democracy," 69.

99. Niebuhr, "Christian Faith and Social Action," 134.

100. Niebuhr, *The Children of Light,* 70–71.

101. Ibid., xv.

102. Niebuhr may have contributed to this view with retrospective observations that his earlier position (in the thirties) was "an abstract idealism which we professed to abhor." See Reinhold Niebuhr, "Farewell . . ." *Christianity and Society* 21, no. 3 (Summer 1956): 3. Perhaps this observation meant he had become more inclined to gradual and ad hoc reform; it cannot have accurately meant that he had previously thought the ideal was directly applicable to social issues or that he had thought it was achievable in history.

a residual capacity for justice. Niebuhr did not change his mind about the impossibility of Christian love, but his doctrine of grace, especially the idea of common grace, made him more appreciative of how democratic freedoms lead to unanticipated possibilities for higher justice. These possibilities are enabled by grace rather than by natural moral capacities, yet they are possibilities for which a consistently realist focus on a political balance of power does not allow.

Ownership of Productive Property

A perception that inequalities of power were endemic to an economic system based on private property was the primary reason Niebuhr had become a socialist in the early thirties.[103] Hence, it is not surprising that his reconception of the balance of power produced nearly simultaneous revisions in his judgments about democracy and ownership of productive property.

In 1938, Niebuhr still argued that the Marxists were essentially correct in claiming that the "communal ownership of the productive process is a basic condition of social health in a technical age."[104] The New Deal was a "whirligig reform" from which "no final good can come."[105] During the late thirties, Niebuhr still saw socialism as the key to economic justice. This was, however, a period of transition and confusion. "Niebuhr was," according to Paul Merkley, "beginning to talk himself into political limbo."[106] In the Spring 1939 issue of *Radical Religion,* Niebuhr criticized New Deal deficit spending as a medicine that "wards off dissolution without giving the patient health,"[107] claimed that socialism is "organically related to our Christian faith,"[108] and called upon readers to conserve "genuine gains" of the Roosevelt administration by supporting the Wagner Act "with grim determination."[109] Despite this waffling about the merits of the New Deal, Niebuhr persisted in the view that palliatives, such as tax reform, could not cure the capitalist patient.[110]

---

103. See *supra,* chapter four, 219.

104. Reinhold Niebuhr, "Russian and Karl Marx," *The Nation* 146, no. 9 (May 7, 1938): 530; see also idem, "Socialist Decision and Christian Conscience," 2.

105. Reinhold Niebuhr, "Roosevelt's Merry-Go-Round," *Radical Religion* 3, no. 2 (Spring 1938): 4.

106. Merkley, *Reinhold Niebuhr,* 111.

107. Reinhold Niebuhr, "New Deal Medicine," *Radical Religion* 4, no. 2 (Spring 1939): 2.

108. Reinhold Niebuhr, "Karl Barth on Politics," *Radical Religion* 4, no. 2 (Spring 1939): 4.

109. Reinhold Niebuhr, "Crisis in Washington," *Radical Religion* 4, no. 2 (Spring 1939): 9.

110. Niebuhr, "New Deal Medicine," 2.

By 1941, Niebuhr had revised this judgment. He wrote, "Social justice will depend increasingly upon taxation schedules in the coming years."[111] And less than a year later: "Taxation schedules . . . will have more to do with the kind of justice we achieve in our society than any other single factor."[112] The fundamental issue was no longer the choice between private and public ownership of industrial property. What had been a palliative had become the most important single factor for achieving relative justice.

In the intervening period, Niebuhr had delivered the Gifford Lectures, which culminated in the publication of his revised understanding of the balance of power in the second volume of *The Nature and Destiny of Man*. It is not overly speculative, I trust, to suggest that Niebuhr's claim that socialism is the key to economic justice dissolved as he began to reconceptualize the balance of power. That reconceptualization enabled Niebuhr to appreciate the balance between economic and political power and to view the task of government as one of refining existing vitalities. By 1942, Niebuhr was observing that government intervention to "tax the rich and pay the poor unemployment benefits" indicates the "gradual ascendancy of politics over economics." This gradual increase in the power of the political organizing center results, he suggested, from the need to respond to the concentrated economic power of technical industry and from government prosecution of the war.[113] Niebuhr had come to believe that a significant shift in power occurred without eliminating private property.

As with democracy, we need to look to *The Children of Light and the Children of Darkness* for Niebuhr's fully articulated revision of his views on ownership of productive property. And again, the argument was based upon Niebuhr's reconceptualization of the balance of power as it reflected the shift to his regulative principles of justice.

His chapter on property begins with a discussion of the history of the application of natural law to the ownership of property. Early Christianity wisely understood the natural law justifying private ownership as a relative law, required by the Fall and existing in tension with the ideal of communism. First Catholicism and then orthodox Protestantism tended to ignore the tension between the relative justice of private property and the ideal of common property. They were inclined to accept private

---

111. Reinhold Niebuhr, "Taxation and the Defense Economy," *Christianity and Society* 6, no. 4 (Fall 1941): 5.

112. Reinhold Niebuhr, "Better Government Than We Deserve," *Christianity and Society* 7, no. 2 (Spring 1942): 10.

113. Reinhold Niebuhr, "Politics and Economics," *Christianity and Society* 7, no. 4 (Autumn 1942): 7–8.

property as absolutely justified by the natural law or by God's providence. By contrast, Protestant sectarians advocated primitive communism on the grounds that it is possible to restore the original innocence of humans. Thus, Christians presented polar views on property, both views ignoring the early Christian tension between the ideal and the actual. Modern liberal and Marxist theories of property completed this trend. They advocated diametrically opposing ideals of property ownership without considering the sinful human condition.[114] On this historical analysis, Niebuhr concluded that the property issue could not be resolved by "a reconsideration of the ideas," that is, by defining the principles of justice. It must be dealt with on the basis of an understanding of the balance of power that corrects "illusions in both the liberal and Marxist theories of property."[115]

Two closely related illusions discredited the bourgeois view of property. First, its "excessive individualism" failed to account for the social character of humans, who cannot be fulfilled except through the harmony and interdependence of self with self. This individualism led to a view that property should be private. It belies the social origins and consequences of wealth, especially wealth in the modern technical industrial society. "The modern factory is a great collective process." Their individualism disables liberals from seeing that "individual control of such centralized power is an invitation to injustice."[116] For Niebuhr, a solution to the property issue must begin with a recognition that it has social effects. Its uses have to be ordered by the community.

The second error of liberal theory compounded the first. Liberals understood the desire for economic power as limited. Thus, they did not understand (as does one who comprehends the depth of sin) "how inordinate and disproportionate economic power may become."[117] They did not understand that property may be a means of dominating others. For Niebuhr, the destructive potential of unrestrained property rights cannot be contained by natural harmonies and equilibria of power. Some social control of property is required to establish a balance of economic power.

These criticisms of liberal theory were merely moderated versions of Niebuhr's early arguments for socialism. There was a change, however, in that Niebuhr's argument against liberal justifications for private property conceded that the power of property can be used "defensively"[118] as well as being a means to dominate others.

---

114. Niebuhr, *The Children of Light,* 91–98.
115. Ibid., 98.
116. Ibid., 103.
117. Ibid., 108.
118. Ibid., 106–107, 113; idem, "Christianity as a Basis of Democracy," 68.

The significance of this change emerged in Niebuhr's criticism of the Marxist view of property. Unlike the liberal theory, Marxists understand the social effects of property.[119] Like the liberalism, Marxism is naive about inordinate power that accompanies some forms of property, in this case, state-owned property.[120] Marxists' naivety arises from their failure to recognize that the roots of sin are in human egotism rather than a corrupt system of property, and from their simple notion that private property is the sole source of unequal economic power.[121] Thus, Marxist theory provides no check against "the excessive power of those who manipulate the socialized economic process."[122] Up to this point, Niebuhr's argument differed only in emphasis from his criticisms of the Marxist illusion in the early thirties. (He did go on to observe that even managers in democratic socialist societies might gain excessive power.)[123] The change occurred in his proposed alternative to correct the Marxists' error. In order to protect against excessive assertions of political and managerial power, modern societies should pursue policies that preserve specific types of private property. Types of property that offer power persons can use to defend themselves against the aggrandizement that others (including government) seek for themselves should remain private.[124]

This proposal reflects Niebuhr's reconception of the balance of power in which political and economic power are intertwined and existing vitalities form a crude equilibrium to be shaped rather than a chaos to be controlled by government. On this view, government ownership of all property is unnecessary in order to effect the most just balance of power. In some cases, state ownership would destroy the "defensive" powers of private property that contribute to an equilibrium of power. The proximate solution to the property problem is for the organizing center of government to refine or mold the given conflicting vitalities into a relatively just balance of power by socializing property on a case by case basis. The process for determining whether public ownership is warranted should be democratic,[125] and it should strike a balance between freedom and equality. "[T]he truth upon this question of property and equality lies somewhere between the traditional Christian [creed, which protected individual freedom to own property] and the utopian Marxist creed."[126] This balance between freedom and equality applies to demo-

---

119. Niebuhr, *The Children of Light*, 104.
120. Ibid., 106.
121. Ibid., 110–111.
122. Ibid., 113.
123. Ibid.
124. Ibid., 115–116.
125. Ibid., 115.
126. Niebuhr, "Christianity as a Basis of Democracy," 68.

cratic socialism as well as Marxist dictatorships. Niebuhr feared that doctrinaire democratic socialism could threaten the future of democracy by being unaware of "the peril in a monopoly of political and economic power in the hands of the omnicompetent state."[127]

Niebuhr had not become a capitalist. He had become "completely pragmatic" about the "institution of property." Property still must be "socialized whenever it is of such a character that it makes for injustice through inordinate centralization of power."[128] There were, nevertheless, instances in which Niebuhr opposed specific socializing practices of democratic socialist countries, such as the British effort to socialize its steel industry.[129] The crucial change was that Niebuhr now eschewed generalizations about socialism (or capitalism) in favor of empirical questions: "[W]hat is the effect of this or that policy in this or that situation; how well does this particular constellation of power satisfy the requirements of justice [equality] and of freedom?"[130] His approach to the issue of property had become ad hoc.

"But the problems of social ethics are not solved merely by an empirical and pragmatic approach. . . . There can . . . be no genuine empiricism without a religious correction" of the tendency to use moral principles and empirical data to further special interests.[131] This passage, from an essay recounting Niebuhr's shift away from Christian socialism, was in part a claim that his ad hoc approach to property was based on a theological understanding of the permanent tension between love and self-love. It was also a call for the relevance of love to reasoning about justice. A just answer to the empirical questions about property cannot be expected unless the attitudes love engenders penetrate the reasoning of the business community and the industrial workers. The business community should be uneasy in its devotion to freedom, and the industrial workers should allow indiscriminate love to temper their confidence in a policy of planning.[132] This essay also implied that enduring justice in property relations cannot be sustained unless individuals occasionally actually sacrifice their "just" interests. Sacrificial love, Niebuhr insisted, is a leaven in the spirit of justice.[133]

---

127. Reinhold Niebuhr, "The Anomaly of European Socialism," *The Yale Review* 42, no. 2 (December 1952): 166; see also idem, "Christianity as a Basis of Democracy," 68.

128. Reinhold Niebuhr, "Frontier Fellowship," *Christianity and Society* 13, no. 4 (Autumn 1948): 3.

129. Reinhold Niebuhr, "Plutocracy and World Responsibilities," *Christianity and Society* 14, no. 4 (Autumn 1949): 8.

130. Niebuhr, "The Anomaly of European Socialism," 166–167.

131. Niebuhr, "Christian Faith and Social Action," 129.

132. Ibid., 133.

133. Ibid., 135.

Niebuhr was vague about how love enters into the determination of just property relations, but that vagueness is consonant with his working standards of justice. Indiscriminate love prohibits principles of justice that define precise property rights. It excludes confident answers to the question of whether public or private control of a particular kind of property is likely to produce a relatively just balance of power. Niebuhr's judgments about particular cases incorporated a high degree of intuition. Despite insisting that relatively just decisions about property control depend on case by case empirical investigations, Niebuhr's numerous judgments about particular cases were, unlike Ryan's, never based on exhaustive empirical analysis. His judgments about British steel, coal, medicine, the Tennessee Valley Authority, and so forth, were made based more on speculations about human character than on data about the economic realities of these situations. Perhaps this approach to judgments reflects Niebuhr's distrust of reason (inductive as well as deductive), a distrust inspired by indiscriminate love. General facts about whether a particular type of property ownership combined the regulative principles of justice in a realistic balance of power were considered. In the end, however, Niebuhr trusted judgments tempered by love more than he did the judgment of persons or groups confident that exhaustive principles and facts could lead to just decisions.

Other Issues

Niebuhr's call for a more empirical approach to justice was not a plea for extensive empirical studies. It meant that relatively narrow policy issues should be examined for their significance in refining the balance of power. He no longer considered these issues trivial. His focus, in the thirties, on whether democracy should survive and how socialism could be achieved, was replaced by concern about what kind of democracy is just and what types of property should be publicly owned. Furthermore, the editorial pages of *Christianity and Society*[134] turned to other narrower issues: taxation, inflation, rationing, price and wage controls, the

---

134. *Radical Religion,* the magazine Niebuhr founded under the auspices of the Fellowship of Socialist Christians in 1935, was renamed *Christianity and Society* in 1940. The editorials in this quarterly magazine, written by Niebuhr, provide an excellent way to monitor changes in his views on issues of economic justice. The Fellowship of Socialist Christians, founded in 1931, was renamed the Frontier Fellowship in 1948, reflecting Niebuhr's withdrawal from socialism, and Christian Action in 1951. After the founding of *Christianity of Crisis* in 1941, *Christianity and Society* was no longer the primary focus of Niebuhr's popular literary efforts. See Fox, *Reinhold Niebuhr,* 196–197. Christian Action and *Christianity and Society* both ceased in 1956.

CIO's organization of unskilled labor, labor legislation, and proper limits on public health care.

A full understanding of Niebuhr's revised conception of justice does not require that we know his position on these issues. His positions changed over time and would be radically different in our context. We do need to understand that these issues became important because Niebuhr thought they could contribute to a balance of power combining freedom, equality, and order in an approximation of love. For example, rationing combined with a sales tax on luxury items was relatively just because it compromised liberty and equality for the purpose of controlling inflation. Controlling inflation was necessary for an ordered community.[135] The Hartley-Taft labor bill was unjust because it proposed to eliminate the closed shop. The closed shop was necessary for labor as a "defensive measure against hostile employers who sought to undermine the power of a union even after it achieved bargaining status." This legislation would have been helpful had it concentrated on bringing democracy to unions, thereby protecting the individual rights of laborers.[136] Niebuhr's concern for a balance of power was clearly operative in this reasoning. Finally, Niebuhr supported a public health delivery system with restrictions on free delivery on the basis, he stated, of answers to empirical questions that emerged from his attempt to apply the law of love in tension with persistent self-love.[137] These illustrations of Niebuhr's ad hoc judgments on narrower economic issues demonstrate how the three working standards I have outlined (i.e., regulative principles, a balance of power, and the indirect relevance of love) were operative in his practical reasoning.

The goal of equality pursued through an economic balance of power had, in the thirties, fixed Niebuhr's attention on the best strategy for socializing property. The regulative principles of justice and a reconceptualized understanding of the balance of power directed him, in the forties and fifties, to these narrower issues as the best means for approximating love. Niebuhr had become convinced that the pragmatic reforms of the New Deal and the labor movement (forces he had earlier considered powerless) had achieved rough justice in America. In his "farewell" editorial in *Christianity and Society,* Niebuhr declared the New Deal a "very significant pragmatic social revolution."[138] In *The Irony of Ameri-*

135. See Reinhold Niebuhr, "Rationing and Democracy," *Christianity and Society* 8, no. 1 (Winter 1942): 8–9; idem, "Taxation and Inflation," *Christianity and Society* 8, no. 4 (Fall 1943): 7–8.

136. Reinhold Niebuhr, "The Republicans and Labor," *Christianity and Society* 12, no. 3 (Summer 1947): 8.

137. Reinhold Niebuhr, "Our Faith and Concrete Political Decisions," *Christianity and Society* 17, no. 3 (Summer 1952): 4.

138. Niebuhr, "Farewell . . . ," 3.

can History, he observed that the rise of the labor movement has been "particularly important" in achieving a tolerably just balance of power,[139] far more just, he conceded, in *"The Self" and the Dramas of History,* than the schemes elaborated by the intellectuals.[140] He no doubt had himself and the Socialist Party in mind.

Niebuhr saw irony in these developments. The forces that produced them had no theory of justice adequate to explain their success. Yet his own theory of a complex balance of power accounted for this irony. It noted the unanticipated progress that could occur through creative vitalities when they are refined and deflected, but not controlled, by the organizing center of government. From this perspective, Niebuhr concluded that piecemeal reforms (attending to issues of tax policy, antitrust legislation, regulation of utilities, social welfare for security and health, etc.) had established "a certain equilibrium in economic society."[141] Even "a very mild socialism" had been proven to be "irrelevant to the American political scene."[142]

This does not mean Niebuhr revised his conception of justice or his ad hoc approach to property ownership after *The Children of Light and the Children of Darkness.* Niebuhr had not become a defender of democratic capitalism. He had rather come to believe, as he wrote in 1957, that, in the American context, piecemeal reforms brought about by the New Deal and labor movement had "solve[d] the over-all problem of justice."[143] These reforms created the balance of power Niebuhr had envisioned since the early forties. Hence, Merkley can claim both that Niebuhr "had not budged an inch to the right" on his understanding of property in *Children* and that he displayed "a pattern of increasing complacency about domestic affairs" from 1945 onward.[144] Compla-

---

139. Niebuhr, *The Irony of American History,* 31; see also idem, "The Teamsters and Labor's Future," *The New Leader* 40, no. 34 (August 26, 1957): 3.

140. Niebuhr, *"The Self" and the Dramas of History,* 196.

141. Niebuhr, *The Irony of American History,* 100–101.

142. Niebuhr, "Farewell . . . ," 3.

143. Niebuhr, "The Teamsters and Labor's Future," 4; cited by Merkley, *Reinhold Niebuhr,* 178. Niebuhr made this comment in the context of an attack on Jimmy Hoffa and the Teamsters Union for seeking power through undemocratic procedures within the union. He believed the remaining problems of justice were to achieve a better balance of power within big business and labor unions. See Niebuhr, "The Teamsters and Labor's Future," 4. He did not mention other economic issues or the race issue.

144. Merkley, *Reinhold Niebuhr,* 179, 177. John C. Bennett deems Merkley's conclusion exaggerated. He cites, among other things, Niebuhr's deep commitment to racial justice. See Bennett, "Reinhold Niebuhr's Social Ethics," in *Reinhold Niebuhr: His Religious, Social, and Political Thought,* 138–140. Herbert O. Edwards, by contrast, although conceding that Niebuhr criticized "racial pride" more often than did other theologians of his time, cites evidence of Niebuhr's complacency on the race issue during the fifties and sixties. See Edwards, "Niebuhr, 'Realism,' and Civil Rights in America,"

cency is not quite accurate, because the indiscriminate criticism of love left Niebuhr uneasy about American justice; but, in the midfifties, he no longer expressed persistent enthusiasm even for specific pragmatic reforms.[145] The irony is that Niebuhr, ostensibly more radical than Ryan and never as enthusiastic about the New Deal, had come to believe that the New Deal had achieved an acceptable justice, whereas Ryan claimed that the New Deal had not gone far enough.

There are numerous plausible explanations for Niebuhr's lack of attention to domestic reforms. Perhaps it was, as John Bennett suggests, partially attributable to his preoccupation with international affairs or his ill health after 1952.[146] Nevertheless, it was also consonant with his conception of justice. Once history demonstrated that piecemeal reforms could produce an equilibrium of power that joined relative equality, freedom, and order, Niebuhr had no criteria sufficiently exact to justify interests in greater equality of income and wealth, economic structures to foster cooperation or character development, better and more equal educational opportunities, and so forth. His theory of justice had always, for theological reasons, resisted refined discriminations among just and unjust interests. All assertions of interests, and the principles or reasons that purport to justify them, are equally unjust when measured by Niebuhr's ideal of love. It is instructive to note that Rauschenbusch and Ryan, who formulated more refined criteria for discriminating among just and unjust interests, ended their careers calling for substantial economic reforms.

Niebuhr was right when he claimed in the midfifties that his conservatism should not be confused with a devotion to the status quo.[147] His continuing commitment to the tension between the ideal of love and the actual assured an uneasiness about American democracy and capitalism. Ironically, this same tension prohibited Niebuhr from formulating crite-

---

Christianity and Crisis 46, no. 1 (February 3, 1986): 12–15. Because my study focuses on economic issues and Niebuhr never made racial justice a major focus, I have not applied his conception of justice to race. A study of Niebuhr's views on racial justice would be valuable, not so much to determine whether he was complacent as to determine whether his modified Christian realist conception of justice enabled him to back strongly the just interests of blacks.

145. The demise of Christian Action and its mouthpiece, *Christianity and Society,* in 1956 was symptomatic of Niebuhr's loss of zeal for domestic reforms. Liston Pope, cochairman of Christian Action, is reported to have commented, "It's difficult to have a parade for a mixed economy." See Fox, *Reinhold Niebuhr,* 248. It is impossible when the leader of the parade is saying the present mixed economy has solved the overall problem of justice.

146. Bennett, "Reinhold Niebuhr's Social Ethics," 138.

147. Reinhold Niebuhr, "Liberalism and Conservatism," *Christianity and Society* 20, no. 1 (Winter 1955): 3–4; Niebuhr, "Reply to Interpretation and Criticism," 510.

ria that could have been the basis for justifying particular claims to justice within a tolerably just balance of power. Consequently, for the same reasons that he could have never become a zealous defender of the American political and economic system, he seemingly lacked grounds for advocating specific policy reforms.

WE HAVE A LEGACY

It is possible to conclude a study of Reinhold Niebuhr and come away without a theological or ethical legacy. Richard Fox's biography is an example. Fox brilliantly portrays a person who devoted his immense energy and considerable intellectual capacity to the cause of justice. Yet no theological or ethical framework emerges; little is bequeathed to us save the remembrance of a virtuoso whom we can admire but are incapable of emulating. Fox reveals a dimension of Niebuhr's acting for justice that necessarily eludes this study. More so than with either Rauschenbusch or Ryan, Niebuhr, the person who commented on, it seems, almost every social problem and was directly involved in many, exceeded his theory and conception of justice.[148] Still, Niebuhr bequeathed to us a highly creative and relatively coherent Christian realist theory of justice. This legacy, properly understood and critically retrieved, can inform our judgments about justice.

From the days when he was a socialist dubious about the future of democracy to his pronouncement that labor and the New Deal had solved the overall problem of justice in America, Niebuhr's judgments about political and economic policies were informed by his Christian realist strategy for approximating the ideal of love. We should not allow Niebuhr's fairly dramatic changes on policies to obfuscate this continuity. For Niebuhr, justice was a matter of approximating the ideal of disinterested or sacrificial love under conditions in which the unchecked human will-to-power pursues its insatiable appetite for power. The

---

148. The reason for this difference is, I think, that an application of Niebuhr's theory and conception of justice depends more heavily on the attitudes and intuitions of an agent responding to a particular situation. Neither Rauschenbusch's nor Ryan's theories and conceptions of justice were sufficiently definitive to indicate precisely what judgments they would make about contemporary issues, but it is hard to imagine right- and left-wing disciples of Rauschenbusch or Ryan, such as we have experienced among Niebuhr's students. This aspect of Niebuhr's thought does not render his theory and conception of justice useless to someone trying to apply it. I have tried to show that right-wing Niebuhrians distort the thinking of their mentor. Doctrinaire socialism is also ruled out by Niebuhr's realism, even in its thirties version. Nevertheless, Niebuhr, as an agent acting for justice, exceeded an analysis of his theory of justice and is nearly impossible for even his most loyal students to emulate.

creative tension between this ideal and these actual conditions precludes reliance on principles to discern an ideal of distributive justice. Consequently, Niebuhr's views may not be recognizable to many as a conception of justice. Nonetheless, his regulative principles (initially the goal of equality), conception of the balance of power, and descriptions of the resources of love constitute "standard[s] whereby the distributive aspects of the basic structure of society are to be assessed."[149] The purpose of these working standards is not to determine which human interests constitute just claims. The social ideal of love judges all interests unjust. These standards are, however, guides and instruments of a strategy for moving the structures of society in the direction toward which justice should move: anarchy and communism in perfect harmony.

Justice was not, for Niebuhr, a problem of discerning the right; it was a problem of which strategy best approximates the ideal. From the thirties onward, that strategy, formed in light of a Christian realist tension between the ideal and the actual, oriented Niebuhr's thinking about justice. His focused attention on Christian doctrine altered this strategy. Nonetheless, his mythical method of interpretation, adopted because it maintained the tension between the transcendent and historical, assured that his conception of justice would remain a strategy for approximating love. The social ideal remained the same. Niebuhr refined his concept of agency and altered his interpretation of history, but his understanding of sin as an insatiable will-to-power remained. If we appropriate Niebuhr's Christian realism, we must judge which version of his strategy is more or less adequate. But there is also a more fundamental question: the adequacy of a conceiving justice as a strategy framed by a Christian realist tension between the ideal and the actual.

From the perspectives of either Rauschenbusch or Ryan, Niebuhr's tension between the ideal and the actual is unwarranted and misconceives the task of justice. It is unwarranted because God has ordered the world to permit human fulfillment through the development of natural interests. Thus, neither love nor communion with God is incompatible with the interests of justice. Moreover, sin, although inevitable and persistent, can be accounted for without compromising the ideal for justice in a balance of power strategy. From this view that lowers the ideal for justice to a theoretical, though not achievable, possibility within history, raising the balance of power to the level of a principle of justice misconceives the task of justice. By focusing on equilibrating power, Niebuhr's balance of power principle obscures the task of discriminating between interests essential for developing the personality and interests

---

149. Rawls, *A Theory of Justice*, 9.

that undermine others' opportunities for development. Niebuhr's working standards of justice fail to consider how institutions can secure opportunities for individuals to develop their natural interests.

From Niebuhr's Christian realism frame of reference, these efforts to discriminate between just and unjust interests foreclose the highest possibilities for which humans are free and dull awareness of the dangers residing in interests disguised by the claim to be just. The claim that an ideal of justice is a possibility in history brings divine fulfillment of human social life into a natural and historical ordering. It robs divine love of its paradoxical character. It is a form of idolatry.

Adequate responses to these disputes must address Niebuhr as a theologian and ethicist who drew upon both various strands of the Christian tradition and upon his experience of sociopolitical events of history. Notwithstanding Niebuhr's well-known self-characterization that he was a social ethicist and itinerant preacher rather than a theologian,[150] part of his legacy is that justice is a theological as well as an ethical problem. And for him, the Christian tradition and experience, as he interpreted them, were the major resources for addressing this theological problem.

In this respect, Rauschenbusch was like Niebuhr, and Ryan was at least half like Niebuhr. Ryan did not draw on an experience of sociopolitical events to revise the theology he received. He made no contributions to Catholic theology. Still, his theory of justice was explicitly grounded in the Catholic Thomism he inherited. Rauschenbusch, like Niebuhr, reformulated his received theology in light of an interpretation of changing social institutions after it had become apparent that his inherited theology could not sustain his thinking about justice. Whatever their differences, the central common legacy of these three protagonists for justice is that a conception of justice appropriate for Christians should be theologically grounded.

---

150. Niebuhr, "Intellectual Autobiography," 3.

8

RETRIEVING LEGACIES

The preceding comparative analysis itself offers, I trust, sufficient reason for attending to the legacy of these ethicists as we attempt to think about justice in the contemporary context. Whether we undertake the task, which we all confront, of applying justice to society's major institutions or attempt the more fundamental work of constructing a theory and conception of justice, the rich legacies of these authors can contribute to our thinking and acting. We will, no doubt, judge the value of these legacies differently, and it has been my intention to present them without injecting, too strongly, my critical assessments. It is worthwhile, however, to draw attention to salient elements of these legacies that, I believe, ought to bear on our contemporary thinking about justice. Though I retrieve elements from all three figures, I will draw upon Rauschenbusch and Ryan to correct what I judge to be significant deficiencies in Niebuhr's theory of justice. In order to interject these legacies into current debates, I will indicate how they bear on various themes in present theological and philosophical thinking about justice.

RETRIEVING THE HISTORICAL RAUSCHENBUSCH

There is a preliminary task. I want to highlight that my analysis corrects misconceptions about Rauschenbusch's social ethic. First, Rausch-

344

enbusch's theory of justice was not based on an idea of a utopian kingdom that transcends all natural (or sinful) human interests. Niebuhr was mistaken when, in his 1956 preface to *An Interpretation of Christian Ethics,* he wrote of the social gospel, and of Rauschenbusch by implication: "[I]t did not have to concern itself very much with the structures of justice and the institutions of society by which men tried to achieve a tolerable justice by managing and balancing competing interests and forces."[1] In contrast to Niebuhr's social ideal, Rauschenbusch's idea of the kingdom requires institutions that justly discriminate among and balance natural human interests.

Second, Rauschenbusch's conception of justice was not grounded in a biblical ethic divorced from a natural ordering of human life. James Gustafson, in his widely read book *Protestant and Roman Catholic Ethics,* exaggerates Rauschenbusch's reliance on the biblical ethics of the prophets and Jesus. Gustafson, emphasizing the contrast between Rauschenbusch's biblically based ethic and Ryan's use of the Catholic natural law tradition, writes that Rauschenbusch's appeal was "not to the nature of man" or "natural law" but to the normative "history that is found in the Bible" and to "the historical Christian movement." For Rauschenbusch, "[j]ustice is part of the message of the prophets and of Jesus; it is not grounded in a theory of natural right and natural moral law."[2]

Gustafson correctly observes that Rauschenbusch's ethic begins with the biblical portrayal of Jesus in relation to the prophets but overlooks that Rauschenbusch's interpretation of Jesus and of the historical Christian movement was informed by a sociology rooted in evolutionary biology. Thus, Rauschenbusch's biblically based ethic is not as starkly in contrast with Ryan's idea of human nature and natural law as Gustafson suggests.[3] To be sure, Rauschenbusch understood the natural order as evolving in history. It can be known satisfactorily only through the redemptive influence of the kingdom. Unlike Niebuhr, however, Rauschenbusch shared with Ryan the idea of a divine natural ordering of human life that is normative for justice.

I agree with Niebuhr that Rauschenbusch's interpretation of history in

---

1. Niebuhr, *An Interpretation,* 9.
2. Gustafson, *Protestant and Roman Catholic Ethics,* 23–25.
3. In an earlier essay, Gustafson notes that Rauschenbusch drew on both scripture and human experience for his understanding of justice. In that article, Rauschenbusch's ethic based on scripture is not cast in such sharp distinction from a natural law ethic, such as Ryan's. See James M. Gustafson, "From Scripture to Social Policy and Social Action," *Andover-Newton Bulletin* 9 (January 1969): 160–169. According to Gustafson, a leading Catholic moral theologian who heard the lecture version of that essay quipped: "It sounds like natural law to me." (From a letter from James Gustafson to Harlan Beckley, 23 August 1990. Copy on file with author.)

light of the redemptive influence of the kingdom of God led him to be overly hopeful about progress toward justice.[4] His interpretation also overstated the role of Christ and Christianity as the historical source of all advances toward justice. Rauschenbusch was wrong to suggest that his era (or any other) might be the time with which historians will begin in their account of how civilization became Christian.[5] Moreover, we have quite properly abandoned the idea that advancing justice requires that we christianize society. Fortunately, these aspects of Rauschenbusch's thought were not based upon Jesus' redemptive influence inducing a new era in history that transcends the created order. Advancing justice, according to Rauschenbusch's understanding of the kingdom, requires that the social order maximize opportunities for individuals to integrate their natural interests through self-development in solidarity with others. This advance depends on redemptive influences in history that improve our capacity for reasoning and acting justly. Still, Rauschenbusch did not believe that the biblical norm for history could raise humans above their conflicting natural interests.

The need to recover the place of natural human interests in Rauschenbusch's theory of justice is the single most important contention in my analysis of him. Understanding this aspect of Rauschenbusch's thought is crucial for properly retrieving other common legacies from Rauschenbusch's and Ryan's theories of justice. It is not, however, the only significant legacy my analysis uncovers.

A COMMON LEGACY: BELIEFS AND JUSTICE

Some of these legacies are common to all three authors. Indeed, students, to whom I assign all three authors, often perceive few significant differences among them. This perception is, in part, grounded in the authors' obvious agreement that significant government intervention in the economy is required to curtail individual liberties that perpetrate injustices against the working class. These students also notice that for all three authors, the criteria for making judgments about just policies are dependent upon beliefs about God, human nature and agency, and the relevant circumstances of justice. These beliefs both justify and inform the application of the criteria for justice.

My analysis of these theories and conceptions of justice illustrates James Gustafson's contention that ethics (in this case the criteria for justice) are dependent on, as John Reeder puts it, "beliefs about the

---

4. Niebuhr, "Walter Rauschenbusch in Historical Perspective," 42–43.
5. Rauschenbusch, *Christianizing the Social Order,* 29.

general and specific contexts of human experience." Gustafson's thesis about the dependence of ethics on these general beliefs applies to all moral theories, nontheological as well as theological. Reeder's nontheological example is John Rawls. Gustafson's ethics differ from those of Rawls, however, in that Gustafson's ethics, but not Rawls's, are dependent upon theological beliefs about "the general and specific contexts of human experience."[6] Because the authors we have examined also use theological interpretations of these contexts of human experience for their theories of justice, the justifications for their conceptions of justice are theologically dependent. Their theories demonstrate how beliefs about God and God's relations to the world will inform any comprehensive and coherent theory of justice formulated by a theist.

These authors manifest dependence upon theology in yet another way. We have seen that the elements in their theories justifying their conceptions or criteria for justice extend into their full understanding of those criteria and into their application to particular policy judgments. We could not, for example, comprehend the radically egalitarian application of Rauschenbusch's principle that income and wealth should be earned without seeing how his description of economic relations as highly interdependent detects privileges for unearned income wherever there are significant economic inequalities.[7] Niebuhr did not think his regulative principles or his understanding of a balance of power could be properly applied as standards of justice by persons who did not share his beliefs about the demands, judgment, and mercy of God's love.[8] Ryan was the only one of these authors who explicitly articulated principles of justice independently of the other base points in his ethics. Even he applied his canons of justice in light of his understanding of human dignity and analysis of economic circumstances, elements of his ethics clearly dependent upon his belief in a divine natural order.[9] In sum, theological elements in these authors' justifications for the criteria of justice extended into their practical reasoning about policies. None of them gave an exclusively theological justification for supporting a policy. They did not receive divine commands for a living wage or socialism. Nonetheless, their practical reasoning about policies was never wholly independent of the theological beliefs they held.

---

6. John P. Reeder, Jr., "The Dependence of Ethics," in *James Gustafson's Theocentric Ethics: Interpretations and Assessments,* ed. Harlan R. Beckley and Charles M. Swezey (Macon, Ga.: Mercer University Press, 1988), 119–122.

7. See *supra,* chapter two, 89–91.

8. See *supra,* chapter seven, 321–323. We should be dubious whether those whom Morton White dubbed "atheists for Niebuhr" could have fully agreed with Niebuhr's criteria for justice while claiming that Niebuhr's views about issues of justice could be separated from his theology. See Merkley, *Reinhold Niebuhr,* vi–ix.

9. See *supra,* chapter three, 165–167.

If all ethics depend upon beliefs so that practical moral reasoning includes, at least implicitly, this intertwining of justifying beliefs (theories of justice) with criteria for practical judgments (conception of justice), two realities for our thinking about justice follow. First, the process of deliberating about what policies are just is far more complex than applying principles of justice to the facts of a given dilemma. My analysis of how these ethicists, especially Niebuhr and Rauschenbusch, arrived at judgments about policies manifests this complexity. Their policy judgments involved attitudes and dispositions, beliefs about the capacities of human agents and about the redemptive or degenerative effects of institutions on persons, preliminary judgments about what circumstances and consequences are relevant to what ends, a preliminary determination of what issues are most crucial for justice, and so forth. One reason for the enduring importance of these ethicists is their appreciation for the complexity of judgments about policies.

Second, agreement on a brief statement of principles of justice is superficial apart from agreement on the beliefs that justify those principles. Persons may ostensibly share principles of justice yet diverge significantly in their practical reasoning about what policies are just. Our authors defy, or make trivial, John Rawls's claim that one may agree with his principles of justice without accepting the contract theory that justifies it.[10] If justifying beliefs permeate the practical application of principles of justice, a sharp distinction between justifying theories and conceptions of justice is not possible. One might agree with an articulation of the principle independent of its justifying beliefs yet not understand it or apply it in the same way. "Atheists for Niebuhr" might, for example, appreciate how his notion of a balance of power accounts for inveterate human egoism, but fail to account for the role that Niebuhr's beliefs regarding divine grace and love played in his understanding and application of the balance of power. This penetration of justifying beliefs into the application of criteria for justice helps explain why significant agreement about just policies is difficult to achieve.

The following chart illustrates the difference between Rawls's separation of a justifying theory and a conception of justice and the shared practice of our ethicists. The superscript numbers indicate different sets of justifying beliefs (sets of beliefs that may be either compatible or incompatible) for a similarly or even identically stated set of principles of justice. To the extent that the different sets of beliefs overlap or are compatible, the policy judgments would coincide, even on our ethicists' understanding of the role of justifying beliefs in policy deliberations. The point is not that Rauschenbusch, Ryan, and Niebuhr held a

---

10. Rawls, *A Theory of Justice,* 15.

common conception of justice, but that the beliefs that justified their standards of justice entered heavily into their moral reasoning about policies.

RAWLS

Theory of Justice

Conception
of Justice

Justifying beliefs^1 ⟶ agreement
Justifying beliefs^2 ⟶ on   ⟶ deliberation ⟶ policy judgments
Justifying beliefs^3 ⟶ principles

RAUSCHENBUSCH, RYAN, AND NIEBUHR

Theory of Justice

Conception
of Justice

Justifying beliefs^1 ⟶ apparent   ⟶ deliberation^1 ⟶ policy judgments^1
Justifying beliefs^2 ⟶ agreement on ⟶ deliberation^2 ⟶ policy judgments^2
Justifying beliefs^3 ⟶ principles   ⟶ deliberation^3 ⟶ policy judgments^3

Even if moral reasoning is dependent on beliefs in this way, agreement among groups with differing pertinent beliefs, such as theists and nontheists, is not impossible. Persons may hold different beliefs that overlap where they are pertinent to justice. Reeder, for example, illustrates how Gustafson's theological rationale for ethics may overlap with nontheists to achieve a convergence in their belief-dependent ethics.[11] There might, therefore, be agreement between theological and non-theological reasoning about justice, even on the view that judgments about justice depend upon beliefs.

Conversely, there might be disagreement among theological theories of justice. We have found significant disagreements among Rauschenbusch, Ryan, and Niebuhr. Despite a common concern for justice for the working class, they have not passed on a common legacy. In the remainder of this chapter, I will highlight some issues that contrasts in their theories raise for contemporary thinking about justice. I will focus

---

11. Reeder, "The Dependence of Ethics," 128.

on five issues: the role of principles of justice in discriminating among conflicting natural interests, the significance of descriptive analysis in formulating and applying principles of justice, the function of equality of opportunity in Rauschenbusch's and Ryan's conceptions of justice, the relevance of theories of justice in determining what policy issues are important, and the place of the church in securing greater justice.

JUST DISCRIMINATIONS AND THE ULTIMATE IDEAL

Clearly, none of our authors used principles or standards of justice as the sole means for determining what policies to advocate. They did, however, use principles quite differently. Rauschenbusch and Ryan used them to guide their discriminations between just and unjust claims on the resources in an ideal society. (For Rauschenbusch, this ideal was confined to the present historical conditions.) They did not perceive these discriminations as intrinsically doomed to fall short of an ideal—that is, uncompromised— arrangement of social relations. Their "channel buoys" or "canons" were intended to assist persons in discerning what would be required by perfect justice. They aimed at perfect justice in the sense that no social ideal stands above it, condemning it as less than God intends. This use of principles does not mean Rauschenbusch and Ryan believed humans could achieve perfect justice or even that they could fully discern what it requires. Nor does it mean that Rauschenbusch and Ryan did not believe that compromises were sometimes necessary in order to approximate justice. Rauschenbusch even elaborated a strategy for advancing justice that rejected a scrupulous examination of the justice of the labor movement's interests. Their use of principles means that perfect justice has to deal with a created natural order in which various interests within the self and conflicting interests in communities are adjusted and balanced. Their ideal for justice did not apply to social relations in which all human interests are transcended, for example, in an "original perfection" before history or an eschatological social ideal beyond history.

Niebuhr understood and used principles differently. He asserted that principles of justice are intrinsically inferior in that they sanction some interests against others. The social ideal of love transcends all human interests. Thus, Niebuhr's working standards for justice were not intended to discriminate among right and wrong claims on society's resources. All such claims reflect individual or group interests. This inferior status of principles does not mean that Niebuhr's approach to justice was limited to dispositions without guidance from standards for discriminating among human interests. He used his regulative principles of justice and his conception of a balance of power to calculate which interests are most likely to advance justice toward the social ideal. These principles, however, were not intended to discern an ideal arrangement of human relations. Niebuhr never doubted that the ideal was perfect liberty, equality, and harmony. Rather, the working standards of justice are *instruments* in a strategy for approximating an impossible ideal, which Christians are presumed to know. Thus, we find Niebuhr's balance of power principle protecting human freedoms, not because they are just, but in order to preserve human vitalities that withstand tyranny and keep open possibilities for the ironies of history that produce justice that humans cannot foresee.

This choice about the use of principles—whether the criteria for our practical judgments about justice function to discriminate between right and wrong conflicting interests or to balance sinful interests in a strategy to approximate an impossible ideal—is an important one. In the first instance, the ideal for human social relations remains within a divine order or ordering of natural human interests. Justice is vulnerable to becoming a tool that sanctions one group's interests over another's. This use of principles can imply divine sanction for a program of justice that truncates our vision of the indeterminate possibilities for human relations. Niebuhr's tension between the ideal and the actual effectively exposes these dangers. He observed how the attempts to construct human relations on the basis of "necessary" natural interests can lead to unjust treatment of classes, sexes, nations, and so forth, in the name of a natural order.[12] Claims that economic productivity depends upon incentives that satisfy humans' natural acquisitive inclinations may be used, for example, to "justify" unjust inequalities. Hence, Niebuhr rejected an understanding of God as orderer. His ideal of divine love stands prior to the beginning of history and beyond the end of history. It enters history only paradoxically and not as part of a natural ordering of history.

Niebuhr's use of principles to envision a balancing of conflicting interests avoids the dangers of inflexible imposition of less than ideal schemes of justice, but at a cost. His use of principles cannot envision even the possibility of an ideal scheme of justice in history. His social ideal defies the possibility of a divine ordering of human nature. Consequently, his standards of justice cannot assert an individual's or group's right to the means to or an equal opportunity for self-development. His working standards for justice cannot be used to discern that laboring-class claims to a living wage or for the abolition of privilege are perfectly just. In the fifties, Niebuhr was able to make only ad hoc judgments in

---

12. See *supra,* chapter six, 266–267.

order to retain and refine the tolerable justice established by the New Deal. Unlike Rauschenbusch and Ryan, Niebuhr had no means for proposing a program to make that tolerably just industrial order more democratic or cooperative.

The appropriate use of principles of justice continues as a matter of dispute among contemporary theological ethicists. Karen Lebacqz— using liberation theology in *Foundations for a Christian Approach to Justice,* her constructive proposal for "justice in an unjust world"— develops a criticism of ideal principles of justice similar to Niebuhr's. According to Lebacqz, "a search for absolute rules of justice is not appropriate. . . . Because justice emerges out of protest against injustice, . . . [i]t is the process of providing new beginnings, not an ideal state of distribution. . . . Justice is a constant process of correction, not a once-and-for-all program." John Rawls's approach to justice "as an issue in rational deliberation" "is not adequate to a world in which rationality itself is distorted by human sin."[13] Like Niebuhr, Lebacqz rejects all attempts to develop a conception of justice on the basis of criteria, such as needs, for what is "due" to persons.[14] Like Niebuhr, Lebacqz offers no positive criteria for justice and no coherent program of policies that could satisfy the demands of justice.

Similar to Niebuhr, Lebacqz rejects a divine natural order from which principles of justice might be inferred. Lebacqz does not claim that the human spirit is free from natural interests or that humans are created in weakness, dependence, and finitude. She argues, however, that the creation stories should be understood in light of God's liberating work in the Exodus so that this "liberating God" is the "God of all creation."[15] Hence, humans are not bound by an order of creation.

As Lebacqz insists, there are important differences between her understanding of justice and Niebuhr's.[16] We do not need to delineate all those differences, but we should observe that her view of God as liberator in history backs a hope for "new beginnings" in justice that Niebuhr's view of a human organic connection to the past foreclosed. Consequently, I doubt that Lebacqz would be fully satisfied with Niebuhr's understanding of principles of justice as guides for a balance of power that compromises the social ideal in order to approximate it. She certainly does not accept present injustice as tolerable. We need a "new beginning." In order to forge this "new beginning," we need to perceive

---

13. Karen Lebacqz, *Foundations for a Christian Approach to Justice: Justice in an Unjust World* (Minneapolis: Augsburg, 1987), 152–153, 157.
14. Ibid., 150, 155.
15. Ibid., 72–73.
16. Ibid., 159.

a positive concept of justice, but only "dimly" and not "directly."[17] The principles of justice proffered in our present "unjust world" cannot envision "an ideal state of distribution" or a program of policies to embody a truly just distribution. The point remains that Lebacqz, like Niebuhr, rejects the view that principles of justice can be used, in the present unjust world, to discriminate between just and unjust interests in order to propose an ideal distribution of benefits and burdens.

Ismael García, also working out of liberation theology in *Justice in Latin American Theology of Liberation,* develops a different understanding of principles of justice. García claims that although Latin American liberation theologians have not developed a positive conception of justice, there are "sources" in their works that enable him to set forth the "criteria [that] give their notions of justice content."[18] The crucial criterion of justice is, according to García, what persons, particularly the poor, "need" in order to be "capable of participating in as many aspects of their social existence as they choose."[19] He specifies the content of need and contrasts this criterion for justice from other conceptions of justice, which he categorizes as natural law, positive law, and natural right conceptions.[20] Despite sharp disagreements with these other conceptions of justice, García adopts their method of using principles to help specify a just distributive pattern. He then uses his criterion of needs to propose a set of economic and political policies, including state ownership of productive property and democratic participation in the productive process.[21]

Despite the obvious similarities with Rauschenbusch's and Ryan's use of principles, the understandings of God and human nature that back García's conception of justice differ sharply from theirs. Like Lebacqz, García understands God, in light of the Exodus event, primarily as a "historico-political" liberator rather than as "a God creating a hierarchically ordered cosmos." It follows, according to García, that liberation theology does not "argue from a substantive notion of human nature." All "interpretations of human nature" are "historically and socially conditioned." Principles inferred from those interpretations impede the formulation of new and better possibilities of life.[22] How, then, can García use his criterion of need to depict a just order that avoids

---

17. Ibid., 154.
18. Ismael García, *Justice in Latin American Theology of Liberation* (Atlanta: John Knox Press, 1987), 11.
19. Ibid., 85, 26.
20. Ibid., 111–138.
21. Ibid., 141–186.
22. Ibid., 117–118.

impeding the same indeterminate possibilities for human nature and relations? He might have drawn upon Rauschenbusch's notion of a divine ordering in which redemption allows for new possibilities without denying natural interests that humans cannot transcend. García's understandings of God and human nature seem not to cohere with his use of principles. Nonetheless, he offers a contemporary theory of justice that, more like Ryan and Rauschenbusch than like Niebuhr, uses principles of justice to propose an ideal within history for just relations among conflicting human interests.

Rauschenbusch's and Ryan's use of principles did not commit them to an absolute and inflexible scheme of justice that they were willing to force on others without amendment. Even Ryan, who believed the divine natural order could be known by natural reason, was not entirely inflexible. His formulation and application of the canons of justice took into account a fairly broad range of changing economic circumstances. Consequently, Ryan remained open to different forms of property ownership and various ways of organizing the economic system, cooperation within industries, and democratic participation in the productive process. Ryan was, of course, convinced that persons who exercised their rational faculties would adopt the crucial features of his program for justice. Rauschenbusch did not share Ryan's confidence in rational deliberation. Rauschenbusch (like Niebuhr, Lebacqz, and García) was able to account for how sin, especially as it is mediated through social institutions, can corrupt moral reason. Perceiving and applying the principles of justice depends upon redemptive forces in history. Rauschenbusch could, therefore, account for corrupted principles of justice and for evolution in the formulation and application of the principles of justice. Yet Rauschenbusch did not believe that the redemptive possibilities in the kingdom of God transcend natural and legitimate human interests in self-preservation, acquisition of material goods, and solidarity. Thus, he used principles of justice to depict a distribution and arrangement of society's benefits and burdens that discriminate between these just interests and interests in liberties, privileges, and so forth, that he unabashedly called unjust.

There were flaws in Ryan's and Rauschenbusch's use of principles, which Niebuhr's theory of justice exposed. Ryan had excessive confidence in the natural capacity of rational agents to know the natural law. Even though Rauschenbusch perceived a need for regenerate reason, his view that religion, under the redemptive influence of Christ, can be defined as "the life of God in the soul of man" led him to identify God too closely with the social movement and a program for justice.[23]

---

23. See *supra*, chapter two, 81–82.

Despite these flaws, there are theological and ethical reasons for adopting modified versions of Rauschenbusch's and Ryan's use of principles. First, their use of principles is based on consent to a divine ordering of life in which human social relations cannot transcend just discriminations among conflicting natural interests. There is an element of species egoism—namely, that human fulfillment is unbounded by natural limitations—in Niebuhr's social ideal and Lebacqz's "new beginnings." Second, by setting forth ideal principles and concomitant policies, Rauschenbusch and Ryan were able to proffer visions, subject to revision, for a just order in history. Their visions had the benefit of challenging policymakers with a reasonable and possible scheme for the highest justice humans can attain, barring new redemptive forces in history. It is a virtue of García's use of principles that it sets a liberation view of justice in critical conversation with alternative conceptions of justice and policy proposals. There are, of course, risks in this use of principles. Both Ryan and Rauschenbusch, for example, held views about women's participation in the family and the economy that are oppressive by most contemporary standards. Those risks are, in my judgment, nevertheless worth taking.

DESCRIPTIVE ANALYSIS AND NORMS OF JUSTICE

Although he posited ideal principles for discriminating among human interests, Rauschenbusch joined Niebuhr in formulating principles of justice in light of a descriptive analysis of changing social forces. There were, for neither, ideal principles in the sense that the norms of justice can be formulated for all times and places. Ryan, on the other hand, grounded his canon of needs on an a priori understanding of the constitution and end of rational human nature. Still, his other canons and the application of his canons were dependent upon his analysis of the economic circumstances of justice. He too used descriptive analysis in forming his conception of justice, but his conception was not informed by an analysis of history.

Our figures' uses of descriptive analyses raise crucial issues for thinking about justice. Because Rauschenbusch is, in my judgment, the most helpful in this regard, I will use his evaluative description of changing and interconnected social institutions as a baseline for assessing this legacy.

Interpreting the Historical Circumstances of Justice

First, Rauschenbusch's "channel buoys" emerged out of his evaluative description of evolving institutions in the United States, namely, the family, the church, and educational, political, and economic institutions. His principles were not derived from a priori reasoning; they were not fully independent of values embodied in the evolving institutions he described. Nor did he apply the ethic of Jesus directly to American democracy and capitalism. That approach to justice would belie Jesus' intention to unleash a redemptive influence that unfolds through the moral forces and institutions of history. For Rauschenbusch, the kingdom of God is not a powerful moral idea for justice until it penetrates the institutions it is intended to redeem. The values of the kingdom cannot be imposed on history; they must be encouraged as they emerge in history.

Rauschenbusch's reliance upon a historical analysis of institutions and movements does not mean that his ethics were based on the prevailing idea of justice in society. His *evaluative* description was informed by his normative idea of the kingdom, an idea in tension with the realities of American capitalism. He sought to align his conception of justice with forces in history that most nearly embodied Jesus' principles of the sacredness of the personality, human solidarity, and partiality for those denied opportunities to develop. Thus, Rauschenbusch's principles of earned income and wealth, democracy, and "socialism" were derived by conjoining descriptive possibilities and the normative demands of Jesus' ethic. Justifying principles of justice is both a descriptive and a normative task.

There was tension between the ideal and the actual in Rauschenbusch's analysis of history, as there was in Niebuhr's. Yet the tension Niebuhr perceived prohibited him from formulating principles intended primarily to distinguish just from unjust interests. Although both conceived justice in light of evaluative descriptions of history, Niebuhr's analysis produced a strategy for justice, not a substantive ideal for justice. This was so for two reasons.

First, because the ethic of Jesus, as Niebuhr understood it, transcends the actual possibilities of history, an ideal for justice could never emerge from institutions and movements in history. Second, a description of history from the perspective of Niebuhr's ethic of Jesus precluded the possibilities for redemption Rauschenbusch perceived. In the thirties, Niebuhr viewed the circumstances of history as offering only the tragic choice between the "vengeance" of the Marxist movement and the "hypocrisy" of democratic capitalism. In the fifties, Niebuhr described history in terms of the irony of grace that allowed for renewals as long as creative vitalities in society were not subdued by conscious attempts to establish the absolute justice of equality.[24] Consequently, on Niebuhr's

---

24. See *supra,* chapter six, 290–291.

analysis of the historical circumstances for justice, the standards of justice are instruments in a strategy for approximating ideal justice. Application of ideal principles of justice would blind us to necessary tragic choices or hinder the ironic possibilities of grace in history.

If our thinking about justice follows either Rauschenbusch or Niebuhr, our analysis of the circumstances of justice must account for the possibilities for justice within history. On Rauschenbusch's analysis, however, redemptive forces provide occasions, though brief, in which social factors allow for an advance in justice by applying principles that envision an uncompromised just social order. Alan Anderson and George Pickering, in *Confronting the Color Line,* develop a contemporary argument for racial justice that accounts for socio-historical circumstances in a way that is reminiscent of Rauschenbusch. Like Rauschenbusch and Niebuhr, Anderson and Pickering do not conceive ethics as "rational criticism of moral ideas abstracted from whatever roles they may play in actual events."[25] Anderson and Pickering begin their moral argument with a description of five ideas about racial justice that have become significant social forces in American society. From their account of the interplay of these ideas in the civil rights struggle in Chicago during the sixties, Anderson and Pickering construct a descriptive and normative argument for "undertaking extensive redistributive policies in the face of the color line."[26] They perceive their argument for these policies as "crossing the boundaries that are usually observed between ethics, history, and the behavioral sciences."[27]

Anderson and Pickering's interpretation of history also differs from Rauschenbusch's and Niebuhr's. It is not theological. Anderson and Pickering conceive the religious dimension of justice broadly to include all competing notions of the nature of and possibilities for meaning in human life. Instead of analyzing history in terms of possibilities enabled by divine grace, they interpret the struggle for racial justice in light of competition between "religious" faiths. Bad faith seeks meaning for human life within limits imposed by the color line. In various versions of democratic faith, human possibilities transcend the color line.[28] Taking their "stand on a socially reconstructed version of the democratic faith,"[29] Anderson and Pickering believe that American history holds a

---

25. Alan B. Anderson and George W. Pickering, *Confronting the Color Line: The Broken Promise of the Civil Rights Movement in Chicago* (Athens, Ga.: University of Georgia Press, 1986), 12.
26. Ibid., 404.
27. Ibid., 12.
28. Ibid., 389–410.
29. Ibid., 17.

possibility for their ideal of racial justice. In these circumstances, their criteria for redistribution can stipulate both a strategy to reform unjust institutions and a vision of ideally just race relations. Thus, Anderson and Pickering offer a contemporary example, similar to Rauschenbusch, of how arguments for a conception of justice might realistically account for social forces in history and yet formulate principles for discriminating among conflicting interests in an ideally just society.

Rauschenbusch, Niebuhr, and Anderson and Pickering are all correct, in my judgment, in attempting to account for the socio-historical possibilities for justice. They all take seriously the notion that arguments for a theory of justice are part of changing events rather than *sub specie aeternitatis.* They see more clearly than Ryan that advances toward justice involve support for existing social forces as well as rational arguments for an ideal conception of justice.

None of these accounts is fully adequate, however. For those who think about justice in the context of ultimate responsibility to God, the analysis of the circumstances of justice must be *theological,* not merely in terms of Anderson and Pickering's broad definition of religious faith. On the other hand, Rauschenbusch's theology of social redemption was too limited to Christian forces in history. Moreover, although he rightly ruled out radical "new beginnings" in history, Rauschenbusch undoubtedly overestimated the possibilities for change in his time and place. The inadequacies of Rauschenbusch's theology of redemption leave us with a question: if we reject Rauschenbusch's hope for a christianized social order, can a theological interpretation of history discern redemptive possibilities that warrant an ideal for justice beyond Niebuhr's mere equilibrium of competing interests? This theological and ethical argument must take seriously Niebuhr's admonitions. A rigid commitment to ideals for justice can lead either to naivety about what can be accomplished or to enforcement of a scheme of justice that undermines the irony of history that makes constant renewal possible.

Interpreting the Economic Circumstances of Justice

A second aspect of Rauschenbusch's analysis of the circumstances of justice also raises a crucial issue for our thinking about justice. Reflecting the highly interdependent ordering of life, Rauschenbusch's descriptions of the circumstances of justice examined individual economic activity in interaction with a broad range of economic and noneconomic actions and institutions. This description of economic activity had a profound influence upon Rauschenbusch's principles of justice. First, production of economic goods is viewed as a communal activity. On this description, unequal distribution of rents, interest, and profits to individuals belies the interdependence of the production process and signifies unearned income derived from special privileges. Consequently, significant inequalities are always perceived as evidence of unjust privileges. Second, management-labor relations and competitive markets are described in the context of individual development in interdependent communities. On this description, democratic production processes and "socializing" competition are important for individual opportunity. Justice cannot be reduced to a fair exchange of goods. Finally, when economic activity is described in interaction with noneconomic realities, remedies for economic injustices are construed in the context of other institutions and forces in society.

Rauschenbusch's socio-historical analysis of economic activities and institutions provides an illuminating contrast with Ryan's narrower economic analysis. We must not overstate their differences. Ryan was never satisfied with economists' descriptions of productivity or with analysis that focused exclusively on economic welfare. Nevertheless, Ryan's use of neoclassical economics, especially in his early years, focused his descriptions on the immediate factors of production and economic efficiency. He gave less attention than Rauschenbusch to more remote contributors to economic value (e.g., a community's contribution to land values) and to values not measured in economic terms (e.g., how cooperation contributes to individual development).

This narrower view of the relevant circumstances impinged on Ryan's conception of justice. Because the canon of needs allowed for proportional and unequal distributions of economic goods, Ryan's other canons, justified largely by his economic analysis, permitted large accumulations of income and wealth through profits. In addition, early in his career, when Ryan confined needs mostly to the material goods necessary for self-development, he perceived the problem of justice largely in terms of a living wage. Except for private property, he did not give much consideration to how institutions bear on individual development. As Ryan expanded the relevant circumstances of justice to include the stability of the whole economy and how institutional arrangements affect opportunities for persons to develop, he also expanded his proposals for economic justice. An increasing emphasis on equality and an interest in policies beyond a living wage brought Ryan closer to Rauschenbusch. Even in the thirties, however, Ryan relied more heavily on traditional economics and remained more concerned with economic efficiency than Rauschenbusch had been. He, for example, stipulated more precisely than Rauschenbusch the limits on labor participation in management. He also retained a place for the profit motive in his proposals for industrial organization. Finally, Ryan's proposals for justice remained focused on economic issues independent of their connections with other institutions and reform movements in society.

Rauschenbusch's and Ryan's differences regarding the relevant circumstances for justice pose an important and difficult issue precisely because they both rejected the narrowest economic analyses of efficiency. (Ryan's concern for economic efficiency was with how it bears on individual dignity.) Rauschenbusch's analysis of economic production in the context of the interdependence of human life helps us to see the role of unmerited privilege where significant inequalities exist. On the other hand, Ryan's attention to economic efficiency demonstrates that some privileges, such as limited hierarchies in management or the potential for profit, may be necessary for a healthy economy, even where those privileges are unmerited. Rauschenbusch's interpretation of a broad range of circumstances on the basis of the advancing kingdom of God appears to have blinded him to these concessions to privilege that Ryan saw as required in order to benefit the most needy persons in society.

John Rawls's difference principle, interpreted and applied in light of the beliefs that underlie it, provides a way of combining these aspects of Rauschenbusch's and Ryan's analyses. The "difference principle" states that social and economic inequalities are justified only where they benefit the least advantaged.[30] Rawls constructs a hypothetical contract situation, the "original position," in which the parties, unaware of their social advantages and their natural talents, consent to the difference principle. These hypothetical restrictions on persons' capacity to consider their social position and natural talents in agreeing to the principles of justice reflect a belief in the interdependence of human activity similar to Rauschenbusch's. These social advantages and natural talents are privileges granted at birth. Possession of these privileges gives persons no claim on society. Indeed, Rawls notes that the difference principle reflects "an agreement to regard the distribution of natural talents as a common asset and to share in the benefits of this distribution." Persons are "to avail themselves of the accidents of nature and social circumstance only when doing so is for the common benefit," more specifically for the benefit of the least advantaged.[31]

In sum, the beliefs underlying Rawls's description of the original position, in which the difference principle is chosen, lead persons to view these privileges that result in inequalities as grants from the community rather than as contributions to production deserving compensation. Yet

---

30. Rawls, *A Theory of Justice,* 83.
31. Ibid., 100–102.

the difference principle also allows inequalities that enhance economic efficiencies for the sake of benefiting the least advantaged. Thus, the difference principle is compatible with economic efficiency and requires consideration of distributive factors that contribute to efficiency.[32] Some undeserved economic privileges might, therefore, be permitted in order to enhance efficiency that benefits the least advantaged. In this way, Ryan's arguments for profits that encourage entrepreneurial competence and risk taking in order to promote economic welfare are relevant for a just distribution. This concern for efficiency holds even if Rauschenbusch is right in noting that the entrepreneur's efforts are made possible by privileges granted by the community. Factors that enhance economic efficiency are relevant to justice even when they are not relevant measures of an agent's distinctive contribution to economic well-being.

Rawls's difference principle combines and balances Rauschenbusch's and Ryan's respective considerations for interdependence and efficiency in economic activity. It does not account, however, for the common concern they exhibited—Ryan came to emphasize this consideration in the thirties—for how economic institutions bear on persons' opportunities for self-development. I have argued that Rauschenbusch's and Ryan's notion of equality of opportunity distinguishes their conceptions of justice from Niebuhr's and represents an important challenge to much of liberal thought. This legacy of their theories of justice deserves special consideration.

EQUAL OPPORTUNITY FOR SELF-DEVELOPMENT

Rawls does not ignore equal opportunity. His difference principle pertains to equality of opportunity as well as to the distribution of income and wealth. The second part of this principle requires that just inequalities must be "attached to offices and positions open to all under conditions of fair equality of opportunity."[33] According to this understanding of equal opportunity, it is not sufficient that positions be open to all qualified persons. A just society must also provide whatever benefits (e.g., education, a minimum level of welfare, affirmative action, etc.)[34] are required

---

32. Ibid., 79–80.
33. Ibid., 83.
34. See, for example, James Sterba, *How to Make People Just: A Practical Reconciliation of Alternative Conceptions of Justice* (Totowa, N.J.: Rowman & Littlefield, 1988), 31–62, esp. 45–52, for an illustration of how Rawls's theories and other theories of justice that Sterba calls "welfare liberal justice" justify welfare policies and affirmative action

for persons to "have the same prospects of success regardless of their initial place in the social system, that is, irrespective of the income class into which they were born."[35] "[T]o provide genuine equality of opportunity, society must give more attention to those with fewer native assets and to those born into less favorable social positions."[36] The crucial point is that fair equality of opportunity goes well beyond equal opportunity understood merely as prohibiting discrimination on the basis of characteristics unrelated to qualifications for a position, such as race or sex. It seeks, so far as possible, to eliminate natural and social contingencies that place some groups at a disadvantage in competing for open positions.

Fair equality of opportunity is not sufficient, however, to secure the opportunity for self-development as Rauschenbusch and Ryan understood it. Fair equality of opportunity does not consider whether the available positions provide the means for persons to develop. Rauschenbusch believed that a competitive, profit-driven economic system overstimulates natural selfish and acquisitive interests. It encourages autocratic management that exploits workers and denies them an opportunity to participate in the productive process. This organization of the economic life stunts the growth of humans' natural interest in solidarity. But even if employers are benevolent, the working class is left with a dependent attitude that hinders desirable "qualities of independence and initiative."[37] Ryan believed that positions open for wage earners in corporations completely controlled by owners and managers fail to provide opportunities for laborers to develop their "creative and directive faculties." Further, laborers who have no opportunities for ownership have no sense of independence, security, or self-respect. Finally, Ryan also argued that the competitive spirit of historical capitalism undercuts the possibilities for cooperation that persons need in order to develop a spirit of social justice.[38]

Rauschenbusch and Ryan believed that a fully adequate notion of equal opportunity requires not only that persons have the means to compete for available positions but that they have access to positions that facilitate the full development of their natural capacities. This understanding of opportunity requires that thinking about justice consider how common values embodied in the constitution and organization

---

programs required to satisfy the right to equal opportunity. Sterba doubts that the difference principle would be chosen by parties in the original position, but he believes that welfare and affirmative action policies would be justified by any conception of justice that might be chosen.

35. Rawls, *A Theory of Justice*, 73.
36. Ibid., 100.
37. Rauschenbusch, *Christianizing the Social Order*, 356.
38. See *supra*, chapter five, 244–245, 248, 249–250.

of institutions impede or cultivate development of desirable qualities of character. This view of opportunity persuaded Rauschenbusch and Ryan that a just economic order requires a democratic organization of corporations and a reorganization of industry to encourage cooperation in pursuit of the common good.

This notion of equal opportunity clearly poses a challenge to liberal conceptions of justice, even egalitarian conceptions such as Rawls's. It accounts for some of the concerns of communitarian critics of liberalism. It shows how justice should attend to the way in which the common good of a society nurtures the virtues of its people.[39] It asserts that respect for the sacredness of the personality or human dignity requires institutions that secure opportunities for persons to develop their natural capacities. This emphasis upon opportunities for individuals, not some prior conception of the common good, led Rauschenbusch and Ryan to consider the common good an important part of a just society.[40] Part of the common good of a society is the values embodied in institutions that foster character development. Unless a society nourishes these values, individuals are denied opportunities for self-development, even if they have been offered a fair opportunity to compete for available positions.

This understanding of opportunity is subject to the liberal criticism that communitarian theories of justice favor a particular view of the good that would be unfairly imposed on those who have reasonable but conflicting life plans.[41] Ryan's "teleology of persons" set forth a particular view of individual excellence that dictated the opportunities he thought institutions should make available for persons. On that basis, he advocated paternalistic policies many persons justly object to. We have noted his judgments about wages and hours for women.[42] He even suggested "labor colonies for those who can but will not work."[43] He supported economic policies that would restrict the availability of "luxury goods" unnecessary for the proper development of the personality.[44]

---

39. See, for example, David Hollenbach, S.J., "The Common Good Revisited," *Theological Studies* 50, no. 1 (March 1989): 77.

40. I do not mean to imply that Rauschenbusch and Ryan believed that advancing the common good should always be constrained by immediate benefits to individuals. Recall that Ryan argued that human welfare considers how the common good furthers individual rights in the *long run* (see *supra,* chapter three, 125–127). Rauschenbusch went even further in separating the common good from benefits to individuals. He believed that there are occasions in which sacrifices must be inflicted on individuals for the sake of advancing toward the kingdom that assures opportunities for all (see *supra,* chapter one, 54–55, and chapter two, 91–92, 110).

41. See, for example, ibid., 77–78.

42. See *supra,* chapter three, 136, 174.

43. Ryan, *The Church and Socialism,* 94.

44. See *supra,* chapter five, 296–297.

Ryan even mildly chastised labor unions for pursuing aggressive collective bargaining for selfish interests rather than cooperating with management to achieve economic democracy.[45] Laborers, thought Ryan, ought to be interested in participation in management that would develop their "creative and directive faculties."

Rauschenbusch did not delineate an explicit account of the ends persons ought to pursue. Nonetheless, his proposals for economic democracy and socialism imply an understanding of the ends persons should seek, for example, cooperation and participation in the productive process. Rauschenbusch assumed that the labor movement shared his view that it should seek economic democracy and fraternity through socialism. History shows that labor unions have sought goals other than those Rauschenbusch and Ryan would have had them pursue. Does this disagreement about goals indicate that Rauschenbusch and Ryan were prepared to impose ends (e.g., cooperation, developing managerial capacities, consumption only for self-development) on persons and groups who were making other reasonable choices about their ends? Does it mean their understanding of the opportunity for self-development restricts liberties for persons to pursue their own life plans using the instrumental goods for which they have a just claim?

Rauschenbusch's analyses of the interdependence of institutions and of how institutions influence qualities of character proffer an important response to these criticisms. In a highly interdependent society where inequalities of power exist, groups and individuals are not free to pursue a life plan of their own choosing. Where competition encourages selfish interests and autocratic management cultivates an excessive sense of dependence, persons are not fully free to envision the goods of cooperation and participation in the productive process. Of more importance, even where persons consciously seek more cooperation and participation, they may not possess the wherewithal to create positions that afford opportunities to develop this kind of life. Have laborers "chosen" not to push harder for some version of economic democracy because they have no interest in greater participation in the productive process? Or have they prudently decided that they lacked the power to bring about participation without sacrificing other interests in wages and more comfortable working conditions? Similar questions can be raised about other positions. They are not easily answered, but they do point out that Rawls's notion of fair equality of opportunity does not, in itself, assure persons the opportunity to pursue a rationally chosen life plan.

Rawls appears to acknowledge Rauschenbusch's observation about

---

45. Ryan, *Declining Liberty*, 214–223.

how the social order enables and limits the ends persons can envision and pursue. In reference to his notion of rational life plans, Rawls recognizes that

> the general facts of social interdependency must be reckoned with. The basic structure of society is bound to encourage and support certain kinds of plans more than others by rewarding its members for contributing to the common good in ways consistent with justice. Taking account of these contingencies narrows down the alternative plans.[46]

In a later essay, Rawls also notes how institutions affect persons' aims and interests.

> Everyone recognizes that the form of society affects its members and determines in large part the kind of persons they want to be as well as the kind of persons they are. . . . Thus an economic regime is not only an institutional scheme for satisfying existing desires and aspirations but a way of fashioning desires and aspirations in the future.[47]

The question is whether these facts about social interdependency and institutions influencing our aims call for a revision in Rawls's principle of fair equality of opportunity.

On Rauschenbusch's account of moral agency in a highly interdependent social order, the equal opportunity for self-development Ryan and Rauschenbusch proposed does not necessarily restrict persons' liberties to pursue their own ends. Their provision for institutional support for self-development may expand these liberties by insisting that society provide for a way of life that is not presently available.

Rauschenbusch and Ryan provide a starting point for us to consider more thoroughly what it means to claim that justice requires equality of opportunity. They demonstrate inadequacies in some liberal conceptions of justice without necessarily rejecting the claim for individuals' freedom not to have a full conception of the good foisted upon them. Rauschenbusch shows, however, that in a highly interdependent social order, the idea that we can have radical pluralism in life-styles is deceptive. Permitting privileges for massive accumulations of wealth and autocratic management may, for example, necessarily inhibit opportunities for participation and cooperation in the economic life.

In addition to posing this important challenge to our thinking about

---

46. Rawls, *A Theory of Justice,* 424–425.
47. John Rawls, "The Basic Structure as Subject," *American Philosophical Quarterly* 14, no. 2 (April 1977): 160.

justice, Rauschenbusch's and Ryan's notions of opportunity have the advantage of drawing on an idea that is deeply entrenched in our culture and institutions. As Anderson and Pickering might put it, equality of opportunity is a moral idea with sufficient social force in our history to create a "moral issue" in relation to our economic and political institutions.[48] A "moral issue" has a powerful hold on us. It gives an idea, such as equality of opportunity, the power to be a social force for justice. Contemporary thinking as diverse as that of Michael Novak and feminist critics of traditionally dominant conceptions of justice appeals to the idea of equality of opportunity. Such appeals indicate that equality of opportunity is a moral issue in our society. These persons, of course, hold views of equal opportunity that differ from each other as well as from the views of Rauschenbusch and Ryan. Novak insists that equality of opportunity can be achieved independently from equality of results,[49] a distinction that is impossible on Rauschenbusch's description of the social order. James Sterba's interpretation of feminists' notion of equal opportunity as requiring "the same right to self-development" has more affinities with Rauschenbusch's and Ryan's. (They, of course, did not extend their idea of equal opportunity fully to include women.) When, however, some feminists claim that equal opportunity requires eradicating biological differences, they go beyond an idea of opportunity based on consent to the natural ordering of human life.[50] The point is that the idea of equal opportunity, though it constitutes a potent social force, must be given common definition in order to become an effective criterion for justice.[51]

Neither Ryan's nor Rauschenbusch's understandings of opportunity should be adopted without revision. Ryan's "teleology of the person" committed him to an understanding of opportunity and to policies that manifest some of the paternalism of which liberal theorists are rightly critical. Rauschenbusch's overestimation of possibilities for redemption through reforming institutions seems to have made him overly sanguine about the opportunities for participation and cooperation in an industrial economy. Recall that Ryan was more cautious than Rauschenbusch regarding how far democratic participation in management could go

---

48. See Anderson and Pickering, *Confronting the Color Line,* 7–15.
49. Novak, *The Spirit of Democratic Capitalism,* 124–125.
50. Sterba, *How to Make People Just,* 67–72.
51. Ryan noted the significance of disagreements about the meaning of equal opportunity in the thirties. Citing a contradiction between Hoover's understanding of opportunity as the freedom to compete and Roosevelt's understanding as a minimum of positive economic goods, Ryan observed that two contrasting philosophies of government followed from "their respective conceptions of 'opportunity.' " See Ryan, *Seven Troubled Years,* 224.

without sacrificing efficiency. Injudicious judgments about the possibilities for self-development continue to plague contemporary understandings of opportunity. Ismael García, for example, goes too far in asserting that justice requires "all that a person lacks to become a person capable of participating in as many aspects of their [sic] social existence as they [sic] choose."[52] We need an understanding of equality of opportunity that enables us to discern how to offer marginal groups the power to forge new positions in economics, education, and politics. This understanding should not, however, stipulate what opportunities persons should want or presume that persons can choose to participate fully in all institutions that impinge on their lives. Here the legacy of Rauschenbusch and Ryan is also a task.

They do not leave us without guidance. A normative idea of opportunity should begin, as Rauschenbusch and Ryan do, with a myriad of legitimate human interests (e.g., in self-preservation, acquiring what one needs for self-development, security, self-reliance, solidarity, etc.) that are rooted in the natural ordering of human life. These potentially conflicting interests must be shaped and balanced in a way that recognizes both the possibilities and limits for self-development in community. Justice requires that a society's institutions offer opportunities for individuals to improve their natural capacities to pursue these interests in concert. Niebuhr's theory of justice offers no such guidance. His social ideal for justice transcends all natural interests. When this ideal is placed in tension with the actual condition of humans, justice seeks an equilibrium of power that balances necessarily sinful interests in equality, freedom, and order. Consequently, justice, for Niebuhr, is not concerned with the opportunities social institutions offer individuals to mold their interests into realized capacities of personality. We should not be surprised that Niebuhr did not share Rauschenbusch's and Ryan's interest in proposals for economic democracy or for organizing the economic system to offer opportunities for cooperation.

JUSTICE AND POLICY ISSUES

All three of our figures demonstrate how a theory of justice informs our determination of what policy issues demand attention and which of these issues are most crucial. A decision to address one policy issue rather than another is not arbitrary. Conceptions of justice not only guide our determination of what policies to advocate; they also form our judg-

---

52. García, *Justice in Latin American Theology of Liberation*, 85.

ments about what issues should be addressed. No conception of justice is applicable to every policy issue that might be raised. One function of a theory of justice is to discern which issues are most important.

This observation leads to another point at which these ethicists had a great deal in common. For all three, concern for a powerless and impoverished working class dictated that justice address issues that could improve the conditions of wage earners. Issues regarding fairness in contracts or what constitutes entitlement to a particular piece of property were not crucial for our authors. Even issues, such as taxation, that deal primarily with the distribution of goods within the existing economic system were not paramount.[53] These issues fail to address deeper structural problems in the economic order. The early Ryan, for whom a living wage was fundamental for distributive justice, is the apparent exception. We should recall, however, that elements in his early theory of justice, especially the canon of human welfare, directed him to address broader issues in the thirties. Furthermore, Ryan's proposal for a minimum wage required substantial changes in the contemporary understanding of property rights, and he expected it to effect a widespread redistribution of income. Present debate about a minimum wage is an issue of almost a different genus from Ryan's call for a living family wage.

Despite these similarities, we can learn more from the differences in the issues these ethicists chose to address and emphasize. I will discuss three points.

Organization of the Productive Process?

First, and of most importance, Rauschenbusch's and Ryan's attention to opportunities for persons to develop their natural interests directed them to advocate changes in the organization of the productive process. Insofar as I know, Niebuhr never discussed economic democracy or how the NRA or other proposals for reorganizing industry might mitigate conflict and encourage cooperation.[54]

---

53. Although Niebuhr, in the early forties, declared taxation the most important single factor for achieving justice (see *supra,* chapter seven, 333), he did not focus on it during the forties and fifties. As his thinking on applied justice unfolded during this period, taxation, along with other narrower issues, was important for him only in the context of an established balance of power among labor, business, and government that dealt with the more fundamental problem of injustice.

54. Niebuhr believed that the NRA was an instrument for enhancing business power over labor. See his comments on the NRA in his "Ex Cathedra" columns in *The World Tomorrow* 17, no. 6 (March 15, 1934): 122; 17, no. 7 (March 19, 1934): 146; 17, no. 8 (April 12, 1934): 170; 17, no. 11 (May 24, 1934): 266. Unlike Ryan, Niebuhr saw no potential for reforming the NRA into a cooperative organization of industry that could protect labor's interests.

In the thirties, Niebuhr considered such proposals counterrevolution-ary. He endorsed the proletarian mission for socialism, not because he expected it to produce participatory or cooperative relations of produc-tion, but as the only strategy capable of securing equal power and income for laborers. A rare comment on the cooperative movement illustrates Niebuhr's attitude toward these issues that were so crucial to Rausch-enbusch and Ryan. In 1936, Niebuhr took the occasion of a visit to the United States by Toyohiko Kagawa, leader of a Rauschenbusch-inspired kingdom of God movement in Japan,[55] to criticize Kagawa's attempt to achieve reform through economic cooperatives. The thrust of Niebuhr's criticism was that the cooperative movement could not be an effective method for achieving justice in an industrialized economy. More drastic measures were required.

On this point, both Rauschenbusch and Ryan agreed with Niebuhr, but they saw in cooperatives a model for the qualities of character an economic organization should encourage. As Rauschenbusch put it, cooperatives "combine a wholesomely selfish desire to get ahead with genuine fraternal sympathy and solidarity."[56] Rauschenbusch and Ryan intended economic democracy to encourage similar qualities by restruc-turing the relations of production in corporations. Niebuhr, by contrast, saw in the cooperative movement only a naive approach to economic reform with the potential for distracting attention from the more signifi-cant issue of how to advance the socialist movement.[57] Neither the cooperative movement nor any other scheme that merely reorganized the relations of production without changing the imbalance of power was pertinent to Niebuhr's strategy for achieving equality of power and income through the proletarian movement.

As Niebuhr's strategy for justice changed in the forties and fifties, issues regarding how the relations of production bear on opportunities for self-development remained peripheral. Narrower issues such as taxation, inflation, health care, labor organization, ownership of property in specific industries, and so forth, became important. Niebuhr's revised strategy took an ad hoc approach to these narrower issues in order to adjust a relatively just equilibrium of power that balanced equality, liberty, and order. The important issues were those that could upset or adjust this equilibrium. Where the purpose of justice is to seek a balance among conflicting sinful interests, thinking about justice does not entertain pro-posals for restructuring the relations of production in order to encourage

55. Sharpe, *Walter Rauschenbusch*, 13, 417.
56. Rauschenbusch, *Christianizing the Social Order*, 387.
57. Reinhold Niebuhr, "The Political Confusions of Dr. Kagawa," *Radical Religion* 1, no. 2 (Winter 1936): 6–7.

persons' interest in self-development. Hence, Niebuhr never addressed economic democracy or proposals for reorganizing industry.

A Coherent Program for Reform?

Differences between Niebuhr's strategy for approximating an impossible ideal and Rauschenbusch's and Ryan's conceptions of an ideal for justice within the limits and possibilities of a natural ordering of human life influenced the issues they addressed in a second way. Both Rauschenbusch and Ryan proposed a set of relatively coherent policies that they believed were appropriate for a piecemeal advance toward justice. Niebuhr did not. In the thirties, Niebuhr agreed with the Marxists that catastrophe would have to precede any real advance toward equality. He rejected the radical argument that policies that ameliorate injustice should be opposed in order to hasten catastrophe and revolution. Nevertheless, he believed that New Deal revisions of capitalist injustice were doomed to failure. The crucial issues were whether one should endorse the proletarian mission and sacrifice democratic procedures for the sake of socialist equality. Ryan was never tempted by this revolutionary socialism. Even in the thirties, he sought to end "historical capitalism" through New Deal legislation. Rauschenbusch, on the other hand, found it necessary to demonstrate differences between his strategy for evolutionary socialism and the dogmatic socialists' focus on issues beyond the impending catastrophe. Consistent with his understanding of an evolutionary advance in the kingdom, Rauschenbusch proposed a set of ameliorative measures to eradicate capitalist privileges and prepare labor for a democratic socialist economy.

Niebuhr's later strategy for justice required attention to narrower issues. But he still had no reason to offer a set of coherent policies. "Progress" toward justice, meaning a better compromise among sinful interests, was possible only by addressing matters that threatened to undermine the highest possible approximation of the social ideal. Unlike Rauschenbusch and Ryan, Niebuhr had no basis to offer a program for justice within a natural ordering of human life. From Niebuhr's perspective, proposals like Rauschenbusch's and Ryan's were either irrelevant or threatened vitalities essential for renewal of the balance of power. Niebuhr's strategy required an ad hoc determination of the issues crucial for sustaining tolerable justice. The irony is that Niebuhr, who was most critical of existing schemes of justice, ended his career asserting that the New Deal had solved the overall problem of justice.[58] By contrast,

---

58. See *supra,* chapter seven, 339–340.

Ryan's tributes for Roosevelt included an agenda for advances toward justice the New Deal had failed to achieve.[59]

Strategies for Achieving Justice?

My third point is that Rauschenbusch's and Niebuhr's insistence on thinking about justice in light of divine grace directed them to consider the means for moving toward justice an important issue. Ryan's belief that rational agents are capable of knowing the natural law coheres with his view that justice can be obtained by addressing arguments for just policies to those responsible for policies. Ryan saw no need to consider what forces in history bear God's judgment on injustice and renew or redeem the capacity to effect justice. On the other hand, both Rauschenbusch and Niebuhr believed reasoning about justice is distorted by sin. Reason, unaided by grace, is incapable of knowing precisely what is just. Further, individuals experience grace mediated by events and forces within history. Consequently, part of the task of justice is to support historical forces that mete out God's judgment and regenerate the human capacity to reason and act justly.

Thus, Rauschenbusch believed the task of justice included support for the socialist and labor movements, without exacting scrutiny of whether their interests are perfectly just. Securing justice also requires sacrificing some legitimate interests in order to advance the cause of justice. Niebuhr, in the thirties, backed the proletarian mission despite its threat to liberty. In the forties and fifties, he countenanced liberties he thought fell short of perfect justice in order to retain the possibility for continuing renewal of social structures that would otherwise tend toward tyranny.

Rauschenbusch's and Niebuhr's differing understandings of grace led to quite different strategies for achieving justice. I have already offered assessments of their strategies. The point in this context is that theories of justice that view reasoning about justice as dependent on divine grace mediated in history will consider issues of strategy part of the subject matter of justice. Justice cannot be reduced to advocating policies that comply with ideal principles of justice. (Although, for Rauschenbusch, justice also included advocating those policies.) Justice also requires policies that can advance a society toward a closer approximation of ideal justice, such as policies that empower the laboring class. Such policies risk subverting the ideal of justice, for example, by sanctioning egoistic interests of the labor movement.[60] Ryan considered such risks

---

59. See *supra,* chapter five, 253.
60. See, for example, *supra,* chapter two, 97–98.

unwarranted and unnecessary, for humans have the capacity to act on rational arguments. Rauschenbusch and Niebuhr considered these policies of strategy necessary means for redeeming or renewing our collective distorted reasoning about justice.

This legacy from our authors' selection of policy issues may resolve some questions and raise others. All three authors demonstrate that justice for the poor and powerless requires that we address issues beyond commutative justice or equivalence of exchange.[61] We also see how Rauschenbusch's and Ryan's theories of justice based on an ordering of natural human interests led them to consider how the relations of production bear on self-development and to formulate a coherent set of policies for reform. These issues were outside the purview of Niebuhr's strategy for approximating an ideal that transcends human interests. Finally, Rauschenbusch and Niebuhr illustrate how attempts to account for the experience of grace in history lead to a concern for strategies to secure justice, which Ryan's confidence in natural reason neglected. I agree that a theological conception of justice should raise these issues of strategy, but neither Rauschenbusch nor Niebuhr adequately resolved which issues are important.

The problem is with their understandings of grace and nature. On Niebuhr's understanding of grace as renewal and forgiveness, justice is reduced to a balance of power strategy for an ongoing approximation of a social ideal beyond history and natural interests. He had no perspective from which to address issues like economic democracy or to develop a program for reform. Rauschenbusch's belief that the forces of grace in history were redeeming society from exaggerated natural self-interest enabled him to develop a set of policies intended to move the social order incrementally toward an ideal for justice. On the other hand, his emphasis upon redemptive possibilities in history led him to focus on

---

61. Jon Gunnemann, in an important essay on "Capitalism and Commutative Justice," argues that "in a capitalist market society we ought chiefly to worry about commutative justice." See Jon P. Gunnemann, "Capitalism and Commutative Justice," in *The Annual of the Society of Christian Ethics,* ed. Alan B. Anderson (Washington, D.C.: Georgetown University Press, 1985): 101. Although this claim appears to contradict our authors, the bulk of Gunnemann's essay addresses the "shared meanings" and "mutual competence" required for just exchanges. On that basis, Gunnemann suggests limitations on what goods may be justly exchanged, such as labor, and restrictions on "the stronger party" in an exchange, ibid., 105–120. Gunnemann addresses the justice of exchange from the perspective Ryan calls human welfare or social justice rather than from an analysis of immediate factors in the exchange itself. Even on this broad understanding of commutative justice, Gunnemann concedes that distributive justice is required in order to account for human needs, ibid., 119. Furthermore, it is difficult to see how even this broad understanding of commutative justice could address the way in which economic institutions affect opportunities for self-development.

realized democracy and fraternity in a future "communistic" economy. He neglected the difficult issues of efficiency and incentives for innovation that Ryan attended to. Rauschenbusch was overly visionary about the future that the socialist and labor movements and the church could effect. This vision was shaped at the expense of addressing more pragmatic issues that his economic proposals raised.

Niebuhr's doctrine of grace pointed to an ideal beyond natural interests that left him without principles addressing issues that involve discriminations among just and unjust interests. Ryan's theory of justice ignored the power of grace in the natural order because he relegated grace to the supernatural level. Rauschenbusch's was too visionary because of his confidence that grace could transform nature into perfection. The task remains of how justice can account for the redemptive possibilities of divine grace within a natural ordering of human life, as Rauschenbusch did, without losing sight of the pragmatic economic issues that Ryan quite properly addressed. James Gustafson's idea of humans as participants in patterns and processes of interdependence in which God is understood as orderer and redeemer, which I explicate briefly below, provides a good framework for dealing with this task.

THE CHURCH AND JUSTICE

Among the future possibilities Rauschenbusch's strategy seriously misjudged was the role of the church in redeeming the social order. None of our figures, save perhaps Niebuhr in the early thirties, deemed the church irrelevant to justice. Ryan believed the church should teach the principles of justice and industrial ethics. Niebuhr's working standards of justice depend upon the church to maintain the creative tension between the ideal and the actual and to sustain an attitude of contrition and a disposition for heedless sacrifice required by love. Yet neither Ryan nor Niebuhr devoted extensive attention to the role of the church in securing justice. Rauschenbusch did. The "new evangelism" of a church, for which service to the kingdom of God was to define mission, was a crucial component in Rauschenbusch's hope for redeeming the social order from injustice.[62] This understanding of the church is not adaptable to contemporary thinking about justice, but it raises an important issue.

Should and how should the church be an agent in efforts to bring about a just social order? Can it take this role without surrendering faithfulness to decisive elements in the ethic of Jesus? Rauschenbusch, of course,

---

62. See *supra,* chapter two, 104–106.

thought the church could help transform the social order. Otherwise, it would either have to choose isolation or be assimilated into the values of an unjust society. For Rauschenbusch, the only viable alternative to isolation or assimilation for the church was for the social order to become more like the kingdom.[63] He thought this transformation was possible through the "new evangelism" of a church that was itself in the process of being redeemed by forces Jesus had unleashed in history.

Rauschenbusch's hope for the church was guarded. His hope, based on his evaluative description of the changing social order, was that the times provided an occasion for the church to become a redemptive agent. He did not claim that the church would inevitably embody the "new evangelism" he envisioned for it. That the church took a different direction than he hoped for does not necessarily disprove Rauschenbusch's claims for the centrality of social redemption in understanding God or for the church's active role in securing justice.

Still, Rauschenbusch's insistence on a socio-historical account of redemption would have required that he reassess the role of the church in securing justice. In our context, that attention to the socio-historical circumstances would require Rauschenbusch to take account of sociological studies such as those by Wade Clark Roof and William McKinney, *American Mainline Religion* (1987), and by Robert Wuthnow, *The Restructuring of American Religion* (1988). These studies provide empirical evidence for what most newspaper readers already suspect. Current churches are moving away from Rauschenbusch's vision of an evangelical mission. Both books take the decade and one half following World War II as the baseline for their observations about the direction religion and the religious institutions are taking. Even that period was not an auspicious time for envisioning the church as a redemptive agent for social reform. In the words of Roof and McKinney, "So wedded were the liberal, mainline churches to the dominant culture that their beliefs, values, and behavior were virtually indistinguishable from the culture."[64] Prospects for the kind of evangelical mission Rauschenbusch hoped for have subsequently deteriorated. Despite differences in these studies, both agree that since the sixties religion has become more private and individualistic, that the churches have split along liberal and conservative moral and political lines, and that the trend is toward greater strength for the religious and political right with no immediate prospect of reversal. Furthermore, if Wuthnow is right about "special

---

63. See *supra*, chapter one, 45.
64. Wade Clark Roof and William McKinney, *American Mainline Religion: Its Changing Shape and Future* (New Brunswick, N.J.: Rutgers University Press, 1987), 22.

purpose groups" weakening denominational unity, churches are no longer organized to heed Rauschenbusch's call for them to sanction character traits that dispose persons to act for justice. Commitment to these groups is based on a single, often narrow, interest. These groups "require relatively limited commitment. . . . When [persons'] interests change, or when a more pressing issue emerges, they can switch to a different organization."[65] This type of organizational structure is hardly suited to molding character. Roof and McKinney organize their study as though denominations were still the dominant religious institutions, but they also note the diminished capacity of denominations and churches to shape shared values and commitments. They claim that individualism has enervated what they call "ascriptive loyalties" or attachments to denominations. "What matters is less the shared experiences and affirmations of a community of like-minded believers and more a person's own spiritual journey and quest."[66] Moreover, these ascriptive loyalties are weakest in liberal churches.[67]

It is difficult to know what one thinking in terms of Rauschenbusch's legacy should make of such studies. Certainly, Rauschenbusch did not permit empirical studies to determine his normative judgments about theology or ethics. Those judgments were rooted in the centrality of the kingdom in Jesus' teaching and ministry as well as sociological descriptions of the social order and institutions. Nonetheless, Rauschenbusch could not have ignored such sociological descriptions. At the very least, he would have had to alter his judgments about the immediate task of the church.

Perhaps these developments in the church—and his parallel misreading of the labor and socialist movements—would have forced Rauschenbusch to revise his theology of redemption and his ecclesiology. Events subsequent to *Christianizing the Social Order* have clearly persuaded others that these aspects of Rauschenbusch's theology are untenable. One could not find a leading theological or religious ethicist willing to defend the view that the church's mission is to be a redemptive agent for christianizing the social order. Indeed, the present trend in North America is away from conceiving the church as an agent for justice. This trend, however, is moving in quite divergent directions. One direction is to ignore the church and seek justice through other forces. Another is to call the church to a faithful witness to the ethic of Jesus that requires it to abandon a participatory role in making the social order just.

---

65. Robert Wuthnow, *The Restructuring of American Religion* (Princeton: Princeton University Press, 1988), 124–125.

66. Roof and McKinney, *American Mainline Religion,* 67.

67. Ibid., 86–87, 184.

Anderson and Pickering's book on racial justice represents the first pole in these opposing trends. They observe that "organized religion" has been relegated to the private sphere of individual lives.[68] Consequently, they do not look to the church as an agent for securing justice. They look to a version of "democratic faith," which they believe has the orientation and social power to effect justice. Because justice is the ultimate test of any faith,[69] Anderson and Pickering hinge their hope for racial justice on a "religious" orientation and force that they believe has the capacity to produce justice. Thus, their thinking about justice is independent of the church and the theological language it sustains.

Stanley Hauerwas represents the other pole of this trend. Hauerwas fears that the "current emphasis upon justice reflects Christian accommodation to liberal social orders and their agendas." Christians should pursue justice "as a claim about the kind of people we ought to be," but not as applied to "social systems."[70] If we make issues of justice fundamental, says Hauerwas, "the contribution of the church is easily lost." "[I]t is not the task of the church to try to develop social theories or strategies to make America work; rather the task of the church in this country is to become a polity that has the character necessary to survive as a truthful society." In carrying out this mission, the church will become a community capable of being a "witness to God's truth in the world."[71]

For Anderson and Pickering, the church is, in Hauerwas's words about those who make justice paramount, "irrelevant to the 'real' issues of social change involved in trying to make a society more just."[72] For Hauerwas, a church faithful in its mission to become a people who can witness to Christ should not pursue justice by trying to reform the social order. These two opposing views represent significant trends in contemporary theological and religious ethics, both of which agree that Rauschenbusch is mistaken in his claim that the church can be an effective agent for justice.[73] Although Rauschenbusch's understanding of how the

---

68. Anderson and Pickering, *Confronting the Color Line*, 396.

69. Ibid., 409.

70. Stanley Hauerwas, "Should Christians Talk So Much About Justice?" *Books and Religion* 14, no. 6 (May–June 1986): 14–15.

71. Stanley Hauerwas, *A Community of Character: Toward a Constructive Christian Social Ethic* (Notre Dame: University of Notre Dame Press, 1981), 3; see idem, *The Peaceable Kingdom*, 112–114, for a similar account of the church's responsibility for justice.

72. Hauerwas, *A Community of Character*, 3.

73. We should note that Anderson's and Pickering's views are based on an analysis of the present situation. They do not claim that the church is constitutionally incapable of being an effective agent for justice. Nevertheless, their fundamental commitment is to justice, not to a faith sustained by any church.

church can be an agent for justice is no longer credible, elements in his theory of justice expose deficiencies in both of these contemporary trends.

First, Rauschenbusch's view that the redemptive influence of Jesus can be sustained only through social institutions and movements requires the church. Although Rauschenbusch recognized advances of the kingdom in movements outside the church, his theory of justice requires an institution that has as its principal mission keeping vital the decisive elements in Jesus' religion and ethic. Anderson and Pickering's stand on democratic faith does not necessarily conflict with the general principles Rauschenbusch drew from Jesus. Rauschenbusch believed that those general principles entailed a version of democracy. Anderson and Pickering's stand, however, neglects a social organization that could keep alive social elements in the redemptive influence of Jesus.

This "religious ethic," bereft of theology and ecclesiology, is not doomed to defending the status quo. Anderson and Pickering do not. The problem is that they provide no means for preserving faithfulness to Jesus or the tradition he spawned. Given the present state of the church, there may be good reasons for not considering it as an agent of justice, but Rauschenbusch demonstrates that we may lose more than we bargain for. Unless the church retains a place in our theories of justice, Christian or theological ethics is destined to become a "religious ethic" that loses the salutary effects faithfulness to God known, at least in part, in Jesus Christ can have on the social order. Religious ethics requires a social organization to sustain it.

Second, despite sharing Hauerwas's emphasis upon faithfulness to Jesus' kingdom ethic, Rauschenbusch's sociological interpretation of Jesus links his evangelical ethic closely to Jesus' redemptive influence through the social and natural order. From the perspective of this sociological interpretation of the kingdom and Rauschenbusch's understanding of human agents as dependent upon social institutions, Hauerwas's views regarding the church and justice do not cohere. Rauschenbusch did not believe it possible for the church to sustain an enduring faithful witness to the ethic of Jesus in the midst of an unjust social order. In order to embody the ethic of Jesus, the church must either isolate itself from the social order, an option Hauerwas rejects, or make the social order like itself, a task Hauerwas thinks the church cannot achieve and should not undertake.[74] Rauschenbusch believed a position like Hauerwas's untenable because human agents cannot sustain qualities of character without support from the social institutions in which they participate. On Rausch-

---

74. See *supra,* chapter one, 45.

enbusch's view of human agents, it is not possible to " 'have character' " merely by "being initiated into a truthful narrative" or "by learning to grow in a truthful narrative."[75] Character cannot be sustained by the ethos of a subculture (or of a culture) alone, for example, by a community in which the story of Jesus is remembered. The development of the personality or character requires support from a network of social institutions in which persons live out their daily lives.[76] In order for the church to sustain radically distinctive Christian virtues, it would have to provide an entire social order isolated from the larger society.

Rauschenbusch, of course, did not believe that assimilation into a social order was immediate or absolute. Social institutions with conflicting characters exist in some tension with each other, such as the church and economic institutions. Like Hauerwas, Rauschenbusch called the church to be more faithful to Jesus' ethic of the kingdom. Nevertheless, if Rauschenbusch's understanding of human agents is correct, the church has a compelling interest either in seeking a more just social order or in separating its members into alternative patterns of living.[77]

Rauschenbusch exposes deficiencies in these two influential contemporary understandings of the relation between the church and justice, but they quite properly reject Rauschenbusch's view that the church can be a principal agent in christianizing the social order. The legacy of Rauschenbusch's thinking on the church and justice leaves us with a puzzle that I doubt can be solved within the framework of a theory of justice that makes the kingdom of God its organizing motif. An adequate understanding of how the church can be an agent for justice requires, I believe, a revision of Rauschenbusch's evaluative description of the social order based, as it is, on the centrality of Christian redemption. This is not the place to undertake such a massive task. I am, however, sufficiently fatuous to proffer a suggestion.

---

75. Hauerwas, *The Peaceable Kingdom,* 43.

76. See *supra,* chapter one, 44; chapter two, 75.

77. See Reinhard L. Hütter's parallel, but dissimilar, comparison and contrast between the ecclesiologies and ethics of Rauschenbusch and John Howard Yoder. Reinhard L. Hütter, "The Church: Midwife of History or Witness of the Eschaton?" *The Journal of Religious Ethics* 18, no. 1 (Spring 1990): 27–54. Hütter's illuminating comparison is more thoroughly developed than mine; but it suffers, in my judgment, from a failure to see how Rauschenbusch's evolutionary sociology was fundamental for his interpretations of Jesus, the church, the kingdom, and eschatology. Hence, Hütter does not account for the importance of a divine ordering of nature and history, including human institutions, in Rauschenbusch's theology and ethics. This omission obfuscates the coherence between the evangelical and social aspects of Rauschenbusch's ethic, distorts the comparison with Yoder, and leads Hütter to identify Rauschenbusch too closely with present-day political and liberation theologies (ibid., 27, 48). See *supra,* 352–354, for my comments on how liberationist themes in Lebacqz and García differ from Rauschenbusch in rejecting a divine ordering of nature and history.

One promising avenue would be to develop James Gustafson's theme of humans, including human communities, as "participant[s] in the patterns and processes of interdependence of life in the world."[78] In an essay written more than a decade before his *Theocentric Ethics,* Gustafson contrasts the role of the church as "participant" with an understanding of its role as "prophet" and as "preserver." As "participant," the church is unquestionably involved in "striving toward the order of life that brings a greater measure of justice."[79] An understanding of the church in accord with Gustafson's metaphor of "participant" raises two important questions in this context. First, can the contemporary church be an effective agent for bringing about greater justice? Anderson and Pickering apparently doubt that it can. Second, can church as "participant"—as distinguished from agent of redemption or witness to God's truth—be faithful to social elements in the ethic of Jesus, as Rauschenbusch and Hauerwas, in different ways, demand?[80] No brief answer to these questions is adequate.

I will not even suggest the direction an answer to the first might take. An answer to the second question requires an understanding of what it means to be faithful to the ethic and religion of Jesus, a matter about which Rauschenbusch, Hauerwas, and Gustafson disagree. We have, then, disagreements about the church's role in securing justice rooted in more fundamental theological differences.

Gustafson believes Hauerwas's attempt to escape the limitations of our social order by staking his ethic on knowledge of God's decisive change of history in Jesus, especially the resurrection, fails to account for God's ordering of nature.[81] For Gustafson, faithfulness to Jesus is devotion to one who "incarnates theocentric piety and fidelity"; that is, one who consents to the divine ordering of human life.[82] From this perspective, Hauerwas's ethic is not faithful to Jesus Christ. When

---

78. Gustafson, *Ethics from a Theocentric Perspective,* vol. 2, 145.

79. James M. Gustafson, "The Theologian as Prophet, Preserver, or Participant," in *Theology and Christian Ethics* (Philadelphia: Pilgrim Press, 1974), 94–95, 78–79, 83.

80. Hauerwas cites the ideal type of "participant" in Gustafson's earlier essay as a turning point in Gustafson's thinking that moves his theological ethics away from a particular historical starting point in Israel, Jesus, and the church. Hauerwas laments that Gustafson develops an ethic that "accepts the limitations of our cultural and social situation." See Stanley Hauerwas, "Time and History in Theological Ethics: The Work of James Gustafson," *The Journal of Religious Ethics* 13, no. 1 (Spring 1985): 10–12, 18–20. For Hauerwas, Gustafson's idea of "participant" threatens to assimilate the church into the present social order.

81. James M. Gustafson, "A Response to Critics," *The Journal of Religious Ethics* 13, no. 2 (Fall 1985): 191.

82. Gustafson, *Ethics from a Theocentric Perspective,* vol. 1, 276; idem, *Ethics from a Theocentric Perspective,* vol. 2, 292.

Hauerwas's ethic "limits the participation of Christians in the ambiguities of moral and social life in the patterns and processes of interdependence in the world,"[83] it neither consents to God's ordering of nature nor is faithful to Jesus' theocentric piety and fidelity. The dispute between them appears to center on the substance of and relation between God's ordering and christology. In response to Gustafson's criticism, Hauerwas continues to insist that the created order should be understood from the eschatological perspective of the resurrection and the kingdom of God.[84] We should note in this context that Rauschenbusch's understanding of Jesus as redeemer focuses on the ministry, teaching, and crucifixion as redeeming, given natural human interests. Rauschenbusch had little to say about the resurrection, and he certainly did not view it as the place where God begins.[85]

The differences between Rauschenbusch and Gustafson are not as wide as appears to be the case for one who makes the kingdom of God the organizing motif of his ethics and another who questions Christian eschatology. Gustafson argues that biblical and contemporary eschatologies are not sustainable if we understand the Deity as divine governance in and through nature and human experience.[86] A crucial theme in my analysis of Rauschenbusch is that he conceived the advance of the kingdom within the limits of a divine natural ordering of human life. Jesus' redemptive influence started with the social and natural forces of his time. Jesus' idea of the kingdom was a redemption of these social and natural interests, not an ideal transcending them.[87] Hence, Rauschenbusch understood the advance of the kingdom in the context of a divine natural ordering.[88]

Gustafson, nevertheless, differs from Rauschenbusch in that divine ordering, not the kingdom and redemption, is central. Yet the divine ordering includes redemptive possibilities. God is redeemer as well as orderer.[89] Moreover, Jesus is a "historical embodiment" of "fidelity to God's governance," which contradicts "conditions of oppression and poverty," enabling new ways of being and acting.[90] Jesus is a redemptive force within the interdependent patterns and processes of nature and

---

83. James M. Gustafson, "The Sectarian Temptation: Reflections on Theology, the Church, and the University," *Proceeding of the Catholic Theological Society* 40 (1985): 84.

84. Stanley Hauerwas, *Christian Existence Today: Essays on Church, World and Living in Between* (Durham, N.C.: Labyrinth, 1988), 16–17.

85. Cf. Hauerwas, "Time and History in Theological Ethics," 19.

86. Gustafson, *Ethics from a Theocentric Perspective*, vol. 1, 268.

87. See *supra*, chapter one, 37–39.

88. See *supra*, chapter two, 84–85.

89. Ibid., 247–251.

90. Ibid., 276.

history. Gustafson's and Rauschenbusch's understandings of faithfulness to the religion and ethics of Jesus combine consent to a divine ordering of human life (a theme Niebuhr rejected) with an affirmation of redemptive possibilities *within* that ordering. They disagree in emphasis, however, and that disagreement is reflected in their views of the church as an agent for justice.

The church as "participant" cannot expect to make the world like itself. It cannot christianize the social order. It will not envision as single-minded an ideal for justice as Rauschenbusch's view of "new evangelism" required. It cannot envision a future social order in total compliance with perfect justice, though it could formulate principles of justice that are not, as Niebuhr's are, inherently inferior to a transcendent social ideal. Churches as "participants" could align themselves with redemptive social movements. There may even be occasions in which large elements of the church unite behind a movement for justice. Churches as "participants" are primarily "communities of moral discourse," not redemptive agents,[91] but they can also be more than teaching communities. Unlike Ryan's idea of the church teaching the natural law, the churches as "participants" can be "redemptively present in the crises, struggles, and transformations of human existence."[92]

The church as "participant" is under the constant threat of assimilation into the social order.[93] Though the church need not consider its principles and schemes of justice inherently inferior to the ethic of Jesus, the "participant" cannot conceive of itself, as Rauschenbusch conceived of redeemed Christians, as possessing fully the mind of God in Christ. Nor can it conceive of itself, or any other collective agent, as a force for redemption in which divine justice is fully immanent.[94] Aware that involvement in transforming the social order holds potential for both corruption and redemption, the "participant" could not give itself as wholeheartedly, as Rauschenbusch demanded, to redemptive movements. Ironically, a church aware of the constant threat of becoming like the world would avoid Rauschenbusch's mistakes of identifying God's purposes with any movement or with the vision of a future "communistic" economic order. It would not claim to satisfy the purity of witness

---

91. Cf. *supra,* chapter two, 106.

92. Gustafson, "The Theologian as Prophet, Preserver, or Participant," 95. The passage cited refers to members of churches, but I see no reason why, on occasion, the churches themselves could not support redemptive movements, for example, during the civil rights movement.

93. Gustafson concedes that his theological ethic "risks" losing "the particularistic historic identity of the Christian religious tradition and the community." See Gustafson, "The Sectarian Temptation," 94.

94. Cf. *supra,* chapter two, 81–83.

that Rauschenbusch or Hauerwas demands. It could, however, keep vital the social elements of Jesus' religion and ethic. By consent to the "power of the gospel," the church's participation in the social and natural order would continue to be "empowered, sustained, renewed, informed and judged by Jesus' incarnation of theocentric piety and fidelity."[95] There are surely occasions in which such a church, in the face of a highly corrupted social order, would seek temporarily to isolate its institutional life as the best way of sustaining its commitment to Jesus' concern for the oppressed and impoverished.[96]

In sum, Rauschenbusch's understanding of the church as an agent for justice exposes deficiencies in alternative views in contemporary theological and religious ethics. Yet Rauschenbusch's call for a "new evangelism" to christianize the social order also manifests problems rooted in the organizing principle of his theory of justice. I have suggested, with little elaboration, that James Gustafson's understanding of the church as "participant" might be an avenue for developing a more plausible claim for the church as an agent for justice. Gustafson's idea of "participant" rests on a different organizing principle for theological ethics. Still, Gustafson, like Rauschenbusch and unlike Ryan or Niebuhr, combines an understanding of divine ordering with an understanding of redemptive possibilities through Christ and the social and natural order. The question remains whether the idea of humans as participants in the patterns and processes of a divine ordering could be developed so as to incorporate the valuable legacies of our ethicists' theories of justice.

LEGACIES AND TASKS

My assessment of these three theories of justice concludes without affirming the organizing framework for ethics in any of them. I concur with the common feature of all three theories: the organizing framework for Christian thinking about justice should be informed and justified by a comprehensive theology. I also believe that the organizing framework

---

95. Gustafson, *Ethics from a Theocentric Perspective*, vol. 1, 276–277.
96. Even Rauschenbusch, with all his emphasis upon the redemptive influence of Jesus in the social order, suggested that the best course for the early church was to isolate itself from the dominant social institutions. He wrote:

> The only course open to Christians was to diminish their points of contact with heathen society and constitute a little social world within the world. Such a mingling in the common life as an effort at social reconstruction would involve, was quite out of the question. The best social service which the Church could render to the heathen world was to counteract and break the power of the demons. (Rauschenbusch, *Christianity and the Social Crisis,* 157).

should, as Rauschenbusch and Ryan do, account for God's ordering of human life through nature and social institutions. The notion of divine ordering is not sufficient, however, for a theory of justice. As "participants" in the ordering of life, humans are enabled by redemptive forces in history to reform unjust orders. Rauschenbusch was right to combine divine ordering and redemption in his theory of justice. The centrality of redemption, however, led Rauschenbusch to a vision of christianizing the social order, through the churches and other social movements, that cannot be sustained by an adequate interpretation of history. Consequently, Rauschenbusch's vision of a future democratic and "socialized" social order did not account for valid concerns in Niebuhr's observations regarding the ironies of history or for Ryan's attention to pragmatic issues of economic efficiency.

Despite deficiencies at this fundamental level in each of these theories of justice, the subjects of this study have left important legacies for our thinking about justice. Although no contemporary Christian should undertake constructive thinking about justice without taking account of Niebuhr's insights, the important achievements of Rauschenbusch and Ryan are in greater danger of being overlooked. Their thinking about justice corrects the view, partially inspired by Niebuhr, that the fulfillment of justice occurs only in a divine love that rises above natural human interests and divine ordering through nature. Rauschenbusch and Ryan articulated criteria for justice that discriminate among human interests without being inherently inferior to divine love. For them, just social institutions are compatible with a divine ordering of human interests. For Rauschenbusch, these just institutions could also be a means of grace.

Their concern for humans to develop natural interests in harmony with one another enabled and informed Rauschenbusch's and Ryan's formulation of quite similar notions of equality of opportunity. Their focus on how social institutions provide opportunities for self-development offers an especially powerful idea for our thinking about justice. The idea of equal opportunity is already a "moral issue" in our society. It has a powerful attraction for many persons with incompatible notions of justice.

This situation calls for greater clarity about what equality of opportunity requires. Rauschenbusch and Ryan can also assist us in this task. They, especially Rauschenbusch, elaborated the ideal of equal opportunity in light of the interdependence in the natural and social ordering of human life. This perspective enabled them to see that equality of opportunity requires collective action that mitigates inequalities created by unrestrained free markets. They also showed how opportunity requires attention to the way in which social institutions and systems hinder or encourage character development. Their understanding of equality of opportunity exposes incoherencies in the view that equality of opportunity involves no more than positions open to the most qualified individuals. This narrow view of equal opportunity leads its proponents to defend liberties and inequalities that hinder the opportunities of many individuals and groups for self-development.

A contemporary formulation and application of Rauschenbusch's and Ryan's understanding of equality of opportunity would, I believe, expose injustices in some of our economic and educational institutions. It would compel us to ask questions that are often neglected. Does a system of financing education that permits grossly unequal per-pupil funding provide equality of opportunity? Does a system of education that treats religious and moral values as private matters of individual preference foster opportunities for persons to develop desirable qualities of character? Is equal opportunity for employment achieved when positions are open to the most qualified, even though many lack the means to become qualified for any but the most menial jobs? Does the opportunity for workers to develop economic skills and important moral qualities require more and new forms of employee participation in management, profits, and ownership?

These are neither novel nor rhetorical questions.[97] Retrieving Rauschenbusch's and Ryan's understanding of equality of opportunity will not revolutionize our thinking about justice nor provide ready answers to policy questions. The point is that it could help us focus these and other similar policy questions that are not asked from the perspective of other theories of justice, including Niebuhr's. In this way, their understanding of equality of opportunity could have significant implications for policies in these and other areas.

---

97. The issue of equitable funding for public education has been in the federal and state courts for more than two decades. Early in this debate, Justice Thurgood Marshall, dissenting from the majority opinion in *San Antonio v. Rodriguez,* raised the issue of equality of opportunity. He charged that the Court, in permitting continuation of the Texas system for financing education, was retreating from a "commitment to equality of educational opportunity." See San Antonio Indep. School Dist. v. Rodriguez, 411 U.S. 1 (1973): 71, see also 90. In a 1989 opinion declaring that the Texas system for financing education violates the Texas State Constitution, Justice Oscar Mauzy wrote: "Children who live in poor districts and children who live in rich districts must be afforded substantially equal opportunity to have access to educational funds." See Edgewood Indep. School Dist. v. Kirby, 777 S.W.2d 391 (Tex. 1989): 97.

One prominent source addressing the issue of worker participation is the American Catholic Bishops' pastoral letter on the U.S. economy. See *Economic Justice for All* (Washington, D.C.: National Conference of Catholic Bishops, 1986), 145–152. The bishops call on labor unions to strive for greater participation within firms and industries and to seek goals that will "enable workers to make positive and creative contributions to the firm, the community, and the larger society in an organized and cooperative way" (150–151).

SELECTED BIBLIOGRAPHY

REINHOLD NIEBUHR
Books and Anthologies

Brown, Robert McAfee, ed. *The Essential Reinhold Niebuhr: Selected Essays and Addresses.* New Haven: Yale University Press, 1986.

Niebuhr, Reinhold. *Beyond Tragedy: Essays on the Christian Interpretation of History.* New York: Charles Scribner's Sons, 1937.

———. *The Children of Light and the Children of Darkness.* New York: Charles Scribner's Sons, 1944.

———. *Christian Realism and Political Problems.* New York: Charles Scribner's Sons, 1953.

———. *Does Civilization Need Religion?* New York: Macmillan, 1927.

———. *Faith and History: A Comparison of Christian and Modern Views of History.* New York: Charles Scribner's Sons, 1949.

———. *Faith and Politics.* Edited by Ronald H. Stone. New York: George Braziller, 1968.

———. *An Interpretation of Christian Ethics.* New York: Harper & Brothers, 1935. Reprint. New York: Meridian Books, 1956.

———. *The Irony of American History.* New York: Charles Scribner's Sons, 1952.

———. *Leaves from the Notebook of a Tamed Cynic.* New York: Richard R. Smith, 1929. Reprint. Louisville, Ky.: Westminster/John Knox Press, 1990.

———. *Love and Justice.* Edited by D. B. Robertson. Cleveland: World Publishing Co., 1957. Reprint. Gloucester, Mass.: Peter Smith, 1976.

———. *Moral Man and Immoral Society.* New York: Charles Scribner's Sons, 1932.

————. *The Nature and Destiny of Man.* Vol. 1, *Human Nature.* New York: Charles Scribner's Sons, 1942.

————. *The Nature and Destiny of Man.* Vol. 2, *Human Destiny.* New York: Charles Scribner's Sons, 1943.

————. *Reflections on the End of an Era.* New York: Charles Scribner's Sons, 1934.

Articles

Niebuhr, Reinhold. "Christian Faith and the Common Life." In *Christian Faith and the Common Life,* edited by Nils Ehrenstrom, M. G. Dibelius, et al., 69–97. Chicago: Willet, Clark & Co., 1938.

————. "Christian Politics and Communist Religion." In *Christianity and the Social Revolution,* edited by John Lewis, Karl Polanyi, and Donald K. Kitchin, 442–472. New York: Charles Scribner's Sons, 1936.

————. "The Problem of a Protestant Social Ethic." *Union Seminary Quarterly Review* 15 (November 1959):1–11.

Secondary Sources

Fox, Richard Wightman. *Reinhold Niebuhr: A Biography.* New York: Pantheon Books, 1985.

Harries, Richard, ed. *Reinhold Niebuhr and the Issues of Our Time.* Grand Rapids, Mich.: Eerdmans, 1986.

Kegley, Charles W., ed. *Reinhold Niebuhr: His Religious, Social, and Political Thought.* New York: Pilgrim Press, 1984.

Lebacqz, Karen. *Six Theories of Justice.* Minneapolis: Augsburg, 1986.

McCann, Dennis P. *Christian Realism and Liberation Theology: Practical Theologies in Conflict.* Maryknoll, N.Y.: Orbis Books, 1981.

Merkley, Paul. *Reinhold Niebuhr: A Political Account.* Montreal: McGill-Queen's University Press, 1975.

Stone, Ronald H. *Reinhold Niebuhr: Prophet to Politicians.* Lanham, Md.: University Press of America, 1981.

WALTER RAUSCHENBUSCH
Books and Anthologies

Hudson, Winthrop S., ed. *Walter Rauschenbusch: Selected Writings.* New York: Paulist Press, 1984.

Rauschenbusch, Walter. *Christianity and the Social Crisis.* Edited by Robert D. Cross. New York: Harper & Row, 1964. Originally published New York: Macmillan, 1907. Reprint. Louisville, Ky.: Westminster/John Knox Press, 1992.

————. *Christianizing the Social Order.* New York: Macmillan, 1912.

————. *Dare We Be Christians?* Boston: Pilgrim Press, 1914.

———. *The Righteousness of the Kingdom.* Edited by Max L. Stackhouse. Nashville: Abingdon Press, 1968.

———. *The Social Principles of Jesus.* New York: Association Press, 1916. Reprint. Darby, Pa.: Arden Library, 1985.

———. *A Theology for the Social Gospel.* New York: Macmillan, 1917. Reprint. Nashville: Abingdon, 1990.

Articles

Rauschenbusch, Walter. "Dogmatic and Practical Socialism." In *The Social Gospel in America, 1870–1920,* edited by Robert T. Handy, 308–322. New York: Oxford University Press, 1966.

———. "The Influence of Historical Studies on Theology." *American Journal of Theology* 11, no. 1 (January 1907): 111–127.

———. "Jesus as an Organizer of Men." *The Biblical World* 11, no. 2 (February 1898): 102–111.

———. "The Kingdom of God." In *The Social Gospel in America, 1870–1920,* edited by Robert T. Handy, 264–267. New York: Oxford University Press, 1966.

———. "The Value and Use of History." *The Rochester Theological Seminary Bulletin: The Record* 65, no. 3 (November 1914): 31–45.

Secondary Sources

Minus, Paul M. *Walter Rauschenbusch: An American Reformer.* New York: Macmillan, 1988.

Sharpe, Dores Robinson. *Walter Rauschenbusch.* New York: Macmillan, 1942.

JOHN A. RYAN
Books and Pamphlets

Ryan, John A. *A Better Economic Order.* New York: Harper & Brothers, 1935.

———. *Can Unemployment Be Ended?* Washington, D.C.: American Association for Economic Freedom, 1940.

———. *The Christian Doctrine of Property.* New York: Paulist Press, 1923.

———. *The Church and Socialism and Other Essays.* Washington, D.C.: The University Press, 1919.

———. *Declining Liberty and Other Papers.* New York: Macmillan, 1927.

———. *Distributive Justice: The Right and Wrong of Our Present Distribution of Wealth.* New York: Macmillan, 1916; 2d ed. 1927; 3d ed. 1942.

———. *Industrial Democracy from a Catholic Viewpoint.* Washington, D.C.: The Rossi-Byrn Co., 1925.

———. *A Living Wage: Its Ethical and Economic Aspects.* New York: Macmillan, 1906.

————. *The Norm of Morality: Defined and Applied to Particular Actions.* Washington, D.C.: National Catholic Welfare Conference, 1944.

————. *Questions of the Day.* Freeport, N.Y.: Books for Libraries Press, 1931.

————. *Seven Troubled Years, 1930–1936: A Collection of Papers on the Depression and on the Problems of Recovery and Reform.* Ann Arbor, Mich.: Edwards Brothers, 1937.

————. *Social Doctrine in Action: A Personal History.* New York: Harper & Brothers, 1941.

————. *Social Reconstruction.* New York: Macmillan, 1920.

————. *Social Reform Along Catholic Lines.* New York: Columbus Press, 1913.

————. *The Supreme Court and the Minimum Wage.* New York: Paulist Press, 1923.

Ryan, John A., and Francis J. Boland, S.J. *Catholic Principles of Politics.* New York: Macmillan, 1940.

Ryan, John A., and Morris Hillquit. *Socialism: Promise or Menace?* New York: Macmillan, 1914.

Ryan, John A., and Moorhouse F. X. Millar, S.J. *The State and the Church.* New York: Macmillan, 1922.

Articles

Ryan, John A. "The Method of Teleology in Ethics." *The New York Review* 2, no. 4 (January–February 1907): 402–429.

————. "Social Objectives of Catholics." *Catholic Charities Review* 13 (April 1929): 114–116.

————. "Two Objectives for Catholic Economists." *Review of Economy* 1, no. 1 (December 1942): 1–5.

Secondary Sources

Broderick, Francis L. *Right Reverend New Dealer: John A. Ryan.* New York: Macmillan, 1963.

Curran, Charles E. *American Catholic Social Ethics: Twentieth-Century Approaches.* Notre Dame: University of Notre Dame Press, 1982.

Gearty, Patrick. *The Economic Thought of Monsignor John A. Ryan.* Washington, D.C.: Catholic University of America Press, 1953.

McShane, Joseph M., S.J. *"Sufficiently Radical": Catholicism, Progressivism, and the Bishops' Program of 1919.* Washington, D.C.: Catholic University of America Press, 1986.

INDEX OF NAMES